# WEBSTER'S EVER READY DICTIONARY
## OF THE ENGLISH LANGUAGE
*Self-Pronouncing*

Based upon the original
foundation laid by

## NOAH WEBSTER, LL.D.

AND OTHER EMINENT
LEXICOGRAPHERS

Compiled, Revised and Edited
BY C. M. STEVENS, PH.D.

This Dictionary is not published by
the original publishers of Webster's
Dictionary, or by their successors.

1928 EDITION

NEW YORK
J. H. SEARS & COMPANY, INC.

Copyright, 1924, by
J. H. SEARS & COMPANY, Inc.

Set up, Printed and Bound by
THE KINGSPORT PRESS
Kingsport         Tennessee
*United States of America*

# WEBSTER'S
*Ever Ready*
# DICTIONARY

## A

**ABAFT** | **ABORIGINES**

**abaft** (a-baft'), adv. and prep. At, toward, or in the direction of the stern of a ship.

**abandon** (a-ban'dun), vt. To give up; desert or forsake utterly.

**a-bas** (a-ba') [French]. Down with.

**abase** (a-bas'), vt. To humble or degrade; debase morally; dishonor.

**abash** (a-bash'), vt. To put to confusion; confound or make ashamed by consciousness of guilt or error.

**abate** (a-bat'), vt. To lessen; suppress.

**abattoir** (a-bat-twar'), n. A public slaughter-house.

**abbe** (a-ba'), n. An ecclesiastic devoted to literature. **[abbess, abbot]**

**abbreviate** (ab-bre'vi-at), vt. To shorten, as by contraction of a word, or the omission of words in a sentence.

**abdicate** (ab'di-kat), vt. To renounce, give up, or withdraw from; to relinquish the crown in favor of a successor.

**abdomen** (ab-do'men), n. The belly; the cavity containing the digestive apparatus or viscera.

**abduce** (ab-dus'), vt. To draw away by persuasion or argument.

**abduct** (ab-dukt'), vt. To carry off by stealth or force; kidnap.

**aberration** (ab-er-ra'shun), n. The act of departing from the usual path, type, or standard; mental derangement.

**abeyance** (a-ba'ans), n. Held or kept back; held over; a state of suspension.

**abhor** (ab-hor'), vt. To hate, loathe, execrate, abominate; be strongly averse to. **[abhorrent]**

**ability** (a-bil'i-ti), n. Power to do anything; talent; skill; in pl. the powers of the mind.

**abiogenesis** (ab'i-o-jen'e-sis), n. The doctrine that living matter may be produced by not-living matter.

**abject** (ab'jekt), a. Mean; despicable.

**abjuration** (ab-ju-ra'shon), n. Act of abjuring; oath taken for that end.

**abjure** (ab-jur'), vt. To renounce upon oath; to reject. **[abjuring, abjured]**

**ablution** (ab-lu'shon), n. A washing away from; a purification by water.

**abnegate** (ab'ne-gat), vt. To deny; to renounce. **[abnegation]**

**abnormal** (ab-norm'al), a. Deviating from a fixed rule; irregular.

**abolish** (a-bol'ish), vt. To destroy; to abrogate. **[abolition]**

**abominable** (a-bom'in-a-bl), a. Loathsome.

**aboriginal** (ab-o-rij'in-al), a. Primitive.

**aborigines** (ab-o-rij'in-ez), n.

# ABORTION — ACCEDE

*pl.* The original inhabitants of a country.

**abortion** (a-bor'shon), n. A miscarriage. [**abortive**]

**abrasion** (ab-ra'zhun), n. The act of wearing or rubbing away; a chafe.

**abridge** (a-brij'), vt. To curtail, shorten, condense, epitomize.

**abroach** (a-broch'), adv. and adj. Letting out; placed in position for yielding the contents.

**abroad** (a-brawd'), adv. Widely; expansively; beyond the limits of house or country; wide of the mark.

**abrogate** (ab'ro-gat), vt. To abolish, annul, or repeal by authority.

**abrupt** (ab-rupt'), adj. Broken; terminating suddenly; steep; precipitous; rough; unceremonious.

**abscess** (ab'ses), n. A collection of morbid matter in the tissues of the body.

**abscond** (ab-skond'), vi. To flee or retire in haste from the place of one's residence or post of duty.

**absence** (ab'sens), n. The state of being absent; the period of being absent.

**absolute** (ab'so-lut), adj. Unlimited in power; fixed, irrevocable; despotic; positive.

**absolution** (ab-so-lu'shun), n. The act of absolving from the consequences of sin.

**absolve** (ab-solv'), vt. To release or set free; clear of crime or guilt.

**absorb** (ab-sorb'), vt. To drink in; imbibe; suck or swallow up; engross or engage wholly. [**absorbent**]

**absorption** (ab-sorp'shun), n. The process or act of absorbing.

**abstain** (ab-stan'), vt. To forbear; refrain; hold aloof; keep away from. [**abstemious**]

**abstergent** (ab-ster'jent), adj. Possessing cleansing or purging properties.

**abstinence** (ab'sti-nens), n. Self-denial; partial or total forbearance from the use of food or drink.

**abstract** (ab-strakt'), vt. To take or draw away; separate; purloin or steal; epitomize; separate from and consider apart.

**abstract** (ab'strakt), n. An epitome; a summary or abstract comprising the essence or principal parts of a larger work. [**abstraction**]

**abstruse** (ab-stroos'), adj. Obscure; hidden; difficult of comprehension; profound.

**absurd** (ab-serd'), adj. Contrary to reason or sense; ridiculous. [**absurdity**]

**abundant** (a-bun'dant), adj. Plentiful.

**abuse** (a-buz'), vt. To use ill; treat rudely or wrongfully; to defile or violate; use violent or abusive language towards; vituperate.

**abuse** (a-bus'), n. Ill-treatment; the excessive or injudicious use of anything; insult; violation.

**abutment** (a-but'ment), n. That which borders upon something else.

**abyss** (a-bis'), n. A bottomless gulf.

**academic** (ak-a-dem'ik), a. Pertaining to an academy. [**academician**]

**acanthous** (a-kan'thus), n. Armed with prickles; spiny.

**acarus** (ak'a-rus), n. A small spider-like insect.

**acataleptic** (a-kat-a-lep'tik), a. Incomprehensible.

**accede** (ak-sed'), vi. To assent; to quicken.

# ACCELERATE — ACONITE

**accelerate** (ak-sel'e-rat), vt. To hasten motion; to quicken. [**accelerative**]

**accent** (ak-sent'), vt. To express or note the accent.

**accent** (ak'sent), n. Modulation of voice.

**accept** (ak-sept'), vt. To receive; to admit. [**acceptable**]

**access** (ak'ses, or ak-ses'), n. Liberty to come to, approach; increase. [**accessible, accession, accessory**]

**accidence** (ak'sid-ens), n. The part of grammar treating of word inflections.

**accident** (ak'sid-ent), n. An unforeseen or unexpected event.

**acclamation** (ak-klam-a'shun), n. A shout of applause. [**acclamatory**]

**acclivity** (ak-kliv'i-ti), n. A slope upwards. [**acclivous**]

**accommodate** (ak-kom'mod-at), v. To adapt; to make suitable; to adjust.

**accompany** (ak-kum'pan-i), vt. To keep company with; to attend.

**accomplice** (ak-kom'plis), n. An associate, esp. in crime.

**accomplish** (ak-kom'plish), vt. To complete; to bring about; to effect.

**accord** (ak-kord'), vi. To agree; to be in correspondence (with).

**accordion** (ak-kor'di-on), n. A portable musical instrument consisting of a hand-bellows.

**accost** (ak-kost'), vt. To speak first to; to address.

**accouchement** (ak-kosh'-mong), n. Delivery in childbed.

**account** (ak-kownt'), vt. To reckon; to judge, value.

**accouter**, vt. To dress or equip.

**accredit** (ak-kred'it), vt. To give credit, countenance, authority, or honor to.

**accrescent** (ak-kres'ent), a. Growing; ever-increasing.

**accrue**, vi. To spring or grow as a natural result.

**accumbent** (ak-kumb'ent), a. Reclining.

**accumulate** (ak-kum'ul-at), vt. To heap or pile up; to amass.

**accurse** (ak-kurs'), vt. To curse; to devote to misery or destruction.

**accusative** (ak-kuz'a-tiv), a. Accursing. n. (gram.) The case which expresses the direct object of transitive verbs (in English, the objective).

**accuse** (ak-kuz'), vt. To bring a charge against; to blame.

**accustom** (ak-kus'tum), v. To make familiar by use.

**ace** (as), n. A single point on cards or dice; a unit.

**acephalous** (a-sef'a-lus), a. Headless; without a head.

**acerbity** (a-ser'bi-ti), n. Sourness; harshness; severity.

**acetate** (as'e-tat), n. The sour principle of vinegar. [**acetous**]

**acetylene** (a-set'i-len), n. Illuminating gas obtained by action of water on calcium-carbide.

**ache** (ak), v. To be in pain.

**achieve** (a-chev'), v. To perform; to accomplish; to obtain.

**aching** (ak'ing), n. Pain; distress; uneasiness.

**achromatic** (ak-ro-mat'ik), a. Destitute of color.

**acid** (as'id), a. Sharp; sour. [**acidity**]

**acknowledge** (ak-nol'ej), v. To admit; to confess.

**acme** (ak'me), n. The highest point; utmost excellence.

**aconite** (ak'o-nit), n. Wolf's-bane; a poison.

**acorn** (a'karn), n. The seed or fruit of the oak.

**acoustic** (a-kos'tik), a. Pertaining to the sense of hearing.

**acquaint** (ak-kwant'), v. To make known; to inform. [acquaintance]

**acquiesce** (ak-kwi-es'), v. To be satisfied with; to consent.

**acquire** (ak-kwir'), v. To gain; to attain; to realize.

**acquisition** (ak-kwi-zish'un) n. The act of acquiring; the thing acquired or gained.

**acquisitiveness** (ak-kwiz'i-tiv-nes), n. Desire of possession.

**acquit** (ak-kwit'), v. To set free; to release; to exonerate.

**acquittal** (ak-kwit'al), n. Discharge from an accusation. [acquittance]

**acre** (a'ker), n. A piece of land containing 160 square rods. [acreage]

**acrid** (ak'rid), a. Sharp; bitter; hot or biting to the taste. [acrimonious]

**acrobat** (ak'ro-bat), n. A rope-dancer; a vaulter.

**acrostic** (a-kras'tik), n. A poem of which the first letters of the lines spell words.

**acta** (ak'ta), n. pl. Proceedings in a court of record, or the minutes of such.

**actiniform** (ak-tin'i-form), a. Having a radiated form.

**actinism** (ak'tin-izm), n. The chemical force of the sun's rays.

**action** (ak'shun), n. A state of acting; activity; a deed; operation; gesture.

**actual** (akt'u-al), a. Real; existing in fact and now.

**actuary** (akt'u-ar-i), n. A registrar; one who makes calculations connected with insurance.

**actuate** (akt'u-at), vt. To put into or incite to action; to influence.

**aculeated** (ak-ul-e-at'ed), p. a. Pointed; pungent; incisive.

**acumen** (ak-u'men), n. Sharpness; penetration.

**acute** (ak-ut'), a. Sharp-pointed; keen; shrewd.

**adage** (ad'aj), n. A proverb.

**adamant** (ad'a-mant), n. A hard stone; a diamond. [adamantine]

**adapt** (a-dapt'), v. To fit one thing to another. [adaptation]

**addendum** (ad-den'dum), n. Something added. pl. Addenda.

**adder** (ad'der), n. A viper.

**addict** (ad-dikt'), v. To practice habitually.

**addition** (ad-dish'un), n. The thing added; increase.

**addle** (ad'dl), v. To make corrupt. a. Barren.

**address** (ad-dres'), v. To speak or write to; to direct to.

**adduce** (ad-dus'), v. To bring forward; to cite.

**adept** (a-dept'), n. A person skilled in any art.

**adequate** (ad'e-kwat), a. Fully sufficient; equal.

**adhere** (ad-her'), v. To stick to; to remain fixed. [adherence]

**adhesion** (ad-he'zhun), n. The state of sticking. [adhesive]

**adieu** (a-du'), ad. Farewell.

**adipose** (ad'i-pos), a. Fatty.

**adit** (ad'it), n. An opening into a mine.

**adjacency** (ad-ja'sen-si), n. Lying close to.

**adjective** (ad'jek-tiv), n. A word added to a noun to qualify it.

**adjoin** (ad-join'), v. To be near; to join.

**adjourn** (ad-jurn'), v. To put off; to postpone.

# ADJUDGE     ADVANTAGE

**adjudge** (ad-juj'), v. To sentence; to judge.

**adjudicate** (ad-jo'di-kat), a. To try judicially.

**adjunct** (ad'junkt), n. Something united to another. a. Added to.

**adjure** (ad-jor'), vt. To charge solemnly on oath.

**adjust** (ad-just'), v. To make; to correspond; to set right.

**adjutant** (ad'jo-tant), n. A military officer who assists the major.

**adjutor** (ad-joo'ter), n. A helper.

**adjuvant** (ad'joo-vant), a. Helping; assisting.

**adminicular** (ad-mi-nik'u-lar), a. Helpful; supplying aid.

**administration** (ad-min-is-tra'shun), n. Executive part of government. [**administrator**]

**administratrix** (ad-min-is-tra'triks), n. A woman that administers.

**admirable** (ad'mi-ra-bl), a. Worthy of admiration; excellent.

**admiral** (ad'mi-ral), n. Principal officer of a fleet or navy. [**admiralty**]

**admiration** (ad-mi-ra'shun), n. Astonishment; wonder; esteem.

**admire** (ad-mir'), vt. To regard with wonder; esteem or prize highly.

**admissible** (ad-mis'i-bl), a. That may be admitted. [**admission**]

**admit** (ad-mit'), vt. To allow; let in; receive as true. [**admittable, admittance**]

**admixture** (ad-miks'tur), n. The compound made by mixing.

**admonish** (ad-mon'ish), vt. To warn; reprove gently; advise.

**admonition** (ad-mon-ish'un), n. Gentle reproof; counsel. [**admonitive, admonitor, admonitory**]

**adnascent** (ad-nas'ent), a. Growing on something else.

**adnate** (ad'nat), a. Growing or attached to by its whole length.

**adobe** (a-do'ba), n. A sun-dried brick.

**adolescence** (ad-o-les'ens), n. State of growing; youth. [**adolescent**]

**adoption** (a-dop'shun), n. The act of adopting. [**adoptive**]

**adorable** (a-dor'a-bl), a. Worthy of adoration; divine. [**adoration**]

**adorn** (a-dorn'), vt. To deck; embellish.

**adrift** (a-drift'), a. or ad. Floating at random.

**adroit** (a-droit'), a. Skilful; expert; dexterous.

**adulation** (ad-u-la'shun), n. Excessive flattery. [**adulatory**]

**adult** (a-dult'), n. A person grown up.

**adulterant** (a-dul'ter-ant), n. The thing or person that adulterates.

**adulterate** (a-dul'ter-at), vt. To debase or corrupt by mixture.

**adulteration** (a-dul-te-ra'shun), n. The act of adulterating. [**adulterer, adulteress, adulterous**]

**adultery** (a-dul'ter-i), n. A violation of the marriage bed.

**adumbrant** (ad-um'brant), a. Giving a faint shadow. [**adumbration**]

**adust** (a-dust'), a. Burnt; hot and fiery; looking as if burnt or scorched.

**advance** (ad-vans'), n. A going forward; promotion; payment beforehand.

**advantage** (ad-van'taj), n. Favorable circumstances; superiority; gain. [**advantageous**]

# ADVENE 6 AFFILIATE

**advene** (ad-ven'), vi. To come or be added to.

**advent** (ad'vent), n. A coming; the season of four weeks before Christmas.

**adventitious** (ad-ven-tish'-us), a. Added; not essentially inherent.

**adventure** (ad-ven'tur), n. An extraordinary event; an enterprise. [adventurer, adventurous]

**adverb** (ad'verb), n. A word which modifies a verb. [adverbial]

**adversary** (ad'ver-sar-i), n. An opponent; enemy.

**adversative** (ad-ver'sa-tiv), a. Denoting opposition. [adverse]

**adversity** (ad-ver'si-ti), n. Misfortune; affliction.

**advert** (ad-vert'), v. To turn or attend to. [advertence]

**advertise** (ad'ver-tiz), v. To inform; to give notice. [advertising]

**advice** (ad-vis'), n. Instruction; notice; advice.

**advisable** (ad-vis'a-bl), a. Fit to be done.

**advise** (ad-viz'), v. To give advice; to inform of; to consider. [adviser]

**advisory** (ad-viz-ur-i), a. Having power to advise.

**advocacy** (ad'vo-ka-si), n. Act of pleading; intercession; defense. [advocate]

**adynamic** (ad-i-nam'ik), a. Weak.

**adytum** (ad'i-tum), n. Sanctum.

**adz, adze**, n. A cutting tool with an arching edge.

**ægis** (e'jis), n. A shield.

**Æolian** (e-o'li-an), a. Belonging to the wind.

**aerate** (a'er-at), v. To combine with air.

**aerial** (a-e'ri-al), a. Belonging to the air; elevated.

**aerie** (a'er-i or e'ri), n. The nest of a bird of prey.

**aeriform** (a'er-i-farm), a. Having the form of air.

**aerodrome** (a'er-o-drome), n. Hangar for a flying machine.

**aerogram** (a'er-o-gram), n. Message sent by wireless telegraphy.

**aerolite** (a'er-o-lit), n. A meteoric stone.

**aerometer** (a-er-om'e-ter), n. An instrument for measuring the density of air and gases.

**aeronaut** (a'er-o-nat), n. An aerial sailor.

**aeronautics** (a-er-o-nat'iks), n. pl. The art or science of sailing in the air.

**aeroplane** (a'er-o-plan), n. A machine for navigating the air.

**aerostatics** (a-er-o-stat'iks), n. pl. Science treating of pressure or equilibrium of the air.

**æsthetics** (es-thet'iks), n. The science of taste.

**affable** (af'fa-bl), a. Of easy manners; courteous.

**affair** (af-far'), n. A business matter.

**affect** (af-fekt'), v. To move the passions; to aim at; to make a show of.

**affectation** (af-fek-ta'shun), n. Insincerity; pretense.

**affection** (af-fek'shun), n. Love; fondness; kindness.

**affective** (af-fek'tiv), a. That affects or excites emotion.

**affeer** (af-fer'), vt. To fix the market value of.

**afferent** (af'fer-ent), a. (anat.) Bringing to, applied to the nerves that convey sensations to the nerve centers.

**affiance** (af-fi'ans), n. Faith pledged; marriage contract; trust.

**affidavit** (af-fi-da'vit), n. A written declaration on oath.

**affiliate** (af-fil'i-at), vt. To

**affinity** (af-fin'i-ti), n. Nearness of kin, agreement, or resemblance.

**affirm** (af-ferm'), vt. To assert confidently or positively.

**affix** (af-fiks'), vt. To fix to; to add.

**afflation** (af-fla'shun), n. A breathing upon.

**afflict** (af-flikt'), vt. To give continued pain, distress, or grief.

**affluent** (af'flo-ent), a. Abounding; wealthy.

**afflux** (af'fluks), n. A flowing to; an accession.

**afforce** (af-fors'), vt. (law). To reinforce (a jury or other deliberate body) by specially skilled persons.

**afford** (af-ford'), vt. To yield or produce.

**affranchise** (af-fran'chiz), vt. To free from slavery, or from some obligation.

**affray** (af-fra'), n. A fight causing alarm; a brawl, or fray.

**affright** (af-frit'), vt. To frighten.

**affront** (af-frunt'), vt. To meet face to face; to insult openly.

**affusion** (af-fu'zhun), n. The act of pouring upon or sprinkling.

**afloat** (a-flot'), adv. or a. Floating; at sea; unfixed.

**aforesaid** (a-for'sed), a. Said or named before.

**afoul** (a-fowl'), a. or adv. Entangled; in collision.

**afraid** (a-frad'), a. Struck with fear; timid.

**African** (af'rik-an), a. Pertaining to Africa.

**aftermath** (af'ter-math), n. Second crop of grass.

**against** (a-genst', a-ganst'), prep. In opposition to; in provision for.

**agamic** (a-gam'ik), a. Not having visible organs of reproduction, as certain plants.

**agape** (a-gap'), ad. With staring eagerness; with surprise.

**agate** (ag'at), n. A kind of quartz.

**agave** (a-ga've), n. The American aloe.

**agency** (a'jensi), n. Quality or state of action; business performed by an agent.

**agenda** (a-jen'da), n. pl. Things to be done; business of the meeting; notebook of such.

**agent** (a'jent), n. A deputy; any active cause or power.

**agglomerate** (a-glom'e-rate) vt. To gather into a ball or mass.

**agglutinate** (a-gloo'ti-nat), vt. To cause to adhere.

**aggrandise** (ag'gran-diz),vt. To make great; exalt.

**aggravate** (ag'ra-vat), vt. To make worse; exaggerate.

**aggregate** (ag're-gat), vt. To collect. a. Formed of parts collected. n. The whole.

**aggress** (a-gres'), vt. To encroach upon with violence. **[aggression, aggressive, aggressor]**

**aggrievance** (a-gre'vans), n. Injury; wrong.

**aggrieve** (a-grev'), vt. To give pain or sorrow to; afflict; oppress; vex.

**aggroup** (a-groop'), vt. To bring together and place in a group.

**aghast** (a-gast'), a. Amazed; terrified.

**agile** (aj'il), a. Quick of motion; nimble; active.

**agility** (a-jil'i-ti), n. Activity; quickness.

**agio** (a'ji-o, aj'i-o), n. The difference in value between metallic and paper money; premium or discount.

## AGITATE     8     ALEMBIC

**agitate** (aj'i-tat). To disturb; to discuss. [**agitator**]

**agnail** (ag'nal), n. A disease of the nails; a whitlow.

**agnate** (ag'nat), a. Related or akin by the father's side.

**agnomen** (ag-no'men), n. An additional name.

**agnostic** (ag-nos'tik), n. One who holds that we can know nothing of God or of the supernatural. [**agnosticism**]

**agonic** (a-gon'ik), a. Not forming an angle.

**agonise** (ag'o-niz), vt. or i. To writhe with pain; put in severe pain.

**agonistic** (ag-o-nist'ik), a. Relating to athletic combats.

**agrarian** (a-gra'ri-an), a. Relating to fields or grounds. [**agrarianism**]

**agree** (a-gre'), vi. [pp. **agreed**]. To be of one mind; come to terms; resemble; suit. [**agreeable**]

**agreed** (a-gred'), pp. Settled by consent; determined. [**agreement**]

**agrestic** (a-gres'tik), a. Relating to the country; rustic; rural.

**agricultural** (ag-ri-kul'tur-al), a. Relating to agriculture. [**agriculture, agriculturist**]

**ague** (a'gu), n. Chilly fit.

**aid** (ad), vt. To help; succor.

**aide-de-camp** (ad'de-kong), n. An officer who conveys the general's orders. pl. **aides-de-camp**.

**aigrette** (a'gret), n. A tuft of feathers. Also **egrette**.

**ail** (al), vt. To affect with uneasiness. [**ailment**]

**aimless** (am'les), a. Without aim.

**air** (ar), n. The fluid we breathe; a tune; affected manner or gesture. pl. **airs**, disdainful mien.

**airy** (ar'i), a. Open to the air; gay; without reality.

**aisle** (il), n. A passageway in a church.

**ajar** (a-jar'), ad. Partly open.

**akimbo** (a-kim'bo), ad. With a crook; arched.

**akin** (a-kin'), a. Related by blood; allied by nature.

**alabaster** (al'a-bas-ter), n. A variety of gypsum or sulphate of lime.

**alack** (a-lak'), interj. Alas! Expression of sorrow.

**alacrity** (a-lak'ri-ti), n. Cheerful willingness or readiness.

**alarm** (a-larm'), n. A notice of danger; sudden terror.

**alas** (a-las'), interj. Expression of sorrow.

**alb** (alb), n. A vestment of white linen.

**albatross** (al'ba-tros), n. A large south-sea bird.

**albeit** (al-be'it), ad. Although; be it so.

**albino** (al-bi'no), n. A white negro; a person unnaturally white.

**album** (al'bum), n. A book used for photographs or autographs.

**albumen** (al-bu'men), n. The white of an egg. [**albuminous**]

**alburnum** (al-bur'num), n. The white or soft part of wood; sap-wood.

**alchemy** (al'ke-mi), n. Occult chemistry.

**alcohol** (al'ko-hol), n. Pure spirit.

**alcoran** (al'ko-ran), n. The book of Mohammedan faith.

**alcove** (al'kov), n. A recess of a room.

**alderman** (al'der-man), n. A city magistrate.

**ale** (al), n. A fermented malt liquor.

**alembic** (a-lem'bik), n. A

**ALERT**     9     **ALLUVIAL**

vessel formerly used for distilling.

**alert** (a-lert'), a. Denoting watchful activity or readiness.

**algebra** (al'je-bra), n. The science of quantity; universal arithmetic.

**alias** (a'li-as), n. A fictitious name; a second writ.

**alibi** (al'i-bi), n. In another place.

**alien** (al'yen), a. Foreign.

**alienate** (al'yen-at), v. To transfer to another; to estrange; to misapply. [**alienation**]

**alight** (a-lit'), v. To fall upon; to get off; to descend.

**alignment** (a-lin'ment), n. The fixing of a line; the line established.

**aliment** (al'i-ment), n. Food; nourishment.

**alimony** (al'i-mon-i), n. The allowance to a wife when legally separated from her husband.

**aliquot** (al'i-kwot), a. That measures exactly; without remainder.

**alkali** (al'ka-li), n. A substance which combines with an acid and neutralizes it, forming a salt. pl. **al'kalis**.

**alkaloid** (al'ka-loid), n. A vegetable principle possessing in some degree alkaline properties.

**Allah** (al'la), n. The Arabic name of the one God.

**allay** (al-la'), vt. To lighten, relieve; to make quiet or calm.

**allege** (al-lej'), vt. To produce as an argument or plea; to assert.

**allegiance** (al-lej'i-ans), n. The duty of a subject to his liege or sovereign.

**allegory** (al'le-gor-i), n. A description of one thing under the image of another.

**allegro** (al-le'gro), adv. and a. (mus.) A word denoting a brisk movement.

**alleviate** (al-lev'i-at), vt. To make light; to mitigate. [**allevia'tion, allev'iator**]

**alley** (al'li), n. A passage in a city narrower than a street.

**All-Fools-Day,** n. The first of April.

**All-Souls-Day,** n. The second of November.

**alliance** (al-li'ans), n. Union by treaty or marriage.

**allied** (al-lid'), part. Connected by agreement, etc.

**alligator** (al'li-ga-tur), n. The American crocodile.

**alliteration** (al-lit-er-a'-shun), n. The beginning of several successive words with the same letter.

**allocate** (al'lo-kat), v. To set apart; to place to. [**allocution**]

**allodial** (al-lo'di-al), a. Not held dependent in a superior.

**allopathy** (al-lop'a-thi), n. The common mode of curing diseases.

**allot** (al-lot'), v. To give by lot; to distribute; to apportion.

**allotropy** (al-lot'ro-pi), n. Property of existing in two or more physical conditions.

**allow** (al-low'), v. To grant. [**allowance**]

**alloy** (al-loi'), v. To mix any metal with another.

**allspice** (al'spis), n. The fruit of the pimento.

**allude** (al-lud'), v. To refer to; to insinuate.

**allure** (al-lur'), v. To tempt by the offer of good; to entice.

**allusion** (al-lu'zhun), n. Indirect reference. [**allusive**]

**alluvial** (al-lu'vi-al), a. Deposited by water. [**alluvium**]

**ally** (al-li'), v. To unite by compact.

**almanac** (al'ma-nak), n. A calendar or register of months, weeks, days, etc.

**almighty** (al-mit'i), a. All-powerful.

**almond** (a'mund), n. The fruit of the almond-tree.

**almoner** (al'mun-er), n. A distributer of alms. [**almonry**]

**alms** (amz), n. sing. and pl. A gift to the poor.

**aloof** (a-loof'), ad. At a distance; apart.

**alpenstock** (al'pen-stok), n. A long stout staff.

**alpha** (al'fa), n. The first letter of the Greek alphabet. [**alphabet**]

**Alpine** (al'pin), a. Pertaining to the Alps.

**already** (awl-red'i), ad. Before this time; now.

**altar** (awl'tar), n. A place for offerings; communion table.

**altarage** (awl'tar-aj), n. Offerings at the altar; a kind of tithes.

**alterable** (awl'ter-a-bl), a. That may be changed; that may vary. [**alterant, alteration**]

**altercate** (al'ter-kat), vi. To contend in words.

**alternate** (al'ter-nat), a. Being by turns. vt. To perform by turns. [**alternation, alternative**]

**altimeter** (al-tim'e-ter), n. An instrument for measuring altitudes.

**altitude** (al'ti-tud), n. The height of a place; elevation.

**alto** (al'to), ad. High. n. The counter tenor.

**alto relievo** (alt'o-re'le-vo), n. High relief; figures that project largely from the surface on which they are sculptured.

**altruism** (al'troo-izm), n. Care or devotion to others; opposed to selfishness.

**alum** (al'um), n. A mineral salt.

**aluminium** (al-u-min'i-um), n. The metallic base of alumina; a light metal resembling silver.

**alumnus** (a-lum'nus), n. A pupil. n. pl. **alumni** (a-lum'ni).

**alveary** (al've-ar-i), n. A bee-hive; the hollow of the ear.

**alveolar** (al-ve'o-lar), a. Pertaining to or resembling the sockets of the teeth.

**alvine** (al'vin), a. Belonging to the belly.

**amalgam** (a-mal'gam), n. A mixture of quicksilver with another metal. [**amalgamate**]

**amanuensis** (a-man-u-en'sis), n. A writer of what another dictates. pl. **amanuenses**.

**amaranth** (am'a-ranth), n. A flower that never fades.

**amass** (a-mas'), vt. To collect into a heap; accumulate.

**amateur** (am-a-tur'), n. One who studies or practises any of the fine arts—not being a professional.

**amatory** (am-a-tur'i), a. Relating to or induced by love.

**amaurosis** (am-aw-ro'sis), n. Decay or loss of sight.

**amaze** (a-maz'), vt. To confound with surprise or wonder.

**Amazon** (am'az-on), n. One of a fabled nation of female warriors; a masculine woman; a virago.

**ambage** (am'baj), n. Roundabout phrases; circuitous paths, windings.

**ambassador** (am-bas'a-dur), n. A diplomatic minister of the highest order

**amber** (am'ber), n. A yellowish fossil resin.

**ambergris** (am'ber-gres), n. A fragrant substance found floating on the sea and in the spermaceti whale.

**ambidexter** (am-bi-deks'ter), a. and n. Able to use both hands with equal facility.

**ambient** (am'bi-ent), a. Going round; surrounding; investing.

**ambiguous** (am-big'u-us), a. Of doubtful signification; indistinct; uncertain. [**ambigu'ity**]

**ambition** (am-bish'un), n. The desire of power, honor, fame, excellence.

**amble** (am'bl), vi. To move as a horse with a peculiar, easy gait.

**ambrosia** (am-bro'zhi-a), n. The fabled food of the gods; any delicious beverage.

**ambulance** (am'bul-ans), n. A carriage which serves as a movable hospital.

**ambuscade** (am'busk-ad), n. A hiding to attack by surprise.

**ambush** (am'boosh), n. and v. Same meanings as **ambuscade**.

**ameer** (a-mer'), n. A title of honor, also of an independent ruler in Mohammedan countries.

**ameliorate** (a-mel'yor-at), vt. To make better; to improve.

**amenable** (a-men'a-bl), a. Easy to be led or governed; liable or subject to.

**amend** (a-mend'), vt. To correct.

**amenity** (am-en'i-ti), n. Pleasantness, as regards situation, climate, manners, or disposition.

**amerce** (a-mers'), vt. To punish by a fine; to deprive of anything, or to inflict loss upon.

**American** (a-mer'ik-an), a. Pertaining to America, esp. to the United States.

**amethyst** (am'eth-ist), n. A bluish-violet variety of quartz.

**amiable** (am'i-a-bl), a. Lovable; worthy of love; of sweet disposition.

**amicable** (am'ik-a-bl), a. Friendly.

**amity** (am'i-ti), n. Friendship; good-will.

**ammonia** (am-mon'i-a), n. A pungent gas.

**ammunition** (am-mu-nish'un), n. Military stores.

**amnesty** (am'nes-ti), n. A general pardon.

**amorous** (am'o-rus), a. Inclined to love; passionate.

**amorphous** (a-mar'fus), a. Of irregular shape.

**amount** (a-mownt'), v. To rise in value; to result in.

**amour** (a-mor'), n. A love intrigue; gallantry.

**amphibious** (am-fib'i-us), a. Able to live on land or in water.

**ample** (am'pl), a. Large; extended; liberal; diffusive; wide; spacious.

**amplification** (am-pli-fi-ka'shun), n. Enlargement; diffuse discourse. [**amplitude**]

**amputate** (am'pu-tat), v. To cut off a limb.

**amulet** (am'u-let), n. A charm worn to prevent evil.

**amuse** (a-muz'), v. To entertain agreeably.

**anabaptist** (an-a-bap'tist), n. One who rejects infant baptism.

**anacronism** (an-ak'ro-nizm), n. An error in the account of events in times past.

**anæsthetic** (an-es-thet'ik), a. Depriving of feeling.

**anagram** (an'a-gram), n. A

new word formed from the letters of another word.
**analogous** (an-al'o-gus), a. Having resemblance.
**analogy** (an-al'o-ji), n. An agreement or correspondence in certain respects between things otherwise different; likeness; proportion.
**analysis** (an-al'i-sis), n. Separation of a body or of a subject into its parts. [**analytic**]
**analytics** (an-a-lit'iks), n. The science of analysis. [**analyze**]
**anarchy** (an'ar-ki), n. Want of government.
**anathema** (a-nath'e-ma), n. An ecclesiastical curse.
**anatomical** (an-a-tom'ik-al), a. Pertaining to anatomy.
**anatomist** (an-at'o-mist), n. One skilled in dissecting. [**anatomy**]
**ancestor** (an'ses-tur), n. One from whom we descend; a forefather. [**ancestry**]
**anchor** (angk'ur), n. An iron instrument for fastening ships at rest in water. [**anchorage**]
**anchovy** (an-cho'vi), n. A dried fish used in seasoning.
**ancient** (an'shent), a. Belonging to former times; not modern; old.
**andiron** (and'i-urn), n. An iron implement to support wood in a fireplace.
**anecdote** (an'ek-dot), n. A short story.
**anemone** (a-nem'o-ne), n. The wind-flower.
**aneurism** (an'u-rizm), n. A rupture of an artery.
**angelic** (an-jel'ik), a. Belonging to or like angels.
**anger** (ang'ger), n. A passion excited by injury.
**angina** (an-ji'na), n. Inflammation of the throat.
**angle** (ang'gl), n. A point or corner where two lines meet; a corner.
**angler** (ang'gler), n. One who fishes with hook and line.
**Anglican** (ang'gli-kan), a. Pertaining to England. [**Anglicize**]
**angrily** (ang'gri-li), ad. In an angry manner.
**angry** (ang'gri), a. Moved with anger; indignant.
**anguish** (ang'gwish), n. Extreme pain.
**angular** (ang'gu-lar), a. Having corners. [**angularity**]
**aniline** (an'i-lin), n. A substance used in dyeing.
**anility** (a-nil'i-ti), n. The old age of woman; dotage.
**animadversion** (an-i-mad-ver'shun), n. Remarks in the way of censure or criticism; reproof; comment. [**animadvert**]
**animalcule** (an-i-mal'kul), n. A very small animal, nearly or quite invisible to the naked eye.
**animate** (an'i-mat), v. To give life to; to enliven.
**animosity** (an-i-mos'i-ti), n. Violent malignity; hatred; malevolence.
**animus** (an'i-mus), n. The feeling that prompts; temper.
**ankle** (angk'l), n. The joint that connects the foot and the leg.
**anklet** (angk'let), n. An ornament for the ankle.
**annalist** (an'nal-ist), n. A writer of annals.
**annals** (an'nalz), n. pl. Histories related in order of time; chronicles.
**anneal** (an-nel'), v. To temper glass or metals by heat.
**annex** (an-neks'), v. To unite; to subjoin; to affix.
**annihilate** (an-ni'hi-lat), v.

# ANNIVERSARY 13 ANTHRACITE

To reduce to nothing; to destroy.

**anniversary** (an-ni-vers'ar-i), a. Returning or happening every year; annual.

**annotate** (an-o-tat), vt. To make comments upon.

**announce** (a-nouns'), vt. To give notice of; proclaim.

**annoy** (a-noi'), vt. To disturb or trouble repeatedly; vex; tease; molest. [annoyance]

**annual** (an'u-al), a. Coming yearly.

**annuity** (a-nu'i-ti), n. A yearly allowance.

**annul** (a-nul'), vt. [pp. annulled]. To make void; abolish.

**annular** (an'u-lar), a. Having the form of a ring; round.

**annulation** (an-u-la'shun), n. A circular, ring-like formation.

**annulet** (an'u-let), n. A little ring.

**annulment** (a-nul'ment), n. The act of annulling.

**annunciate** (a-nun'si-at), vt. To bring tidings; announce. [annunciation]

**anodic** (a-nod'ik), a. Proceeding upwards; ascending.

**anodyne** (an'o-din), n. Medicine to assuage pain and dispose to sleep.

**anoint** (a-noint'), vt. To rub with oil; consecrate.

**anomalous** (a-nom'a-lus), a. Deviating from rule or analogy. [anomaly]

**anon** (a-non'), ad. Soon; quickly.

**anonymous** (a-non'i-mus), a. Wanting a name; nameless.

**anserine** (an-se'rin), a. Belonging to the goose family.

**answer** (an'ser), vi. To speak in reply; succeed. [answerable]

**antagonise** (an-tag'o-niz), vi. To act in opposition. [antagonist]

**antalgic** (an-tal'jik), a. Alleviating pain.

**antarctic** (ant-ark'tik), a. Opposite to the arctic.

**ante** (ante). In compound words signifies before.

**anteact** (an'te-akt), n. A preceding act.

**antecede** (an-te-sed'), vi. To precede; to go before in time, etc. [antecedence, antecedent]

**antechamber** (an'te-chamber), n. A room leading to another.

**antediluvian** (an-te-di-loo'vi-an), a. Being before the flood in Noah's days.

**antelucan** (an-te-loo'kan), a. Before light or the dawn of day.

**antemeridian** (an-te-me-rid'i-an), a. Being before noon.

**antemundane** (an-te-mun'dan), a. Being before the creation.

**antennæ** (an-ten'e), n. pl. The feelers of insects.

**antenuptial** (an-te-nup'shal), a. Being before marriage.

**antepaschal** (an-te-pas'kal), a. Before Easter.

**antepast** (an'te-past), n. A foretaste.

**antepenult** (an-te-pe-nult'), n. The last syllable but two of a word.

**anteposition** (an-te-po-zish'un), n. Placing a word before another.

**anterior** (an-te'ri-er), a. Going before in time or place; prior; previous.

**anthem** (an'them), n. A hymn sung in parts and set to words from Scripture.

**anthology** (an-thol'o-ji), n. A collection of flowers, or of poems.

**anthracite** (an'thra-sit), n. A sort of hard coal.

**anthrax** (an'thraks), n. A carbuncle; an ulcer.

**anthropoid** (an'thro-poid), a. Resembling the human form.

**anthropology** (an-thro-pol'o-ji), n. The natural history of the human species.

**anthropomorphism** (an-thro-po-mor'fizm), n. The ascription to God of a human form, passions, and affections.

**antic** (an'tik), a. Odd; fanciful.

**anticipant** (an-tis'i-pant), a. That anticipates.

**anticipate** (an-tis'i-pat), vt. To take before; foretaste; foresee.

**anticlimax** (an-ti-kli'maks), n. A falling off or sinking; bathos.

**anticlinal** (anti-kli'nal), a. Dipping or sloping in opposite directions.

**antidotal** (an-ti-dot'al), a. Efficacious against. [**antidote**]

**antipathy** (an-tip'a-thy), n. Aversion; dislike; repugnance.

**antipode** (an'ti-pod), n. pl. **antipodes** (an-tip'o-dez). One of those on the opposite side of the globe. [**antip'odal**]

**antiquarian** (an'ti-kwa'ri-an), a. Pertaining to antiquity. [**an'tiquary**]

**antique** (an-tek'), a. Old; ancient; of old fashion. [**antiq'uity**]

**antiseptic** (an'ti-sep'tik), a. Opposing putrefaction.

**antithesis** (an-tith'e-sis), n. Opposition of words or sentiments; contrast.

**antitoxin** (an'ti-toks'in), n. A substance used to inoculate against diseases caused by bacteria, as diphtheria.

**antler** (ant'ler), n. A branch of a stag's horn.

**anvil** (an'vil), n. An iron block to hammer on.

**anxious** (ank'shus), a. Greatly concerned or solicitous; distressed.

**aorta** (a-or'ta), n. The great artery from the heart.

**apathy** (ap'a-thy), n. Want of feeling; insensibility; unconcern. [**apathet'ic**]

**aperient** (a-pe'ri-ent), a. Tending to open; gently purgative.

**aperture** (ap'er-tur), n. An opening; a hole.

**apetalous** (a-pet'al-us), a. Having no petals.

**aphorism** (af'o-riz'm), n. A precept expressed in few words; axiom; maxim; adage.

**apiary** (a'pi-a-ry), n. A place for keeping bees.

**apiece** (a-pes'), adv. To each; to the share of each.

**apologue** (ap'o-log), n. A moral fable.

**apology** (a-pol'o-jy), n. Something said to defend.

**apoplexy** (ap'o-plex-i), n. Sudden loss or diminution of sensation and of the power of voluntary motion.

**apostasy** (a-pos'ta-si), n. Desertion of one's faith, religion, party, or principles.

**apostle** (a-pos'l), n. One of the twelve chosen by Christ to proclaim his gospel (Matt. x, 2-4).

**apostrophe** (a-pos'tro-fe), n. Omission indicated; digressive address.

**apothecary** (a-poth'e-ke-ri), n. A druggist; pharmacist.

**apothegm** (ap'o-them), n. A terse, instructive, practical saying.

**apotheosis** (ap'o-thi'o-sis), n. Exaltation to divine honors; deification.

# APPAL     15     AQUEDUCT

**appal**, vt. To fill with dismay or horror; terrify; shock.

**apparatus**, n. A set of tools, appliances, etc.

**apparel**, vt. To clothe.

**apparent** (ap-par'ent), a. That may be seen; evident.

**apparition** (ap-a-rish'un), n. Specter.

**appeal** (ap-pel'), vt. Remove a cause to a higher court; invoke aid, pity or mercy.

**appear** (ap-per'), vi. Become visible; seem probable. [**appear'ance**]

**appease** (ap-pez'), vt. Pacify; quiet; allay.

**appellant** (ap-pel'ant), n. One who appeals. [**appellation**]

**append** (ap-pend'), vt. Attach; subjoin. [**append'age, append'ix**]

**appendicitis** (ap-pen-di-si'tis), n. Inflammation of the vermiform appendix.

**appertain** (ap-er-tan'), vi. Belong; relate.

**appetite** (ap'e-tit), n. Natural desire; physical or mental craving. [**appetizer**]

**applaud** (ap-plad'), vt. and vi. Praise; express approval. [**applause**]

**appliance** (ap-pli'ans), n. Act of applying.

**applicable** (ap'li-ka-bl), a. That may be applied; suitable; relevant.

**applicant** (ap'li-kant), n. One who applies; candidate. [**application**]

**apply** (ap-pli'), vt. Employ; devote; have reference.

**appoint** (ap-point'), vt. Assign; equip.

**apportion** (ap-por'shun), vt. Divide in share.

**apposition** (ap-o-zish'un), n. Annexing one noun to another in the same case or relation.

**appraise** (ap-praz'), vt. Value.

**appreciable** (ap-pre'sh-i-a-bl), a. That may be estimated.

**appreciate** (ap-pre'shi-at), vt. Rise in value. [**appreciation**]

**apprehend** (ap-pre-hend'), vt. Comprehend; expect with fear.

**apprentice** (ap-pren'tis), vt. Bind to a trade; learner; beginner.

**apprise, apprize** (ap-priz'), vt. Give notice; inform.

**approach** (ap-proch'), vt. Come near to; make advances to.

**approbation** (ap-pro-ba'shun), n. Commendation.

**appropriate** (ap-pro'pri-at), vt. Take to one's self. a. Suitable; peculiar.

**approve** (ap-prov'), vt. Commend; sanction.

**approximate** (ap-prox'i-met), v. To approach or cause to approach closely without exact coincidence.

**appurtenance** (ap-pur'te-nans), n. Something belonging or attached to something else as an accessory or adjunct.

**apricot**, n. A fruit intermediate between the peach and the plum.

**April**, n. The fourth month.

**apron**, n. A covering to protect or adorn the front of a person's clothes.

**apropos** (a'pro-po'), a. Pertinent; opportune.

**aptitude** (apt'i-tiud), n. Natural or acquired adaptation.

**aqua**, n. Water.

**aquarium** (a-cwe'ri-um), n. A tank or building for aquatic animals or plants.

**aquatic** (a-cwat'ic), a. Pertaining to, living, growing in, or adapted to the water.

**aqueduct** (ac'we-duct), n. A

water-conduit for supplying a community from a distance.

**aqueous** (a'cwe-us), a. Watery.

**aquiline** (ac'wi-lin), a. Of or like an eagle or an eagle's beak; curving; hooked.

**Arab** (ar'ab), n. One of the Arabian race. [**Ara'-bian**]

**arable** (ar'a-b'l), a. Fit for tillage.

**arbiter** (ar'bi-ter), n. An umpire; a judge. [**ar'bitrary, ar'bitra'tion, ar'bitra'tor**]

**arbor** (ar'ber), n. A bower; a shaded seat. [**arbo'reous**]

**arc** (ark), n. Part of the circumference of a circle or curve.

**arcade** (ar-kad'), n. A series of arches; an arched passage.

**arch** (arch), a. Cunning or sly; roguish; chief; of the first class; principal; a curved or vaulted structure.

**archæology** (ar'ke-ol'o-jy), n. The science of antiquities.

**archaic** (ar-ka'ik), a. Obsolete; antiquated.

**archer** (ar'cher), n. One who shoots with a bow and arrow. [**ar'chery**]

**archipelago** (ar-ki-pel'a-go), n. Sea abounding in small islands.

**architect** (ar'ki-tekt), n. One who designs buildings and superintends their erection. [**architecture**]

**archives** (ar'kivz), n. pl. Place where public papers and records are kept.

**arctic** (ark'tik), a. Northern; pertaining to the region round the north pole.

**ardent** (ar'dent), a. Intense; eager.

**ardor** (ar'dur), n. Warmth of passion or feeling.

**arduous** (ar'du-us), a. Difficult to accomplish.

**area** (a're-a), n. Plain surface included within limits.

**arena** (a-re'na), n. Place for public action or contest.

**argent** (ar'jent), a. Made of or like silver.

**argosy** (ar'go-si), n. Large merchant vessel.

**argue** (ar'gu), vt. Prove by argument.

**argument** (ar'gu-ment), n. Reason offered as proof.

**arid** (ar'id), a. Dry; parched. [**arid'ity**]

**Aries** (a'ri-ez), n. Constellation of the zodiac.

**aristocracy** (ar-is-tok'ra-si), n. Government by the nobles.

**aristocrat** (ar-is'to-krat), n. One who belongs to or favors an aristocracy.

**arithmetic** (a-rith'me-tik), n. Science of numbers. [**arithmeti'cian**]

**ark** (ark), n. Large boat; chest.

**armada** (ar-ma'da or ar-ma'da), n. Fleet of warships.

**armistice** (ar'mis-tis), n. Truce.

**armor** (ar'mur), n. Defensive arms or dress; plating of ships.

**aroma** (a-ro'ma), n. Fragrance. [**aromat'ic**]

**arouse** (a-rowz'), vt. Wake; stir.

**arraign** (ar-ran'), vt. Accuse; call to account in court.

**arrange** (ar-ranj'), vt. Put in order.

**array** (ar-ra'), vt. Arrange; deck.

**arrear** (ar-rer'), n. That which remains overdue.

**atmosphere** (at'mos-fer), n. The air that surrounds the earth.

**atoll** (at-ol'), n. A ring-shaped coral island with central lagoon.

**atom** (at'om), n. A minute particle.

**atomizer**, n. Instrument for converting liquids into spray.

**atone** (a-ton'), vt. To expiate, or make satisfaction for.

**atrocious** (a-tro'shus), a. Extremely cruel or wicked. [atrocity]

**atrophy** (at'ro-fi), n. A wasting away.

**attach** (at-tach'), vt. To fasten to; seize by legal process.

**attack** (at-tak'), vt. To assail.

**attain** (at-tan'), vt. To reach by efforts.

**attaint** (at-tant'), vt. To disgrace.

**attar** (at'tar), n. A fragrant volatile oil, esp. of roses.

**attempt** (at-temt'), vt. To try; make trial of, or an effort upon.

**attend** (at-tend'), vt. To accompany. [attendance, attendant]

**attention** (at-ten'shun), n. The act of heeding.

**attentuate** (at-ten'yu-at), vt. To render thin.

**attest** (at-test'), vt. and vi. To bear witness to; to affirm. [attestation]

**attic** (at'tik), n. The low topmost story of a house.

**Attic** (at'tik), a. Pertaining to Attica; elegant; classical.

**attire** (at-tir'), vt. To dress; to array.

**attitude** (at'ti-tud), n. Posture.

**attorney** (at-tur'ni), n. One who acts for another; a lawyer.

**attract** (at-trakt'), vt. To draw to; to allure. [attraction, attractive]

**attribute** (at-trib'yut), vt. To ascribe; impute.

**attribute** (at'trib-ut), n. Inherent quality or property.

**attrition** (at-trish'un), n. Act of rubbing or wearing.

**attune** (at-tun'), vt. To bring into harmony; to tune.

**auburn** (a'burn), a. Reddish brown.

**auction** (ak'shun), n. A public sale to the highest bidder. [auctioneer]

**audacious** (a-da'shus), a. Bold; daring; impudent.

**audible** (ad'i-bl), a. That may be heard.

**audience** (ad'i-ens), n. A hearing; an assembly of hearers.

**audit** (ad'it), vt. To adjust accounts by authority. [auditor]

**auditorium** (ad-it-o'ri-um), n. That part of a public building occupied by the audience.

**auditory** (ad'it-o-ri), a. Pertaining to the sense of hearing.

**auger** (a'ger), n. A tool for boring holes.

**aught** (at), n. Anything.

**augment** (ag-ment'), vt. and vi. To increase. [augmentation]

**augur**, n. A diviner; a soothsayer. [augury]

**August**, n. The eighth month of the year.

**auricular** (a-rik'yu-lar), a. Pertaining to the ear.

**auriferous** (a-rif'e-rus), a. Yielding gold.

**aurora** (a-ro'ra), n. The goddess of morning.

**aurora borealis**, n. The northern light.

**auspice**, n. An omen.

**auspicious** (as-pish'us), a. Ominous of good; fortunate.

**austere** (as-ter'), a. Harsh; severe. [**austerity**]

**austral** (as'tral), a. Southern.

**authentic** (a-then'tik), a. Genuine; trustworthy. [**authenticity**]

**author** (a'thor), n. One who produces; an originator.

**authorize, -ise** (a'thor-iz), vt. To furnish with authority.

**authority** (a-thor'i-ti), n. Power; sway; rule; source; permission.

**autobiography** (a-to-bi-og'ra-fi), n. The narration of one's own life.

**autocracy** (a-tok'ra-si), n. Absolute government.

**autograph** (a'to-graf), n. A person's own handwriting or signature.

**automatic** (a-to-mat'ik), a. Like an automaton; self-moving.

**automobile** (a-to-mo'bil), n. A self-propelled road-carriage.

**autonomy** (a-ton'o-mi), n. Self-government.

**autopsy** (a'top-si), n. The examination of a body after death.

**autumn** (a'tum), n. The third season of the year.

**auxiliaries** (ag-zil'ya-riz), n. pl. Troops aiding the forces of another nation.

**auxiliary** (ag-zil'ya-ri), a. Helping; assisting.

**avail** (a-val'), vt. To aid; benefit. [**available**]

**avalanche**, n. A falling or gliding mass of snow or ice.

**avarice** (av'a-ris), n. Excessive love of gain. [**avaricious**]

**avenge** (a-venj'), vt. To take vengeance.

**avenue** (av'e-nu), n. A way; alley of trees.

**average** (av'er-aj), n. A mean proportion; proportional distribution.

**averse** (a-vers'), a. Turned away; disinclined. [**aversion**]

**avert** (a-vert'), vt. To turn away; to prevent.

**aviator** (a'vi-a-ter), n. An operator of machines navigating the air.

**avidity** (a-vid'i-ti), n. Eagerness.

**avocation** (av-o-ka'shun), n. Occupation other than one's principal business.

**avoid** (a-void'), vt. To keep away from; to shun. [**avoidable, avoidance**]

**avoirdupois** (av-er-dyu-poiz'), a. or n. A weight of which the pound contains 16 ounces, or 7,000 grains.

**avouch** (a-vouch'), vt. To avow; to affirm.

**avow** (a-vou'), vt. To declare openly; to own. [**avowal**]

**award** (a-ward'), vt. To adjudge.

**awe** (a), n. Reverential fear. [**awful**]

**awkward** (ak'ward), a. Clumsy; unskilful.

**awl** (al), n. A pointed tool for piercing leather or wood.

**awning** (an'ing), n. A covering to shelter from the sun.

**axe** (aks), n. A tool for chopping.

**axial** (aks'i-al), a. Pertaining to, or revolving about, an axis.

**axiom** (aks'i-om), n. A self-evident proposition.

**axis** (aks'is), n. The line on which a body revolves. pl. **axes**.

**axle** (aks'l), n. The shaft on which a wheel turns.

**ay, or aye** (ai), adv. Yes.

**aye** (a), adv. Always; ever.

**azimuth** (az'i-muth), n. Angular distance from the north or south point of the horizon.

**azure** (azh'ur or a'zhur), a. Clear blue.

# B

**babel**, n. Confusion; confused clamor.

**baboon**, n. A large monkey of Asia and Africa.

**baccalaureate** (bak-ka-la'-re-at), n. The degree or position of a Bachelor of Arts.

**bachelor** (bach'e-lor), n. An unmarried man; one who has taken the first degree at a university.

**bacillus** (ba-sil'us), n. One of a genus of bacteria.

**bacon** (ba'kun), n. Hog's flesh cured with salt and smoke.

**bade** (bad). Past tense of **bid**.

**badge** (baj), n. A mark of distinction.

**badger** (baj'er), n. A quadruped; to worry.

**badinage** (bad-i-naj'), n. Playful discourse.

**baffle** (baf'l), vt. To elude or defeat by artifice.

**bagatelle** (bag-a-tel'), n. A thing of no importance.

**baggage** (bag'aj), n. Utensils of an army; clothing; lumber.

**bagnio** (ban'yo), n. A bathing-house; enclosure for slaves.

**bail** (bal), n. A surety for another's appearance.

**bailiff** (ba'lif), n. An executive officer.

**bait** (bat), vt. or i. To put on a hook so as to catch fish; provoke or harass.

**bakshish** (bak'shesh), n. A gratuity.

**balance** (bal'ans), n. A pair of scales; the difference of accounts.

**balcony** (bal'ko-ni), n. A frame or gallery before a window.

**bald** (bawld), a. Without hair; naked; mean; unadorned.

**balderdash** (bal'der-dash), n. A jumble of words.

**bale** (bal), n. A pack of goods. **[baleful]**

**ballad** (bal'ad), n. A little song.

**ballast** (bal'ast), n. Weight to steady a ship. vt. To load with ballast.

**balloonist** (bal-loo'nist), n. One who ascends in a balloon.

**ballot** (bal'ut), n. A ball or ticket used in voting.

**baluster** (bal'us-ter), n. A rail; a small pillar or column.

**balustrade** (bal'us-trad), n. A row of balusters or rails.

**bamboozle** (bam-boo'zl), vt. To deceive.

**banal** (ban'al), a. Commonplace; trite, stale.

**banana** (ba-na'na), n. A plantain tree, and its fruit.

**bandage** (ban'daj), n. A fillet.

**bandana** (ban-dan'a), n. A kind of silk handkerchief.

**bandit** (ban'dit), n. An outlaw; a robber.

**bandy** (ban'di), n. A club for striking a ball. vt. or i. To beat about.

**baneful** (ban'fool), a. Poisonous; hurtful.

**barter** (bar'ter), vt. To traffic by exchanging articles.

**bashful** (bash'fool), a. Wanting confidence; modest; shy.

**basin** (ba'sn), n. A small vessel; a dock; a pond.

**basis** (ba'sis), n. Foundation; support. pl. **bases**.

**bask** (bask), vi. To lie in warmth.

**bas-relief** (bas-re-lef'), n. Sculpture in which the figures do not stand far out from the surface.

**bass** (bas), n. A fish; a species of tree.
**bastard** (bas'tard), n. A spurious child.
**baste** (bast), vt. To beat; sew lightly; drip butter.
**bastinado** (bas-ti-na'dc), vt. To beat with a cudgel.
**bastion** (bast'yun), n. A mass of earth standing out from a rampart.
**batch** (bach), n. Quantity of bread baked at one time; number produced or despatched.
**bateau** (ba-to'), n. A long light boat.
**bathe** (bath), vt. To wash in a bath.
**bathos** (ba'thos), n. Descent in poetry.
**baton** (bat'un), n. A staff; a club.
**battalion** (ba-tal'yun), n. A division of an army.
**batten** (bat'n), vt. or i. To make fat.
**batting** (bat'ing), n. Cotton or wool in sheets for quilting.
**bawdiness** (baw'di-nes), n. Obscenity.
**bawl** (bawl), vt. or i. To speak loud; proclaim, as a crier.
**bayonet** (ba'o-net), n. A dagger fixed to a musket.
**bayou** (ba'oo), n. Outlet of a lake, etc.
**bazaar** (ba-zar'), n. A market-place for sale of goods.
**beach** (bech), n. A sandy shore; strand.
**beacon** (be'kn, be'kun), n. A light to direct seamen; lighthouse.
**bead** (bed), n. A little globule strung on thread, used for necklaces.
**beadle** (be'dl), n. A crier; a messenger.
**beadsman** (bedz'man), n. One who prays for others.
**beagle** (be'gl), n. A hunting dog.

**beak** (bek), n. The bill of a bird; anything like a beak.
**beaker** (be'ker), n. A drinking-cup.
**beam** (bem), n. A main timber; part of a balance.
**bean** (ben), n. The name of many kinds of pulse.
**bear**, vt. To bring forth, as young. n. A wild animal; a stock-jobber interested in depressing stocks.
**beard** (berd), n. Hair on the chin.
**beat** (bet), vt. To strike with repeated blows.
**beatific** (be-a-tif'ik), a. Making happy.
**beatification** (be-at-i-fi-ka'-shun), n. Admission to heavenly honours.
**beatitude** (be-at'i-tud), n. Blessedness; perfect felicity.
**beau** (bo), n. An attendant on a lady; a fop.
**beautiful** (bu'ti-fol), a. Pleasing to the sight or the mind.
**beauty** (bu'ti), n. Gracefulness.
**because**, conj. By cause; for the reason that.
**beckon** (bek'un), v. To make a sign to another; to summon.
**become** (be-kum'), v. To fit or befit.
**bedlam** (bed'lam), n. An asylum for lunatics.
**bedstead** (bed'sted), n. The frame of a bed.
**beech** (bech), n. A species of tree, bearing a nut of triangular shape.
**beef** (bef), n. The flesh of an ox, bull, or cow.
**beeswax** (bez'waks), n. The wax collected by bees.
**beet** (bet), n. A vegetable.
**befoul** (be-fowl'), v. To make foul; to make dirty.
**beget** (be-get'), v. To procreate; to produce.

**beggar** (beg'gar), n. One who begs, or lives by begging. v. To bring to want; to impoverish. **[beggary]**

**begrime** (be-grim'), v. To soil deeply with dirt.

**begrudge** (be-gruj'), v. To envy the possession of.

**beguile** (be-gil'), v. To impose upon by craft; to deceive; to amuse.

**behave** (be-hav'), v. To bear, or carry; to conduct; to act. **[behavior]**

**behest** (be-hest'), n. An order; a command; an injunction.

**beholden** (be-hold'n), a. Indebted; obliged.

**behoof** (be-hof'), n. Profit; advantage; necessity.

**behoove** (be-hov'), v. To be fit, right, or necessary for.

**belch** (belch), v. To eject wind; to eructate.

**beleaguer** (be-le'ger), v. To besiege.

**belfry** (bel'fri), n. A tower where bells are hung.

**belie** (be-li'), v. To speak falsely of; to slander.

**belief** (be-lef'), n. Credit given to evidence; the thing believed; credence; faith. **[believe]**

**belle** (bel), n. A handsome, gay young lady.

**belles-lettres** (bel-let'r), n. pl. Polite literature, including poetry, fiction, criticism, æsthetics, etc.

**bellicose** (bel'ik-os), a. Contentious, war-like.

**belligerent** (bel-ij'er-ent), a. Carrying on regular war. n. A party or person waging such.

**bemean** (be-men'), vt. To make mean.

**beneath** (be-neth'), prep. Under, or lower in place.

**benedict** (ben'e-dikt), n. A newly married man.

**benediction** (ben-e-dik'shun) n. A solemn invocation of the divine blessing on men or things.

**benefaction** (ben-e-fak'shun), n. The act of doing good.

**benefice** (ben'e-fis), n. An ecclesiastical living.

**beneficence** (be-nef'i-sens), n. Active goodness; kindness; charity.

**beneficial** (ben-e-fish'al), a. Useful.

**benevolence** (ben-ev'ol-ens), n. Disposition to do good; generosity.

**benign** (ben-in'), a. Favorable, esp. in astrology, as opposed to malign; gracious.

**benzene** (ben'zen), n. A compound of carbon and hydrogen, found among the products of the destructive distillation of a great many organic bodies, especially coal-tar.

**bequeath** (be-kweth'), vt. To leave by will to another; to transmit to posterity.

**bequest** (be-kwest'), n. A legacy.

**berate** (be-rat'), vt. To scold or chide vigorously.

**bereave** (be-rev'), vt. To rob of anything valued; to leave destitute.

**berth**, n. A sleeping-place.

**beseech** (be-sech'), vt. To entreat; to implore.

**besom** (be'zom), n. A broom.

**besought** (be-sat'), pt. and pp. of **beseech**.

**bestial** (best'yal), a. Pertaining to or resembling a beast; degraded; filthy.

**bestowal** (be-sto'al), n. Act of bestowing.

**bestride** (be-strid'), vt. To stand or sit, having a leg on each side the object.

**betray** (be-tra'), vt. To deliver up treacherously;

# BETROTH 24 BIVOUAC

**be a traitor to. [betrayal, betrayer]**

**betroth** (be-troth'), vt. To plight marriage to.

**bevel** (bev'l), n. A slant or inclination not a right angle.

**beverage** (bev'er-age), n. Liquor for drinking.

**bevy** (bev'i), n. A flock of birds; an assemblage.

**bewail** (be-wal'), vt. To lament; mourn for.

**beware** (be-war'), vt. To regard with distrust.

**bewilder** (be-wil'der), vt. To perplex; confuse.

**bewitch** (be-wich'), vt. To lay a spell or charm upon; to enchant.

**bias**, n. A leaning; inclination.

**bibliography** (bib-li-og'ra-fi), n. The history or knowledge of books.

**bibulous** (bib'yul-us), a. Apt to imbibe or absorb.

**biceps** (bi'seps), n. Large flexor muscle of the upper arm.

**bicker** (bik'er), vi. To contend petulantly.

**bicycle** (bi'sik-l), n. Vehicle with two wheels propelled by the feet of the rider.

**biennial** (bi-en'ni-al), a. Lasting two years.

**bier** (ber), n. Carriage or frame for bearing the dead.

**bifurcate** (bi-fur'kat), a. Having two prongs or branches. **[bifurcation]**

**bigamist** (big'a-mist), n. One guilty of having two wives or husbands at the same time. **[bigamy]**

**bigot** (big'ot), n. One blindly devoted to a party or creed. **[bigotry]**

**bile** (bil), n. Gall.

**bilingual** (bi-ling'gwal), a. Expressed in, or speaking, two languages.

**bilious** (bil'yus), a. Affected by bile; melancholy.

**billet** (bil'let), n. A small note; small log of wood.

**billet-doux** (bil-e-doo'), n. A love-letter.

**billiards** (bil'yardz), n. A game played on a table with balls and cues.

**billingsgate** (bil'ingz-gat), n. Foul language.

**billion** (bil'yun), n. A thousand millions (Fr. & Am.); a million millions (Eng.).

**binary** (bi'na-ri), a. Composed of two; assorted in pairs.

**bindery** (bind'er-i), n. The place where books are bound.

**binocular** (bin-ok'yu-lar), a. Pertaining to, or to be used with, both eyes.

**biographer** (bi-og'ra-fer), n. One who writes biography.

**biography** (bi-og'ra-fi), n. A history of a life.

**biology** (bi-ol'o-ji), n. The science of life.

**bipartite** (bip'ar-tit), a. Divided into two parts.

**biped** (bi'ped), n. An animal having but two feet.

**birth** (berth), n. The act of being born; origin.

**biscuit** (bis'kit), n. Hard or unleavened bread in cakes; unglazed earthenware.

**bisect** (bi-sekt'), vt. To divide into two equal parts.

**bishop** (bish'op), n. The head of a diocese.

**bison** (bi'zon), n. The American buffalo.

**bisque** (bisk), n. Unglazed earthenware; a kind of odds at tennis.

**bissextile** (bis-seks'til), n. Leap-year. a. Intercalary.

**bitch**, n. The female of the dog, wolf, or fox.

**bivalve** (bi'valv), n. A shell-fish having a shell in two valves or parts.

**bivouac** (biv'u-ak), vi. To

**bizarre** (bi-zar'), a. Odd; fantastical.
**blackamoor** (blak'a-moor), n. A negro.
**blackguard** (blag'gard), n. A low, scurrilous fellow.
**black-mail** (blak'mal), n. Money paid to robbers or ill-doers to purchase their forbearance.
**bladder** (blad'er), n. A thin bag distended with liquor or air.
**blain** (blan), n. A boil or blister.
**blanch** (blanch), vt. and vi. To whiten.
**blandish** (bland'ish), vt. To flatter; wheedle; caress.
**blare** (blar), n. A sonorous blast; glare of light.
**blarney** (blar'ni), n. Wheedling or cajoling talk.
**blaspheme** (blas-fem'), vi. To utter profane or impious speech. [**blasphemy**]
**blatant** (blat'ant), a. Offensively loud or clamorous.
**blazon** (bla'zon), vt. To publish ostentatiously.
**blazonry** (bla'zon-ri), n. Art of blazonry; heraldry; armorial devices.
**bleach** (blech), vt. To whiten.
**bleak** (blek), a. Unsheltered; cold.
**blear** (bler), vt. To inflame or dim the eyes.
**bleat** (blet), vi. To cry like a sheep.
**blew** (bloo), pt. of blow.
**blight** (blit), n. A withering disease; mildew.
**blithe** (blith), a. Gay; airy; joyous.
**blizzard** (bliz'ard), n. A violent snowstorm with intense cold.
**bloat** (blot), vt. To cause a swell.
**blockade** (blo-kad'), n. A close siege.

pass the night on guard in the open air.

**blonde** (blond), n. Fair complexion, light hair and eyes.
**blouse** (blouz), n. A light loose outer garment.
**bludgeon** (bluj'un), n. A short, thick club.
**blue** (bloo), n. One of the primary colours.
**blunt**, a. Dull on the edge or point; rude; abrupt.
**blur**, n. A blot; spot; stain.
**blurt**, vt. To utter inadvertently.
**blush** (blush), vi. To redden in the face.
**boar** (bor), n. A male swine.
**board** (bord), n. A piece of timber sawn thin and broad; a table; food; a council.
**boarder** (bor'der), n. One who pays for food taken at another's table; one who enters a ship by force.
**boast** (bost), vt. or i. To talk ostentatiously.
**boat** (bot), n. A small open vessel.
**boatswain** (bo'sn, bot'-swan), n. An officer in a ship who has charge of the boats and rigging.
**bode** (bod), vt. or i. To presage; foreshow.
**bodice** (bod'is), n. A close-fitting garment for the body, worn by women.
**boding** (bo'ding), n. An omen.
**bodyguard** (bod'i-gard), n. A guard of a person.
**Boer** (boor), n. A Dutch farmer at the Cape.
**boggle** (bog'l); vi. To hesitate from fear of difficulties.
**boggy** (bog'i), a. Marshy; swampy.
**bogus** (bo'gus), a. Counterfeit; spurious.
**bohemian** (bo-he'mi-an), n. An artist or literary man who lives a free, unconventional life.

**boil** (boil), n. A sore swelling.

**boiler** (boi'ler), n. A vessel for boiling.

**boisterous** (bois'ter-us), a. Violent; noisy.

**bole** (bol), n. The body or stem; any cylindrical body.

**bolshevik** (bol'she-vek), n. Radical; socialist.

**bolster** (bol'ster), n. A long pillow. vt. To pad; support.

**bolt** (bolt), n. Bar of a door; an arrow; lightning; a piece of canvas of 38 yards.

**bolus** (bo'lus), n. A large pill.

**bomb** (bom), n. An iron shell to be filled with powder and discharged from a mortar.

**bombardment**, n. An attack with bombs.

**bombast**, n. High-sounding language.

**bombastic**, a. Inflated, extravagant.

**bona fide** (bo'na fid'e), adv. and a. In good faith, genuine.

**bonanza**, n. Any mine of wealth or stroke of luck.

**bonbon**, n. A sweetmeat.

**boniface** (bon'i-fas), n. Landlord, host.

**bonnet** (bon'net), n. A headdress; a cap.

**bonny** (bon'ni), a. Handsome.

**bonus** (bo'nus), n. A premium.

**bony** (bo'ni), a. Full of bones.

**boodle** (bo'dl), n. Bribes paid to politicians to affect votes or win influence.

**boomerang** (bom'e-rang), n. An Australian weapon, which, when thrown, returns toward the thrower.

**boon** (bon), a. Gay; merry. n. A gift; present; a favor.

**boor** (bor), n. A clown; a countryman; a rustic.

**booth** (both), n. A slight temporary shelter; a stall in a fair.

**booty** (bot'i), n. Plunder, spoil; pillage.

**borax** (bo'raks), n. Boracic acid and soda, used as a styptic.

**border** (bar'der), n. An edge; boundary.

**boreal** (bo're-al), a. Northern.

**borne** (born), pr. Carried; supported.

**borough** (bur'o), n. A corporate town.

**boscage** (bosk'aj), n. Underwood. a. Representation of woods.

**bosh** (bosh), n. Silly talk; nonsense.

**botany** (bot'a-ni), n. The science that treats of plants.

**botch** (boch), n. Swelling; work badly done. [**botchery**]

**bother** (both'er), v. To tease, or perplex.

**bots**, n. pl. Small worms in the entrails of horses.

**boudoir** (bo'dwar'), n. A lady's private apartment.

**bough** (bow), n. A branch.

**bought**, pr. Purchased.

**boulevard** (bol'e-vard), n. A fine broad street, usually paved and bordered with trees.

**bounce** (bowns), v. To jump; to spring.

**boundary** (bownd'a-ri), n. A limit; bound; barrier.

**bounteous** (bown'te-us), a. Liberal; kind. [**bountiful**]

**bounty** (bown'ti), n. Liberality in giving; a premium.

**bouquet** (bo-ka'), n. A bunch of flowers.

**bourse** (bors), n. A French exchange.

**bout** (bowt), n. A turn; trial; attempt.

**bovine** (bo'vin), a. Pertaining to cattle.

**bow** (bo), n. An instrument to shoot arrows; a fiddlestick; anything arched or curved.

**bowels** (bow'elz), n. pl. The intestines of animals.

**bower**, n. An arbor.

**bowery** (bow'er-i), a. Shady; having bowers.

**bowl** (bol), n. A deep vessel; a large wooden ball used in a game.

**bowlder** (bol'der), n. A large roundish rock.

**bowsprit** (bo'sprit), n. The fore spar of a ship's head.

**boycott** (boi'kot), v. Conspiracy to destroy a person's or company's trade.

**bracelet** (bras'let), n. An ornament for the wrist.

**bracket** (brak'et), n. A small support of wood. pl. Marks [ ] for inclosing words.

**brackish** (brak'ish), a. Somewhat salt; saltish.

**braggadocio** (brag-a-do'she-o), n. A vain boaster.

**braggart** (brag'art), n. A boaster; a vain fellow.

**braid** (brad'), vt. To weave three or more strands to form one.

**brain** (bran), n. Soft substance within the skull; the understanding.

**brakeman** (brak'man), n. One who manages the brake on railroads.

**bran** (bran), n. The outer coats of grain separated from the flour.

**brand**, vt. To burn with a hot iron; to stigmatize.

**brandish** (brand'ish), vt. To wave; to flourish.

**brandy** (bran'de), n. A spirit distilled from wine, cider, or fruit.

**brasier** (bra'zher), n. One who works in brass; a pan for holding coals.

**bravado** (bra-va'do), n. An arrogant threat; boasting fellow.

**bravery** (brav'er-e), n. Courage; heroism.

**bravo** (bra'vo), n. A daring villain.

**brawl** (brawl), vi. To make a great noise; to quarrel noisily. **[brawler]**

**brawn** (brawn), n. A boar's flesh. **[brawny]**

**brazen** (bra'zn), a. Made of brass; bold.

**breach** (brech), n. A gap; quarrel.

**breadstuff** (bred'stuf), n. That of which bread is made.

**breadth** (bredth), n. Width.

**breakage** (brak'aj), n. Allowance for things broken.

**breakfast** (brek'fast), n. The first meal in the day.

**breast-work** (brest'wurk), n. A low parapet for defence.

**breath** (breth), n. Life; air respired.

**breathe** (breth), vi. To respire; to live; to utter softly.

**bred** (bred), pret. and pp. of **breed.**

**breeches**, n. A garment worn by men upon the legs.

**breed** (bred), vt. or i. [pret. and pp., **bred**]. To generate; to hatch; to bring up. n. Offspring; progeny. **[breeding]**

**breeze** (brez), n. A gentle wind.

**brethren** (breth'ren), n. pl. of **brother.**

**brevet** (bre-vet'), n. A commission which entitles an officer to rank above his pay.

**breviary** (bre've-ar-e), n. The prayer-book of the Roman Catholic church.

**brevity** (brev'e-te), n. Conciseness.
**brew** (broo), vi. To make beer. [**brewer**]
**bribe** (brib), n. Gift to corrupt the conduct. [**bribery**]
**brick-kiln** (brik-kil), n. A kiln for burning brick.
**bridal** (brid'al), a. Belonging to marriage.
**bridegroom** (brid'groom), n. A man newly married or about to be married.
**bridewell** (brid'wel), n. A house of correction.
**bridle** (bri'dl), n. An instrument to restrain a horse.
**brief** (bref), a. Short; concise.
**brier** (bri'er), n. A prickly shrub.
**briery** (bri'er-e), a. Full of briers; rough.
**brigade** (brig-ad'), n. Troops under a brigadier.
**brigadier** (brig-a-der'), n. The officer commanding a brigade.
**brigand** (brig'and), n. An armed robber; a freebooter. [**brigandage**]
**brilliant** (bril'yant), a. Glittering; splendid.
**brimful** (brim'ful), a. Full to the brim.
**brimstone** (brim'ston), n. Sulphur.
**brindled** (brin'dld), a. Marked with streaks.
**brine** (brin), n. Salt water; the sea.
**bristle** (bris'l), n. A strong, stiff hair.
**brittle** (brit'l), a. Easily broken; fragile.
**broach** (broch), vt. To tap, as a cask; to enter upon a subject.
**broad** (brad), a. Extended from side to side; wide.
**broadcast** (brad'kast), a. Scattered widely. adv. Widely.
**broadside** (brad'sid), n. The side of a ship.

**brocade** (bro-kad'), n. Silk stuff with an embroidered pattern.
**brochure** (bro-shur'), n. A book or pamphlet sewed, not bound.
**brogan**, n. A stout, coarse shoe.
**brogue** (brog), n. A coarse shoe; a Celtic accent in pronunciation.
**broker** (brok'er), n. One who buys or sells on commission; an agent.
**brokerage** (brok'er-aj), n. Commission of a broker.
**bronchial** (brongk'i-al), a. Relating to the air-tubes of the lungs.
**bronchitis** (bron-ki'tis), n. Disease of the air-tubes of the lungs.
**bronze** (bronz), n. An alloy of copper and tin.
**brooch** (broch), n. An ornamental pin.
**brood** (brood), vi. To cover in order to hatch.
**brow** (brou), n. The ridge above the eyes; forehead; edge of a hill.
**browbeat** (brou'bet), vt. To overbear with arrogance or harshness.
**browse** (brouz), vi. To feed on the sprouts of plants.
**bruise** (bruz), vt. To crush or indent by a heavy blow.
**bruit** (brut), n. Noise; rumor; report.
**brumal** (bru'mal), a. Pertaining to winter.
**brunette** (bru-net'), n. A woman of a dark complexion.
**brunt** (brunt), n. Shock; onset.
**brusque** (brusk), a. Blunt; abrupt.
**brutal**, a. Barbarous; cruel; inhuman. [**brutal'ity**]
**buccaneer**, n. A pirate of the Spanish main; a pirate.
**buckle** (buk'l), n. An in-

## BUCKLER — BURIAL

strument for fastening straps, etc.

**buckler** (buk'ler), n. A shield.

**buckram** (buk'ram), n. A kind of canvas stiffened with glue.

**buckskin** (buk'skin), n. Soft-dressed skin of a deer.

**bucolic** (bu-kol'ik), a. Relating to shepherds; pastoral.

**budge** (buj), vi. To stir; go; move.

**budget** (buj'et), n. A bag; a pouch; the annual financial statement made by the Chancellor of the Exchequer.

**buffalo** (buf'a-lo), n. A kind of wild ox.

**buffer** (buf'er), n. An apparatus with strong springs to deaden concussion as at the end of a railway carriage.

**buffet** (buf'et), vt. To box; beat; strike with the fist.

**buffo** (buf'o), n. A comic singer in Italian opera.

**buffoon** (bu-foon'), n. An arch fellow. [**buffoonery**]

**bugbear** (bug'bar), n. A frightful object.

**buggy** (bug'i), a. Full of or having bugs. n. A light carriage.

**bugle** (bu'gl), n. Military instrument of music; a glass bead.

**builder** (bil'der), n. One who builds.

**bulbous** (bul'bus), a. Having round roots or heads.

**bulge** (bulj), vi. To swell in the middle.

**bulk** (bulk), n. Size; substance in general; main mass or body.

**bulletin** (bool'e-tin), n. Official report.

**bullion** (bool'yun), n. Uncoined silver or gold.

**bullirag** (bool'i-rag), n. To abuse; badger.

**bullock** (bool'uk), n. A young bull.

**bulwark** (bool'wark), n. A fortification.

**bumper** (bum'per), n. A glass filled to the brim.

**bumpkin** (bump'kin), n. An awkward person; a clown.

**bumptious** (bump'shus), a. Self-important; forward.

**bun** (bun), n. A small cake, or sweet bread.

**bung** (bung), n. A stopper for a barrel.

**bungalow** (bung'ga-lo), n. A country house in India.

**bungle** (bung'gl), n. A gross blunder.

**bunion** (bun'yun), n. An excrescence on the toe.

**bunker** (bung'ker), n. A bin or receptacle; a kind of chest.

**buoy** (boi), n. A piece of wood or cork floating on the water for a direction, or to bear a cable.

**buoyancy** (boi'an-si), n. The quality of floating.

**bur** (bur), n. The prickly head of a plant.

**burdensome** (bur'dn-sum), a. Grievous to be borne; heavy; oppressive.

**bureau** (bu-ro', bu'ro), n. A chest of drawers for holding papers or clothes; an office or department of government.

**bureaucracy** (bu-ro'kra-si), n. Government by departments under the control of a chief.

**burgeon** (burj'on), vi. To sprout; put forth.

**burgess** (bur'jes), n. A member of a municipal body.

**burgher** (burg'er), n. A freeman of a city or borough; a citizen.

**burglar**, n. One who feloniously breaks into a house. [**burglary**]

**burial** (ber'i-al), n. The act of laying a dead body in the grave; interment.

**burke** (berk), vt. To murder, esp. by stifling hence (fig.) to put an end to quietly.

**burlap** (ber'lap), n. A coarse canvas for wrappings, hangings, etc.

**burlesque** (ber-lesk'), n. A ludicrous representation—in speaking, acting, writing, drawing; a satire or lampoon.

**burly** (ber'li), a. Bulky; boisterous, bluff.

**burnish**, vt. To polish by friction.

**burrow** (bur'o), n. A lodge under ground dug by certain animals.

**bury**, vt. To hide in the ground.

**bushel** (bosh'el), n. A dry measure of eight gallons.

**busily** (biz'i-li), ad. Actively; earnestly.

**business** (biz'nes), n. Employment; occupation.

**bustle** (bus'sl), v. To be busy.

**busy** (biz'i), a. Employed with earnestness; meddling. [**busybody**]

**butcher** (boch'er), n. One who kills animals to sell. [**butchery**]

**butt** (but), n. A mark to shoot at; the thick end.

**butte** (but), n. A solitary hill or ridge.

**butterine** (but'er-en), n. A fatty compound sold as a substitute for butter.

**buttery** (but'ter-i), n. A place for provisions.

**buttock** (but'tuk). Upper part of the thigh.

**buttonhole** (but'n-hol), n. The slit in which the button is caught.

**buttress** (but'tres), n. A projection from a wall to give strength and support.

**buxom** (buks'um), a. Gay; lively; brisk; wanton.

**buyer** (bi'er), n. A purchaser.

**buzz** (buz), n. A humming sound.

**buzzard** (buz'ard), n. A species of hawk; a blockhead.

**by-and-by** (bi-and-bi), ad. Presently; soon; before long.

**bygone** (bi'gan), a. Past.

**by-law** (bi'la), n. A law of a town or society.

**bystander** (bi'stand-er), n. A looker-on.

# C

**cabal** (ka-bal'), n. A party of plotters; a plot. vi. To plot.

**cabalistic** (kab-a-list'ik), a. Pertaining to the Cabala, or Jewish secret science; mystic.

**cabbage** (kab'aj), n. A biennial vegetable with a head of thick leaves.

**cabin** (kab'in), n. A hut or cottage. [**cabinet**]

**cable** (ka'bl), n. A strong rope or chain.

**caboose** (ka-bos'), n. A ship's cook-room; the living car of a freight-train crew.

**cache** (kash), n. A hiding-place.

**cackle** (kak'l), n. The sound made by a hen or goose.

**cactus** (kak'tus), n. A prickly American plant.

**cad** (kad), n. A low, mean, or vulgar fellow.

**cadaverous** (ka-dav'er-us), a. Looking like a dead body; sickly-looking.

**caddie** (kad'i), n. A lad who attends a golfer at play, carrying his clubs.

**caddy** (kad'i), n. A small box for holding tea.

**cadence** (ka'dens), n. Tone, sound, modulation.

**cadet** (ka-det'), n. A student in a military or naval school.

**cairn** (karn), n. A monumental pile of stones.

**caisson** (ka'son), n. Box for military stores.

**caitiff** (ka'tif), n. A low villain; a base wretch.

**cajole** (ka-jol'), vt. To deceive by flattery.

**calamity** (ka-lam'i-ti), n. Misfortune; disaster; affliction.

**calcareous** (kal-ka're-us), a. Like or containing lime.

**calcine** (kal'sin), vt. To reduce to a calx.

**calculable** (kal'kyu-la-bl), a. That may be reckoned. [**calculation**]

**caldron** (kal'drun), n. A large kettle.

**calendar** (kal'en-dar), n. A register of successive days; an almanac.

**calender** (kal'en-der), vt. To make smooth by passing through rollers.

**calends** (kal'endz), n. The first day of the Roman month (more properly **kalends**).

**calibre** (kal'i-ber), n. Size of the bore of a gun or tube.

**calipers** (kal'i-perz), n. pl. Compasses with curved legs.

**calisthenics** (kal-is-then'-iks), n. pl. Exercises for promoting gracefulness of carriage.

**calix** (ka'liks), n. The outer cup of a flower.

**callosity** (kal-os'i-ti), n. A hard swelling; thickening of the skin.

**callous** (kal'us), a. Hardened; unfeeling. n. **callousness**.

**callow** (kal'o), a. Unfledged; featherless.

**calm** (kam), a. Still; quiet; undisturbed.

**calomel** (kal'o-mel), n. A preparation of mercury.

**caloric** (ka-lor'ik), n. The principle or element of heat.

**calumniate** (ka-lum'ni-at), vt. To accuse falsely. [**calumniation, calumniator**]

**calumny** (kal'um-ni), n. Malicious accusation.

**Calvary** (kal'va-ri), n. A place of skulls.

**Calvinism** (kal'vin-izm), n. The doctrine of Calvin. [**Calvinist**]

**calyx** (ka'liks), n. A covering of a flower.

**camarilla** (kam-ar-il'a), n. A body of men, intriguing in secret against the king's ministers; secret intriguers; a small room.

**cambric** (kam'brik), n. A fine linen or cotton.

**camel** (kam'el), n. An animal of Arabia.

**cameo** (kam'e-o), n. A precious stone sculptured in relief.

**camera** (kam'er-a), n. An apparatus used in taking pictures by photography.

**camisole** (kam'i-sol), n. A jacket; a woman's wrapper.

**camouflage** (cam'ou-flaj), v. To conceal with a device intended to deceive.

**campaign** (kam-pan'), n. The time an army keeps the field. [**campaigner**]

**campanulate** (kam-pan'u-lat), a. Bell shaped.

**camphor** (kam'fur), n. A solid white gum.

**canaille** (ka-nal'), n. The lowest order of the people.

**canal** (ka-nal'), n. A watercourse; a pipe.

**canard** (ka-nard'), n. An idle rumour or report.

**canary** (ka-na'ri), n. A species of singing-bird.

**canaster** (kan-as'ter), n. A rush basket used in South

America for packing tobacco.

**cancel** (kan'sel), vt. To blot out; efface; obliterate. [**cancellation**]

**cancer** (kan'ser), n. A sign in the zodiac; a virulent ulcer.

**cancerous** (kan'se-rus), a. Consisting of, or relating to, a cancer.

**candelabrum** (kan-de-la'-brum), n. A candlestick with branches.

**candid** (kan'did), a. Frank; ingenuous.

**candidate** (kan'di-dat), n. One who sues or is proposed for an office. [**candidature**]

**candle** (kan'dl), n. A light made of tallow or wax.

**Candlemas** (kan'dl-mas), n. A feast of the Church of Rome on 2nd February.

**candour** (kan'dur), n. Fairness; frankness.

**cane** (kan), n. A reed; the sugar-plant; a walking-stick.

**canine** (ka-nin'), a. Having the properties of a dog.

**canker** (kang'ker), n. A disease in animals and plants. [**cankerous**]

**cannel-coal** (kan'l-kol), n. A hard bituminous coal which burns without smoke.

**cannibal** (kan'i-bal), n. A man-eater. [**cannibalism**]

**cannon** (kan'un), n. A great gun for throwing balls or other instruments of destruction by the force of gunpowder. [**cannonade**]

**canoe** (ka-noo'), n. A boat made of the trunk of a tree, or of bark and skins.

**canon** (kan'un), n. A church law or rule; the genuine books of the Bible.

**canonical** (ka-non'i-kal), a. According to canons; ecclesiastical.

**canopy** (kan'o-pi), n. A covering over the head, throne, or bed.

**cant** (kant), vi. To speak with affected solemnity. n. Inclination from the level.

**cantaloup** (kan'ta-loop), n. A species of muskmelon.

**cantata** (kan-ta'ta), n. A poem set to music.

**canteen** (kan-ten'), n. A tin vessel for liquors; the sutler's shop in a garrison.

**canter** (kan'ter), vi. To move in a moderate gallop.

**cantilever**, n. A bracket for supporting a cornice or balcony.

**cantle** (kan'tl), n. A corner; a portion; the hind part of a saddle.

**canto** (kan'to), n. A division of a poem.

**canton** (kan'ton), n. A division of a country.

**cantonment** (kan'tun-ment), n. A district occupied by soldiers.

**canvas** (kan'vas), n. A coarse cloth for sails, etc.

**canvass** (kan'vas), vt. or i. To examine; solicit votes. [**canvasser**]

**caoutchouc** (koo'chook), n. India-rubber or gum elastic.

**capability** (ka-pa-bil'i-ti), n. Capacity; qualification.

**capacious** (ka-pa'shus), a. Wide; large.

**capacitate** (ka-pas'i-tat), vt. To make capable.

**capacity** (ka-pas'i-ti), n. The power of receiving and containing.

**cap-a-pie** (kap-a-pe'), ad. From head to foot.

**caparison** (ka-par'i-sun), n. Trappings for a horse.

**caper** (ka'per), n. Bud of the caper-bush; a leap.

**capillary** (kap'i-lar-i, kap-

## CAPILLOSE — CARNIVAL

**il'ar-i)**, a. Resembling a hair.

**capillose** (kap'i-los), a. Hairy; rough.

**capital** (kap'i-tal), n. Principal sum; stock; large letter; chief city; upper part of a column.

**capitalise** (kap'i-tal-iz), vt. To convert into capital.

**capitalist** (kap'i-tal-ist), n. One who employs or has capital.

**capitation** (kap-i-ta'shun), n. Numeration by heads; a poll-tax.

**capitol** (kap'i-tol), n. A temple in Rome; a government house.

**capitulate** (ka-pit'u-lat), vi. To surrender on conditions. [capitulation]

**capote** (ka-pot'), n. A long cloak worn by ladies.

**caprice** (ka-pres'), n. Sudden or unreasonable change of mind or humour. [capricious]

**Capricorn** (kap'ri-korn), n. One of the signs in the zodiac.

**capsize** (kap-siz'), vt. To overturn.

**capstan** (kap'stan), n. A machine to raise great weights, principally used in ships for raising an anchor.

**capsule** (kap'sul), n. The seed-vessel of a plant; a small dish.

**captain** (kap'tan, kap'tin), n. A commander in the army or navy. [captaincy]

**caption** (kap'shun), n. Act of legal seizure; arrest; the writ or warrant for it. [captious]

**captivate** (kap'ti-vat), vt. To take prisoners; please exceedingly; fascinate.

**captive** (kap'tiv), n. One taken in war. [captivity]

**capture** (kap'tur), n. Seizure of a prize.

**carafe** (ka-raf'), n. A glass water-bottle for the table or toilet.

**caramel** (kar'a-mel), n. Burnt sugar used for colouring spirits.

**carat** (kar'at), n. A weight of 4 grains.

**caravan** (kar'a-van), n. A company of travelers or merchants proceeding in a body for greater safety.

**caravansary** (kar-a-van'sa-ri), n. A kind of inn for travelers in Asia.

**carbine** (kar'bin), n. Short light gun.

**carbon** (kar'bun), n. Pure charcoal. [carbonic]

**carbuncle** (kar'bungk-l), n. An inflamed ulcer; a precious stone of red color.

**carcass** (kar'kas), n. A dead body; an old frame.

**cardiac** (kar'di-ak), a. Belonging to the heart.

**cardinal** (kar'di-nal), a. Principal; chief. n. A dignitary in the Roman Catholic church; a short cloak.

**careen** (ka-ren'), v. To incline to one side.

**career** (ka-rer'), n. Course of action; procedure.

**careful** (kar'fol), a. Full of concern; cautious; watchful; saving.

**caress** (ka-res'), n. Act or expression of endearment.

**caricature** (kar'i-ka-tur), n. A ludicrous representation. v. To represent very ugly or ludicrously.

**carmine** (kar'min), n. A bright crimson color.

**carnage** (kar'naj), n. A great slaughter or massacre.

**carnal** (kar'nal), a. Fleshly; sensual.

**carnation** (kar-na'shun), n. The color of flesh; a flower of flesh-color.

**carnival** (kar'ni-val), n. A festival in Roman Catholic countries before Lent.

**carnivorous**(kar-niv'o-rus), a. Flesh eating.

**carol** (kar'ul), n. A song of joy or praise. v. To sing or warble.

**carotid** (ka-rot'id), a. A term describing the two great arteries of the neck which carry the blood from the heart to the head.

**carousal** (ka-rouz'al), n. Feast, noisy drinking bout.

**carouse** (ka-rouz'), vt. To drink freely and noisily.

**carping** (karp'ing), a. Finding fault peevishly.

**carriage** (kar'aj), n. A vehicle; conveyance; behavior.

**carrier** (kar're-er), n. One who carries parcels; a porter.

**carrion** (kar'ri-un), n. The dead and putrid body or flesh of any animal.

**carrot** (kar'ut), n. A garden vegetable of a yellowish color.

**cartilage** (kar'te-laj), n. A tough elastic substance softer than bone; gristle.

**cartridge** (kar'trij), n. A paper case, containing the charge for a gun or pistol.

**Cartesian**(kar-te'zhi-an), a. Relating to the French philosopher Des Cartes, or his philosophy.

**cascade** (kas'kad), n. A waterfall; a jet of water.

**casement** (kas'ment), n. The frame of a window; a window that opens on hinges; a hollow moulding.

**cashier** (kash-er'), n. A cash-keeper; an officer of a bank; one who has charge of money.

**casket** (kas'ket), n. A small box for holding jewels.

**casque** (kask), n. A helmet.

**cassimere** (kas'i-mer), n A twilled woollen cloth

**cassock** (kas'ok), n. A close frock-coat for clergymen; a loose cloak or gown.

**castanet** (kas'ta-net), n. The hard shells strung in pairs which are struck together to make dance music.

**castaway** (kast'a-wa), n. One abandoned to destruction.

**caste** (kast), n. A tribe of the same profession; a distinction prevalent in India.

**castigation**(kas-ti-ga'shun) n. Repressive remedy; chastisement; punishment.

**castle** (kas'sl), n. A fortified house or fortress.

**castor-oil** (kas'ter-oil), n. A gentle aperient oil, obtained from a tropical plant.

**casual** (kazh'u-al), a. Happening by chance; incidental; fortuitous. [casualty]

**cataclysm** (kat'a-klizm), n. A deluge; a vast flood.

**catacomb** (kat'a-kom), n. A cave in the earth or rocks for interring dead bodies.

**catalepsy** (kat'a-lep-si), n. A disease which suddenly suspends motion and sensation.

**catalogue** (kat'a-log), n. A list of names, books, &c.

**catamount**(kat'a-mount), n. A wild cat; Am. tiger.

**catapult** (kat'a-pult), n. An ancient military engine for throwing darts, stones, &c.

**cataract** (kat'a-rakt), n. A large waterfall; a disorder in the eye which comes on as if a veil fell before it.

**catarrh** (ka-tar'), n. Great secretion from a mucous

**catastrophe** (ka-tas'tro-fe), n. Final event; unfortunate conclusion; calamity.

**catechise** (kat'e-kiz), vt. To question; to examine; to teach by question and answer. [**catechism**]

**category** (kat'e-gor-i), n. A class, rank, or order of ideas; state or situation; a predicament.

**cater** (ka'ter), vi. To provide.

**caterpillar** (kat'er-pil-ar), n. A grub that lives upon the leaves of plants.

**caterwaul** (kat'er-wawl), n. The shriek or cry emitted by the cat.

**cathartic, -al** (kath-art'ik, -al), a. Having the power of cleansing the stomach and bowels; purgative.

**cathedral** (kath-ed'ral), n. The principal church of a diocese.

**cattle** (kat'l), n. pl. Beasts of pasture.

**Caucasian** (kaw-ka'zhi-an), a. Pertaining to Mount Caucasus or the country around it. n. The fair type of man as opposed to the Mongolic or yellow type.

**caucus** (kaw'kus), n. A private meeting of representatives of a party.

**caudal** (kaw'dal), a. Pertaining to the tail.

**caul** (kawl), n. A net or covering for the head.

**cauliflower** (kaw'li-flow-er), n. A variety of cabbage —the eatable part is the deformed inflorescence or head.

**cause** (kawz), n. That which produces an effect.

**causerie** (koz'ri), n. Small talk or gossip.

**causeway** (kawz'wa), n. A raised way through a marsh.

**caustic** (kaws'tik), a. Burning: (fig.) bitter, severe, cutting.

**cauterize** (kaw'ter-iz), vt. To burn with caustic or a hot iron.

**caution** (kaw'shun), n. Heedfulness; security; warning.

**cavalcade** (kav-al-kad'), n. A procession on horseback.

**cavalier** (kav-al-er'), n. A knight; a gallant.

**cavalry** (kav'al-ri), n. Horse-soldiers.

**caveat** (ka've-at), n. A notice or warning.

**cavern** (kav'ern), n. A deep hollow place in the earth.

**caviare** (kav-i-ar'), n. An article of food made from the salted roes of the sturgeon, etc.

**cavil** (kav'il), vi. To raise false or trifling objections; carp.

**cavity** (kav'i-ti), n. A hollow place.

**cayenne** (ka-en'), n. A pungent pepper.

**cease** (ses), vi. To stop; leave off.

**cedar** (se'dar), n. An evergreen tree.

**cede** (sed), vt. To yield; give up.

**ceiling** (se'ling), n. Covering of the inner roof.

**celebrate** (sel'e-brat), vt. To praise; extol; observe; commemorate. [**celebration**]

**celebrity** (se-leb'ri-ti), n. Fame; distinction; a person of distinction or fame.

**celerity** (se-ler'i-ti), n. Swiftness; speed.

**celery** (sel'er-i), n. A plant cultivated for the table.

**celestial** (se-lest'yal), a. Heavenly.

**celibacy** (sel'i-ba-si), n. Single life; unmarried state.

**cell** (sel), n. A small room;

any small cavity or hollow place.

**cellar** (sel'ar), n. A room under a house.

**Celtic** (sel'tik), a. Pertaining to the primitive inhabitants of Western Europe.

**cement** (se-ment', sem'ent), n. An adhesive substance which unites bodies.

**cemetery** (sem'e-ter-i), n. A place where the dead are buried.

**censer** (sen'ser), n. An incense-pan.

**censor** (sen'ser), n. A Roman magistrate; one who examines manuscripts for the press; a severe critic. [censorial, censorious]

**censual** (sen'shual), a. Relating to the census.

**censure** (sen'shur), n. Blame.

**census** (sen'sus), n. An official enumeration of inhabitants.

**centaur** (sen'tawr), n. A fabulous monster, half man, half horse.

**centenary** (sen'ten-a-ri), n. Pertaining to a hundred.

**centigrade** (sen'ti-grad), a. Divided into a hundred degrees.

**centipede** (sen'ti-ped), n. An insect with many legs.

**central** (sen'tral), a. Relating to the centre; near the centre. [centralisation]

**centre** (sen'ter), n. The middle point.

**centrifugal** (sen-trif'u-gal), a. Tending from the centre.

**centripetal** (sen-trip'e-tal), a. Tending to the centre.

**centurial** (sen-tur'i-al), a. Pertaining to a century.

**centurion** (sen-tur'i-un), n. A Roman officer over a hundred men.

**century** (sen'tu-ri), n. A hundred years.

**cereal** (se're-al), a. Pertaining to grain. n. An edible grain.

**cerement** (ser'ment), n. Cloth dipped in wax, used in embalming.

**ceremonial** (ser-e-mo'ni-al), a. Relating to rites. n. Outward form. [ceremonious, ceremony]

**cerise** (se-rez'), a. Cherry-coloured.

**certain** (ser'tin), a. Sure; regular. [certainty]

**certificate** (ser-tif'i-kat), n. A testimony in writing.

**certify** (ser'ti-fi), v. To give certain notice; to inform; to declare in writing. [certitude]

**cerulean** (se-ro'le-an), a. Sky blue; sea green.

**cessation** (ses-sa'shun), n. Stop; pause; respite.

**cession** (sesh'un), n. A giving up; surrendering.

**cesspool** (ses'pol), n. A receptacle for liquid filth.

**cetaceous** (se-ta'shus), a. Of the whale kind.

**chafe** (chaf), v. To fret; to gall; to rage. n. A heat; passion.

**chaff** (chaf), n. The husks of grain; worthless matter.

**chaffer** (chaf'fer), v. To bargain; to buy.

**chagrin** (sha-grin'), n. Ill-humor; vexation.

**chain** (chan), n. A line of links.

**chair** (char), n. A movable seat.

**chalice** (chal'is), n. A cup or bowl; a communion-cup.

**chalk** (chak), n. Carbonate of lime.

**challenge** (chal'lenj), v. To claim; to call to fight; to object to a juror.

**chamber** (cham'ber), n. An upper room; a hollow or cavity.

**chamois** (sham'mi), n. A kind of antelope or goat

**chamomile** (kam'o-mil), n. A bitter medicinal plant.
**champagne** (sham-pan'), n. A light, sparkling wine.
**champaign** (sham-pan'), n. A flat, open country.
**champion** (cham'pi-un), n. A defender; leader; hero.
**chance** (chans), n. An unforeseen occurrence; a possibility.
**chancel** (chan'sel), n. A part of a church where the communion-table is placed.
**chancellor** (chan'sel-lur), n. An officer of state; judge of a Court of Chancery.
**chandelier** (shan-de-ler'), n. A hanging fixture for lights.
**changeable** (chanj'a-bl), a. Fickle; inconstant.
**channel** (chan'nel), n. A watercourse; a furrow; strait.
**chant** (chant), v. To sing.
**chanticleer** (chant'i-kler), n. The male fowl; a cock.
**chaos** (ka'os), n. A confused, shapeless mass; disorder. [chaotic]
**chapel** (chap'el), n. A place of religious worship.
**chaperon** (shap'er-on), v. To attend on a lady in public.
**chaplain** (chap'lan), n. A clergyman who officiates in Congress, in a regiment, a public institution, a family or a chapel.
**chaplet** (chap'let), n. A garland or wreath for the head; a rosary.
**char** (char), vt. To reduce to coal or carbon.
**character** (kar'ak-ter), n. A letter, sign or figure; peculiar quality; reputation. [characteristic]
**charade** (sha-rad'), n. A kind of riddle in which a word and each syllable contain an enigma.
**charcoal** (char'kol), n. Coal made by charring or burning wood under turf.
**charge** (charj), vt. To exhort; to command; to impute to; to put to the account of; to load; to make an onset. [chargeable]
**charitable** (char'i-ta-bl), a. Liberal to the poor; inclined to overlook faults and judge leniently.
**charity** (char'i-ti), n. Liberality; alms; candor; universal love; benevolence.
**charlatan** (shar'la-tan), n. A quack; an empiric; a mere talking pretender.
**charnel** (char'nel), a. Containing flesh or carcasses.
**chary** (char'i), a. Wary; cautious; careful; sparing; nice; scrupulous.
**chase** (chas) vt. To hunt; to pursue; to drive away; to incase; to enchase; to emboss.
**chasm** (kazm), n. A cleft; gap.
**chaste** (chast), a. Modest; refined; virtuous; clear. [chasten]
**chastise** (chas-tiz'), vt. To correct; to punish; to afflict; to reduce to order or obedience.
**chastity** (chas'ti-ti), n. Purity of body, conduct, morals, language, taste, or design.
**chateau** (sha-to'), n. A castle or country seat.
**chattel** (chat'l), n. Any kind of property not freehold.
**chatter** (chat'ter), vi. To talk idly or rapidly; to sound as the teeth when one shivers.
**chaw** (chau), vt. To champ; to crush with the teeth.
**cheap** (chep), a. Low in price or value; common.
**cheat** (chet), n. A trick; a deceiver.
**check** (chek), vt. To curb, rebuke, reprove, or restrain.

**checker** (check'er), vt. To diversify; vary; mix.

**checkers** (chek'erz), n. pl. A game at draughts or chess on a checkered board.

**checkmate** (check'mat), n. A movement in chess that ends the game.

**cheery** (cher'i), a. Sprightly; animated; with bright and pleasant manners and spirits.

**cheese** (chez), n. Curd of milk coagulated, pressed and hardened.

**chef** (shef), n. A head or chief person; master cook.

**chemise** (she-mez'), n. An undergarment for females; a shift.

**chemist** (kem'ist), n. One versed in chemistry.

**chemistry** (kem'is-tri), n. The science which investigates the nature and property of bodies, drugs, or plants.

**cherish** (cher'ish), vt. To treat with tenderness and affection; to encourage certain thoughts.

**cherry** (cher'i), n. Small red stone fruit.

**cherub** (cher'ub), n. A celestial spirit; a beautiful child.

**chestnut** (ches'nut), n. A fruit or nut enclosed in a prickly case.

**chevalier** (shev-a-ler'), n. A gallant man.

**chew** (chu), vt. To grind with the jaws and teeth.

**chicane** (shi-kan'), n. Shift; trickery; evasion.

**chide** (chid), vt. To reprove; to blame mildly; to scold.

**chief** (chef), a. Highest in office; leading; principal.

**chiffonier** (chif'fon-er), n. Ornamental cupboard.

**chilblain** (chil'blan), n. A sore on the hands or feet caused by frost or cold.

**chill** (chil), n. Cold that causes shivering; ague-fit. [chilly]

**chime** (chim), n. A set of bells; harmony of bells.

**chimera** (ki-me'ra), n. A fabulous monster; idle fancy. [chimerical]

**chimney** (chim'ni), n. A flue or passage for smoke.

**chimpanzee** (chim-pan'zi), n. African anthropoid ape.

**chinch** (chinch), n. An insect of an offensive smell.

**Chinese** (chi-nez'), a. Belonging to China.

**chink** (chingk), n. A crack; narrow opening.

**chipmunk** (chip'mungk), n. A small squirrel-like animal; ground squirrel.

**chirography** (ki-rog'ra-fi), n. Handwriting.

**chiropodist** (ki-rop'o-dist), n. A corn-doctor; operator on the feet.

**chirrup** (chir'up), vi. To chirp merrily; chatter gaily.

**chisel** (chiz'el), n. A cutting tool, used by carpenters, etc.

**chivalrous** (chiv'al-rus), a. Pertaining to chivalry; knightly; gallant. [chivalry]

**chloroform** (klo'ro-form), n. A volatile liquid, composed of chlorine and formyl.

**chocolate** (chok'o-lat), n. A preparation of cacao nuts, or the beverage made from it.

**choice** (chois), n. Alternative; preference; the preferable or best part.

**choir** (kwir), n. A chorus or band of singers, esp. those belonging to a church.

**choke** (chok), vt. To throttle; to suffocate; to stop or obstruct; to suppress.

**choler** (kol'er), n. The bile; anger; irascibility.

**cholera** (kol'er-a), n. A highly infectious and

**choose** (choz), vt. To take in preference to another; to select.

**chord** (kord), n. (mus.) The simultaneous and harmonious union of sounds of a different pitch.

**chore** (chor), n. A job of domestic work; a petty task.

**chorus** (ko'rus), n. A band of singers and dancers, aiding the principals in a musical play.

**chowder** (chow'der), n. A stew of fish, clams, etc.

**Christmas** (kris'mas), n. An annual festival in memory of the birth of Christ, held on the 25th of December.

**chromatic** (kro-mat'ik), a. Relating to colors; colored; (mus.) relating to notes in a melodic progression, and also to chords in which such notes occur.

**chronic** (kron'ik), a. Lasting a long time; of a disease, deep seated or long continued, as opposed to acute.

**chronicle** (kron'i-kl), n. A bare record of events in order of time.

**chronology** (kron-ol'o-ji), n. The science of time.

**chrysanthemum** (kris-an'the-mum), n. A genus of composite plants with single large-stalked flowers or many small ones.

**chuckle** (chuk'l), n. A kind of laugh.

**chute** (shot), n. A waterfall, rapid; a channel down which to pass water, logs, rubbish, etc.

**chyle** (kil), n. A white fluid drawn from the food while in the intestines.

**chyme** (kim), n. The pulp to which the food is reduced in the stomach.

**cicatrix** (sik'a-triks), n. The scar over a wound after it is healed.

**cicerone** (sis-e-ro'ne), n. One who shows strangers the curiosities of a place; a guide.

**cider** (si'der), n. A drink made from apples.

**ci-devant** (se-de-von'), a. Former. [Fr.]

**cigar** (si-gar'), n. A roll of tobacco-leaves for smoking.

**Cimmerian** (sim-e'ri-an), a. Relating to the Cimmerii, a tribe fabled to have lived in perpetual darkness; extremely dark.

**cinch** (sinch), n. A saddle-girth; a game of cards, pedro or high-five.

**cincture** (singk'tur), n. A girdle or belt; a molding round a column.

**cinder** (sin'der), n. The refuse of burned coals; anything charred by fire.

**cinematograph.** Motion picture photography.

**cinerary** (sin'e-ra-ri), a. Pertaining to ashes.

**Cingalese** (sing'ga-lez), n. A native of Ceylon. a. Belonging to Ceylon.

**cinnamon** (sin'a-mon), n. The spicy bark of a laurel in Ceylon.

**cinque** (singk), n. The number five, as on dice.

**cipher** (si'fer), n. The figure (0); initial letter of a name inwoven; a secret writing.

**circle** (ser'kl), n. A round figure; a ring; a sphere; surrounding company.

**circuit** (ser'kit), n. That which encircles. [circuitous]

**circular** (ser-ku'lar), a. Round; like a circle.

**circulate** (ser'ku-lat), vi. To move round. [circulation, circulatory]

**circumference** (ser-kum'fer-ens), n. The line that bounds a circle.

**circumlocution** (ser-kum-lo-ku'shun), n. The use of indirect expression.

**circumnavigable** (ser-kum-nav'i-ga-bl), a. That may be sailed around. [**circumnavigate, circumnavigation**]

**circumspect** (ser'kum-spekt), a. Guarded; prudent. [**circumspection, circumspective**]

**circumstance** (ser'kum-stans), n. Something pertaining to a fact, but not essential thereto; event; incident. [**circumstantial**]

**circumvent** (ser-kum-vent'), vt. To get round or outwit; delude. [**circumvention**]

**circus** (ser'kus), n. An enclosed place for games or feats of horsemanship.

**cistern** (sis'tern), n. A large vessel for water, etc.; reservoir.

**citable** (si'ta-bl), a. That may be cited.

**citadel** (sit'a-del), n. A fortress in a city.

**citation** (si-ta'shun), n. A summons; quotation.

**cite** (sit), vt. To summon; quote.

**citizen** (sit'i-zn), n. An inhabitant of a city; a freeman.

**citric** (sit'rik), a. Belonging to lemons.

**citron** (sit'run), n. A species of lemon.

**civics** (siv'iks), n. That branch of science which concerns itself with the training and duties of citizens.

**civil** (siv'il), a. Pertaining to society. [**civilian, civilisation**]

**civilise** (siv'il-iz), vt. To reclaim from barbarism.

**claim** (klam), vt. To demand. n. Demand as of right; thing claimed. [**claimable, claimant**]

**clairvoyance** (klar-voi'ans), n. Discernment of things through mesmeric influence.

**clammy** (klam'i), a. Viscous; sticky.

**clamorous** (klam'ur-us), a. Noisy with the tongue; loud.

**clamp** (klamp), n. An iron fastening.

**clan** (klan), n. A family; tribe; sect.

**clandestine** (klan-des'tin), a. Concealed.

**clangour** (klang'gur), n. A loud, harsh sound.

**clannish** (klan'ish), a. United and mutually helpful; like a clan.

**claque** (klak), n. A term used to denote a body of hired applauders in a French theatre.

**clarification** (klar-i-fi-ka'shun), n. Act of making clear or fining.

**clarion** (klar'i-un), n. A kind of trumpet, of a shrill, clear tone.

**classic** (klas'ik), n. An author of rank.

**classification** (klas-i-fi-ka'shun), n. Act of arranging in classes.

**classify** (klas'i-fi), vt. To arrange; put in its proper class.

**clatter** (klat'ter), n. A rattling noise.

**clause** (klawz), n. Part of a sentence, contract, bill, etc.

**clavicle** (klav'i-kl), n. The collar-bone.

**clayey** (kla'i), n. Consisting of clay; abounding in or resembling clay.

**clean** (klen), n. Free from dirt; pure. [**cleanliness**]

**cleanse** (klenz), vt. To purify.

**clear** (kler), a. Free from mixture; pure; indisputable.

**clearance** (kler'ans), n. Act of removing; free space or profit; permit to sell.

**cleat** (klet), n. A piece of wood in joinery nailed on

| CLEAVE | 41 | COALESCE |

to strengthen or fasten.
**cleave** (klev), vi. To stick; adhere.
**cleavage** (kle'vij), n. Act of cleaving; quality of splitting or dividing naturally.
**clef** (klef), n. A character in music to determine position and pitch of scale.
**cleft** (kleft), pp. or a. Split; divided.
**clemency** (klem'en-si), n. A disposition to treat with lenity; mildness; tenderness.
**clement** (klem'ent), a. Mild; kind; indulgent.
**clergy** (kler'ji), n. The ministers of the gospel.
**clerical** (kler'i-kal), a. Pertaining to the clergy, or to a writer or transcriber.
**clerk** (klerk), n. A writer for another.
**clever** (klev'er), a. Quick-witted; dexterous.
**clew** (kloo), n. A ball of thread; anything serving to discover or solve; the corner of a sail.
**client** (kli'ent), n. The employer of an attorney; a dependent of a patron.
**clientele** (kli'en-tel), n. Clients or customers collectively.
**climacteric** (kli-mak'te-rik, kli-mak-ter'ik), n. A critical period of human life.
**climate** (kli'mat), n. Condition of a country in respect of temperature, atmospheric changes, etc.
**climax** (kli'maks), n. Gradation; ascent; the highest point; acme.
**climb** (klim), vt. or i. To mount by the hands and feet.
**clime** (klim), n. A climate.
**clinch** (klinsh), vt. To gripe; hold fast.
**cling** (kling), v. To adhere, or stick close to; to hang upon.

**clinic** (klin'ik), a. Pertaining to a sick-bed.
**clink** (klingk), v. To make a ringing sound.
**clinker** (klingk'er), n. Slag which forms in furnaces.
**clip** (klip), v. To cut short with scissors; to curtail.
**clique** (klek), n. A party; a coterie; a gang; a set or party.
**cloak** (klok), v. To cover with a cloak; to disguise.
**clog** (klog), v. To hinder in motion.
**cloister** (klois'ter), n. A place of religious retirement.
**close** (kloz), v. To shut; to end; to finish; to join.
**closet** (kloz'et), n. A private apartment; secluded; hidden.
**cloth** (klath), n. A stuff formed by weaving.
**clothe** (kloth), v. To furnish with clothes; to dress.
**clothier** (kloth'i-er), n. One who makes or sells clothing.
**cloud** (klowd), n. A mass of vapor in the atmosphere.
**cloven** (klo'vn), a. Divided in two parts; cleft; split.
**clown** (klown), n. A rustic; a fool, or buffoon.
**cloy** (kloi), v. To fill to loathing; to glut, or satiate.
**clue** (klo), n. A ball of thread.
**clumsy** (klum'ze), a. Awkward.
**cluster** (klus'ter), n. A bunch.
**clutch** (kluch), n. A gripe; grasp; claw.
**clutter** (klut'er), n. A noise; confusion.
**coagulate** (ko-ag'u-lat), vt. or i. To curdle [**co-agu-lation**]
**coal** (kol), n. Wood charred; a fossil.
**coalesce** (ko-a-les'), vi. T

grow together; to unite. **[coalescence]**
**coalition** (ko-a-lish'un), n. Union of persons, particles, or states.
**coarse** (kors), a. Gross; rude; rough.
**coast** (kost), n. Land next the sea.
**coaster** (kost'er), n. A person or vessel that sails near a coast.
**coat** (kot), n. A man's upper garment.
**coax** (koks), vt. To wheedle; to persuade by flattery.
**cobble** (kob'l), n. A roundish stone.
**cobbler** (kob'ler), n. A mender of shoes.
**cockade** (kok-ad'), n. A knot of ribbon worn on the hat.
**cockroach** (kok'roch), n. A troublesome insect; a kind of beetle.
**cocoa** (ko'ko), n. The chocolate-tree, and a decoction of the nut or the paste.
**cocoanut** (ko'ko-nut), n. The nut of a kind of palm-tree.
**cocoon** (ko-koon'), n. A ball spun by the silkworm.
**coddle** (kod'l), vi. To parboil.
**code** (kod), n. A system; a digest of laws.
**codger** (kod'jer), n. A clownish fellow.
**codicil** (kod'e-sil), n. Supplement to a will.
**codification** (ko-di-fi-ka'shun), n. Act of reducing laws to a system.
**codify** (ko'di-fi), vt. To reduce to a code.
**coefficiency** (ko-e-fish'en-si), n. Joint operation. **[coefficient]**
**coerce** (ko-ers'), vt. To restrain by force; compel; constrain. **[coercion]**
**coffin** (kof'in), n. A chest for a dead human body.

**cogency** (ko'jen-si), n. Power; urgency; strength. **[cogent]**
**cogitate** (koj'i-tat), vi. To think; meditate. **[cogitation]**
**cognisance** (kog'ni-zans, kon'i-zans), n. Knowledge; judicial notice; jurisdiction; a badge or crest. **[cognisant]**
**cognition** (kog-nish'un), n. Knowledge.
**cognomen** (kog-no'men), n. Family name; surname.
**cohabitation** (ko-hab-i-ta'shun), n. A living together.
**cohere** (ko-her'), vi. To stick together; be well connected or consistent. **[coherence]**
**cohesion** (ko-he'zhun), n. State of union; union. **[cohesive]**
**cohort** (ko'hort), n. A body of soldiers.
**coif** (koif), n. A headdress.
**coiffure** (koif'ur), n. A head-dress.
**coigne** (koin), n. A corner; a corner-stone; a wedge.
**coil** (koil), vt. To wind into a ring.
**coin** (koin), n. Money stamped. **[coinage]**
**coincide** (ko-in-sid'), vi. To agree; concur. **[coincidence]**
**coke** (kok), n. Mineral coal charred.
**colic** (kol'ik), n. A pain in the bowels.
**collapse** (ko-laps'), vi. To fall together.
**collar** (kol'ar), n. Something worn around the neck.
**collate** (ko-lat'), vt. To compare; gather and place in order; present to a benefice.
**collateral** (ko-lat'e-ral), a. Being side by side; indirect.
**collation** (ko-la'shun), n. A

repast; gift; act of comparing.
**colleague** (kol'eg), n. An associate in office.
**collect** (kol-lekt'), v. To gather; to bring together; to assemble.
**collect** (kol'lekt), n. A short prayer of the church service.
**collection** (kol-lek'shun), n. That which is collected; a contribution. [**collective, collector**]
**college** (kol'ej), n. An assembly or community engaged in a common pursuit. [**collegian**]
**collide** (kol-lid'), v. To strike or dash together.
**collier** (kol'yer), n. One who works in a coal-mine; a ship that carries coal.
**colliery** (kol'yer-i), n. A coal-mine; the coal-trade.
**collision** (kol-lizh'un), n. A clashing together.
**collocate** (kol'lo-kat), v. To set in order; to place.
**colloquial** (kol-lo'kwi-al), a. Used in common conversation. [**colloquialism**]
**colloquy** (kol'lo-kwi), n. Mutual discourse; a dialogue.
**collude** (kol-lud'), v. To act in concert; to conspire.
**collusion** (kol-lu'zhun), n. A secret agreement.
**colon** (ko'lon), n. A mark [:] of punctuation indicating the next greatest pause to that of the period.
**colonel** (kur'nel), n. The chief commander of a regiment.
**colonial** (ko-lo'ni-al), a. Pertaining to a colony. [**colonist, colonize**]
**colonnade** (kol-on-ad'), n. A row of columns.
**colony** (kol'o-ni), n. A body of people who settle in a distant country, continuing subject to the parent state.
**color** (kul'ur), n. The appearance that a body presents to the eye; a paint. [**colorable**]
**colors** (kul'urz), n. pl. A banner; flag; ensign.
**colossal** (ko-los'sal), a. Very large; gigantic.
**colossus** (ko-los'us), n. A gigantic statue.
**colt** (kolt), n. A young horse.
**column** (kol'um), n. Round pillar or shaft; a perpendicular section of a printed page; a body of troops in subdivisions.
**coma** (ko'ma), n. Nebulous covering of a comet; a tuft or bunch; propensity to sleep; lethargy.
**comatose** (ko'ma-tos), a. Drowsy; dozing without natural sleep; lethargic.
**comb** (kom), n. An instrument for adjusting hair, wool, flax, etc.
**combat** (kom'bat), n. A battle; a fight; a duel.
**combatant** (kom'bat-ant), n. One who fights.
**combination** (kom-bi-na'shun), n. Close union or connection.
**combine** (kom-bin'), v. To unite intimately; to coalesce.
**combustible** (kom-bus'ti-bl) a. That will take fire and burn. [**combustion**]
**comedian** (ko-me'di-an), n. An actor, or player in comedy.
**comedy** (kom'e-di), n. A dramatic representation of an amusing character.
**comely** (kum'li), a. Becoming; handsome; graceful.
**comet** (kom'et), n. A heavenly body that emits a long train of luminous matter.
**comfit** (kum'fit), n. A confection; dry sweetmeat.

**comfort** (kum'fort), vt. To relieve from pain or distress; cheer; console. **[comfortable]**

**comforter** (kum'fort-er), n. One who or that which comforts; wrapper for the neck.

**comic** (kom'ik), a. Relating to comedy; inspiring mirth.

**comical** (kom'ik-al), a. Ludicrous; droll.

**comity** (kom'i-ti), n. Courtesy; civility.

**comma** (kom'a), n. The mark (,) in punctuation.

**command** (kom-mand'), vt. To order; govern.

**commemorate** (kom-mem'o-rat), vt. To call to remembrance by a solemn act.

**commence** (kom-mens'), vt. To begin.

**commencement** (kom-mens'ment), n. Beginning; time when students receive degrees.

**commendable** (kom-mend'a-bl), a. Worthy of praise. **[commendation, commendatory]**

**commensurate** (kom-men'-shur-at), a. Of equal measure; in proportion with.

**comment** (kom'ment), n. An explanatory note or remark; observation. **[commentary, commentator]**

**commerce** (kom'mers), n. Interchange of commodities; traffic; intercourse. **[commercial]**

**commination** (kom-mi-na'-shun), n. A solemn threat.

**commingle** (kom-ming'gl), vt. and vi. To mix together.

**comminute** (kom'min-ut), vt. To reduce to small fragments or particles.

**commiserate** (kom-miz'er-at), vt. To feel pity for. **[commiseration]**

**commissary** (kom'mis-a-ri), n. One to whom a charge is committed.

**commission** (kom-mish'un), n. Act of committing; writing conferring powers; authority; charge. **[commissioner]**

**commit** (kom-mit'), vt. To intrust; consign. **[commitment, committal]**

**committee** (kom-mit'e), n. Persons appointed to manage any business.

**commode** (kom-mod'), n. A small sideboard; small article of furniture.

**commodious** (kom-mo'di-us) a. Suitable; convenient.

**commodity** (kom-mod'i-ti), n. Convenience; an article of traffic.

**common** (kom'on), a. Belonging to several; public; general; usual; of small value.

**commonweal** (kom'un-wel), n. Government of a free State; whole body of the people.

**commotion** (kom-mo'shun), n. Disturbance; agitation.

**commune** (kom-mun'), vi. To interchange thoughts or feelings.

**communicable** (kom-mu'ni-ka-bl), a. That may be communicated.

**communicate** (kom-mu'ni-kat), vt. To impart; reveal. **[communication]**

**communism** (kom'un-izm), n. State of holding property in common; doctrine that all property should belong to the State. **[communist]**

**community** (kom-mu'ni-ti), n. Possession in common; the public; people of any place.

**commutation** (kom-mu-ta'-shun), n. Exchange, esp. of a penalty or rate from a greater to a less, or from one kind to another.

**commute** (kom-mut'), vt.

**COMPACT** 45 **COMPONENT**

To exchange; exchange a penalty or rate.
**compact** (kom-pakt'), a. Closely united; firm; brief.
**companion** (kom-pan'yun), n. An associate, or partner. [**companionable**]
**company** (kum'pa-ni), n. Persons assembled together.
**comparable** (kom'pa-ra-bl), a. That may be compared.
**compare** (kom-par'), v. To examine together; to be like. [**comparison**]
**compartment** (kom-part'ment), n. A division.
**compass** (kum'pas), v. To surround; to obtain; to contrive.
**compasses** (kum'pas-ez), n. pl. An instrument with which circles are drawn, figures measured, etc.
**compassion** (kom-pash'un), n. Pity; mercy; fellow-feeling. [**compassionate**]
**compatibility** (kom-pat-i-bil'i-ti), n. Consistency; agreement; suitableness.
**compatriot** (kom-pa'tri-ut), n. A fellow-countryman.
**compeer** (kom-per'), n. An equal; companion; colleague.
**compel** (kom-pel'), v. To force; to constrain.
**compendium** (kom-pen'di-um), n. An abridgment; a summary; an epitome.
**compensate** (kom'pen-sat), v. To make amends; to recompense. [**compensation**]
**compete** (kom-pet'), v. To strive to rival; to claim to be equal.
**competence** (kom'pe-tens), n. Sufficiency; legal power or capacity; fitness. [**competent**]
**competition** (kom-pe-tish'un), n. Strife for superiority; rivalry.
**competitor** (kom-pet'i-tur), n. A rival; a contester.

**compile** (kom-pil'), v. To select from various authors.
**complacency** (kom-pla'sen-si), n. Pleasure; satisfaction; civility. [**complacent**]
**complain** (kom-plan'), v. To murmur; to accuse.
**complainant** (kom-plan'ant), n. One who complains; a prosecutor.
**complaint** (kom-plant'), n. A murmuring; an accusation; a bodily ailment.
**complaisance** (kompla'zans) n. Obliging treatment.
**complaisant** (kom'pla-zant), a. Civil; polite; courteous; affable.
**complement** (kom'ple-ment) n. The full number or quantity. [**complemental**]
**complete** (kom-plet'), a. Finished; perfect; entire.
**complex** (kom'pleks), a. Composed of many parts; difficult; intricate; not simple.
**complexion** (kom-plek'shun) n. The color or hue of the skin, especially the face; texture; temperature; general appearance.
**compliance** (kom-pli'ans), n. A yielding to a request; assent or consent; obedience.
**compliant** (kom-pli'ant), n. Yielding, civil, submissive; obliging; complaisant. a. Compliable.
**complicate** (kom'pli-kat), vt. To twist together; to make intricate; to entangle.
**complicity** (kom-plis'i-ti), n. Being an accomplice.
**compliment** (kom'pli-ment) n. Act or expression of civility; delicate flattery.
**comply** (kom-pli'), vt. To yield to; be obsequious to; accord or suit with.
**component** (kom-pon'ent), a. Helping to form a compound.

**comport** (kom-port'), vt. or i. To agree, suit or put up (with), behave; conduct.

**compose** (kom-poz'), vt. To soothe; quiet; allay; to write or dictate, as a book or music; to constitute, as parts of a whole; to put in order; to set up printing type.

**composite** (kom'poz-it), a. Composed of two or more distinct parts.

**composition** (kom-po-zish'-un), n. Act of composing or of setting types; a work in literature, art, music or painting; a mass formed of different ingredients; union; combination.

**compost** (kom'post), n. A mixture for manures, &c.

**compound** (kom'pound), a. Formed of several ingredients; not simple.

**comprehend** (kom-pre-hend') vt. To comprise; include; understand.

**comprehensible** (kom-pre-hen'si-bl), a. That may be comprehended; intelligible. **[comprehension, comprehensive]**

**compress** (kom-pres'), vt. To press together; squeeze.

**compress** (kom'pres), n. A pad of cloth used in surgery.

**compressible** (kom-pres'i-bl), a. That may be compressed or condensed. **[compression]**

**comprise** (kom-priz'), vt. To contain; include.

**compromise** (kom'pro-miz), n. A settlement by reciprocal concession.

**compulsion** (kom-pul'shun), n. Force; necessity.

**compunction** (kom-pungk'-shun), n. Remorse; reproach of conscience.

**computable** (kom-put'a-bl), a. That may be computed. **[computation]**

**comrade** (kom'rad), n. A companion; associate.

**concave** (kon'kav), a. Having a curved hollow.

**conceal** (kon-sel'), vt. To keep secret; hide.

**concede** (kon-sed'), vt. To give up; admit; grant.

**conceit** (kon-set'), n. Imagination; notion; vanity.

**conceivable** (kon-sev'a-bl). a. That may be conceived or believed.

**concentrate** (kon-sen'trat), vt. To bring to a common centre, or closer union; to condense.

**conception** (kon-sep'shun), n. Act of conceiving; notion; idea.

**concern** (kon-sern'), vt. To affect interest.

**concert** (kon-sert'), vt. To arrange together; plan.

**concession** (kon-sesh'un), n. Act of conceding; allowance; grant.

**conch** (kongk), n. Convolute marine shell.

**conciliate** (kon-sil'i-at), vt. To make friendly; win over; reconcile.

**concise** (kon-sis'), a. Brief; terse.

**conclave** (kon'klav), n. Meeting of cardinals to choose a pope; any close assembly.

**conclude** (kon-klod'), vt. End; infer.

**concoct** (kon-kokt'), vt. Prepare. **[concoction]**

**concord** (kong'kard), n. Harmony. **[concordance]**

**concordat** (kon-kar'dat), n. Compact, esp. between a state and the Pope.

**concourse** (kong'kors), n. Assembly.

**concrete** (kon'kret or kong'-), a. Formed into one mass; material; individual.

**concrete** (kon-kret'), vi. Unite into a mass. **[concretion]**

**concur** (kon-kur'), vi. Meet;

**concussion** (kon-kush'un), n. Collision; violent shock.

**condemn** (kon-dem'), vt. Pronounce guilty or unfit. [**condemna'tion**]

**condense** (kon-dens'), vt. Reduce in volume. [**condensa'tion**]

**condescend** (kon-de-send'), vi. Descend from a superior position. [**condescen'sion**]

**condign** (kon-din'), a. Well merited.

**condiment** (kon'di-ment), n. Seasoning served at table.

**condition** (kon-dish'un), n. Situation; required quality.

**condole** (kon-dol'), vi. Sympathize. [**condo'lence**]

**condone** (kon-don'), vt. Forgive.

**condor** (kon'dor), n. Large vulture.

**conduce** (kon-dus'), vi. Contribute. [**condu'cive**]

**conduct** (kon'dukt), n. Act or method of managing.

**conduct** (kon-dukt'), vt. Lead; direct; carry. [**conduct'or**]

**conduit** (kon'dit), n. Pipe to convey water.

**cone** (kon), n. A solid body, tapering to a point from a circular base.

**confection** (kon-fek'shun), n. A preparation of fruit, etc., with sugar; a comfit.

**confederate** (kon-fed'er-at), a. United in a league; engaged in a confederacy. [**confed'eracy**]

**confer** (kon-fer'), vt. To bestow; to grant; to award. [**con'ference**]

**confess** (kon-fes'), vt. and i. To acknowledge or avow (a fault, crime, debt, etc.); to assert; to attest; to make confession.

**confidant** (kon'fi-dant'), n. A friend to whom secrets are intrusted.

**confide** (kon-fid'), vi. To put faith; to believe. [**con'fidence**]

**confine** (kon-fin'), vt. To restrain within limits; to bound; to restrict. [**confine'ment**]

**confirm** (kon-ferm'), vt. To make firm; to verify; to corroborate; to assure.

**confiscate** (con'fis-ket or con-fis'ket), vt. To appropriate as forfeited to the public use or treasury.

**conflagration** (con'fla-gre'-shun), n. A great or extensive fire.

**conflict** (con-flict'), vi. To come into collision; be in mutual opposition; clash; contend.

**conflict** (con'flict), n. A contest; strife.

**confluent** (con'flu-ent), a. Flowing together so as to form one; blended into one.

**confuse** (con-fiuz'), vt. To perplex; bewilder; abash; disconcert.

**confute** (con-flut'), vt. To prove to be false or invalid; refute successfully.

**congeal** (con-jil'), vt. and vi. To convert or be converted from a fluid to a solid condition; coagulate; stiffen; harden; freeze.

**congenial** (con-ji'nial), a. Having similar character or tastes; sympathetic.

**congenital** (con-jen'i-tal), a. Born with one; existing from birth.

**congestion** (con-jes'chun), n. An excessive accumulation, as of blood in the blood-vessels, or of population; overcrowded condition.

**conglomerate** (con-glom'er-et), vt. and vi. To gather into a cohering mass.

**congratulate** (con-grat'yu-let), vt. To express sympathetic pleasure in the joy or good fortune of (another).

**congregate** (con'gre-get), vt. and vi. To bring or come together into a crowd; assemble. [**congrega'tion**]

**congress** (con'gres), n. An assembly or conference; the national legislative body of the United States.

**congruent** (con'gru-ent), a. Having mutual agreement or conformity; correspondent; appropriate.

**congruous** (con'gru-us), a. Harmoniously.

**conjecture** (con-jek'tur), n. Opinion based on imperfect knowledge; presumption; guess. [**conjec'tural**]

**conjoin** (kon-join'), vt. and i. To connect; to unite; to join; to associate.

**conjugal** (kon'ju-gal), a. Relating to marriage; nuptial.

**conjugate** (kon'ju-gat), vt. To inflect, as verbs.

**conjunct** (kon-junkt'), a. United; conjoined; concurrent. [**conjunc'tion**]

**conjure** (kon-jur'), vt. To call on or summon solemnly; to adjure. [**conjur'er**]

**conjure** (kun'jur'), vt. To charm; to enchant; to bewitch. [**con'jurer**]

**connate** (kon'nat), a. Born with another; united in origin.

**connect** (kon-nekt'), vt. and i. To knit together; to unite; to join.

**connive** (kon-niv'), vi. To close the eyes upon; to wink at; to purposely fail to see. [**conniv'ance**]

**connubial** (kon-nu'bi-al), a. Pertaining to marriage; conjugal; nuptial.

**conquer** (kon'ker), vt. and i. To overcome; to subdue; to master. [**con'quest**]

**conscience** (kon'shens), n. Self-knowledge; sense of right and wrong; truth. [**conscien'tious**]

**conscious** (kon'shus), a. Able to know one's own thoughts; aware; sensible.

**conscript** (kon'skript), a. Enrolled; written; registered.

**consecrate** (kon'se-krat), vt. To dedicate; to declare sacred; to dignify.

**consecutive** (kon-sek'u-tiv), a. Following in order; successive.

**consent** (kon-sent'), vi. To agree in opinion; to assent; to comply; to concur.

**consequence** (kon'se-kwens), n. That which follows; effect; result; importance.

**conserve** (kon-serv'), vt. To save; to protect; to preserve (fruit, etc.) with sugar.

**conservatism** (-tiz'm), n. Opposition to change; desire to preserve what is established.

**conserve** (kon-serv'), vt. Keep entire; retain; preserve.

**consider** (kon-sid'er), vt. Deliberate on.

**considerate** (kon-sid'er-at), a. Thoughtful of others; prudent.

**consign** (kon-sin'), vt. Transfer, in trust for sale or custody. [**consign'or, consignee'**]

**consist** (kon-sist'), vi. Be composed of. [**consist'ency**]

**console** (kon-sol'), vt. Give solace or comfort.

**consolidate** (kon-sol'i-dat), vt. and vi. Form into a compact mass; unite into one.

**consort**, n. Partner; companion

# CONSPICUOUS — CONTRABAND

**conspicuous** (kon-spik'u-us) a. Clearly seen; prominent.

**conspire** (kon-spir'), vi. Plot or scheme together. [**conspiracy**]

**constable** (kun'sta-bl), n. Peace officer.

**constant** (kon'stant), a. Fixed; continual; faithful. [**con'stancy**]

**constellation** (kon-stel-la'-shun), n. Group of stars.

**consternation** (kon-ster-na'-shun), n. Terror; confusion.

**constipate** (kon'stip-at), vt. Clog, esp. the intestine.

**constituent** (kon-stit'u-ent), a. Constituting; forming; essential. [**constit'uency**]

**constitute** (kon'sti-tut), vt. Establish. [**constitution**]

**constrain** (kon-stran'), vt. Force.

**constrict** (kon-strikt'), vt. Bind together; contract.

**construct** (kon-strukt'), vt. Build; put together. [**construc'tion**]

**construe** (kon'stro), vt. Translate; explain.

**consul** (kon'sul), n. Government agent abroad. [**con'sular**]

**consulate**, n. Office, residence or jurisdiction of a consul.

**consult** (kon-sult'), vt. and vi. Consider together. [**consulta'tion**]

**consume** (kon-sum'), vt. Use up.

**consummate** (kon-sum'at or kon'-), vt. Raise to the summit; perfect or finish.

**consumption** (kon-sum'-shun), n. Act of using up; disease destroying the lungs; phthisis.

**contact** (kon'takt), n. Touch; meeting.

**contagion** (kon-ta'jun), n. Transmission of a disease or evil by contact. [**conta'gious**]

**contain** (kon-tan'), vt. Hold; restrain.

**contaminate** (kon-tam'i-nat), vt. Defile; infect. [**contamina'tion**]

**contemn** (kon-tem'), vt. Despise.

**contemplate** (kon-tem'plat or kon'-), vt. Consider; intend. [**contempla'tion**]

**contemporaneous** (kon-tem-po-ra'ne-us), a. Living, happening, or being at the same time. [**contemporary**]

**contempt** (kon-temt'), n. Scorn. [**contempt'ible, contempt'uous**]

**contend** (kon-tend'), vi. Strive; debate.

**content** (kon'tent), n. That which is contained; capacity; extent.

**content** (kon-tent'), a. Satisfied.

**contention** (kon-ten'shun), n. Strife; debate. [**conten'tious**]

**contest** (kon-test'), vt. Call in question; strive (for).

**context** (kon'tekst), n. Parts which precede or follow a passage.

**contiguous** (kon-tig'u-us), a. Touching; adjoining; near.

**continence** (kon'ti-nens), n. Restraint; chastity.

**continent** (kon'ti-nent), n. One of the great divisions of the land surface of the globe.

**contingent** (kon-tin'jent), a. Dependent; accidental.

**continue** (kon-tin'u), vt. Prolong; extend; persist in [**contin'uous, continu'ity**]

**contort**, vt. To twist violently; wrench out of place or shape. [**contor'tion**]

**contour** (con'tur), n. The line bounding a figure or body; outline.

**contraband** (con'tra-band), a. Prohibited or excluded,

as by military law; forbidden.
**contract**, vt. To shorten by drawing together; narrow; limit; condense.
**contract**, n. A formal agreement, or the writing containing it.
**contractor** (con-tract'or), n. One of the parties to a contract.
**contradict**, vt. To deny (a statement) directly or by implication.
**contradiction** (-dik'shun), n. A gainsaying; denial; opposition; contrariety.
**contralto** (kon-tral'to), n. and a. Alto or counter tenor.
**contrary** (kon'tra-ry or -tra-ry), a. Opposite; opposing; contradictory; perverse.
**contrast** (kon'trast), n. Opposition of things or qualities; comparison by contrariety of qualities.
**contravene** (kon'tra-ven'), vt. To contradict; to cross; to obstruct; to oppose.
**contribute** (kon-trib'ut), vt. To participate in giving. [**contrib'utor**]
**contrite** (kon'trit), a. Broken down with grief; penitent; humble; sorrowful.
**contrive** (kon-triv'), vt. and vi. To devise; to plan; to project.
**control** (kon-trol'), n. Power to check or govern; restraint; direction; superintendence.
**controversy** (kon'tro-ver'-sy), n. Dispute; debate; discussion; strife; hostility. [**con'trover'sial**]
**controvert** (kon'tro-vert), vt. To dispute; to debate; to contest.
**contumacy** (kon'tu-ma-sy), n. Persistent obstinacy; stubborn perverseness. [**con'tuma'cious**]
**contumely** (kon'tu-me-ly), n. Insolent contempt; reproach; disdain; disgrace. [**con'tume'lious**]
**contuse** (kon-tuz'), vt. To beat; to pound; to bruise; to injure by beating. [**contusion**]
**conundrum** (ko-nun'drum), n. A riddle suggesting resemblance between things quite unlike; a quibble; a puzzle.
**convalesce** (kon'va-les'), vi. To recover health and strength after sickness. [**con'vales'cence**]
**convene** (kon-ven'), vt. To collect; to assemble; to unite. [**conven'ient**]
**convent** (kon'vent), n. A community of religious recluses.
**convention** (kon-ven'shun), n. Custom; usage; an assembly of representatives for deliberative purposes; a temporary treaty. [**conven'tional**]
**converge** (kon-verj'), vi. To tend to one point; to incline and approach nearer together. [**conver'gence**]
**converse** (kon-vers'), vi. To keep company; to talk familiarly; to chat. [**con'-verse**]
**converse** (kon'vers), a. Converted or reversed in order or relation; turned about; reciprocal.
**convert** (kon-vert'), vt. and vi. To change to another form or state; to turn; to alter. [**con'vert**]
**convex** (kon'veks), a. Rising or swelling into a rounded form.
**convey** (kon-va'), vt. To carry; to bear; to transfer. [**convey'ance**]
**convict** (kon-vikt'), vt. To prove or find guilty; to confute; to detect; to confound.
**convict** (kon'vikt), n. One proved guilty of crime; a malefactor; a culprit; a

felon; a criminal. [**con-vic'tion**]
**convince** (kon-vins'), vt. To satisfy by evidence; to persuade.
**convivial** (kon-yiv'i-al), a. Festive; jovial; social; gay.
**convoke** (kon-vok'), vt. To call together; to summon; to assemble; to convene. [**con'voca'tion**]
**convolve** (kon-volv'), vt. To roll or wind together; to twist.
**convoy** (kon-voi'), vt. To accompany for protection.
**convoy** (kon'voi), n. Escort.
**convulse** (kon-vuls'), vt. To draw or contract violently; to agitate; to shake; to rend. [**convul'sion**]
**cony** (ko'ny or kun'y), n. A rabbit.
**coop** (koop), n. A barrel or cask; a grated inclosure for small animals or poultry.
**co-ordinate** (ko-or'di-nat), a. Equal in rank or order; not subordinate. [**co-ordina'tion**]
**cope** (kop), vi. & t. To combat; to encounter.
**copier** (kop'i-er), n. One who copies; imitator.
**coping** (ko'ping), n. The top course of a wall.
**copious** (ko'pi-us), a. Large in quantity or amount; abundant; full.
**coppice** (kop'pis), n. A wood of small growth; underwood or brushwood.
**copse** (kops), n. A coppice; a thicket.
**copula** (kop'u-la), n. A word uniting the subject and predicate of a proposition.
**copyright** (kop'i-rit), n. Exclusive right to publish an author's work.
**coquet** (ko-ket'), vi. Attempt to excite love; make eyes; flirt. [**coquet'ry, coquette**]
**cordate** (kar'dat), a. Heart-shaped.
**cordial** (kar'jal), a. Hearty; affectionate.
**cordon**, n. Line of military or police.
**corduroy** (kar'du-roi), n. Thick cotton stuff with ribbed surface.
**core** (kor), n. Inner part of a thing.
**cork**, n. Outer bark of the cork tree.
**corn**, n. Kernel; grain; maize.
**corner**, n. Point where two lines meet.
**cornet**, n. Horn-shaped wind instrument.
**cornice**, n. Highest projection of a wall.
**cornucopia** (kar-nu-ko'pi-a), n. Conical receptacle.
**coronation** (kor-o-na'shun), n. Act of crowning.
**coroner** (kor'o-ner), n. Officer who inquires into accidental or suspicious deaths.
**corporal**, n. Lowest non-commissioned army officer.
**corporal** (kar'po-ral), a. Relating to the body.
**corporate** (kar'po-rat), a. Legally incorporated. [**corpora'tion**]
**corporeal** (kar-po're-al), a. Material.
**corps** (kor), n. Body of soldiers or co-workers.
**corpse**, n. Dead body of a human being.
**corpulent**, a. Fleshy. [**cor'pulence, cor'pulency**]
**corral** (kor-ral'), vt. Drive into a pen.
**correct** (kor-rekt'), vt. Make right. [**correction**]
**correlative** (kor-rel'a-tiv), a. Mutually or reciprocally related.
**correspond** (kor-re-spond'), vi. Be similar; hold in-

tercourse by letters. [**correspond'ence**]

**corridor** (kor'i-dor), n. Passage.

**corroborate** (kor-rob'o-rat), vt. Confirm. [**corroboration**]

**corrode** (kor-rod'), vt. Rust. [**corrosion**]

**corrugate** (kor'ro-gat), vt. Wrinkle; fold.

**corrupt** (kor-rupt'), vt. Make putrid; debase. [**corrupt'ible, corrup'tion**]

**corsage** (kar'saj), n. Bodice.

**corsair** (kar'sar), n. Pirate.

**corset** (kar'set), n. Stays; bodice.

**cortege** (kar-tazh'), n. Train of attendants.

**coruscate** (kor'us-kat or ko-rus'kat), vi. Sparkle.

**cosmetic** (koz-met'ik), n. Preparation for the complexion.

**cosmopolitan** (koz-mo-pol'i-tan), n. Citizen of the world.

**costive** (kos'tiv), a. Constipated.

**costume** (kos'tum), n. Manner of dressing.

**cotemporaneous** (ko-tem-po-ra'ne-us), a. Being at the same time with another. [**cotemporary**]

**coterie** (ko'te-ri), n. A fashionable association.

**cotillion** (ko-til'yun), n. A brisk, lively dance and tune.

**cottage** (kot'aj), n. A small house; a hut.

**cotton** (kot'n), n. Vegetable wool; cloth made from it. a. Consisting of cotton.

**couch** (kouch), vi. To lie or squat down; stoop, as in fear.

**cough** (kof), n. Effort of the lungs to throw off phlegm.

**council** (koun'sil), n. An assembly for consultation. [**councillor**]

**counsel** (koun'sel), n. Advice; an advocate. [**counsellor**]

**count** (kount), vt. or i. To reckon; number; esteem; be counted; rely on.

**countenance** (koun'te-nans), n. The face; air; look; support.

**counteract** (koun-ter-akt'), vt. To act in opposition to. [**counteractive**]

**counterfeit** (koun'ter-fit), vt. To copy; imitate; forge. [**counterfeiter**]

**countermand** (koun'ter-mand), n. A contrary order.

**countersign** (koun-ter-sin'), vt. To sign as secretary or subordinate official.

**countervail** (koun-ter-val'), vt. To act against equally.

**countess** (koun'tes), n. The lady of an earl or count.

**countless** (kount'les), a. Numberless; innumerable.

**country** (kun'tri), n. Land around a city; a kingdom or state; native place.

**county** (koun'ti), n. A shire; a district.

**couple** (kup'l), n. Two; a pair; a brace.

**coupon** (koo'pong), n. An interest certificate attached to transferable bonds.

**courage** (kur'aj), n. Boldness to encounter danger; bravery; daring. [**courageous**]

**courier** (koo'ri-er), n. A messenger sent in haste; a travelling servant.

**course** (kors), n. A passing or running; career; progress; a race; ground run over; series or range; a service of part of a dinner.

**courser** (kor'ser) n. A swift horse.

**court** (kort), n. Residence or retinue of a prince; a legal tribunal; the judges; polite attention; a yard or area.

**courteous** (kurt'yus), a. Polite; civil; complaisant.

**courtesy** (kur'te-si), n. Politeness; civility.

**courtier** (kort'yer), n. One who frequents the court; one who solicits favours.

**courtly** (kort'li), a. Polite; elegant.

**courtship** (kort'ship), n. Solicitation in marriage.

**cousin** (kuz'n), n. The son or daughter of an uncle or aunt.

**cove** (kov), n. A small inlet of the sea; a bay; a cavern or rocky recess.

**covenant** (kuv'e-nant), n. A mutual agreement; the writing containing the agreement.

**cover** (kuv'er), vt. To hide; to clothe.

**coverlet** (kuv'er-let), n. A bedcover.

**covet** (kuv'et), vt. To desire or wish for eagerly; to wish for what is unlawful.

**covey** (kuv'i), n. A brood or hatch of partridges; a small flock of birds.

**coward** (kow'ard), n. A faint-hearted person; one without courage. [cow'-ardice]

**cower** (kow'er), vi. To sink down through fear, etc.; to crouch, for protection or in fear.

**coy** (koy), a. Modest; bashful; shy.

**coyote** (ko-yot'e), n. A prairie wolf.

**cozen** (kuz'n), vt. To flatter; to cheat.

**cozy, cosy** (ko'zi), a. Snug.

**crackle** (krak'l), vi. To give out slight but frequent cracks.

**cradle** (kra'dl), n. A bed or crib in which children are rocked.

**craft** (kraft), n. Cunning; artifice; dexterity; art; trade; occupation; small ships.

**crag** (krag), n. A rough steep rock or point.

**cram** (kram), vt. To press close; to stuff; to fill to superfluity.

**cramp** (kramp), n. An involuntary and painful contraction of a voluntary muscle or group of muscles; restraint.

**cranium** (kra'ni-um), n. The skull; the bones inclosing the brain.

**crayon** (kra'on), n. A pencil of colored chalk; drawing made with crayons.

**craze** (kraz), vt. To weaken: to derange.

**crazy** (kra'zi), a. Feeble; ruinous; insane.

**creak** (krek), vi. To make a sharp, grating sound.

**cream** (krem), n. The fatty part of milk; the best part. [creamery]

**crease** (kres), vt. To mark by folding. n. Mark of a fold.

**create** (kre-at'), vt. To make from nothing; to form; produce. [creation]

**creator** (kre-at'or), n. One who creates.

**creature** (kret'yur), n. A being or thing created; one entirely subservient to another.

**credence** (kre'dens), n. Belief; trust.

**credential** (kre-den'shal), n. That which gives a title to credit; in pl.esp. letters or documents supporting any one's pretensions.

**credible** (kred'i-bl), a. Worthy of belief.

**credit** (kred'it), n. Belief; trust; reputation; time allowed for payment; record of payment; amount due.

**creditable** (kred'it-a-bl), a. Trustworthy; reputable.

**creditor** (kred'i-tor), n. One to whom a debt is due.

**credulity** (kre-du'li-ti), n. Over-readiness to believe. [credulous]

# CREED 54 CRUCIFY

**creed** (kred), n. Belief; summary of articles of belief.

**creel** (krel), n. A fishing-basket.

**cremate** (kre'mat), vt. To burn to ashes. [**crema'tion**]

**crematory** (krem'a-to-ri), n. Building or apparatus for burning bodies.

**creole** (kre'ol), n. One born in a country but of foreign blood; usually a person born in America or the West Indies, of pure French or Spanish blood.

**crepitate** (krep'i-tat), vi. To crackle in burning.

**crescendo** (kre-shend'o), a. Increasing in loudness or power.

**crescent** (kres'ent), a. Increasing.

**cress** (kres), n. A plant with pungent edible leaves.

**crevasse** (kre-vas'), n. Rift in an embankment or a glacier.

**crevice** (krev'is), n. A crack; narrow opening.

**crew** (kru), n. A company of people; ship's company.

**crew** (kru), pt. of crow.

**crier** (kri'er), n. An officer who makes public proclamation.

**crime** (krim), n. A wicked violation of law. [**criminal**]

**crimson** (krim'zn), n. A deep red inclined to purple; red in general.

**cringe** (krinj), vi. To bow or crouch with servility; to fawn.

**cripple** (krip'l), n. A lame person.

**crisis** (kri'sis), n. A decisive point or time. pl. **crises**.

**crisp** (krisp), a. Curled; wrinkled; brittle.

**criterion** (kri-te'ri-on), n. A standard of judging.

**critic** (krit'ik), n. One who judges, esp. in literature or the fine arts.

**critical** (krit'ik-al), a. Relating to criticism; discriminating; captious; indicating a crisis; decisive; important.

**criticise, -ize** (krit'i-siz), vt. To examine and judge; pass judgment on; censure. [**criticism**]

**croak** (krok), n. Cry of a frog or raven. vi. To utter a sound like a frog; forebode evil.

**crochet** (kro-sha'), n. Knitting done with a small hook.

**crock** (krok), n. A wide-mouthed earthen vessel. [**crockery**]

**crocodile** (krok'o-dil), n. An amphibious animal of the lizard kind.

**crone** (kron), n. An old woman.

**crony** (kron'e), n. An old acquaintance.

**croquet** (kro-ket'), n. An out-door game for ladies and gentlemen.

**crotch** (kroch), n. The forking of a tree.

**crotchet** (kroch'et), n. A note of half a minim; a whim.

**crouch** (krouch), vi. To stoop low; to cringe.

**croup** (kroop), n. A disease in the throat; buttocks of a horse.

**crucial** (kroo'she-al), a. Transverse; intersecting.

**cruciate** (kroo'she-at), vt. To torture.

**crucible** (kroo'se-bl), n. A chemical vessel.

**crucifier** (kroo'se-fi-er), n. One who crucifies. [**crucifix**]

**crucifixion** (kroo-se-fik'-shun), n. A nailing to a cross.

**cruciform** (kroo'se-form), a. In form of a cross.

**crucify** (kroo'se-fi), vt. To

fasten and put to death on a cross.

**crude** (krood), a. In a raw or rough state. [**crudity**]

**cruel** (kroo'el), a. Inhuman; void of pity.

**cruelty** (kroo'el-te), n. Inhumanity.

**cruet** (kroo'et), n. A vial for sauces.

**cruise** (krooz), vi. To rove back and forth on the sea. [**cruiser**]

**crumb** (krum), n. A fragment or piece, as of bread.

**crumple** (krum'pl), vt. To draw into wrinkles.

**crupper** (krup'er), n. A leather to hold a saddle back; buttocks of a horse.

**crural** (kroo'ral), a. Pertaining to the leg.

**crusade** (kroo-sad'), n. A military expedition to recover the holy land. [**crusader**]

**cruse** (krooz), n. A small cup or vial.

**crutch** (kruch), n. A staff for cripples.

**crypt** (kript), n. A cell or chapel under a church.

**cryptic** (krip'tik), a. Hidden; secret.

**crystal** (kris'tal), n. A regular solid transparent body; a watch-glass.

**crystalline** (kris'tal-in), a. Consisting of crystal.

**cube** (kub), n. A regular solid body with six equal sides; the third power of a root.

**cubic** (kub'ik), a. Having the form of a cube.

**cubit** (kub'it), n. The fore arm; measure of a man's arm from the elbow to the wrist, 18 inches.

**cuckold** (kuk'old), n. Husband of an adulteress.

**cucumber** (ku'kum-ber), n. A garden plant.

**cud** (kud), n. A portion of food or of tobacco chewed.

**cuddle** (kud'dl), vi. To lie close or snug.

**cudgel** (kud'jel), n. A thick heavy stick.

**cue** (ku), n. The end or tail of a thing.

**cuff** (kuf), n. A blow; part of a sleeve.

**cuirass** (kwe-ras'), n. A breastplate.

**culinary** (ku'lin-ar-e), a. Belonging to the kitchen.

**cull** (kul), vt. To select from others.

**culm** (kulm), n. The stem of grasses; a kind of coal.

**culminate** (kul'min-at), vi. To be in the meridian.

**culpability** (kulp-a-bil'e-te), n. Blamableness; faultiness; guilt.

**culprit** (kul'prit), n. One arraigned for a crime.

**cultivate** (kul'te-vat), vt. To till; to dress; to foster; to ameliorate.

**cultivated** (kul'te-vat-ed), pp. or a. Improved or raised by culture. [**cultivation**]

**cultivator** (kul'te-vat-er), n. One who tills.

**culture** (kul'tur), n. Act of cultivating.

**culvert** (kul'vert), n. An arched drain.

**cumber** (kum'ber), vt. To clog; to burden. [**cumbersome**]

**cumbrance** (kum'brans), n. Burden; clog. [**cumbrous**]

**cumulate** (kum'u-lat), vt. To heap together; to accumulate.

**cumulus** (ku'mu-lus), n. A heap of cloud common in summer, consisting of rounded heaps with a darker horizontal base.

**cuneal** (ku'ne-al), **cuneate.** (ku'ne-at), a. Of the form of a wedge.

**cunning** (kun'ing), a. Knowing; skilful; artful.

**cupel** (ku'pel), n. A small vessel used by goldsmiths in assaying.

**cupidity** (ku-pid'i-ti), n. Inordinate desire; avarice.

**cupola** (ku'po-la), n. An arched vault; a dome.

**cur** (kur), n. A worthless dog; a churl.

**curable** (kur'a-bl), a. That may be cured.

**curate** (kur'at), n. A clergyman who performs duties for a rector or vicar.

**curative** (kur'a-tiv), a. Tending to cure.

**curb** (kurb), vt. To subdue; restrain; control by a curb.

**curdle** (kurd'l), vt. and vi. To coagulate; congeal.

**cure** (kur), n. Act of healing; remedy.

**curfew** (kur'fu), n. An evening bell anciently rung as a signal for putting out fires and lights; an evening bell.

**curiosity** (ku-ri-os'i-ti), n. Inquisitiveness. [curious]

**curl** (kurl), n. A ringlet of hair, or anything like it.

**curmudgeon** (kur-muj'un), n. A miser; churl.

**currant** (kur'ant), n. A small kind of grape.

**currency** (kur'en-si), n. Circulation; money of a country; general acceptation.

**current** (kur'ent), a. Circulating; generally received; passing.

**curriculum** (kur-rik'yu-lum), n. A course, esp. course of study at a university.

**cursive** (kurs'iv), a. Running; flowing. [cursory]

**curt** (kurt), a. Short; concise; abrupt.

**curtail** (kur-tal'), vt. To cut off a part; abridge.

**curtain** (kur'tin), n. Hanging cloth for a bed or window.

**curtsey, curtsy** (kurt'si), n. Gesture of salutation made by women.

**curvature** (kurv'at-yur), n. A curving or bending; deflection from a straight line.

**cushion** (kush'un), n. Bag or case filled with soft materials for resting on; elastic rim of a billiard table.

**cusp** (kusp), n. Point; horn of a crescent; angle formed by intersecting curves.

**cuspidate** (kusp'i-dat), a. Ending in a cusp or point.

**cuspidor** (kusp'i-dor), n. An ornamental spittoon.

**custard** (kus'tard), n. Dish composed of milk, eggs, sugar, etc.

**custodian** (kus-tod'i-an), n. One who has care of anything, esp. of a public building. [custody]

**custom** (kus'tom), n. Usage; habit; repetition; regular trade or dealing. pl. Duties on imports and exports.

**customer** (kus'tom-er), n. An accustomed buyer; a purchaser.

**custom-house** (kus'tom-hous), n. Place where duties are collected.

**cutaneous** (kyu-ta'ne-us), a. Belonging to the skin.

**cuticle** (ku'ti-kl), n. Outer skin; scarf-skin.

**cutlet** (kut'let), n. Small slice of meat for cooking.

**cycle** (si'kl), n. Recurring period of time; circle or orbit.

**cyclone** (si'klon), n. A rotary storm of extended circuit.

**cyclopean** (si-klo-pe'an), a. Pertaining to the one-eyed Cyclops; vast; gigantic.

**cyclopedia** (si'klo-pe'di-a), n. A body of sciences, and the books containing them.

**cylinder** (sil'in-der), n. Long circular body of uniform diameter.

**cymbal** (sim'bal), n. A hollow, brass, basin-like, musical or tinkling instrument, beaten together in pairs.

**cynic** (sin'ik), n. A morose, surly man; a snarler.

**cynosure** (si'no-shoor), n. The dog's tail, a constellation containing the north-star;—hence, anything that strongly attracts attention.

**cyst** (sist), n. Bag of morbid matter in animal bodies.

# D

**dainty** (dan'ti), a. Toothsome; fastidious; pleasant to the palate; delicious; elegant; tender.

**dairy** (da'ri), n. The place where milk is kept and butter and cheese made.

**dais** (da'is), n. A raised floor with a seat and canopy.

**daisy** (da'zi), n. A flower which closes at night and opens in the morning.

**dale** (dal), n. A low place or valley between hills.

**dalliance** (dal'i-ans), n. Act of fondness; delay.

**dally** (dal'li), vi. To delay; trifle; fondle; play.

**damage** (dam'aj), n. Injury; hurt; loss; harm to property or person. pl. Compensation for loss or injury.

**damp** (damp), a. Moist; humid; watery.

**damsel** (dam'zel), n. A young maiden; a girl.

**dance** (dans), v. To move with measured steps to music; to leap and frisk about.

**dandelion** (dan'de-li-un), n. A plant with a naked hollow stalk.

**dandle** (dan'dl), v. To shake on the knee; to fondle; to amuse.

**dandruff** (dan'druf), n. A scaly scurf on the head.

**danger** (dan'jer), n. Exposure to evil, or risk; peril. [**dangerous**]

**dangle** (dang'gl), v. To hang loose and swinging.

**dank** (dangk), a. Very humid; close and damp.

**dapper** (dap'er), a. Little; active; brisk; neat.

**dapple** (dap'l), a. Of various colors; marked with spots.

**dare** (dar), v. To have courage; to venture; to defy; to provoke.

**dastard** (das'tard), n. One who meanly shrinks from danger; coward; poltroon.

**data** (da'ta), n. pl. Propositions given and admitted.

**date** (dat), n. The time of an event; the fruit of the palm-tree.

**daub** (dawb), vt. To smear with mortar; paint coarsely.

**daughter** (daw'ter), n. A female child.

**daunt** (dant, also dawnt), vt. To check by fear of danger; intimidate; dishearten.

**dawn** (dawn), vi. To begin to grow light.

**daze** (daz), vt. To confuse; stupefy.

**dazzle** (daz'l), vt. To overpower with light or splendour.

**deacon** (de'kn), n. (1) In Episcopal churches, the order of clergy below priesthood. (2) In Presbyterian churches, an officer (not an elder) who attends to the secular affairs of the congregation. (3) In Congrega-

**deaf** (def), a. Wanting the sense of hearing.

**deaf-mute** (def'mut), n. One who is both deaf and dumb.

**deal** (del), n. A part; quantity; boards, etc.; distribution.

**dean** (den), n. The second dignitary of a diocese; the head of a college or faculty.

**debar** (de-bar'), vt. To hinder from entering or enjoying.

**debark** (de-bark'), vt. or i. To disembark. [**debarkation**]

**debase** (de-bas'), vt. To degrade; adulterate; vitiate.

**debatable** (de-ba'ta-bl), a. Disputable.

**debate** (de-bat'), vt. or i. To dispute; discuss. n. Public discussion.

**debauch** (de-bawch'), n. Unrestrained indulgence of the appetites. vt. To corrupt; seduce.

**debauchee** (deb-o-she'), n. A drunkard; a rake.

**debauchery** (de-baw'cher-i), n. Seduction from duty, etc.; habitual intemperance or lewdness.

**debenture** (de-ben'tur), n. A writing acknowledging a debt; a certificate entitling to a draw back.

**debilitate** (de-bil'i-tat), vt. To weaken.

**debit** (deb'it), n. The debtor side of an account book.

**debonair** (deb-o-nar'), a. Of pleasing manners; courteous.

**debouch** (de-boosh'), vi. To issue from a narrow pass.

**debris** (da-bre'), n. Fragments; ruins.

tional churches, an officer who advises the minister, sees to the charitable concerns of the congregation, and distributes the elements at the Communion. [**deaconess**]

**debt** (det), n. Anything owed or due. [**debtor**]

**debut** (da-bu'), [or French u], n. Beginning; first public appearance.

**decade** (dek'ad), n. An aggregate of ten; period of ten years.

**decadence** (de-ka'dens), n. State of decay or decline.

**decalogue** (dek'a-log), n. The ten commandments.

**decamp** (de-kamp'), vi. To leave an encampment; go away.

**decanter** (de-kant'er), n. An ornamental bottle for liquors.

**decapitate** (de-kap'i-tat), vt. To behead.

**decay** (de-ka'), vi. To waste away; become decomposed.

**decease** (de-ses'), vi. To die.

**deceit** (de-set'), n. Anything that deceives; fraud.

**deceitful** (de-set'ful), a. Disposed or tending to deceive

**deceive** (de-sev'), vt. To mislead; impose on; cheat.

**December** (de-sem'ber), n. The twelfth month of the year.

**decency** (de'sen-si), n. Propriety; modesty.

**decennial** (de-sen'i-al), a. Lasting ten years; happening every ten years.

**decent** (de'sent), a. Seemly; proper; modest.

**decentralize, -ise** (de-sent'-ral-iz), vt. To distribute powers that have been concentred.

**deception** (de-sep'shun), n. Act of deceiving; fraud; illusion. [**deceptive**]

**decide** (de-sid'), vt. To determine; settle.

**deciduous** (de-sid'yu-us), a. Falling off in autumn, as leaves; shedding leaves in the autumn.

**decimal** (des'i-mal), a.

Proceeding by tens or powers of ten.

**decimate** (des'i-mat), vt. To take or put to death one in every ten.

**decipher** (de-si'fer), vt. To read secret writing

**decision** (de-sizh'un), n. Determination; settlement; firmness.

**decisive** (de-si'siv), a. Final; conclusive; positive.

**declaim** (de-klam'), vt. and vi. To speak oratorically. [declamation]

**declamatory** (de-klam'a-tori), a. Rhetorical.

**declaration** (dek-la-ra'shun), n. Open affirmation.

**declare** (de-klar'), vt. To make known; affirm openly.

**declension** (de-klen'shun), n. Descent; decay; in gram. inflection by cases.

**declination** (dek-li-na'shun), n. Descent; in astr. distance from the celestial equator.

**decline** (de-klin'), vt. and vi. To bend from, or down; to fail or decay; refuse; in gram. to inflect by cases.

**declivity** (de-kliv'i-ti), n. Inclination downward; slope.

**decoction** (de-kok'shun), n. Boiling; extract made by boiling.

**decompose** (de-kom-poz'), vt. and vi. To resolve or separate into elements. [decomposition]

**decorate** (dek'o-rat), vt. To ornament; embellish. [dec'orator]

**decorous** (de-ko'rus), a. Becoming; suitable.

**decorum** (de-ko'rum), n. Propriety of conduct; decency.

**decoy** (de-koi'), vt. To entice; allure into a snare.

**decrease** (de-kres'), vt. To make less.

**decree** (de-kre'), n. An order; edict.

**decrepit** (de-krep'it), a. Infirm; worn out by age. [decrepitude]

**decry** (de-kri'), vt. To cry down; condemn.

**decumbent** (de-kum'bent), a. Lying down.

**dedicate** (ded'i-kat), vt. To consecrate; devote. [dedication]

**deduce** (de-dus'), vt. To infer; infer a special from a general truth.

**deducible** (de-dus'i-bl), a. That may be deduced.

**deduction** (de-duk'shun), n. Inference; abatement.

**deductive** (de-duk'tiv), a. That is or may be deduced; proceeding by deduction.

**deface** (de-fas'), vt. To disfigure; obliterate.

**defalcate** (de-fal'kat), vi. To show a deficiency of funds intrusted to one's care.

**defamation** (def-am-a'shun), n. Injurious report; slander.

**default** (de-falt'), n. Fault; failure; neglect; non-appearance in court. [defaulter]

**defeasible** (de-fez'i-bl), a. That may be annulled.

**defeat** (de-fet'), vt. To frustrate; overthrow.

**defect** (de-fekt'), n. Deficiency; blemish; fault.

**defection** (de-fek'shun), n. A falling away; desertion.

**defective** (de-fek'tiv), a. Incomplete; insufficient.

**defend** (de-fend'), vt. To guard; protect; maintain against attack; resist in law. [defendant]

**defense, defence,** (de-fens'), n. Protection.

**defensive** (de-fens'iv), a. Serving to defend.

**defer** (de-fer), vt. To put off; delay.

**deference** (def'er-ens), n. Respectful submission.

**defiance** (de-fi'ans), n. A challenge; contempt of danger.

**deficient** (de-fish'ent), a. Wanting; imperfect.

**deficit** (de'fi-sit), n. Want; balance on the wrong side.

**defile** (de-fil), n. A narrow passage; lane; vt. To pollute; &c.; defilement, foulness.

**definition** (def'i-nish'un), n. A description of the essential properties of a thing; an explanation of the exact meaning of a word, term, &c.

**definitive** (de-fin'it-iv), a. Determinate; final.

**deflect** (de-flekt'), vi. or t. To turn aside; bend from a right line; dip.

**deflorate** (de-flo'rat), a. Past the flowering state, as an anther after it has shed its pollen.

**deflour** (de-flour'), vt. To deprive of flowers; to take away original grace and beauty; to ravish.

**defoliation** (de-fo-li-a'shun), n. Falling of leaves.

**deform** (de-form'), vt. To mar; to disfigure in form.

**defraud** (de-frawd'), vt. To cheat or deceive; to deprive of by fraud; to withhold wrongfully; a. Defraud'ed.

**defray** (de-fra'), vt. To bear or pay, as expenses.

**defunct** (de-fungkt'), a. Deceased; dead; lifeless.

**defy** (de-fi'), vt. To dare; challenge; treat with contempt; disown; brave. a. Defi'ant, bold, saucy.

**degenerate** (de-jen'er-at), a. Having declined in moral worth.

**deglutition** (deg-loo-tish'un), n. Act or power of swallowing.

**degradation** (deg-ra-da'shun), n. A depriving of rank; degeneracy.

**degrade** (de-grad), vt. To deprive of rank or title; to lessen.

**degree** (de-gre'), n. A step; extent; the 360th part of a circle.

**deification** (de-if-ik-a'shun), n. The act of enrolling among the deities.

**deify** (de'e-fi), vt. To exalt to the rank of deity.

**deign** (dan), vi. To condescend. vt. To grant.

**deism** (de'izm), n. A denial of revelation. [**deist**]

**deject** (de-jekt'), vt. To dispirit; to discourage.

**delay** (de-la'), vt. To put off; to detain.

**dele** (de'le), vt. To blot out.

**delectable** (de-lekt'a-bl), a. Delightful.

**delegate** (del'e-gat), vt. To send away. [**delegation**]

**deleterious** (del-e-te're-us), a. Destructive; highly injurious.

**deliberate** (de-lib'er-at), vt. or i. To weigh in the mind; to hesitate.

**deliberative** (de-lib'er-at-iv), a. Apt to consider.

**delicacy** (del'e-ka-se), n. Refinement of sensibility or taste.

**delicate** (del'e-kat), a. Nice; pleasing to the taste; effeminate.

**delicious** (de-lish'e-us), a. Sweet to the palate or other sense.

**delight** (de-lit'), n. Great joy or pleasure.

**delineate** (de-lin'e-at), vt. To draw the outline.

**delineation** (de-lin-a'shun), n. Act of drawing the outline of a thing.

**delineator** (de-lin'e-at-er), n. One who delineates.

**deliquate** (del'e-kwat), vt. or i. To melt.

**delinquency** (de-lin'kwen-

# DELIQUESCE 61 DENUDE

**se), n.** Failure of duty; fault.
**deliquesce** (del-e-kwes'), vi. To melt.
**delirious** (de-lir'e-us), a. In a state of delirium.
**delirium** (de-lir'e-um), n. Derangement.
**deliver** (de-liv'er), vt. To free; to release; to utter. [**deliverance**]
**delude** (de-lud'), vt. To deceive.
**deluge** (del'uj), n. A general inundation.
**delusion** (de-lu'zhun), n. Act of deluding.
**delusive** (de-lu'siv), a. Tending to deceive.
**demagogue** (dem'a-gog), n. A ringleader of the rabble.
**demain** (de-man'), n. A manorhouse and land; also written **demesne.**
**demand** (de-mand'), vt. To claim. n. A claim by right.
**demarcation** (de-mar-ka'-shun), n. A division; a fixed limit.
**demean** (de-men'), v. To behave; to conduct; to debase. [**demeanor**]
**demented** (de-men'ted), a. Crazy; mad; infatuated.
**demerit** (de-mer'it), n. Fault; crime; guilt.
**demigod** (dem'i-god), n. A fabulous hero, half divine.
**demise** (de-miz'), n. Death; decease; a lease.
**democracy** (de-mok'ra-si), n. Government by the people. [**democrat, democratic**]
**demolish** (de-mol'ish), v. To destroy; to raze; to ruin.
**demolition** (dem-o-lish'un), n. Act of overthrowing; destruction; ruin.
**demon** (de'mun), n. An evil spirit; a bad genius.
**demonetize** (de-mon'e-tiz), v. To deprive of standard value, as money.
**demoniac** (de-mo'ni-ak), n. One possessed by an evil spirit.
**demonstrate** (de-mon'strat or dem'on-strat), v. To point out clearly; prove with certainty. [**demonstration**]
**demoralize** (de-mor'al-iz), vt. To corrupt in morals; to deprive of spirit and confidence; to throw into confusion.
**demulcent** (de-mul'sent), a. Soothing.
**demur** (de-mer'), vi. To hesitate; to object.
**demure** (de-mur'), a. Sober; staid; modest; affectedly modest; making a show of gravity.
**denial** (de-ni'al), n. Contradiction; refusal.
**denim** (den'im), n. A colored twilled fabric for overalls, etc.
**denizen** (den'i-zn), n. An inhabitant.
**denominate** (de-nom'in-at), vt. To give a name to; to call.
**denote** (de-not'), vt. To note or mark off; to indicate by a sign.
**denouement** (da-no'mon), n. The unraveling of a plot or story; the issue.
**denounce** (de-nowns'), vt. To inform against or accuse publicly.
**dense** (dens), a. Thick, close, compact; impenetrably stupid.
**dental** (den'tal), a. Belonging to the teeth; produced by the aid of the teeth.
**dentate** (den'tat), a. Toothed; notched; set as with teeth.
**dentifrice** (den'ti-fris), n. A substance used in rubbing or cleaning the teeth.
**dentist** (den'tist), n. One who remedies diseases of the teeth, or inserts artificial teeth.
**denude** (de-nud'). vt. To

**DEODORIZE**    62    **DEROGATE**

make nude or naked; to lay bare.

**deodorize** (de-o'dor-iz), vt. To take the odor or smell from.

**depart** (de-part'), vt. To go away; to quit or leave; to die.

**department** (de-part'ment), n. A part or portion; a separate part of business or duty; a section of the administration.

**depend** (de-pend'), vi. To hang down; to be sustained by or connected with anything; to be pending; to rely.

**depict** (de-pikt'), vt. To paint carefully; to make a likeness of; to describe.

**deplete** (de-plet'), vt. To empty, reduce, exhaust.

**deplore** (de-plor'), vt. To feel or express deep grief for.

**deploy** (de-ploy'), vt. To unfold; to open out or extend.

**depopulate** (de-pop'u-lat), vt. To deprive of population.

**deport** (de-port'), vt. To exile; to behave.

**depose** (de-poz'), vt. To remove from a high station; to degrade; to strip; to attest.

**deposit** (de-poz'it), vt. To put or set down; to place; to lay up or past; to intrust.

**deposition** (dep-o-zish'un), n. Declaration, testimony taken authoritatively; removal.

**depot** (de'po, or dep'o), n. A place of deposit; a storehouse; a military station; a railroad station.

**depravation** (dep-ra-va'shun), n. Depravity.

**deprave** (de-prav'), vt. To make bad or worse; corrupt.

**depravity** (de-prav'i-ti), n. Wickedness; moral corruption.

**deprecate** (dep're-kat), vt. To desire earnestly, or entreat, that something may not be.

**deprecative** (dep're-kat-iv), a. Tending to deprecate.

**depreciate** (de-pre'si-at), vt. To lower the value of; disparage.

**depreciation** (de-pre-si-a'shun), n. Decline in value.

**depredate** (dep're-dat), vt. To plunder; prey upon; lay waste.

**depress** (de-pres'), vt. To press down; lower; cast down. [depression]

**deprivation** (dep-ri-va'shun), n. Loss; want.

**deprive** (de-priv'), vt. To take from; bereave.

**depth** (depth), n. Deepness; profundity; a deep place.

**deputation** (dep-yu-ta'shun), n. Act of deputing; persons deputed.

**depute** (de-put'), vt. To appoint as an agent.

**deputy** (dep'yu-ti), n. One appointed to act for another.

**derail** (de-ral'), vt. To cause to run off the rails.

**derange** (de-ranj'), vt. To put out of order; confuse.

**derangement** (de-ranj'ment), n. Disorder; insanity.

**derelict** (der'e-likt), a. Abandoned.

**derision** (de-rizh'un), n. Mockery.

**derivation** (der-i-va'shun), n. Act or process of deriving.

**derivative** (de-riv'a-tiv), a. Derived.

**derive** (de-riv'), vt. To draw from; receive from a source; deduce; trace a word to its origin.

**derogate** (der'o-gat), vi. To lessen by taking away; detract. [derogation]

**derogatory** (de-rog'a-to-ri), a. Tending to derogate; detracting.

**derrick** (der'ik), n. Machine for hoisting heavy weights.

**dervish** (der'vish), n. A religious mendicant of the Mohammedan faith.

**descant** (des-kant'), vt. To discourse or comment at large.

**descend** (de-send'), vi. To go or come down. [descendant]

**descendent** (de-send'ent), a. Proceeding downwards.

**descent** (de-sent'), n. Motion downward; slope; invasion; derivation from an ancestor.

**describe** (de-skrib'), vt. To represent by words; trace.

**descry** (de-skri'), vt. To discover; espy.

**desecrate** (des'e-krat), vt. To divert from a sacred purpose; profane.

**desert** (de-zert'), n. Merit; reward.

**desert** (de-zert'), vt. To leave; forsake.

**desert** (dez'ert), a. Desolate; uninhabited; barren.

**desertion** (de-zer'shun), n. Being deserted.

**deserve** (de-zerv'), vt. To earn by service; merit.

**desiccate** (des'i-kat), vt. and vi. To dry up or out.

**desideratum** (de-sid-e-ra'tum), n. Something wanted. pl. **desiderata**.

**design** (de-zin'), vt. and vi. To draw; sketch; contrive; plan; purpose; intend.

**designate** (des'ig-nat), vt. To point out; name.

**desirable** (de-zir-a-bl), n. Worthy of desire.

**desist** (de-sist'), vi. To stop; forbear.

**desolation** (des-o-la'shun), n. Waste; destruction.

**despair** (de-spar'), vi. To be without hope.

**despatch** (des-pach'), vt. To send off; put to death; dispose of.

**desperado** (des-per-a'do), n. A desperate or reckless man; ruffian.

**desperate** (des'per-at), a. Hopeless; reckless; furious.

**desperation** (des-per-a'shun), n. Recklessness of consequences; fury.

**despicable** (des'pi-ka-bl), a. Deserving to be despised.

**despise** (de-spiz'), vt. To scorn; view with contempt.

**despiteful** (de-spit'ful), a. Full of spite or malice.

**despoil** (de-spoil'), vt. To strip; bereave; rob.

**despond** (de-spond'), vt. To lose courage, or hope. [despondent]

**despot** (des'pot), n. An absolute sovereign; tyrant. [despotism]

**dessert** (dez-ert'), n. Service of fruit, etc., at the close of a meal.

**destination** (des-ti-na'shun), n. Appointed end or goal; place to which one is going.

**destine** (des'tin), vt. To ordain or appoint to a purpose; to doom. [destiny]

**destitute** (des'ti-tut), a. In utter want; needy.

**destroy** (de-stroi'), vt. To demolish; ruin; put an end to.

**destructible** (de-struk'ti-bl), a. Liable to be destroyed.

**desuetude** (des'we-tud), n. Disuse.

**desultory** (des'ul-to-ri), a. Unconnected; rambling; loose.

**detach** (de-tach'), vt. To unfasten; separate.

**detachment** (de-tach'ment), n. Unfastening; separation; body of troops separated from the army.

**detail** (de-tal'), vt. To re-

**detain** (de-tan'), vt. To hold back; withhold; delay.

**detect** (de-tekt'), vt. To discover; find out.

**detective** (de-tek'tiv), n. A policeman in plain clothes.

**detention** (de-ten'shun), n. Detaining.

**deter** (de-ter'), vt. To prevent; hinder.

**deteriorate** (de-te'ri-u-rat), vt. or i. To impair; become worse. [deterioration]

**determinable** (de-ter'mi-na-bl), a. That may be decided.

**determinate** (de-ter'mi-nat) a. Limited; definite; conclusive.

**determination** (de-ter-mi-na'shun), n. Resolution taken; end; decision.

**deterrent** (de-ter'ent), n. That which hinders or prevents.

**detest** (de-test'), vt. To hate extremely; abhor.

**detestable** (de-tes'ta-bl), a. Very hateful. [detestation]

**dethrone** (de-thron'), vt. To divest of royalty; depose.

**detonate** (det'u-nat), vt. To cause to explode.

**detour** (de-toor'), n. A winding; a circuitous route.

**detract** (de-trakt'), vt. or i. To lessen; disparage; defame; take away. [detraction]

**detriment** (det'ri-ment), n. Loss; damage.

**detritus** (de-tri'tus), n. Fragments or particles of rock or soil carried down and deposited by floods or rivers.

**detruncate** (de-trung'kat), vt. To lop off; shorten by cutting.

**deuce** (dus), n. A card or die with two spots; the devil.

**devastate** (dev'as-tat), vt. To lay waste; ravage.

**develop** (de-vel'up), vt. To disengage; lay open to view.

**deviate** (de'vi-at), vi. To wander; go astray.

**device** (de-vis'), n. Scheme; contrivance; an emblem or motto.

**devious** (de'vi-us), a. Going astray.

**devisable** (de-vi'za-bl), a. That may be devised or contrived; that may be bequeathed.

**devise** (de-viz'), vt. To contrive; bequeath.

**devitalise** (de-vi'tal-iz), vt. To deprive of living power.

**devoid** (de-void'), a. Not possessing; void; empty; destitute.

**devoir** (dev-wawr'), n. Duty; act of civility.

**devolution** (de-vo-lu'shun), n. Transference.

**devolve** (de-volv'), vt. or i. To roll down; fall by succession.

**devote** (de-vot'), vt. To dedicate; appropriate by vow.

**devotee** (dev-u-te'), n. One devoted; a bigot.

**devour** (de-vour'), vt. To eat up ravenously; consume or destroy rapidly.

**devout** (de-vout'), a. Pious; religious.

**dew** (du), n. A moisture on the earth deposited at night.

**dewy** (du'i), a. Moist with dew.

**dexter** (deks'ter), a. Right, as opposed to left.

**dexterity** (deks-ter'i-ti), n. Activity and expertness; adroitness; skill. [dexterous]

**diabetes** (di-a-be'tez), n.

Excessive discharge of urine.

**diabolical** (di-a-bol'i-kal), a. Devilish.

**diadem** (di'a-dem), n. A crown.

**diæresis** (di-e're-sis), n. A mark (..) placed over one of two vowels to note that they are pronounced separately.

**diagnosis** (di-ag-no'sis), n. The science or art of distinguishing one disease from another by means of its symptoms.

**diagonal** (di-ag'u-nal), n. A right line drawn from angle to angle.

**diagram** (di'a-gram), n. A figure or drawing made to illustrate a statement, or facilitate a demonstration.

**dial** (di'al), n. A plate to show the hour by the sun's shadow; any face or plate with a movable index or pointer.

**dialect** (di'a-lekt), n. Language; peculiar or local form of speech.

**dialectics** (di-a-lek'tiks), n. pl. The science of reasoning; the forms and rules of argument.

**dialogue** (di'a-log), n. Discourse between two or more.

**diameter** (di-am'e-ter), n. A right line passing through the centre of a circle.

**diamond** (di'a-mund), n. The hardest and costliest of gems; a rhomboidal figure; the smallest printing type.

**diaphragm** (di'a-fram), n. The midriff.

**diarrhœa** (di-a-re'a), n. Morbidly frequent evacuation of the intestines.

**diary** (di'a-ri), n. A register of daily events or transactions.

**diatribe** (di'a-trib), n. A continued discourse or disputation; an invective.

**dice** (dis), n. pl. of **die**.

**dictate** (dik'tat), vt. To tell another what to do, say, or write; prescribe or direct authoritatively.

**dictator** (dik-ta'ter), n. One temporarily invested with absolute power.

**dictatorial** (dik-ta-to'ri-al), n. Unlimited in power; imperious.

**diction** (dik'shun), n. Manner of expression; choice of words; style.

**dictionary** (dik'shun-ar-i), n. A book in which words are explained.

**dictum** (dik'tum), n. An authoritative word or assertion. pl. **dicta**.

**didactic** (di-dak'tik), a. Intended to instruct.

**diet** (di'et), n. Food; an assembly of princes.

**dietary** (di'et-a-ri), n. Course or order of diet.

**dietetic** (di-e-tet'ik), a. Relating to diet.

**dietetics** (di-e-tet'iks), n. pl. The science pertaining to food.

**differ** (dif'fer), v. To be unlike; to vary; to disagree; to contend.

**difference** (dif'fer-ens), n. Distinction; disagreement. [different]

**differentiate** (dif-fer-en'shi-at), v. To find the differential of.

**difficult** (dif'fi-kult), a. Not easy; hard to be done. [difficulty]

**diffidence** (dif'fi-dens), n. Want of confidence; modesty; reserve; distrust of one's self.

**diffinitive** (dif-fin'i-tiv), a. Final; conclusive.

**diffuse** (dif-fuz'), v. To pour out; to spread; to circulate.

**diffuse** (dif-fus'), a. Copiously full; widely spread. [diffusion]

**diffusive** (dif-fu'siv), a. That spreads widely.

**digest** (di'jest), n. A complication, abridgment or summary of laws.

**digest** (di-jest'), v. To dissolve food in the stomach; to think over; to arrange.

**digestible** (di-jest'i-bl), a. Capable of being digested. [**digestion**]

**digit** (dij'it), n. Three-fourths of an inch; the 12th of the diameter of the sun or moon; any number under ten.

**dignified** (dig'ni-fid), a. Noble; exalted; grave; lofty. [**dignify**]

**dignity** (dig'ni-ti), n. Nobleness or elevation of mind; grandeur of mien; preferment; high office.

**digraph** (di'graf), n. Two vowels with only one sound.

**digress** (di-gres'), v. To go from the main point of subject; to introduce unnecessary matter.

**digressive** (di-gres'iv), a. Leaving the subject.

**dihedron** (di-he'dron), n. A figure having two sides or surfaces.

**dike** (dik), n. A ditch; a mound raised to prevent inundation.

**dilapidate** (di-lap'i-dat), v. To fall into decay; to go to ruin.

**dilatation** (dil-a-ta'shun), n. Act of expanding.

**dilate** (di-lat'), v. To expand; to extend; to enlarge.

**dilatory** (dil'a-to-ri), a. Tending to delay; slow; tardy.

**dilemma** (di-lem'a), n. A state of perplexity how to decide.

**dilettante** (dil-et-tan'ta), n. An admirer of the fine arts.

**diligence** (dil'i-jens), n. Steady application; industry. [**diligent**]

**dilute** (di-lut'), v. To weaken or make thinner.

**dilution** (di-lu'shun), n. Act of making thin or more.

**diluvium** (di-lu'vi-um), n. A deposit of clay or earth caused by a flood.

**dimension** (di-men'shun), n. Size; extent; bulk.

**diminish** (di-min'ish), v. To lessen; to make or become less; to abate; to subside.

**diminution** (dim-i-nu'shun), n. The act of lessening or making smaller; decrease.

**diminutive** (di-min'u-tiv), a. Small; little; contracted.

**dimity** (dim'i-ti), n. A kind of cotton cloth; ribbed.

**dimple** (dim'pl), n. A small natural depression on the face. v. To form dimples.

**dinginess** (din'ji-nes), n. A dark dusky hue.

**dingy** (din'ji), a. Dusky; dull; brown; soiled; foul.

**diocese** (di'o-ses), n. Jurisdiction of a bishop.

**diptheria** (dif-the'ri-a, dip), Disease in which the air-passages are coated with a membranous substance.

**diphthong** (dif'thong), n. Union of two vowel-sounds in one syllable.

**diploma** (di-plo'ma), n. Writing conferring some honor or privilege.

**diplomacy** (di-plo'ma-si), n. Art or conduct of negotiation, esp. between states or sovereigns. [**diplomatist**]

**dipsomania** (dip-so-man'-i-a), n. Diseases characterized by an insane thirst for spirituous liquors.

**direct** (di-rekt'), a. Straight; straight forward; lineal

**direction** (di-rek'shun), n. Aim; course; relative position; order; address.

**director** (di-rekt'or), n. One who directs; manager.

**directory** (di-rekt'o-ri), n. Book of names and addresses.

**dirge** (derj), n. A funeral song or hymn.

**disability** (dis-a-bil'i-ti), n. Want of power or qualification.

**disable** (dis-a'bl), vt. To deprive of power; disqualify.

**disabuse** (dis-a-buz'), vt. To undeceive.

**disadvantage** (dis-ad-vant'aj), n. Unfavorable state or position; injury.

**disaffect** (dis-af-fekt'), vt. To make unfriendly.

**disaffection** (dis-af-fek'shun), n. Unfriendliness; alienation.

**disagree** (dis-a-gre'), vi. Not to agree; to differ; be at variance.

**disagreeable** (dis-a-gre'a-bl), a. Unpleasant.

**disagreement** (dis-a-gre'ment), n. Want of agreement; difference; dispute.

**disallow** (dis-a-lou'), vt. To refuse to grant; deny the authority of.

**disappear** (dis-ap-per'), vi. To vanish.

**disappointment** (dis-appoint'ment), n. Defeat of expectation or hope.

**disapprove** (dis-ap-proov'), vt. Not to approve; to censure; reject.

**disaster** (diz-as'ter), n. An unfortunate event; calamity.

**disastrous** (diz-as'trus), a. Unlucky; calamitous.

**disbar** (dis-bar'), vt. To deprive of the right of pleading in a court.

**discern** (di-zern'), vt. To perceive; see; distinguish.

**discernible** (di-zern'i-bl), a. That may be discerned; perceptible.

**discernment** (di-zern'ment), n. Act or power of discerning; penetration.

**discharge** (dis-charj'), vt. To unload; set free; dismiss; emit; fire, as a gun.

**disciple** (dis-si'pl), n. A learner; follower.

**disciplinarian** (dis-si-plin-a'ri-an), n. One who enforces discipline.

**disclaim** (dis-klam'), vt. To renounce claim to; deny; reject.

**disclose** (dis-kloz), vt. To lay open; reveal. [**disclosure**]

**discoloration** (dis-kul-or-a'shun), n. Change of color.

**discomfit** (dis-kum'fit), vi. To disconcert; defeat. [**discomfiture**]

**discomfort** (dis-kum'fort), n. Want of comfort; uneasiness; distress.

**discompose** (dis-kom-poz'), vt. To disarrange.

**disconsolate** (dis-kon'so-lat), a. Without consolation; uncomforted; sad.

**discontent** (dis-kon-tent'), a. Not content; dissatisfied.

**discord** (dis'kord), n. Disagreement; want of harmony; union of inharmonious sounds.

**discount** (dis'kount), n. Deduction made from a payment; interest paid in advance.

**discount** (dis-kount'), vt. To lend money on, deducting interest.

**discountenance** (dis-koun'te-nans), vt. To abash; discourage; disfavor. n. Disfavor.

**discourage** (dis-kur'aj), vt. To dishearten; repress by disfavor.

**discourse** (dis-kors'), n.

Speech; talk; an address; treatise.

**discourteous** (dis-kurt'yus), a. Uncivil; rude.

**discourtesy** (dis-kurt'e-si), n. Want of courtesy; incivility.

**discovery** (dis-kuv'er-i), n. Finding out; something discovered.

**discredit** (dis-kred'it), n. Want of credit or reputation; disgrace.

**discreditable** (dis-kred'it-a-bl), a. Not creditable; disgraceful.

**discrepant** (dis-krep'ant, dis'-), a. Disagreeing; not consistent.

**discrete** (dis-kret'), a. Separate; distinct.

**discretional** (dis-kresh'un-al), **discretionary** (dis-kresh'un-a-ri), a. Left to discretion; unrestrained.

**discriminate** (dis-krim'i-nat), vt. and vi. To distinguish; make a distinction.

**discursion** (dis-kur'shun), n. Desultory discourse.

**discursive** (dis-kurs'iv), a. Rambling; diffuse.

**discuss** (dis-kus'), vt. To disperse; examine in debate. [**discussion**]

**disdain** (dis-dan'), vt. To scorn. n. Scorn; haughtiness.

**disease** (diz-ez'), n. Malady; sickness; ailment.

**disembark** (dis-em-bark'), vt. and vi. To take out of, or land from, a ship.

**disembody** (dis-em-bod'i), vt. To divest of a body.

**disembogue** (dis-em-bog'), vt. and vi. To discharge at the mouth, as a stream.

**disenchant** (dis-en-chant'), vt. To free from enchantment.

**disencumber** (dis-en-kum'ber), vt. To free from encumbrance.

**disfavor** (dis-fa'vor), n. Want of favor, dislike.

**disfranchise** (dis-fran'chiz), vt. To deprive of citizenship.

**disgorge** (dis-gorj'), vt. To vomit; give up what has been taken.

**disgrace** (dis-gras'), n. State of being out of favor; dishonor.

**disguise** (dis-giz'), n. Dress which prevents the wearer from being recognized; false appearance.

**disgust** (dis-gust', diz-), n. Aversion; strong dislike; loathing.

**dishearten** (dis-hart'n), vt. To discourage.

**dishevel** (di-shev'l), vt. To disorder the hair.

**dishonor** (dis-on'or, diz-), n. Want of honor; disgrace; shame.

**disincline** (dis-in-klin'), vt. To make unwilling; indispose.

**disinfect** (dis-in-fekt'), vt. To free from infection.

**disinfectant** (dis-in-fekt'-ant), n. Anything that disinfects.

**disingenuous** (dis-in-jen'yu-us), a. Not frank; not candid.

**disinherit** (dis-in-her'it), vt. To cut off from inheriting.

**disintegrate** (dis-in'te-grat), vt. To separate into parts or particles.

**disinterested** (dis-in'ter-est-ed), a. Not interested; free from bias.

**disjunction** (dis-jungk'shun), n. Separation; disjoining.

**disjunctive** (dis-jungk'tiv), a. Tending to disjoin; in gram. uniting words but separating sense.

**dislike** (dis-lik'), n. Absence of affection; aversion.

**dislocate** (dis'lo-kat), vt. To displace; put out of joint. [**dislocation**]

**dislodgment** (dis-loj'ment), n. Displacement; removal.

**disloyalty** (dis-loi'al-ti), n. Want of fidelity; treacherousness.

**dismal** (diz'mal), a. Dark; gloomy; sorrowful; dreadful.

**dismantle** (dis-man'tl), vt. To strip of dress, furniture, or outworks.

**dismay** (dis-ma'), vt. To discourage.

**dismiss** (dis-mis'), vt. To send away; discharge; despatch; reject.

**dismissal** (dis-mis'al), n. Discharge; dismission. [**dismission**]

**dismount** (dis-mount'), vi. To alight from a horse, etc.

**disobedience** (dis-o-bed'yens), n. Neglect or refusal to obey.

**disobedient** (dis-o-be'dient), a. Refusing to obey.

**disobey** (dis-o-ba'), vt. To refuse or neglect to obey; break the commands of.

**disorder** (dis-or'der), n. Confusion; disease. vt. To throw into confusion; make sick.

**disorganise** (dis-or'ga-niz), vt. To derange an organised body.

**disown** (dis-on'), vt. To disavow; renounce.

**disparage** (dis-par'ij), vt. To match unequally; detract from.

**disparate** (dis'pa-rat), a. Unequal; unlike.

**disparity** (dis-par'i-ti), n. Inequality in form, character, years, etc.

**dispassionate** (dis-pash'un-at), a. Cool; calm; impartial.

**dispatch.** See **despatch**.

**dispel** (dis-pel'), vt. To drive away; scatter; dissipate.

**dispensible** (dis-pen'sa-bl), a. That may be dispensed.

**dispensary** (dis-pen'sa-ri), n. A place for dispensing medicine.

**dispense** (dis-pens'), vt. To deal out in portions; distribute; administer.

**disperse** (dis-pers'), vt. To scatter; spread abroad.

**dispersion** (dis-per'shun), n. Scattering, or being scattered.

**dispersive** (dis-per'siv), a. Tending to disperse.

**dispirit** (dis-pir'it), vt. To discourage.

**display** (dis-pla'), vt. To spread wide; open; exhibit.

**displease** (dis-plez'), vt. To give offence to.

**displeasure** (dis-plezh'ur), n. Slight anger; irritation; cause of offence.

**disport** (dis-port'), n. Play; sport; pastime.

**disposal** (dis-po'zal), n. Power of bestowing; management.

**dispose** (dis-poz'), vt. To place; incline; adapt or fit.

**disposition** (dis-po-zish'un), n. Order; distribution; temper; deed of gift.

**dispraise** (dis-praz'), n. Censure; blame; dishonour.

**disproof** (dis-proof'), n. Refutation.

**disproportion** (dis-pro-por'shun), n. Want of proportion or symmetry.

**disprove** (dis-proov'), vt. To show to be false; confute.

**disputable** (dis'pu-ta-bl), a. That may be disputed.

**disputant** (dis'pu-tant), n. One who disputes.

**disputation** (dis-pu-ta'shun) n. Act of disputing; contest in argument.

**dispute** (dis-put'), vt. or i. To debate; call in question.

**disqualification** (dis-kwol-i-fi-ka'shun), n. That which disqualifies.

**disquiet** (dis-kwi'et), vt. To disturb; to make anxious.

**disquisition** (dis-kwi-zish'un), n. A careful and formal inquiry into any matter by arguments, &c.; an elaborate essay; writing.

**disregard** (dis-re-gard'), n. Want of attention; neglect.

**disreputable** (dis-rep'u-ta-bl), a. Disgraceful; shameful; unbecoming.

**disrespect** (dis-re-spekt'), n. Want of reverence; incivility.

**disruption** (dis-rup'shun), n. A breaking asunder.

**dissatisfy** (dis-sat'is-fi), vt. To displease; make uneasy.

**dissect** (dis-sekt'), vt. To cut in pieces; divide a body.

**dissemble** (dis-sem'bl), vt. or i. To conceal real views, motives, or facts; to disguise; play the hypocrite.

**disseminate** (dis-sem'i-nat), vt. To spread; to sow or scatter abroad; to propagate.

**dissent** (dis-sent'), vi. To express objections; to think differently; to disagree in opinion.

**dissertation** (dis-ser-ta'-shun), n. A formal discourse; an essay.

**disservice** (dis-serv'is), n. Injury done; mischief.

**dissever** (dis-sev'er), vt. To part in two; disunite.

**dissident** (dis'si-dent), a., n. Dissenting; not agreeing.

**dissimilar** (dis-sim'i-lar), a. Unlike; different in nature, properties, and external form; not similar.

**dissimulation** (dis-sim-u-la'-shun), n. A dissembling; hypocrisy; deceit; guile.

**dissipate** (dis'si-pat), vt. To scatter, spread, squander.

**dissipation** (dis-si-pa-shun) n. Dispersion; scatter attention; waste of property; a licentious course of life.

**dissociate** (dis-so'shi-at), vt. To disunite; to separate.

**dissolute** (dis'o-lut), a. Loose in morals, etc.; lewd; licentious.

**dissolution** (dis-o-lu'shun), n. The breaking up of an assembly; change from a solid to a liquid state; a melting; decomposition; separation into original elements; ruin; end; death.

**dissolve** (diz-zolv'), vt. or i. To melt; separate; break up, as a legislature, &c.; destroy; waste away; perish; crumble.

**dissonant** (dis'so-nant), a. Discordant; harsh; jarring.

**dissuade** (dis-swad'), vt. To advise against a course or measure.

**dissyllable** (dis-sil'la-bl), n. A word of two syllables.

**distaff** (dis'taf), n. A stick to hold the bunch of flax, tow, or wool, in spinning.

**distance** (dis'tans), n. Remoteness; space between bodies; length; period; reserve of manner. vt. To leave behind, as in a race.

**distemper** (dis-tem'per), n. Morbid state of the body or mind; disease, esp. of animals; ill-humor; a coarse mode of painting.

**distend** (dis-tend'), vt. To stretch; extend; swell. a. Disten'sible, elastic.

**distention** (dis-ten'shun), n. A stretching; an extension.

**distil** (dis-til'), vt. or i. To drop gently; to extract spirit. [distillation]

**distinct** (dis-tingkt'), a. Separate; different; clear; not confused. [distinction]

**distinguish** (dis-ting'gwish) v. To note the difference; to signalize.

**distort** (dis-tart'), v. To twist; to writhe. [distortion]

**distract** (dis-trakt'), v. To draw different ways; to

**DISTRAIN** 71 **DOLOROUS**

perplex; to confound; to confuse. [distraction]

**distrain** (dis-tran'), v. To seize goods for debt.

**distraint** (dis-trant'), n. A seizure for debt.

**distress** (dis-tres'), n. Act of distraining goods; extreme pain; anguish; adversity.

**distribute** (dis-trib'ut), v. To divide among several; to deal or allot. [distribution]

**distributive** (dis-trib'u-tiv), a. That distributes.

**district** (dis'trikt), n. A circuit; region; a portion of country.

**distrust** (dis-trust'), v. To doubt or suspect. n. Doubt or suspicion; want of confidence.

**disturb** (dis-turb'), v. To start; to perplex; to disquiet. [disturbance]

**disunion** (dis-un'yun), n. Want of concord or agreement.

**disunity** (dis-u'ni-ti), n. A state of separation.

**ditch** (dich), n. A trench dug in the ground; a moat.

**ditto** (dit'to), n. The same as above; the same thing.

**ditty** (dit'ti), n. A sonnet.

**diurnal** (di-ur'nal), a. Pertaining to or performed in a day; daily.

**diverge** (di-verj'), v. To go from one point. [divergence]

**divergent** (di-ver'jent), a. Receding from each other.

**divers** (di'verz), a. Various; sundry; many; several.

**diverse** (di-vers' di-vers'), a. Different; various; unlike.

**diversify** (di-ver'si-fy), v. To make different.

**diversion** (di-ver'shun), n. That which diverts; a. Turning aside; sport; recreation.

**diversity** (di-ver'si-ti), n. Difference; unlikeness; variety.

**divert** (di-vert'), vt. To turn aside; change the direction of; draw off the attention; amuse.

**divest** (di-vest'), vt. To strip or deprive.

**dividend** (div'i-dend), n. Number or sum to be divided; share of a sum divided.

**divination** (div-i-na'shun), n. Art or practice of divining; prediction.

**divine** (di-vin'), a. Pertaining to God or a deity; sacred.

**divinity** (di-vin'i-ti), n. Godhead; a deity; theology.

**divisible** (di-viz'i-bl), a. That may be divided.

**divisor** (di-viz'or), n. Number which divides another.

**divorce** (di-vors'), n. Legal separation of husband and wife; separation.

**divulge** (di-vulj'), vt. To make public; reveal.

**docile** (dos'il), a. Easily taught or managed.

**doctor** (dok'tor), n. One who has received the highest degree of a university; a physician.

**doctorate** (dok'tor-at), n. A doctor's degree.

**doctrine** (dok'trin), n. Something taught; tenet.

**document** (dok'yu-ment), n. Written evidence or information.

**doggerel** (dog'er-el), n. Worthless or low verses.

**dogma** (dog'ma), n. A settled opinion; tenet; article of doctrine. [dogmatic]

**dogmatism** (dog'ma-tizm), n. Positive assertion of opinion.

**dogwood** (dog'wud), n. An American tree with very compact wood.

**doily** (doi'li), n. A small napkin used at dessert.

**dolorous** (dol'or-us), a. Painful; afflicting; sad.

**domain** (do-man'), n. Territory; estate.

**domestic** (do-mes'tik), a. Belonging to the house; tame; not foreign. n. A house-servant.

**domicile** (dom'i-sil), vt. To establish in a domicile.

**dominate** (dom'i-nat), vt. To rule.

**domination** (dom-i-na'shun), n. Rule; authority; tyranny.

**domineer** (dom-i-ner'), vi. To rule or overbear arrogantly.

**dominion** (dom-in'yun), n. Lordship; sovereignty; the country governed; region.

**donor** (do'nor), n. One who gives.

**dormant** (dor'mant), a. Sleeping; resting; not in use.

**dormitory** (dor'mi-to-ri), n. Place or room for sleeping in.

**dorsal** (dor'sal), a. Pertaining to the back.

**dotage** (dot'age), n. A doting; childishness of old age; excessive fondness.

**double** (dub'l), a. Twofold; twice as much; of extra weight, size, or quality; in pairs; acting two parts, insincere.

**doubt** (dout), vi. To hesitate.

**dough** (do), n. A mass of flour or meal moistened and kneaded, but not baked.

**doughty** (dow'ti), a. Able, strong; brave.

**dour** (dor), a. (Scot.) Obstinate; bold.

**douse** (dows), vt. To plunge into water.

**dowager** (dow'a-jer), n. A widow with a dower or jointure.

**dowdy** (dow'di), a. Untidy, carelessly dressed, soft and slack in habit.

**doxology** (doks-ol'o-ji), n. A hymn giving praise to God.

**doze** (doz), v. Slumber; to be drowsy.

**dozen** (duz'n), a. or n. Twelve things.

**dozy** (do'zi), a. Sleepy; drowsy.

**drachm** (dram), n. One-eighth of an ounce.

**draft** (draft), n. A drawing; order for money; a rough sketch; a detachment.

**drag** (drag), v. To pull or carry with force.

**draggle** (drag'l), v. To be drawn on the ground.

**dragon** (drag'un), n. A fabulous winged serpent.

**dragoon** (dra-gon'), n. A horse soldier.

**drain** (dran), n. A channel for water.

**drainage** (dran'aj), n. A drawing off.

**drake** (drak), n. A male duck.

**dram** (dram), n. A glass of spirits; eighth of an ounce.

**drama** (dra'ma), n. The action of a play; a play.

**dramatic** (dra-mat'ik), a. Belonging to the drama. **[dramatist]**

**dramatize** (dram'a-tiz), v. To compose, like a drama.

**drapery** (dra'per-i), n. Cloth, clothes or garments.

**drastic** (dras'tik), a. Powerful; acting rapidly and violently.

**draught** (draft), n. Act of drawing; act of drinking; quantity drunk; delineation.

**draughts** (drafts), n. pl. A game, played on a checkered board.

**dread** (dred), n. Great fear; awe; terror.

**dream** (drem), n. Thoughts in sleep; a fancy; a whim.

**drear** (drer), a. Mournful; dismal; gloomy; sad.

**dredge** (drej), n. An oyster-net.

**dregs** (dregz), n. pl. Lees; refuse; sediment; dross.

**drench** (drench), v. To soak;

**dribble** (drib'l), v. To slaver; to drivel; to let fall in drops.
**drivel** (driv'el), vi. To slaver. n. Slaver; spittle.
**driveller** (driv'el-er), n. Simpleton.
**drizzle** (driz'l), vi. To fall in small drops.
**drollery** (drol'er-e), n. Buffoonery; low sport.
**dromedary** (drum'e-dar-e), n. A camel with one hunch.
**drone** (dron), n. The male bee; a sluggard.
**droop** (droop), vi. To pine; to languish; to be dispirited.
**dropsical** (drop'se-kal), a. Disease with dropsy.
**dropsy** (drop'se), n. A collection of water in the body.
**dross** (dros), n. The scum of metals.
**drought** (drout), n. Dry weather; dryness; thirst.
**drown** (drown), vt. To suffocate in water; to overflow.
**drowsy** (drowz'e), a. Sleepy; heavy.
**drub** (drub), n. A thump, a blow.
**drudge** (druj), vi. To labour in mean offices; to toil.
**drudgery** (druj'er-e), n. Hard labour; toil.
**drug**, n. Any substance used in the composition of medicine.
**druid** (dro'id), n. A priest among the ancient Celts of Britain, Gaul, and Germany.
**dual** (du'al), a. Consisting of two.
**dubious** (du'bi-us), a. Doubtful; undetermined; causing doubt; of uncertain event or issue.
**duchy** (duch'i), n. The territory of a duke, a dukedom.
**duct** (dukt), n. A tube conveying fluids in animal bodies or plants.
**ductile** (duk'til), a. Easily led; yielding; capable of being drawn out into threads.
**dudgeon** (duj'un), n. Resentment; grudge.
**due** (du), a. Owed; that ought to be paid or done to another; proper; appointed, under engagement to be ready, arrive, etc.
**duel**, n. A prearranged combat between two persons; any fight or struggle between two parties.
**duet** (du-et'), **duetto** (du-et'o), n. A composition in music for two voices or instruments.
**duffer** (duf'er), n. A dull plodding person; a fogy, useless old fellow.
**dulcet** (duls'et), a. Sweet to the taste, or to the ear; melodious, harmonious.
**duly** (du'li), adv. Properly; fitly; at the proper time.
**dumb** (dum), a. Without the power of speech; silent; soundless.
**dump** (dump), vt. To throw down; to unload.
**dunce** (duns), n. One slow at learning; a stupid person.
**dungeon** (dun'jun), n. A close, dark prison; a cell under ground.
**dunnage** (dun'aj), n. On shipboard, loose wood of any kind used to keep cargoes steady; baggage.
**duo** (du'o), n. Song in two parts.
**duodecimal** (du-o-des'i-mal), a. Computed by twelves; twelfth.
**dupe** (cup), n. One easily cheated; one who is deceived or misled.
**duplex** (du'pleks), a. Twofold; double.
**durable** (dur'a-bl), a. Able

**duress** (dur'es, or dur-es'), n. Constraint; imprisonment; constraint illegally exercised.

**duty** (du'ti), n. That which is due; what one is bound by any obligation to do; obedience; military service; respect or regard; one's proper business; tax on goods.

**dwarf** (dwawrf), n. An animal or plant that does not reach the ordinary height.

**dwindle** (dwin'dl), vi. To become less; diminish; grow feeble; degenerate.

**dye** (di), vt. To colour; stain. n. Colouring liquor; tinge.

**dyeing** (di'ing), ppr. Staining. n. Art of colouring cloths.

**dying** (di'ing), ppr. Expiring.

**dynameter** (di-nam'e-ter), n. An instrument used to determine the magnifying power of a telescope.

**dynamics** (di-nam'iks), n. That branch of mechanics which treats of bodies in motion.

**dynamite** (di'na-mit), n. A highly explosive compound of nitro-glycerine and a siliceous earth.

**dynasty** (din'as-ti), n. A race of kings of the same family; sovereignty.

**dysentery** (dis'en-ter-i), n. A bloody flux.

**dyspepsia** (dis-pep'si-a), n. Indigestion or difficulty of digestion.

# E

**each** (ech), a. and pron. Denoting every one separately.

**eager** (e'ger), a. Keenly desirous; ardent; impetuous; sharp.

**eagle** (e'gl), n. A bird of prey.

**ear** (er), n. The organ of hearing; a spike of corn.

**earache** (er'ak), n. Pain in the ear.

**earing** (er'ing), n. Ploughing of land.

**earnest** (er'nest), a. Determined; eager; intent; sincere.

**earnest** (er'nest), n. A pledge; token.

**earth** (erth), n. Soil; dry land; the world.

**earthquake** (erth'kwak), n. A shaking or heaving of the ground.

**ease** (ez), n. Freedom from pain or disturbance; rest; facility.

**easel** (ez'l), n. Frame to support a picture while painting.

**Easter** (est'er), n. Feast commemorating Christ's resurrection.

**eastern** (est'ern), a. Pertaining to the east.

**easy** (e'zi), a. Free from pain or anxiety; not difficult; not straitened.

**ebriety** (e-bri'e-ti), n. Drunkenness.

**ebullition** (eb-ul-ish'un), n. Act of boiling; outbreak.

**eccentric** (ek-sen'trik), a. Deviating from the centre; not having the same centre; odd; queer.

**ecclesiastic** (ek-kle-zi-as'tik), a. Pertaining to the church, priesthood, or clergy.

**echo** (ek'o), n. A sound reflected from, or repeated by, some object.

**eclat** (a-kla'), n. A striking effect; distinction; renown.

**eclectic** (ek-lek'tik), a. Selecting; choosing.

**eclipse** (e-klips'), n. Obscuration of the light of a heavenly body; darkness. vt. To intercept the light of; darken.

**ecliptic** (e-klip'tik), n. The apparent path of the sun.

**economize** (e-kon'o-miz), vt. To use frugally.

**economy** (e-kon'o-mi), n. Management; frugal use of money, etc.; system of operations.

**ecstasy** (ek'sta-si), n. Transport; extreme joy or pleasure.

**ecumenical** (ek-yu-men'i-kal), a. Pertaining to the inhabited world; general.

**eddy** (ed'i), n. Circular motion of water; whirlpool.

**edgewise** (ej'wiz), adv. In the direction of the edge.

**edible** (ed'i-bl), a. Fit to be eaten.

**edict** (e'dikt), n. A decree; command.

**edification** (ed-i-fi-ka'shun), n. A building-up; increase in virtue or wisdom.

**edifice** (ed'i-fis), n. A large house.

**edify** (ed'i-fi), vt. To improve in virtue or wisdom.

**edit** (ed'it), vt. To prepare for publication.

**edition** (e-dish'un), n. Number of copies of a book published at one time. [editor]

**educate** (ed'yu-kat), vt. To cultivate the mental powers of; to train. [educator, education]

**educe** (e-dus'), vt. To lead or draw out.

**eel** (el), n. A fish in shape like a serpent.

**efface** (ef-fas'), vt. To rub or blot out; erase; wear away.

**effect** (ef-fekt'), n. Something done; results; operation; impression. pl. property.

**effective** (ef-fekt'iv), a. Causing something; serviceable.

**effectual** (ef-fekt'yu-al), a. Producing an effect; successful.

**effeminate** (ef-fem'i-nat), a. Womanish; soft; luxurious; unmanly.

**effervesce** (ef-er-ves'), vi. To bubble or froth up, as if boiling.

**effete** (ef-fet'), a. Exhausted; barren.

**efficacy** (ef'fi-ka-si), n. Power to produce effects; virtue; energy. [efficient]

**effigy** (ef'i-ji), n. Image or likeness of a person.

**effloresce** (ef-flo-res'), vi. To burst into bloom; to fall into powder by exposure to the air, as some salts.

**effluvium** (ef-flu'vi-um), n. Exhalation; odor.

**effort** (ef'ort), n. Exertion; attempt.

**effulgence** (ef-ful'jens), n. Great splendor or brightness.

**effusion** (ef-fu'zhun), n. Act of pouring forth; that which is poured forth.

**effusive** (ef-fuz'iv), a. Pouring forth; gushing.

**egotism** (eg'o-tizm, e'-), n. Self-importance, vanity. [egotist]

**egregious** (e-gre'jus), n. Remarkable; extravagant.

**egress** (e'gres), n. Act or power of going out; place of exit.

**Egyptian** (e-jip'shan), a. Pertaining to Egypt.

**either** (e'ther, i'ther), a. or pron. One or the other; one of two; each.

**ejaculate** (e-jak'u-lat), vt. To throw out; utter suddenly and briefly. [ejaculation]

**eject** (e-jekt'), vt. To cast out; dismiss; expel.

**elaborate** (e-lab'u-rat), vt. To produce with labour.

**elaboration** (e-lab-u-ra'shun), n. A producing with labour; a natural process of growth in living organisms.

**elapse** (e-laps'), vi. To pass away.

**elastic** (e-las'tik), a. Having elasticity.

**elasticity** (e-las-tis'i-ti), n. The property by which bodies recover a former state after being bent or compressed.

**elate** (e-lat'), a. Flushed with success. vt. To puff up.

**elation** (e-la'shun), n. Self-esteem; vanity; pride.

**elect** (e-lekt'), vi. To choose for office; prefer.

**election** (el-ek'shun), n. Power of choosing; choice; preference.

**electioneer** (e-lek-shu-ner'), vt. To make interest for office.

**elective** (e-lek'tiv), a. Relating to or regulated by choice.

**elector** (e-lek'ter), n. One who elects or has the right of voting. [electoral]

**electric** (e-lek'trik), n. A substance that exhibits electricity by friction; a non-conductor.

**electrician** (e-lek-trish'an), n. One versed in electricity.

**eleemosynary** (el-e-mos'i-na-ri), a. Given in or living on charity.

**elegance** (el'e-gans), n. State or quality of being elegant.

**elegy** (el'e-ji), n. A funeral poem; a song, expressing sorrow.

**element** (el'e-ment), n. One of the essential parts of anything. [elementary]

**elephant** (el'e-fant), n. The largest quadruped. [elephantine]

**elevate** (el'e-vat), v. To raise to higher position. [elevation, elevator]

**elicit** (e-lis'it), v. To draw out; to extract; to deduce.

**elide** (e-lid'), v. To cut off or suppress a vowel or syllable.

**eligibility** (el-i-ji-bil'i-ti), n. Fitness to be chosen. [eligible]

**eliminate** (e-lim'i-nat), v. To set at liberty; to get rid of.

**elision** (e-lizh'un), n. The cutting off of a vowel.

**elite** (a-let'), n. A chosen or select part.

**elixir** (e-liks'er), n. A refined spirit.

**ellipse** (el-lips'), n. An oval figure bounded by a regular curve.

**ellipsis** (el-lips'is), n. The omission of a word or phrase.

**elliptic** (el-lip'tik), a. Having the form of an ellipse; defective; having a part understood.

**elocution** (el-o-ku'shun), n. Proper delivery of words.

**elogium** (e-lo'ji-um), n. Eulogy; a panegyric.

**elongate** (e-lang'gat), v. To draw out; to lengthen.

**elope** (e-lop'), v. To run away secretly; to escape privately.

**eloquence** (el'o-kwens), n. Elegance and appropriateness of language.

**else** (els), a. Other; besides.

**elucidate** (e-lu'si-dat), v. To make clear; to explain.

**elude** (e-lud'), v. To escape by artifice; to evade.

**elysian** (e-lish'i-an), a. Very delightful; blissful.

**elysium** (e-lizh'i-um), n. A place of delight.

**emaciate** (e-ma'shi-at), v. To lose flesh; to waste; to pine.

**emaciation** (e-ma-shi-a'shun), n. Becoming lean.

**emanate** (em'a-nat), v. To flow or proceed from.

**emancipate** (e-man'si-pat), v. To free from slavery.

**embalm** (em-bam'), v. To fill with preserving fluids.

**embank** (em-bangk'), v. To defend or protect by a mound.

**embargo** (em-bar'go), n. Prohibition of vessels from sailing.

**embark** (em-bark'), vt. To enter on board; to engage in.

**embarrass** (em-bar'as), vt. To perplex. [embarrassment]

**embassy** (em'bas-e), n. Message to a foreign nation.

**embattle** (em-bat'l), vt. To form for battle.

**embellish** (em-bel'ish), vt. To make beautiful by adornment.

**embers** (em'berz), n. pl. Hot cinders.

**embezzle** (em-bez'l), vt. To appropriate by breach of trust.

**emblazon** (em-bla'zn), vt. To adorn with figures of heraldry; to deck in glaring colours.

**emblem** (em'blem), n. A picture or representation imaging forth a truth; a type.

**embody** (em-bod'e), vt. To form into a body.

**embolden** (em-bol'n), vt. To give courage to.

**embonpoint** (ong-bong-pwaw'), n. Plumpness of body.

**emboss** (em-bos'), vt. To adorn with protuberances.

**embrace** (em-bras'), vt. To clasp in the arms; to adopt.

**embroider** (em-broid'er), vt. To ornament with designs in needlework, originally on the border.

**embroil** (em-broil'), vt. To involve in a broil, or in perplexity (with); to entangle; to distract.

**embryo** (em'bri-o), n. The young of an animal in its earliest stages of development; the part of a seed which forms the future plant; the beginning of anything.

**emend**, vt. To remove faults or blemishes from; to correct or improve.

**emerge** (e-merj'), vi. To rise out of; to issue or come forth; to reappear after being concealed.

**emeritus** (e-mer'i-tus), a. Honorably discharged from the preformance of public duty.

**emetic** (e-met'ik), a. Causing vomiting. n. A medicine that causes vomiting.

**emigrate** (em'i-grat), vt. To remove from one country to another as a place of abode.

**eminent**, a. Rising above others; conspicuous; distinguished; exalted in rank or office.

**emit** (e-mit'), vt. To send out; to issue out; to throw or give out; to issue.

**emollient** (e-mol'yent), a. Softening; making supple.

**emolument** (e-mol'u-ment), n. Advantage; profit arising from employment.

**emotion** (e-mo'shun), n. A moving of the feelings; agitation of mind.

**emphasis** (em'fa-sis), n. Stress of the voice on particular words or syllables to make the meaning clear; impressiveness of expression or weight of thought; intensity.

**empire** (em'pir), n. Supreme control or dominion; the territory under the dominion of an emperor.

**employ** (em-ploy'), vt. To occupy the time or attention of; to use as a means or agent; to give work to.

**emporium** (em-po'ri-um), n. A place to which goods

**EMPOWER** 78 **ENFORCE**

are brought from various parts for sale; a store; a great mart.

**empower** (em-pow'er), vt. To authorize.

**empty** (emp'ti), a. Having nothing in it; unfurnished; without effect; unsatisfactory; wanting substance; foolish.

**empyreal** (em-pir'e-al), a. Formed of pure fire or light; pertaining to the highest and purest region of heaven.

**emulate** (em'u-lat), vt. To strive to equal or excel; to imitate, with a view to equal or excel; to rival.

**emulsion** (e-mul'shun), n. A milky liquid prepared by mixing oil and water by means of another substance that combines with both.

**enable** (en-a'bl), vt. To make able; to give power, strength, or authority to.

**enact** (en-akt'), vt. To perform; to act the part of; to establish by law.

**enamel** (en-am'el), n. The name given to vitrified substances applied chiefly to the surface of metals; any smooth hard coating, esp. that of the teeth.

**enamour** (en-am'er), vt. To inflame with love; to charm.

**encaustic** (en-kaws'tik), a. Having the colors burned in.

**enchant** (en-chant'), vt. To act on by songs or rhymed formulas of sorcery; to charm; to delight in a high degree.

**encomium** (en-ko'mi-um), n. High commendation; a eulogy.

**encompass** (en-kum'pas), vt. To surround or inclose.

**encore** (an-kor'), adv. Again; once more.

**encounter** (en-kown'ter), vt. To meet face to face, esp. unexpectedly; to meet in contest; to oppose.

**encourage** (en-kur'ij), vt. To give courage to; animate. [**encouragement**]

**encroach** (en-kroch'), vi. To intrude on another's rights; infringe. [**encroachment**]

**encumber** (en-kum'ber), vt. To impede action by a load or burden. [**encumbrance**]

**encyclopedia** (en-si-klo-pe'di-a), n. A work that embodies the whole circle of sciences.

**endeavour** (en-dev'ur), n. Effort; attempt. vi. To exert oneself; labour; try.

**endive** (en'div), n. A garden vegetable.

**endogenous** (en-doj'en-us), a. Increasing by internal growth, as the palm, etc.

**endorse**. See indorse.

**endowment** (en-dou'ment), n. Act of settling a fund; property or revenue; talent; gift.

**endurance** (en-dur'ans), n. Continuance; suffering; patience.

**endure** (en-dur'), vi. To continue.

**enema** (e-ne'ma), n. An injection of fluid into the bowels by the rectum.

**energetic** (en-er-jet'ik), a. Operating with vigour; active; effective; vigorous.

**energise** (en'er-jiz), vi. To act with energy. vt. To employ with energy.

**energy** (en'er-ji), n. Internal strength; force of expression; vigour; spirit; resolution.

**enervation** (en-er-va'shun), n. Act of weakening.

**enfeeblement** (en-fe'bl-ment), n. A weakening; enervation.

**enfilade** (en-fi-lad'), n. A straight line.

**enforce** (en-fors'), vt. To put in execution.

**enforcible** (en-for'si-bl), a. Capable of being enforced.

**enfranchise** (en-fran'shiz), vt. To set free; admit to civil and political privileges.

**engage** (en-gaj'), vt. To encounter; bind by contract.

**engender** (en-jen'der), vt. To beget; produce.

**engineer** (en-ji-ner'), n. One skilled in mathematics and mechanics, and who superintends work for military or civil objects.

**engorge** (en-gorj'), vt. or i. To swallow greedily; devour.

**engrain** (en-gran'), vt. To dye in grain; dye deep.

**engrave** (en-grav'), vt. To cut with a chisel or graver; impress deeply. [**engraver, engraving**]

**engross** (en-gros'), vt. To seize or buy the whole; write in a large hand.

**engulf** (en-gulf'), vt. To throw or absorb, as in a gulf.

**enhance** (en-hans'), vt. To heighten in price; aggravate. vi. To grow larger; swell.

**enigma** (e-nig'ma), n. An obscure question; riddle; anything unaccountable.

**enjoin** (en-join'), vt. To command; order; forbid judicially.

**enjoyment** (en-joi'ment), n. Possession with pleasure; fruition.

**enlargement** (en-larj'ment), n. Increase of bulk; release.

**enlighten** (en-li'tn), vt. To illuminate; instruct.

**enlistment** (en-list'ment), n. Act of enlisting.

**enmity** (en'mi-ti), n. Ill-will; hatred; hostility.

**ennoble** (e-no'bl), vt. To make noble.

**ennui** (a'nu-e), n. Lassitude; languor; dullness of spirit.

**enormity** (e-nor'mi-ti), n. Atrociousness.

**enormous** (e-nor'mus), a. Beyond all natural or ordinary limits; immense; excessive.

**enough** (e-nuf'), a. Sufficient.

**enrage** (en-raj'), vt. To irritate; provoke to fury.

**enrapture** (en-rap'tur), vt. To throw into rapture.

**enravish** (en-rav'ish), vt. To throw into ecstasy.

**enshrine** (en-shrain'), vt. To place in or as in a shrine; cherish devoutly; be a shrine for.

**enshroud** (en-shraud'), vt. To cover with a shroud; hence, to enwrap or conceal.

**ensiform** (en'si-form), a. Sword-shaped, as certain leaves.

**ensign** (en'sain), n. A distinguishing flag or banner; standard; a military or naval officer.

**ensilage** (en'si-lej), n. The process of preserving succulent fodder in airtight pits or silos.

**ensue** (en-siu'), vt. & vi. To follow; result.

**ensure**, v. Same as **insure**.

**entail**, vt. To leave or fix, by or as by entail, upon a successor; bring upon another as a consequence or legacy; limit by entail.

**entangle** (en-tan'gl), vt. To catch in or as in a snare; hamper; perplex.

**enter**, v. To pass from without to the interior of; pass inward through, as a gate; penetrate; be initiated into; join.

**enterprise** (en'ter-praiz), n. Any projected task or work; an undertaking.

**entertain**, v. To receive and care for, as a guest.

**enthrall** (en-throl'), vt. To

**ENTHUSIASM**     80     **EPOCH**

**bring** under any overmastering influence; enslave.

**enthusiasm** (en-thu'zi-azm), n. Earnest and fervent feeling; ardent zeal for a person or cause.

**entice** (en-tais'), vt. To draw or attempt to draw (especially into evil), through the desires, hopes, etc.; allure.

**entire** (en-tair'), a. Complete in all its parts; undivided; unbroken; unqualified; whole.

**entitle** (en-tai'tl), vt. To give title to; to authorize to receive or require.

**entity** (en'ti-ti), n. Anything that exists or may be supposed to exist; being.

**entomb** (en-tum'), vt. To place in a tomb; bury.

**entomology** (en'to-mol'o-ji), n. The branch of zoology that treats of insects, or a treatise upon it.

**entrance** (en'trans), n. Door; beginning.

**entrance** (en-trans'), vt. Put into a trance.

**entrap** (en-trap'), vt. Catch in a trap.

**entreat** (en-tret'), vt. Ask earnestly; implore. [**entreaty**]

**entree** (ang-tra'), n. Entry; dish served between courses.

**entrust.** See **intrust**.

**entry** (en'tri), n. Entering; passage into; item entered.

**enumerate** (e-nu'mer-at), vt. Count; name. [**enumera'tion**]

**enunciate** (e-nun'si-at), vt. State formally; pronounce distinctly. [**enuncia'tion**]

**envelop** (en-vel'up), vt. Roll or fold in; surround.

**envelope** (en'vel-op), n. Cover of a letter.

**enviable** (en'vi-a-bl), a. Capable of exciting envy.

**envious** (en'vi-us), a. Feeling envy; prompted by envy.

**environ** (en-vi'run), vt. Surround. [**envi'ronment, envi'rons**]

**envoy** (en'voi), n. Messenger.

**envy** (en'vi), vt. Look upon grudgingly.

**epaulet** (ep'al-et), n. Shoulder-piece indicating official rank.

**ephemeral** (ef-em'er-al), a. Existing only for a day; short-lived.

**epic** (ep'ik), n. Heroic poem.

**epicure** (ep'i-kur), n. One devoted to the luxuries of the table. [**epicure'an**]

**epidemic** (ep-i-dem'ik), a. Affecting a whole people.

**epidermis** (ep-i-der'mis), n. Outer layer of skin, cuticle or scarfskin.

**epiglottis** (ep-i-glot'is), n. Cartilaginous appendage that closes the opening of the larynx when food or drink is swallowed.

**epigram** (ep'i-gram), n. Short witty poem. [**epigrammat'ic**]

**epilepsy** (ep'i-lep-si), n. Nervous affection attended by convulsions; falling sickness. [**epilep'tic**]

**epiphany** (e-pif'a-ni), n. Christian festival on Jan. 6, in commemoration of the appearance of the wise men of the East.

**episcopacy** (e-pis'ko-pa-si), n. Government of the church by bishops.

**episode** (ep'i-sod), n. Interesting incident.

**epistle** (e-pis'l), n. Letter.

**epitaph** (ep'i-taf), n. Inscription on a tomb.

**epithet** (ep'i-thet), n. Adjective expressing some quality.

**epitome** (e-pit'o-me), n. Short summary. [**epit'omize**]

**epoch** (ep'ok), n. Period of

**EQUABLE** 81 **ESTUARY**

time made remarkable by some event.
**equable** (e'kwa-bl), a. Equal.
**equal** (e'kwal), a. Alike; adequate; just; uniform. [equality]
**equanimity** (e-kwa-nim'i-ti), n. Evenness of mind or temper.
**equation** (e-kwa'shun), n. Statement of the equality of two quantities.
**equator** (e-kwa'tur), n. Imaginary circle passing round the middle of the globe, and dividing it into equal parts.
**equestrian** (e-kwes'tri-an), a. Pertaining to horses or horsemanship.
**equilibrium** (e-kwi-lib'ri-um), n. Equality of weight or force; state of rest.
**equine** (e'kwin), a. Pertaining to a horse or horses.
**equinoctial** (e-kwi-nok'shal), a. Pertaining to the equinoxes, or to the regions about the equator.
**equinox** (e'kwi-noks), n. Time when day and night are of equal length.
**equip** (e-kwip'), vt. Fit out. [equipage]
**equipoise** (e'kwi-poiz), n. Equality of balance.
**equitable** (ek'wi-ta-bl), a. Just. [eq'uity]
**equivalent** (e-kwiv'a-lent), n. Thing equal in value.
**equivocate** (e-kwiv'o-kat), vi. Use ambiguous words.
**era** (e'ra), n. Epoch.
**eradicate** (e-rad'i-kat), vt. Destroy.
**erase** (e-ras'), vt. Efface. [era'sure]
**ere** (ar), adv., prep. and conj. Before.
**erect** (e-rekt'), vt. Set upright; build.
**err** (er), vi. Be mistaken.
**errand** (er'and), n. Message; commission. [errat'ic]
**errant** (er'ant), a. Wandering.

**error** (er'ur), n. Inaccuracy; mistake. [erroneous]
**erudite** (er'o-dit), a. Learned. [erudition]
**erupt** (e-rupt'), vt. and vi. Break or throw out. [erup'tion, erupt'ive]
**erysipelas** (er-i-sip'e-las), n. Inflammatory disease, generally in the face.
**escalator** (es'ka-la-tur), n. Moving stairway.
**escapade** (es-ka-pad'), n. Capering of a horse; prank.
**escape** (es-kap'), vt. and vi. Flee; leak out; remain unharmed; flight.
**eschew** (es-cho'), vt. Shun.
**escort** (es'kart), n. Guard.
**esculent** (es'ku-lent), a. Toothsome.
**escutcheon** (es-kuch'un), n. Coat of arms.
**Eskimo, Esquimau** (es'ki-mo), n. One of a tribe of Arctic America.
**esophagus** (e-sof'a-gus), n. Gullet.
**especial** (es-pesh'al), a. Special.
**espouse** (es-pouz'), vt. Betroth; embrace, as a cause.
**espy** (es-pi'), vt. Catch sight of.
**essay** (es'a), n. Experiment; written composition.
**essence** (es'ens), n. True substance; distinctive characteristic; extracted virtues of a drug. [essential]
**establish** (es-tab'lish), vt. Settle; fix; found.
**estate** (es-tat'), n. Fixed condition; property, esp. in land.
**esteem** (es-tem'), vt. Value.
**estimable** (es'tim-a-bl), a. Worthy of esteem.
**estimate** (es'tim-at), vt. Calculate. [estima'tion]
**estrange** (es-tranj'), vt. Alienate.
**estuary** (es'tu-ar-i), n. Pas-

sage where the tide meets the current.

**etch** (ech), vt. and vi. Make designs on metal, glass, etc.

**eternal** (e-ter'nal), a. Without beginning or end. [eter'nity]

**ether** (e'ther), n. Subtle universal medium; light, volatile, inflammable fluid. [ethe'real]

**ethic** (eth'ik), a. Relating to duty. [eth'ics]

**ethnology** (eth-nol'o-ji), n. Science of human races.

**etiquette** (et'i-ket), n. Forms of ceremony or decorum.

**etymology** (et-i-mol'o-ji), n. Science of the origin and history of words.

**eucharist** (u'ka-rist), n. Sacrament of the Lord's Supper.

**eulogy** (u'lo-ji), n. Speech or writing in praise. [eu'logize]

**euphony** (u'fo-ni), n. Agreeable sound. [euphonious]

**European** (u-ro-pe'an), a. Belonging to Europe.

**evacuate** (e-vak'u-at), vt. Empty; withdraw from.

**evade** (e-vad'), vt. Escape; avoid.

**evanescent** (ev-an-es'ent), a. Fleeting; fading away.

**evangel** (e-van'jel), n. Good news. [evan'gelist]

**evaporate** (e-vap'o-rat), vi. Escape in vapor.

**evasion** (e-va'zhun), n. Attempt to evade; excuse. [eva'sive]

**event** (e-vent'), n. That which happens.

**evict** (e-vikt'), vt. Dispossess by law. [evic'tion]

**evidence** (ev'i-dens), n. Proof; testimony.

**evil** (e'vil), a. Wicked; unfortunate. [worse, worst]

**evince** (e-vins'), vt. Prove; show.

**evoke** (e-vok'), vt. Summon forth.

**evolve** (e-volv'), vt. and vi. Unroll, develop. [evolu'tion]

**ewe** (u), n. Female of the sheep.

**exact** (egz-akt'), a. Precise.

**exaggerate** (egz-aj'er-at), vt. Overstate. [exaggera'tion]

**exalt** (egz-alt'), vt. Raise high.

**examine** (egz-am'in), vt. Inspect; question.

**example** (egz-am'pl), n. Specimen; illustration.

**exasperate** (egz-as'per-at), vt. Make angry.

**excavate** (eks'ka-vat), vt. Hollow out.

**exceed** (ek-sed'), vt. Surpass; go beyond.

**excel** (ek-sel'), vt. Surpass.

**excelsior** (ek-sel'si-ur), a. Higher.

**except** (ek-sept'), vt. Exclude.

**excess** (ek-ses'), n. Intemperance. [excess'ive]

**exchange** (eks-chanj'), vt. Give in return for some equivalent.

**excise** (ek-siz'), n. Duty or tax on goods.

**excision** (ek-sizh'un), n. A cutting off; extirpation.

**excite** (ek-sit'), vt. To stir up; stimulate to action.

**exclaim** (eks-klam'), vi. To cry out; speak vehemently.

**exclamation** (eks-kla-ma'shun), n. A loud outcry; an uttered expression of surprise, pain, &c.

**exclude** (eks-klud'), vt. To shut out; debar; reject; except; eject.

**exclusive** (eks'klu'siv), a. Peculiar; debarring from participation; sole; not taking into account.

**excommunicate** (eks-kom-mu'ni-kat), vt. To expel from church communion.

**excrescence** (eks-kres'ens), n. Preternatural growth or protuberance; a wart or tumor; a superfluous part.

**excrete** (eks-kret'), vt. To eject from the pores; to perspire.

**excruciate** (eks-kroo'shi-at) vt. To torture; to rack.

**exculpate** (eks-kul'pat), vt. To clear from a charge of crime or a fault; excuse; justify.

**excursion** (eks-kur'shun), n. A ramble; journey.

**excuse** (eks-kuz'), vt. To pardon; justify; free from accusation or an obligation; make an apology for.

**execrable** (eks'e-kra-bl), a. Detestable; accursed; bad.

**execute** (eks'e-kut), vt. To give effect to; complete; to sign one's name to a deed; put to death by law.

**executive** (egz-ek'u-tiv), a. Carrying into effect.

**executor** (egz-ek'u-tor), n. One who performs; one who settles the estate of a testator. fem. exec'-utrix.

**exegesis** (eks-e-je'sis), n. Science of interpretation; exposition of the Scriptures, &c.

**exemplify** (egz-em'pli-fi), vt. To illustrate by example; prove by an attested copy.

**exempt** (egz-emt'), a. Free.

**exercise** (eks'er-siz), n. Exertion of the body for health or amusement, use; practice; a lesson; a task.

**exert** (egz-ert'), vt. To use strength; to strain; set in action; afflict; to bring into operation.

**exfoliate** (eks-fo'li-at), vi. To come off in scales.

**exhale** (egz-hal'), vt. or i. To breathe out; emit vapor; evaporate; be given off, as steam. [ex-hala'tion]

**exhaust** (egz-haust'), vt. To drain to emptiness; expend the whole strength of; wear or tire out; treat of or develop completely.

**exhibit** (egz-hib'it), vt. To present to view; to show formally or publicly.

**exhilarate** (egz-hil'ar-at), vt. To make cheerful, brisk, merry; to enliven.

**exhort** (egz-ort'), vt. & i. To advise; to warn; to caution. [ex'horta'tion]

**exhume** (eks-hum'), vt. To dig up (from a grave); to disinter.

**exile** (eks'il), n. Forced separation from one's country; banishment; one banished from his country.

**exist** (egz-ist'), vi. To be; to live; to have life [exist'ence]

**exit** (eks'it), n. A departure (from the stage of action or of life); death; passage out of a place.

**exodus** (eks'o-dus), n. A departure.

**exonerate** (egz-on'er-at), vt. To relieve (from a charge, obligation, or blame); to absolve; to acquit; to discharge.

**exorbitant** (egz-or'bi-tant), a. Excessive; enormous; irregular.

**exorcise** (eks'or-siz), vt. To drive away (an evil spirit) by conjuration. [ex'-orcism]

**exotic** (egz-ot'ik), a. Introduced from abroad; foreign.

**expand** (eks-pand'), vt. & i. To open; to dilate; to enlarge; to extend. [expanse]

**expatiate** (eks-pa'shi-at), vi. To move at large; to enlarge in discourse.

**expatriate** (eks-pa'tri-at), vt. To banish. [expa'tria'tion]

**expect** (eks-pekt'), vt. To wait for; to await; to anticipate. [expect'ant]

**expectorate** (eks-pek'to-rat), vt. & i. To discharge (phlegm, etc.) from the throat or lungs; to spit.

**expedient** (eks-pe'di-ent), a. Suitable; advisable. [expe'dience]

**expedite** (eks'pe-dit), vt. Hasten; send forth. [expedition]

**expel** (eks-pel'), vt. Drive out.

**expend** (eks-pend'), vt. Lay out; spend. [expend'iture]

**expense** (eks-pens'), n. Outlay; cost. [expen'sive]

**experience** (eks-pe'ri-ens), n. Personal observation; knowledge.

**experiment** (eks-per'i-ment) n. Trial; practical test.

**expert** (eks-pert'), a. Experienced; skillful.

**expiate** (eks'pi-at), vt. Atone for. [expia'tion]

**expire** (eks-pir'), vt. Breathe out. vi. Die; come to an end. [expiration]

**explain** (eks-plan'), vt. Make plain. [explana'tion]

**expletive** (eks'ple-tiv), n. Oath.

**explicit** (eks-plis'it), a. Not obscure or ambiguous; distinctly stated.

**explode** (eks-plod'), vt. vi. Burst with a loud report.

**exploit** (eks-ploit'), n. Great achievement.

**explore** (eks-plor'), vt. Search through.

**explosion** (eks-plo'zhun), n. Sudden violent burst. [explo'sive]

**exponent** (eks-po'nent), n. Representative of a principle or party.

**export** (eks-port'), vt. Ship goods out of a country.

**expose** (eks-po-sa'), n. Exposure.

**expostulate** (eks-pos'tu-lat) vi. To remonstrate earnestly.

**exposure** (eks-po'zhur), n. An exposing; position as to points of the compass, climate, etc.

**expound** (eks-pound'), vt. To explain; to interpret.

**express** (eks-pres'), vt. To press or squeeze out; to exhibit (opinion or feeling); to send by express messenger.

**expulsion** (eks-pul'shun), n. Expelling; being expelled. [expul'sive]

**expunge** (eks-punj'), vt. To blot out; to wipe out; to destroy; to efface; to erase; to cancel.

**exquisite** (eks'kwi-zit), a. Carefully selected; nice; delicate; refined; perfect.

**exsert** (eks-sert'), a. Standing out; projecting.

**extant** (eks'tant), a. Standing out above the surface; in being; now existing.

**extemporaneous** (eks-tem'po-ra'ne-us), a. Performed or uttered without previous study; unpremeditated. [extem'pore]

**extend** (eks-tend'), vt. & i. To stretch out; to spread; to reach; to diffuse.

**extensible** (-ten'si-b'l), a. Capable of being extended [exten'sive]

**extenuate** (eks-ten'u-at), vt. To draw out; to make thin, lean, or slender; to lessen.

**exterior** (eks-te'ri-er), a. External; outside; foreign.

**exterminate** (eks-ter'mi-nat), vt. To drive away; to eradicate; to eliminate.

**external** (eks-ter'nal), a. Outward; exterior; accidental; irrelevant; foreign.

**extinct** (eks-tinkt'), a. Extinguished; put out; quenched; terminated; closed. [extinc'tion]

**extinguish** (eks-tin'gwish), vi. To smother; to quench; to put an end to; to destroy.

**extirpate** (eks-ter'pat), vt. To pull up by the roots; to eradicate; to destroy; to expel.

**extol** (eks-tol'), vt. To elevate by praise; to eulogize; to laud; to glorify.

**extort** (eks-tort'), vt. & i. To gain by force; to exact. [extor'tion]

**extra** (eks'tra), a. Over and above; uncommon; superior.

**extract** (eks-trakt'), vt. To draw out or forth; to withdraw by distillation, or other chemical process; to take by selection.

**extradition** (ex'tra-dish'un) n. The surrender of an accused person to the justice of another government.

**extraordinary** (ex'tror'di-ne-ri or ex'tra-or'di-ne-ri), a. Being beyond or out of the common order; remarkable; special.

**extravagant** (ex-trav'a-gant), a. Exceeding ordinary limits; immoderate; fantastic; unrestrained.

**extreme**, a. Being of the highest degree.

**extricate** (ex'tri-ket), vt. To liberate from entanglement.

**extrinsic** (ex-trin'sic), a. Being outside of the nature of an object or case; foreign.

**exuberant** (ex-yu'ber-ant), a. Marked by plentifulness; producing copiously.

**exude** (ex-yud'), vt. & vi. To discharge; ooze or trickle forth, as through pores.

**exult** (egz-ult'), vi. To rejoice in or as in triumph; take a lively delight.

# F

**fable**, n. A brief tale embodying a moral, with animals or inanimate things as speakers and actors.

**fabric**, n. A woven, felted, or knitted material, as cloth, felt, etc.; a system or structure; also, workmanship; texture.

**fabulous** (fab'yu-lus), a. Belonging to fable; fictitious; mythical; incredible; false.

**facetious** (fa-si'shus), a. Witty; jocose; droll; funny; humorous.

**facial** (fa'ci-al), a. Of, near, or affecting the face.

**facile** (fas'il), a. Easy; pliant; yielding; dexterous; skilful.

**facility** (fa-sil'i-ti), n. Ease or readiness in doing; dexterity.

**facsimile** (fac-sim'i-li), n. An exact copy or reproduction.

**faction** (fac'shun), n. A party within a party; an irregular association of partizans; a cabal. [fac'tious]

**factitious** (fac-tish'us), a. Artificial; conventional.

**factor**, n. A commission merchant; agent.

**factory** (fac'to-ri), n. A manufactory.

**factotum** (fac-to'tum), n. A man of all work.

**faculty** (fac'ul-ti), n. Any special power of mind or body; the members of a profession, or the instructors in an educational institution, collectively.

**failure** (fal'ur), n. Deficiency; omission; decay; want of success; bankruptcy.

**fain** (fan), ad. Gladly.

**faint** (fant), a. Weak; languid; indistinct; feeble.

**familiarise** (fa-mil'ya-riz), vt. To accustom; make

easy by practice or study. [familiarity]

**family** (fam'i-li), n. Household; lineage; class.

**famine** (fam'in), n. A general scarcity of food; dearth. [famish]

**famous** (fa'mus), a. Renowned; noted.

**fanatic** (fa-nat'ik), n. An enthusiast; a bigot. [fanaticism]

**fancied** (fan'sid), a. Imaginary; liked.

**fancy** (fan'si), n. Notion; groundless opinion; preference; taste.

**fanfare** (fan'far), n. A flourish of trumpets.

**fanfaronade** (fan'far-o-nad) n. A vain boasting; ostentation.

**fantastic** (fan-tas'tik), a. Fanciful; whimsical. [fantasy]

**farce** (fars), n. A ludicrous play.

**farcial** (far'si-kal), a. Belonging to a farce.

**farinaceous** (far-in-a'shi-us), a. Consisting of meal or flour; mealy.

**farrago** (far-ra'go), n. A medley.

**farther** (far'ther), a. Being at a greater distance.

**fascinate** (fas'i-nat), vt. To charm; captivate. [fascination]

**fashion** (fash'un), n. Form; custom; mode. [fashionable]

**fastidious** (fas-tid'i-us), a. Difficult to please; squeamish.

**fasting** (fas'ting), n. Abstinence from food; religious mortification.

**fatal** (fa'tal), a. Deadly; destructive; necessary. [fatalism]

**fatalist** (fa'tal-ist), n. One who holds to fatalism. [fatality]

**fates** (fats), n.pl. The destinies supposed to preside over men.

**fathom** (fath'um), n. Six feet; depth.

**fatigue** (fa-teg'), n. Great weariness; toil.

**fatuous** (fat'u-us), a. Foolish; weak; silly.

**fauces** (faw'sez), n.pl. Back part of the mouth.

**faucet** (faw'set), n. A pipe for drawing liquors.

**fault** (fawlt), n. A defect; offence.

**faulty** (fawl'ti), a. Guilty of a fault; defective.

**favor**, n. Kind regard; good will; act of kindness.

**favorable** (fa'vor-a-bl), a. Inclined to favor; propitious; advantageous.

**favorite** (fa'vor-it), n. Person or thing especially favored or preferred. [favoritism]

**fawn** (fan), n. A young deer.

**fealty** (fe'al-ti), n. Loyalty or fidelity to a superior.

**fear** (fer), n. Alarm; apprehension of evil.

**feasible** (fez'i-bl), a. That may be done; practicable.

**feast** (fest), n. A holiday; rich banquet.

**feat** (fet), n. An exploit; trick; notable performance.

**feather** (feth'er), n. One of those growths which form the covering of birds.

**feature** (fet'yur), n. Prominent trait of anything.

**febrifuge** (feb'ri-fuj), n. Remedy for fever. [febrile]

**February** (feb'ru-a-ri), n. Second month of the year.

**feculent** (fek'yu-lent), a. Containing dregs or filth; foul.

**fecund** (fek'und), a. Fruitful; prolific. [fecundity]

**federal** (fed'er-al), a. Pertaining to a league or compact.

**feign** (fan), vt. and vi. To pretend; counterfeit.

**feint** (fant), n. False show;

**pretense**; pretended attack.

**felicitate** (fe-lis'i-tat), vt. To make happy; congratulate. [felicitous]

**felicity** (fe-lis'i-ti), n. Happiness; delight.

**feline** (fe'lin), a. Pertaining to cats; catlike.

**felon** (fel'on), n. One guilty of felony; painful swelling caused by inflammation of the periosteum.

**felony** (fel'o-ni), n. A heinous or capital crime.

**feminine** (fem'i-nin), a. Pertaining to, or resembling, women; tender; delicate.

**femoral** (fem'or-al), a. Pertaining to the thigh.

**fence** (fens), n. A structure for inclosing land.

**fennel** (fen'el), n. An aromatic plant.

**ferment** (fer'ment), n. Agitation; yeast or leaven. [fermentation]

**ferocious** (fe-ro'shus), a. Savage; fierce.

**ferret** (fer'et), n. A kind of weasel.

**ferry** (fer'i), n. Place for crossing a river, etc., in a boat.

**fertile** (fer'til), a. Fruitful; productive.

**ferule** (fer'ul), n. Rod used for punishing children.

**fervent** (fer'vent), a. Warm; ardent.

**fervid** (fer'vid), a. Very hot; fiery; ardent. [fervor]

**festal** (fes'tal), a. Pertaining to a feast.

**fester** (fes'ter), vi. To rankle; corrupt; suppurate. n. A suppurating sore or wound.

**festival** (fes'ti-val), n. A feast; joyful celebration. [festivity]

**festoon** (fes-toon'), n. Garland, ribbon, etc., suspended between two points.

**fetch** (fech), vt. To bring; go for and bring obtain, as a price.

**fete** (fat), n. A festival.

**fetid**, a. Smelling offensively.

**fetish**, n. Object to which supernatural powers are ascribed.

**feud** (fud), n. Family quarrel; continued hostility. [feudal, feudalism]

**fiance** (fe-ang-sa'), n. A betrothed man. fem. [fiancee]

**fibre** (fi'ber), n. Fine thread or thread-like substance.

**fibrous** (fi'brus), a. Consisting of, or containing, fibers.

**fickle** (fik'l), a. Inconstant; variable.

**fiction** (fik'shun), n. An invented story. [fictitious]

**fidelity** (fi-del'i-ti), n. Faithfulness; loyalty; constancy.

**fidget** (fij'et), vi. To move restlessly or nervously.

**fiduciary** (fi-du'shi-a-ri), a. Of the nature of a trust.

**field** (feld), n. Open ground; inclosed land; place of a battle; battle; space for action; expanse.

**fiend** (fend), n. A devil; demon.

**fierce** (fers), a. Violent; ferocious; angry.

**fiery** (fi'e-ri), a. Impetuous; quick-tempered.

**fife** (fif), n. A shrill wind-instrument.

**figment** (fig'ment), n. Invention; fiction.

**figurative** (fig'yur-a-tiv), a. Containing figures; metaphorical.

**filament** (fil'a-ment), n. A slender thread.

**filch** (filch), vt. To steal; pilfer.

**filial** (fil'yal), a. Pertaining to, or becoming, a child; bearing the relation of a child.

**filigree** (fil'i-gre), n. Orna-

**Filipino** (fil'i-pe'no), n. pl. **Filipinos** (noz). A native of the Philippine Islands, esp. one of Spanish descent.

**fillet** (fil'let), n. A little band or twist; esp., a band encircling the hair.

**film**, n. A thin skin; a pellicle; a slender thread, as in a cobweb; a ribbon of celluloid for motion photography.

**filter**, n. Strainer for purifying liquids.

**filth** (filth), n. Foul matter; dirt; nastiness.

**filtrate** (fil'trat), vt. To filter.

**final**, a. Ending; last; ultimate; terminating; conclusive.

**finance** (fi-nans'), n. Income of a ruler or of a state; revenue; science of raising and expending public money; pl. funds. [**finan'cial**]

**finesse** (fi-nes'), n. Subtility; contrivance; artifice; stratagem.

**finical** (fin'i-kal), a. Affectedly fine; foppish.

**finis**, n. An end; conclusion.

**finite** (fi'nit), a. Limited in quantity, degree, or capacity; bounded.

**firm** (ferm), a. Fixed; solid; compact; dense; stable; robust; sturdy; steady; resolute. [**fir'mament**]

**fiscal** (fis'kal), a. Pertaining to the public treasury or revenue.

**fissure** (fish'ur), n. A cleft; a longitudinal opening.

**flaccid** (flak'sid), a. Flabby; lax; easily yielding to pressure; soft and weak.

**flagellate** (flaj'el-at), vt. To whip or scourge.

**flagitious** (fla-jish'us), a. Grossly wicked; guilty of enormous crimes.

**flagon** (flag'un), n. A vessel with a narrow neck, for holding liquids.

**flagrant** (fla'grant), a. Glaring; notorious; enormous.

**flail** (flal), n. An implement for threshing grain.

**flambeau** (flam'bo), n. A flaming torch.

**flamboyant** (flam-boi'ant), a. Gorgeously colored.

**flange** (flanj), n. A projecting or raised edge or flank, as of a wheel or of a rail.

**flannel** (flan'el), n. A soft woolen cloth of loose texture.

**flatulent** (flat'u-lent), a. Affected with air in the stomach; apt to generate such; empty; vain.

**flaunt** (flawnt), vi. To fly or wave in the wind to move or display ostentatiously to carry a gaudy or saucy appearance.

**flavor** (fla'ver), n. That quality of anything which affects the smell or the palate; a smack or relish.

**flea** (fle), n. A well-known wingless insect of great agility, ectoparasitic on warm-blooded animals.

**fleck** (flek), n. A spot or speckle; a little bit of a thing.

**fledge** (flej), vt. To furnish with feathers or wings.

**flee** (fle), vt. To run away, as from danger; to disappear.

**fleece** (fles), n. The coat of wool shorn from a sheep at one time; anything like a fleece.

**fleet** (flet), n. A number of ships in company, esp. ships of war; a division of the navy, commanded by an admiral.

**fleet** (flet), vi. To flit, pass swiftly.

**fleurdelis** (fler-de-le'), n. The flower of the lily; a design supposed to resemble the lily.

**flicker** (flik'er), vi. To flutter and move the wings, as a bird; to burn unsteadily.

**flier, flyer** (fli'er), n. One who flies or flees.

**flimsy** (flim'ze), a. Thin.

**flinch** (flinsh), vi. To draw back; to shrink from irresolution.

**flippancy** (flip'an-se), n. Volubility of tongue. [**flippant**]

**flirt** (flert), n. A jerk; a volatile girl. [**flirtation**]

**flit** (flit), vi. To flutter; to dart along; to remove.

**float** (flot), n. Something that swims; a raft.

**floculence** (flok'u-lens), n. Adhesion in small locks.

**flock** (flok), n. A collection of small animals; a lock of wool.

**floe** (flo), n. A mass of floating ice.

**flog** (flog), vt. To whip; to lash; to chastise.

**flood** (flud), n. Flow of tide; the sea; inundation.

**floodgate** (flud'gat), n. A gate to stop or let out water.

**floral** (flo'ral), a. Pertaining to flowers.

**florescence** (flo-res'ens), n. The season of flowering in plants.

**florid** (flor'id), a. Flushed with red.

**floriferous** (flo-rif'er-us), a. Producing flowers.

**florist** (flor'ist), n. One who cultivates flowers.

**flota** (flo'ta), n. A fleet of Spanish ships.

**flotilla** (flo-til'la), n. A little fleet.

**flotsam** (flot'sam), n. Goods found floating on the sea.

**flounce** (flouns), vt. To deck with flounces; to jerk or dash. [**flounder**]

**flour** (flour), n. Fine part of grain.

**flourish** (flur'ish), vi. or t. To thrive; to embellish; to brandish.

**flout** (flout), vt. To treat with contempt.

**flowery** (flow'er-e), a. Full of flowers; highly ornamented.

**fluctuate** (fluk'tu-at), vi. To waiver; to rise and fall. [**fluctuation**]

**flue** (flu), n. A passage for smoke.

**fluency** (flu'en-se), n. Facility of utterance. [**fluent**]

**fluid** (flu'id), a. Having parts which easily move, as water; liquid.

**flume** (flum), n. A channel for water.

**flummery** (flum'er-e), n. A kind of jelly; flattery.

**flurry** (flur're), n. A hasty blast; sudden commotion.

**flutter** (flut'er), vi. To move or flap the wings rapidly.

**fluvial** (flu've-al), a. Of or pertaining to a river.

**flux** (fluks), n. A flowing; looseness.

**foal** (fol), n. The young of a mare.

**foam** (fom), vi. To froth; to be in a rage.

**focal** (fo'kal), a. Belonging to a focus.

**focus** (fo'kus), n. The point in which rays of light meet when reflected, or refracted; pl. **focuses, foci.**

**fodder** (fod'er), n. Food for cattle.

**foe** (fo), n. An enemy; an adversary; an ill-wisher.

**foible** (foi'bl), n. A moral weakness.

**foil**, vt. To frustrate. Defeat; a blunt sword; a thin leaf of metal.

**foist** (foist), vt. To insert wrongfully or secretly.

**fold** (fold), n. A doubling; a plait; a pen for sheep.

**folder** (fold'er), n. An instrument to fold paper.

**foliage** (fo'le-aj), n. Leaves of trees.

**foliation** (fo-le-a'shun), n.

# FOLIO 90 FORTUITOUS

The beating into plates.
**folio** (fo'le-o), n. A book of two leaves to a sheet; a page; pl. folios.
**folk** (fok), n. People in general; pl. folks.
**folly** (fol'le), n. Absurd action; criminal weakness.
**foment** (fo-ment'), vt. To apply lotions; to encourage or abet.
**fond** (fond), a. Foolish; silly; loving.
**fondle** (fon'dl), vt. or i. To doat on.
**font** (font), n. A baptismal basin; an assortment of types.
**forage** (for'aj), n. Food for horses and cattle; provisions.
**foray** (for'a'), n. An excursion into an enemy's country.
**forbear** (far-bar'), v. To refrain from; to cease; to abstain [forbearance]
**forbid** (far-bid'), v. To prohibit; to obstruct.
**force** (fors), n. Active power; vigor; violence; troops; armament.
**forceps** (far'seps), n. An instrument used by surgeons.
**forcible** (for'si-bl), a. Having great force; violent.
**forebode** (for-bod'), v. To foretell; to predict.
**foreclosure** (for-klo'zhur), n. A foreclosing; a deprivation of the power of redeeming a mortgage.
**forehead** (for'ed), n. The upper part of the face.
**foreign** (for'in), a. Belonging to another country; external; alien; not to the purpose. [foreigner]
**forensic** (fo-ren'sik), a. Relating to courts of judicature.
**forest** (for'est), n. An extensive wood; a wilderness; wild land.
**forestall** (for-stawl'), vt. To buy ahead of the market, to anticipate; to displant.
**forfeit** (for'fit), vi. To lose by an offense; to lose all right to.
**forgery**, n. Act of counterfeiting money, a writing or a signature.
**forget** (for-get'), vt. To lose the remembrance of; slight; neglect.
**forgive** (for-giv'), vt. To pardon; remit.
**formal** (form'al), a. Having the form only; stiff; ceremonious; external; proper.
**formation** (for-ma-shun), n. Act of forming; creation; production; strata.
**former** (form'er), n. One who makes.
**formidable** (for'mi-da-bl), a. Causing fear; dreadful; imposing.
**formula** (form'u-la), n. Prescribed form; routine of doctrines; a general expression for solving problems; symbols expressing the chemical compounds of a body; pl. form'ulæ.
**fornication** (for-ni-ka'shun) n. Incontinence of unmarried persons.
**forsake** (for-sak'), vt. To quit entirely; abandon.
**forsooth** (for-sooth'), ad. In very truth; certainly.
**forswear** (for-swar'), vt. or i. To deny or renounce upon oath; to swear falsely.
**forth** (forth), ad. Forward; abroad.
**fortification** (for-ti-fi-ka'shun), n. Works for defence.
**fortitude** (for'ti-tud), n. Firmness of mind which enables one to meet danger or endure pain resolutely.
**fortnight** (fort'nit), n. The space of two weeks.
**fortuitous** (for-tu'i-tus), a. Depending upon causes

**fortunate** (for'tu-nat), a. Lucky; successful.

**forum** (fo'rum), n. A court of justice; a tribunal.

**fossil** (fos'sil), n. and a. Remains of plants and animals dug out of the strata of the earth in a petrified state.

**foster** (fos'ter), vt. To nurse; feed; incite; cherish.

**foul** (foul), a. Dirty; loathsome; profane; impure; stormy; unfair; running against; entangled.

**foundry** (found'er-i), n. A place for casting metals.

**fowl** (fowl), n. Creature that flies; poultry; cock or hen. [**fowler**]

**foyer** (fow-ya'), n. In theaters, a public room opening on the lobby.

**fracas** (fra'kas), n. Uproar; a noisy quarrel.

**fraction** (frak'shun), n. A fragment or very small piece.

**fragile** (fraj'il), a. Easily broken; frail; delicate.

**fragment** (frag'ment), n. A piece broken off; an unfinished portion.

**fragrant** (fra'grant), a. Sweet-scented.

**frail** (fral), a. Wanting in strength or firmness; weak; unchaste.

**frail** (fral), n. A rush; a basket made of rushes.

**franchise** (fran'chiz or-chiz) n. Liberty; a right or privilege belonging to the people, esp. the right to vote; a particular privilege granted to an individual or corporation.

**frank** (frangk), a. Free, open; open or candid in expression.

**frantic** (fran'tik), a. Mad; raving; wild.

**fraternal** (fra-ter'nal), a. Pertaining to, or becoming, brothers; brotherly. [**fraternity**]

**fratricide** (frat'ri-sid), n. Murder, also the murder, of a brother.

**fraud** (frad), n. Deception; deceit; guile; trick; cheat; fraudulent procedure; breach of trust. [**fraudulent**]

**fraught** (frat), a. Freighted; laden; filled; full; stored.

**freak** (frek), n. A sudden, causeless change of the mind; a whim; a caprice.

**freckle** (frek'k'l), n. A spot of yellowish color in the skin; a small discoloration.

**freeze** (frez), vt. & i. To congeal with cold; to chill.

**freight** (frat), n. Lading (of a ship, car, etc.); cargo; price for transportation of merchandise.

**frenzy** (fren'zy), n. Violent agitation; madness; rage.

**frequent** (fre'kwent), a. Often done or happening; habitual; persistent. [**frequency**]

**fricassee** (frik'as-se'), n. A dish of fowls or small animals stewed or fried.

**friction** (frik'shun), n. A rubbing one body against another; attrition; abrasion.

**friend** (frend), n. One attached to another by esteem, respect, and affection.

**frigate** (frig'at), n. A ship of war, larger than a sloop of war, and less than a ship of the line.

**fright** (frit), n. Sudden and violent fear; terror; consternation.

**frigid** (frij'id), a. Cold; of low temperature; impotent.

**fringe** (frinj), n. A trimming consisting of loose threads; a border; a confine.

**frisk** (frisk), vi. To skip, dance, or gambol.
**fritter** (frit'ter), n. A pancake of fried batter; a fragment; shred; small piece.
**frivolous** (friv'o-lus), a. Of little weight, worth, or importance; trivial; unimportant; petty.
**frolic** (frol'ik), a. Full of pranks; gay; merry.
**frontal** (fron'tal), a. Belonging to the front.
**frontier** (fron'ter), n. Part of a country which fronts or faces another country; the border.
**frost** (frost), n. Act of freezing; cold or freezing weather; frozen dew.
**froth** (froth), n. Bubbles collected on liquids; spume; foam; empty show; unsubstantial matter.
**frouzy** (frou'zy), a. Fetid; musty; rank.
**froward** (fro'ward), a. Perverse; disobedient; refractory.
**frown** (frown), n. A look of displeasure. v. To scowl at or on.
**frozen** (fro'zn), a. Congealed by cold; frosty.
**fructification** (fruk-ti-fi-ka'shun), n. Act of rendering productive of fruit.
**frugal** (fro-gal), a. Economical in living; sparing. [**frugality**]
**fruit** (frot), n. Whatever the earth produces for food, clothing, or profit; effect; consequence. [**fruitage, fruiterer**]
**fruition** (fro-ish'un), n. Enjoyment; pleasure.
**frustrate** (frus'trat), v. To disappoint; to defeat.
**fuchsia** (fu'shi-a), n. A plant with pendulous flowers.
**fudge** (fuj), n. Nonsense; kind of candy.

**fuddle** (fud'dl), v. To make tipsy.
**fuel** (fu'el), n. Anything that feeds fire.
**fugitive** (fu'ji-tiv), a. Apt to flee away; wandering.
**fugue** (fug), n. A succession in music.
**fulcrum** (ful'krum), n. That which supports a lever.
**fulfill** (fol-fil'), v. To perform what was promised; to complete.
**fuller** (fol'ler), n. One who fulls or whitens cloth.
**fully** (fol'li), ad. To the full; entirely; completely.
**fulminate** (ful'min-at), v. To utter denunciation; to explode; to roar.
**fulsome** (ful'sum), a. Disgusting; offensive; nauseous.
**fumble** (fum'bl), v. To do awkwardly; to grope.
**fume** (fum), n. Smoke; vapor; passion; rage. v. To smoke; to rage.
**fumiferous** (fu-mif'er-us), a. Producing fumes or smoke.
**fumigate** (fu'mi-gat), v. To smoke; to perfume.
**function** (fungk'shun), n. Office; employment; charge. [**functional, functionary**]
**fund** (fund), n. Stock; capital; supply. pl. Money for supplies.
**fundamental** (fun-da-men'tal), a. Relating to the foundation; essential.
**funeral** (fu'ner-al), n. The ceremony of burying.
**funereal** (fu-ne're-al), a. Suiting to a funeral.
**fungous** (fung'gus), a. Soft; spongy.
**funnel** (fun'el), n. Passage for smoke; a tube for pouring liquids into bottles.
**funny** (fun'i), a. Droll; whimsical; comical.
**fur** (fur), n. Soft hair or

skin of animals; morbid matter on the tongue.

**furbish** (fur'bish), v. To polish.

**furcate** (fur-kat), a. Forked.

**furious** (fu-ri-us), a. Impetuous, raging with passion.

**furioso** (fu-ri-o'so), ad. In music, furiously.

**furl** (furl), v. To roll up in a long bundle, as a sail.

**furlong** (fur-lang), n. The eighth of a mile.

**furlough** (fur-lo), n. Temporary leave of absence.

**furnace** (fur'nas), n. An inclosed fire-place.

**furnish** (fur'nish), v. To supply; to provide; to store.

**furniture** (fur'ni-tur), n. Goods, vessels, utensils.

**furor** (fu'rur), n. Rage; fury.

**furrier** (fur'rier), n. A dealer in furs.

**furrow** (fur'ro), n. The small channel made by a plough.

**furry** (fur'ri), a. Covered with fur.

**further** (fur'ther), a. More distant; beyond this; additional.

**furtherance** (fur'ther-ans), n. Helping forward.

**furtive** (fur'tiv), a. Gotten by stealth.

**fury** (fu're), n. Madness; passion; a raging woman.

**fuse** (fuz), vt. To liquefy by heat.

**fusible** (fuz'e-bl), a. That may be melted.

**fusion** (fu'zhun), n. The operation of converting a solid into a liquid by heat; union, as of parties.

**fussy** (fus'e), a. Bustling in small matters.

**fusty** (fus'te), a. Mouldy; ill-smelling.

**futile** (fu'til), a. Trifling; worthless; ineffectual.

**futility** (fu-til'e-te), n. Worthlessness.

**future** (fu'tur), a. That is to come or be hereafter. [futurity]

**fuzz** (fuz), vi. To fly off in small particles.

# G

**gabble** (gab'l), vi. To talk fast or without meaning.

**gable** (ga'bl), n. Triangular part of the end of a house, &c.

**gadder** (gad'er), n. One who walks the streets often and idly.

**gadfly** (gad'fli), n. A fly that stings cattle, and deposits its eggs in their skin.

**gaff** (gaf), n. A light spear; a small boom.

**gage** (gaj), n. A pledge or pawn.

**gaily.** See **gayly.**

**gainful** (gan'fool), a. Producing profit; lucrative.

**gainsay** (gan'sa), vt. To deny; to oppose; to contradict.

**gairish** (gar'ish), a. Gaudy; showy.

**gait** (gat), n. Manner of walking.

**gala** (ga'la), n. Show; festivity.

**galaxy** (gal'ak-se), n. The milky way; a splendid assemblage.

**gale** (gal), n. A strong wind.

**gall** (gawl), n. Bile; rancour; an excrescence on the oak.

**gallant** (gal-lant'), n. A lover; an attendant.

**gallantry** (gal'lant-re), n. Bravery; nobleness; civility to ladies.

**gallery** (gal'er-e), n. A covered walk.

**galley** (gal'e), n. A low flat-built vessel; a frame

which receives the types from a composing-stick. pl. galleys.

**gallicism** (gal'e-sizm), n. A French idiom.

**gallon** (gal'un), n. A measure of four quarts.

**gallop** (gal'up), vi. To move by leaps, as a horse.

**gallows** (gal'us), n. A frame for the execution of criminals.

**galoche** (ga-losh'), n. An overshoe.

**galvanic** (gal-van'ik), a. Pertaining to galvanism.

**galvanise** (gal'va-niz), vt. To affect by galvanism; electro-plate; restore to activity. [galvanism]

**gamble** (gam'bl), vi. To play for money.

**gamut** (gam'ut), n. A scale of notes in music.

**gander** (gan'der), n. The male of the goose kind.

**gang** (gang), n. A crew; a band.

**ganglion** (gang'gli-un), n. A tumour in the tendinous parts.

**gangrene** (gang'gren), n. Mortification of flesh.

**gangway** (gang'wa), n. A narrow passage of any kind.

**gaol** (jal), n. A jail.

**garage** (gar'azh), n. A depot for storing and repairing motor cars.

**garbage** (gar'bij), n. Offals of animals; refuse matter.

**garble** (gar'bl), vt. To pick out or sift; select or suppress for a purpose.

**gargle** (gar'gl), vt. To wash the throat.

**gargoyle** (gar'goil), n. A projecting water-spout in ancient buildings, carved grotesquely.

**garish** (gar'ish), a. Gaudy; dazzling; flighty.

**garland** (gar'land), n. A wreath of flowers; principal thing; choice collection.

**garner** (gar'ner), n. A store-house for grain.

**garnish** (gar'nish), vt. To adorn; ornament or set off with something; furnish; warn; give notice.

**garniture** (gar'ni-tur), n. Furniture; ornament.

**garret** (gar'et), n. A room directly under the roof.

**garrison** (gar'i-sn), n. A body of troops in a fort.

**garrote** (ga-rot'), n. Strangling by a collar screwed tight round the neck; a mode of capital punishment in Spain.

**garrulous** (gar'u-lus), a. Disposed to talk much; talkative; loquacious.

**garter** (gar'ter), n. A band to hold up a stocking; the highest order of knighthood in England.

**gastric** (gas'trik), a. Belonging to the stomach.

**gaud** (gawd), n. Ornament; trinket.

**gaudy** (gaw'di), a. Showy; ostentatiously fine.

**gauge** (gaj), vt. To measure the contents of a cask.

**gaunt** (gant), a. Lean; thin;

**gauntlet** (gant'let), n. An iron glove.

**gauze** (gawz), n. A thin silk or linen.

**gavel**, n. A mallet used by the chairman of a meeting, for rapping to attract attention or call to order.

**gawky** (gaw'ki), a. Foolish; awkward.

**gaze** (gaz), vi. To look intently.

**gazelle** (ga-zel'), n. A species of antelope.

**gazette** (ga-zet'), A newspaper.

**gear** (ger), n. The moving parts taken together which form a mechanical whole.

**gender** (jen'der), n. Sex. vt. to beget.

**genealogist** (jen-e-al'o-jist)

n. One skilled in genealogy. [genealogy]

**genera** (jen'er-a), n. pl. of **genus** (je'nus).

**general** (jen'er-al), a. Common; prevalent; public; vague. [generalissimo]

**generation** (jen-er-a'shun), n. Act of producing; people of one period; race or family. [generative, generator]

**generic** (jen-er'ik), a. Pertaining to, or distinguishing, a genus.

**generosity** (jen-er-os'i-ti), n. Nobleness; liberality. [generous]

**genesis** (jen'e-sis), n. Origin.

**genial** (jen'i-al), a. Vivifying; healthful; cheerful.

**genius** (je-ni-us), n. Good or evil spirit presiding over one's destiny. pl. **genii**; Special taste or faculty; inborn mental power; person endowed with special powers of mind.

**genre** (zhongr), Denoting a style of art that deals with every-day subjects.

**genteel** (jen-tel'), a. Wellbred; respectable.

**Gentile** (jen'til), n. One not a Jew.

**gentility** (jen-til'i-ti), n. Good birth; goodbreeding; respectability.

**genuine** (jen'yu-in), a. Real; pure; authentic.

**genus** (je'nus), n. Group containing several species. pl. **genera**.

**geocentric** (je'o-sen'trik), a. Having the centre of the earth as its centre.

**geography** (je-og'ra-fi), n. Science which treats of the world and its inhabitants.

**geologist** (je-ol'o-jist), n. One versed in geology.

**geology** (je-ol'o-ji), n. Science which treats of the structure of the earth.

**geometry** (je-om'e-tri), n. Science which treats of the properties and relations of magnitude.

**germ** (jerm), n. Bud; embryo; origin; first principle.

**german** (jer'man), a. Of the first degree, as **cousin-german**.

**germane** (jer-man'), a. Relevant; appropriate.

**germinate** (jer'mi-nat), vi. To begin to grow; sprout.

**gesticulate** (jes-tik'yu-lat), vi. To make gestures.

**gesture** (jest'yur), n. Action; motion of the body or limbs.

**gewgaw** (gu'ga), n. A showy trifle; bauble.

**geyser** (gi'ser), n. A spring which boils with explosions.

**ghastly** (gast'li), a. Deathlike; hideous.

**gherkin** (ger'kin), n. A small cucumber.

**ghost** (gost), n. The soul; apparition of a deceased person.

**ghoul** (gool), n. A fabulous monster supposed to devour human carcases.

**giant** (ji'ant), n. A man of extraordinary size. fem. **giantess**.

**gibberish** (gib'er-ish), n. Unmeaning articulations.

**gibbet** (jib'et), n. A gallows.

**gibbous** (gib'us), a. Hunched; swelling; convex.

**gibe** (jib), vt. and vi. To mock; jeer.

**giblets** (jib'lets), n. pl. Internal eatable parts of a fowl.

**giddy** (gid'i), a. Dizzy; causing giddiness; thoughtless.

**gigantic** (ji-gan'tik), a. Enormous.

**giggle** (gig'l), n. Half-suppressed, or silly, laughter.

**gilding** (gild'ing), n. Art

**gill** (jil), n. One-fourth of a pint.
**gills** (gilz), n. pl. The breathing organs in fishes.
**gilt**, a. Overlaid with gold.
**gimlet** (gim'let), n. Small tool for boring.
**gipsy** (jip'si), See gypsy.
**giraffe** (ji-raf'), n. The camelopard; a long-necked African quadruped.
**gird** (gerd), vt. To bind round; surround.
**girder** (gerd'er), n. Chief timber supporting a floor.
**girdle** (ger'dl), n. A band for the waist; inclosure.
**girlish** (gerl'ish), a. Of, or like, a girl.
**gist** (jist), n. Main point, pith of a matter.
**gizzard** (giz'ard), n. Muscular stomach of a fowl.
**glacial** (gla'shal), a. Pertaining to ice; icy.
**glacier** (gla'sher, glas'i-er), n. Large field of ice among mountains.
**glade** (glad), n. Open space in a wood.
**gladiator** (glad'i-a-tor), n. A swordsman; one who fought for the public entertainment.
**glamour** (glam'ur), n. Magical illusion; fascination.
**glance** (glans), n. Sudden flash of light; momentary view.
**gland** (gland), n. Secreting organ in animals or plants.
**glandular** (gland'yu-lar), a. Pertaining to, or consisting of, glands.
**glare** (glar), n. A dazzling light; fierce look.
**gleam** (glem), n. A shoot of light; beam; ray.
**glean** (glen), vt. & i. To gather after a reaper; to collect with minute labor.
**glebe** (gleb), n. Turf; soil; land belonging to a parish church.

**glimpse** (glims), n. A sudden flash; a short, hurried view.
**glisten** (glis''n), vi. To sparkle; to shine with a mild and fitful luster.
**glitter** (glit'ter), vi. To sparkle with light; to gleam; to glare.
**gloam** (glom), vi. To grow dusk.
**gloat** (glot), vi. To look steadfastly; to gaze with malignant satisfaction, passionate desire, lust, avarice, etc.
**glossary** (glos'ar-e), n. A vocabulary for explaining obsolete or peculiar words.
**glossy** (glos'e), a. Smooth and shining; bright.
**gloze** (gloz), vt. To flatter.
**glue** (gloo), n. A tenacious substance.
**gluey** (gloo'e) a. Glutinous.
**glut** (glut), vt. To cloy; to overload.
**glutinous** (gloo'tin-us), a. Viscous; viscid.
**glutton** (glut'n), n. A voracious eater. [gluttonous]
**gnarled** (narld), a. Full of knots.
**gnash** (nash), vi. or t. To strike the teeth together.
**gnat** (nat) n. A small insect that bites.
**gnaw** (naw), vt. To bite off; to corrode.
**goad** (god), n. A pointed stick to drive oxen.
**goal** (gol), n. A starting-post.
**goblin** (gob'lin), n. An evil spirit; apparition; fairy.
**goggle** (gog'l) vi. To strain or roll the eyes.
**goitre** (goi'ter), n. An enlargement of the thyroid gland, or swelled neck.
**gondola** (gon'do-la), n. A long, narrow pleasure boat.
**gong** (gong), n. A circular piece of metal, producing,

when struck, a loud harsh sound.

**gore** (gor), n. Clotted blood; triangular piece of cloth or land.

**gorge** (gorj) n. The throat; that which is swallowed; a narrow passage between mountains, &c.; a concave moulding.

**gorgeous** (gor'jus), a. Fine; splendid; showy; magnificent.

**gorilla** (gor-il'a), n. Large anthropoid ape of Western Africa, which grows from 5 to 7 feet in height.

**gormand** (gor'mand), n. A glutton; epicure.

**gospel** (gos'pel), n. System of religious truth; Christian revelation; the four Scriptural narratives of the life of Christ.

**gossamer** (gos'a-mer), n. Down or spider threads floating in the air; silk.

**gossip** (gos'ip), n. One who tattles; idle talk.

**gouge** (gowj), n. A chisel with a hollowed blade.

**gourd** (gord), n. A plant and its fruit; the rind.

**gout** (gout), n. Severe pains in joints or toes.

**govern** (guv'ern), vt. To rule; regulate; influence; to administer the laws.

**governess** (guv'er-nes), n. A female who instructs.

**government** (guv'ern-ment) n. System of laws; the ruling power; self-restraint. [governor]

**gown** (gown), n. A woman's garment; official robe.

**grab** (grab), vt. To seize.

**grace** (gras), n. Favor; religious affections; a short prayer; a trait; beauty; refinement; elegance; three extra days on a note. pl. Fine manners; the three Graces.

**gracious** (gra'shus) a. Condescending; kind; merciful.

**gradation** (gra-da'shun), n. Regular progress; order; series.

**grade** (grad) n. A step or degree in rank, order or dignity; the rise and descent of a road.

**gradual** (grad'u-al), a. Proceeding slowly and step by step.

**graduate** (grad'u-at), vt. To receive an academical degree.

**graft** (graft), n. A scion inserted in a stock.

**granary** (gran'ar-i), n. A storehouse for grain, &c.

**grandeur** (grand'ur), n. State; magnificence; loftiness of thought or deportment.

**grandsire** (grand'sir), n. A grandfather; ancestor.

**granite** (gran-it), n. A stone composed of quartz, feldspar, &c.

**granular** (gran'u-lar), a. Like or consisting of grains.

**graphic, graphical** (graf'ik-al), a. Pertaining to writing or delineating; descriptive; picturesque.

**grapple** (grap'l), vt. To seize; to lay fast hold of.

**grasp** (grasp), vt. To seize and hold by clasping with the fingers or arms; to catch at; to comprehend.

**grate** (grat), n. A framework composed of bars with interstices, esp. one of iron bars for holding fuel while burning.

**grate** (grat), vt. To rub hard or wear away with anything rough; to make a harsh sound; to irritate or offend.

**grateful** (grat'fool) a. Causing pleasure; acceptable; delightful; thankful; having a due sense of benefits.

**gratis**, adv. For nothing; without payment or recompense.

**gratitude** (grat'i-tud), n.

Warm and friendly feeling towards a benefactor. [**gratuity**]

**gravamen** (grav-a'men), n. Grievance; the substantial or chief ground of complaint or accusation.

**gravel**, n. Small stones often intermixed with sand; small collections of gravelly matter in the kidneys or bladder.

**gravity** (grav'i-ti), n. Weightiness; that attraction between bodies, or acceleration of one toward another, of which the fall of a body to the ground is an example.

**gravy** (grav'i), n. The juices from meat while cooking.

**gray, grey** (gra), a. Of a white color mixed with black; ash-colored; (fig.) aged, gray-haired, mature.

**graze** (graz), vt. To eat or feed on grass; to feed or supply with grass.

**grease** (gres), n. Soft thick animal fat; oily matter of any kind.

**gregarious** (gre-ga'ri-us), a. Associating in flock or herds.

**grewsome, gruesome** (gru'-sum) a. Frightful; ghastly; horrible.

**grey** (gra), see **gray**.

**griddle** (grid'l), n. Plate or shallow pan for baking cakes.

**gridiron** (grid'i-urn), n. Small iron grate for broiling.

**grief** (gref), n. Sorrow; regret; affliction. [**grievance, grieve, grievous**]

**grill** (gril), vt. To broil on a gridiron.

**grimace** (gri-mas'), n. Distortion of the face.

**grimalkin** (gri-mal'kin), n. An old cat.

**grisly** (griz'li), a. Frightful; hideous.

**grist** (grist), n. Corn ground or for grinding, at one time.

**gristle** (gris'l), n. Elastic animal tissue; cartilage. a. **gristly**.

**groan** (gron), vi. To utter a deep moan; be afflicted.

**grocer** (gros'er), n. A dealer in tea, sugar, spices, etc. [**grocery**]

**groin** (groin), n. Junction of the belly and the thigh; junction of intersecting arches.

**groom** (groom), n. One who has the charge of horses; a bridegroom.

**groove** (groov), n. A narrow furrow.

**grope** (grop), vi. To feel about in the dark.

**gross** (gros), a. Coarse; large; palpable; obscene.

**grotesque** (gro-tesk'), a. Extravagantly formed; ludicrous.

**ground** (ground), n. Surface of the earth; soil; land; foundation; in pl. dregs.

**group** (groop), n. Cluster; assemblage.

**grout**, n. A mixture of cement and broken stone.

**grovel** (grov'l), vi. To crawl on the ground; abase one's self.

**growl** (groul), vi. To grumble; snarl.

**growth** (groth), n. Increase in size; development; vegetation.

**grub** (grub), vt. and vi. To dig. n. Larva of a beetle, etc.

**grudge** (gruj), vt. To give unwillingly; envy.

**gruel** (gru'el), n. Meal boiled in water.

**grumble** (grum'bl), vi. To murmur with discontent; growl.

**grunt** (grunt), vi. To make a sound like a hog.

**guano** (gwa'no), n. Dung of sea-fowl.

**guarantee** (gar-an-te'), n.

Surety for the performance of a contract; charge for insuring payment of a debt. [**guarantor, guaranty**]
**guard** (gard), vt. To watch; defend; protect. [**guardian**]
**gubernatorial** (gu-ber-na-tor'i-al), a. Pertaining to a governor.
**guerdon** (gerd'on), n. Recompense.
**guerilla** (ger-il'a), n. Irregular war by small bands.
**guess** (ges), vt. To conjecture; solve, as a riddle.
**guest** (gest), n. A visitor entertained.
**guffaw** (guf-a'), n. A boisterous laugh.
**guidance** (gid'ans), n. Direction; leading.
**guide** (gid), vt. To lead; direct.
**guild** (gild), n. An association of workmen or others.
**guile** (gil), n. Cunning, deceit.
**guillotine** (gil'o-ten), n. A machine for beheading.
**guilt** (gilt), n. Crime; sin.
**guilty** (gilt'i), a. Criminal; wicked.
**guise** (giz), n. Manner; appearance; dress.
**guitar** (gi-tar'), n. Musical stringed instrument played with the fingers.

**gulf** (gulf), n. Large bay; chasm.
**gullet** (gul'et), n. Passage conveying food from the mouth to the stomach.
**gullible** (gul'i-bl), a. Easily deceived.
**gully** (gul'i), n. Channel worn by water.
**gulp** (gulp), vt. To swallow eagerly.
**gurgle** (gur'gl), vi. To gush or flow with a bubbling noise.
**gusset** (gus'et), n. A piece of cloth inserted in a garment to strengthen it, or fill an angle.
**guttural** (gut'ur-al), a. Pertaining to, or formed in, the throat.
**guy** (gi), n. Rope to guide or steady a suspended weight.
**guzzle** (guz'l), vt. To drink greedily or frequently.
**gymnasium** (jim-na'zi-um), n. Place for athletic exercises; school. [**gymnast, gymnastic, gymnastics**]
**gypsy** (jip'si), n. One of a wandering Asiatic race, now scattered over Europe.
**gyrate** (ji'rat), vt. To move in a circle or spiral.
**gyroscope** (ji'ro-skop), n. A revolving instrument or toy.
**gyve** (jiv), n. A fetter or shackle for the leg.

# H

**haberdasher** (hab'er-dash-er), n. A dealer in small wares.
**habiliment** (hab-il'i-ment), n. Garment; dress.
**habitable** (hab'it-a-bl), a. That may be dwelt in.
**hackney** (hak'ni), n. A horse for general use, esp. for hire.
**hades** (ha'dez), n. The unseen world; the abode of the dead indefinitely, hell.
**haft** (haft), n. A handle.
**haggard** (hag'ard), a. Lean; hollow-eyed.
**haggle** (hag'l), vt. To cut unskilfully.
**hair** (har), n. A small animal filament.
**hairiness** (har'e-nes), n. State of being hairy.

**hairy** (har'e), a. Full of hair; made of hair.

**halcyon** (hal'se-un), a. Calm; quiet.

**half** (haf), n. One of two equal parts. pl. **halves**.

**halleluiah** (hal-le-loo'ya), n. Praise ye the Lord; also written **hallelujah**.

**halloo** (hal-loo'), vi. or t. To cry out.

**hallow** (hal'o), vt. To consecrate.

**hallucination** (hal-lu-sin-a'shun), n. A delusion of the imagination.

**halo** (ha'lo), n. A circle round the sun. pl. **halos**.

**halter** (hawlt'er), n. A rope to tie a horse; a hangman's rope.

**halves** (havz), n. pl. of **half**.

**hamlet** (ham'let), n. A small village.

**hammer** (ham'er), n. An instrument for driving nails.

**hammock** (ham'uk), n. A hanging bed used in ships.

**hamper** (ham'per), n. A covered basket.

**handicraft** (hand'e-kraft), n. Manual occupation.

**handkerchief** (hang'kerchif), n. A cloth used for the face or neck.

**handle** (hand'l), vt. To touch; to manage; to treat of.

**handsome** (hand'sum, han'sum), a. Well-formed; beautiful; generous.

**handy** (hand'e), a. Ready; dexterous.

**hangar** (hahng'gahr), Shelter for aircraft.

**hanger** (hang'er), n. A broad-sword; that by which anything hangs.

**happiness** (hap'e-nes), n. State of enjoyment.

**harangue** (ha-rang'), n. A noisy speech; an oration.

**harass** (har'as), vt. To vex with bodily labour; to perplex.

**harbinger** (har'bin-jer), n. A forerunner.

**harbour** (har'ber), n. A haven for ships.

**hardihood** (hard'e-hood), n. Boldness.

**hardiness** (hard'e-nes), n. Firm intrepidity; assurance.

**hardship** (hard'ship), n. Severe toil; oppression.

**hardware** (hard'war), n. Wares made of iron, &c.

**hare** (har), n. A small timid animal.

**harelip** (har'lip), n. A divided lip like a hare's.

**harem** (ha'rem), n. Ladies' apartment in a seraglio.

**harlequin** (har'le-kwin), n. A buffoon.

**harlot** (har'lot), n. A lewd woman.

**harmful** (harm'fool), a. Hurtful.

**harmonical** (har-mon'ik-al), a. Relating to harmony; musical.

**harmonious** (har-mo'ne-us), a. Agreeing together; musical.

**harness** (har'nes), n. Furniture for a horse, etc.

**harpoon** (har-poon'), n. A barbed spear.

**harpy** (har'pi), n. A fabulous animal; an extortioner.

**harrow** (har'o), n. An instrument to break or smooth land.

**harry** (har'i), vt. or i. To plunder; pillage; ravage.

**harsh** (harsh), a. Rough to the touch, taste, ear, or feelings.

**hart** (hart), n. A stag or male deer.

**hartshorn** (harts'horn), n. Salammonia.

**harvest** (har'vest), n. The season for gathering ripe grain; the crop gathered; effects.

**hash** (hash), vt. To mince; chop.

**haste** (hast), n. Celerity of motion or action; hurry; speed; despatch. **[hasty]**

**hatches** (hach'ez), n. pl. The opening in a ship's deck.

**hatchet** (hach'et), n. A small axe.

**hatchway** (hach'wa), n. An opening in a ship's deck.

**hatred** (ha'tred), n. Ill-will; hate.

**haughty** (haw'ti), a. Proud and overbearing.

**haul** (haul), vt. To draw with force.

**haunch** (hansh), n. The thigh.

**haunt** (hant), vt. or i. To frequent.

**haven** (ha'vn), n. A harbour.

**haversack** (hav'er-sak), n. Strong cloth bag, in which a soldier carries his rations.

**havoc** (hav'uk), n. Waste; destruction.

**hawk** (hawk), vt. or i. To force up phlegm; cry goods.

**hawser** (haw'zer), n. A small cable; a large rope.

**hazard** (haz'ard), n. Risk of loss or evil; danger. **[hazardous]**

**haze** (haz), n. A thin mist or fog.

**hazel** (ha'zl), n. A shrub bearing nuts.

**hazy** (ha'zi), a. Foggy; misty; obscure.

**headache** (hed'ak), n. Pain in the head.

**headquarters** (hed'kwawr-terz), n. pl. Quarters of a chief commander.

**headstone** (hed'ston), n. Corner stone of a building; stone at the head of a grave.

**heady** (hed'i), a. Hasty; rash; wilful; intoxicating.

**heal** (hel), vt. To cure.

**health** (helth), n. Freedom from sickness; sound state of body and mind.

**healthy** (hel'thi), a. Free from disease.

**hear** (her), vt. To perceive by the ear.

**hearken** (har'kn), vi. To listen; lend the ear; attend to; grant.

**hearse** (hers), n. A carriage to bear the dead.

**heart** (hart), n. The organ of the blood's motion; inner part; seat of love; spirit.

**heartache** (hart'ak), n. Deep sorrow.

**heartburn** (hart'burn), n. An acrid sensation in the stomach.

**hearth** (harth), n. Place on which fire is made.

**hearty** (har'ti), a. Healthy; sincere.

**heat** (het), n. Great warmth; glow.

**heath** (heth), n. A shrub; a place overgrown with shrubs.

**heathen** (he'thn), n. A pagan. **[heathenish, heathenism]**

**heave** (hev), vt. To lift; cause to swell; pant; cast.

**heaven** (hev'n), n. The region of the air; expanse of the sky; place of the blessed.

**heavy** (hev'i), a. Weighty; grievous; dull; burdensome; stiff; dense; copious; gloomy; expensive.

**hebe** (he'be), n. The goddess of youth.

**hebetude** (heb'e-tud), n. Bluntness; dullness.

**hebraic** (he-bra'ik), a. Pertaining to the Hebrews.

**hectic** (hek'tik), n. A kind of fever attending consumption.

**hector** (hek'ter), n. A bully.

**hedge** (hej), n. A thicket of shrubs.

**heifer** (hef'er), n. A young cow.

**height** (hit), n. Distance

from a point below; an elevated place; summit; utmost degree.

**heinous** (ha'nus), a. Characterised by great wickedness; atrocious; flagrant.

**heir** (ar), n. He who inherits the property of another.

**heiress** (ar'es), n. A female heir.

**heirloom** (ar'loom), n. Any movable property which descends to the heir.

**heliograph** (he'li-u-graf), n. An apparatus for telegraphing by the sun's rays.

**helm** (helm), n. The instrument by which a ship is steered.

**helot** (he'lot, hel'ut), n. A Spartan slave.

**hemisphere** (hem'i-sfer), n. The half of a sphere.

**hemlock** (hem'lok), n. A poisonous plant.

**hemorrhage** (hem'u-rij), n. A flowing of blood from a rupture.

**hemp** (hemp), n. A plant whose fibers are used for cloth and cordage.

**henbane** (hen'ban), n. A poisonous plant, sometimes used for opium.

**henceforth** (hens'forth), ad. From this time.

**henchman** (hensh'man), n. An attendant; a page.

**hepatic** (he-pat'ik), a. Belonging to the liver.

**heptagonal** (hep-tag'u-nal), a. Having seven sides.

**heptarchy** (hep'tar-ki), n. Government by seven rulers.

**herb** (erb or herb), n. A plant having a soft or succulent stem, that dies every year. [herba'ceous]

**herd** (herd), n. A collection of beasts; a drove; a crowd; a rabble.

**hereditary** (he-red'i-ta-ry), a. Descended by inheritance; ancestral; patrimonial.

**heresy** (her'e-sy), n. Opinion opposed to usually received doctrine; lack of orthodox belief. [her'etic]

**hermaphrodite** (her-maf'rodit), n. An animal or plant, uniting both sexes.

**hermetic** (her-met'ik), a. Chemical; perfectly close; airtight.

**hermit** (her'mit), n. A recluse; an anchoret; one who lives in solitude from religious motives. [her'mitage]

**hernia** (her'ni-a), n. Protrusion of any internal part through the inclosing membrane; rupture.

**hero** (he'ro), n. pl. **heroes** (-roz). A man of great valor, intrepidity, enterprise, etc.; principal personage in a poem, story, etc.

**herring** (her'ring), n. A small fish which migrates in great shoals from northern latitudes to the shores of Europe and America, where they are taken and salted.

**hesitate** (hez'i-tat), vi. To stop or pause; to doubt; to waver; to falter; to stammer.

**heterodox** (het'er-o-doks), a. Contrary to some acknowledged standard; not orthodox.

**heterogeneous** (het'er-o-je'ne-us), a. Differing in kind.

**hiatus** (hi-a'tus), n. A gap; a chasm; a defect.

**hibernal** (hi-ber'nal), a. Pertaining to winter.

**hibernian** (hi-ber'ni-an), a. or n. A native of Ireland.

**hiccough** (hik'up), n. Spasmodic affection of the stomach.

**hickory** (hik'or-i), n. The name of several nut-bearing trees, which have a

**HIDDEN** 103 **HOMOLOGOUS**

very hard wood suitable for carriages, &c.
**hidden** (hid'n), a. Not seen or known; mysterious.
**hide** (hid), vt. or i. To conceal; keep close; to lie in safety.
**hidebound** (hid'bound), a. Having the skin too tight.
**hideous** (hid'e-us), a. Ugly; frightful; ghostly. n. hideousness.
**hierarch** (hi'er-ark), n. The chief of a sacred order. [hierarchy]
**hieroglyphic** (hi-er-o-glif'-ik), n. A sacred symbol; the picture-writing of ancient Egypt.
**hilarity** (hi-lar'i-ti, hi-lar'-i-ti), a. Mirth; gayety; joyousness.
**hinderance** (hin'der-ans), n. Act of hindering; impediment.
**hippodrome** (hip'o-drom), n. Circus for equestrian performances.
**hippopotamus** (hip-o-pot'a-mus), n. Large African quadruped.
**hire** (hir), n. Price paid for service or use.
**hirsute** (her-sut', soot), a. Hairy; shaggy.
**histology** (his-tol'o-ji), n. Science which treats of the tissues of organisms.
**historian** (his-to'ri-an), n. A writer of history.
**histrionic** (his-tri-on'ik), a. Pertaining to stage-playing.
**hoar** (hor), **hoary** (hor'i), a. Gray; white.
**hoard** (hord), n. Hidden store.
**hoarhound, horehound** (hor'-hound), n. A bitter herb of the mint family.
**hoarse** (hors), a. Having a rough, indistinct voice; harsh.
**hoax** (hoks), n. A deception for sport.
**hobble** (hob'l), vi. To walk lamely.
**hobby** (hob'i), n. A nag;

figure of a horse for a child to ride; pet pursuit or idea.
**hobgoblin** (hob'gob'lin), n. A goblin; ugly apparition.
**hobnail** (hob'nal), n. Nail with thick head, used in a shoe.
**hockey** (hok'i), n. A game played with curved clubs and a block or ball.
**hoe** (ho), n. Tool for loosening the earth.
**hogshead** (hogz'ed), n. A large cask; measure of 63 gallons.
**hoist** (hoist), vt. To raise; lift.
**holiday** (hol'i-da), n. Festival day; day of amusement.
**hollo** (ho-lo'), int. Calling attention.
**hollow** (hol'o), a. Not solid; vacant; concave; insincere.
**holly** (hol'i), n. An evergreen tree with prickly leaves.
**holocaust** (hol'o-kast), n. A whole burnt-offering.
**holster** (hol'ster), n. Horseman's case for a pistol.
**homage** (hom'aj), n. Act of fealty; reverence; worship.
**homeopathy, homœ**opathy (ho-me-op'a-thi), n. System of treating disease by drugs which cause similar symptoms.
**homestead** (hom'sted), n. Family home.
**homicide** (hom'i-sid), n. Act of killing a human being; one who kills another.
**homily** (hom'i-li), n. A serious discourse; sermon.
**hominy** (hom'i-ni), n. Maize hulled and broken.
**homogeneous** (ho-mo-je'-ne-us), a. Of the same kind; of similar elements.
**homologous** (ho-mol'o-gus),

a. Similar in plan but different in function.
**homonym** (hom'o-nim), n. A word like another in sound, but different in meaning.
**honest** (on'est), a. Just in dealing; sincere.
**honey** (hun'i), n. Sweet liquid collected by bees from flowers.
**honeysuckle** (hun'i-suk-l), n. Climbing shrub with tubular flowers.
**honor** (on'or), n. Esteem paid to worth; respect; nobleness of character; integrity; distinction. In pl. Privileges of rank; academic distinction; four highest trump cards.
**hoodwink** (hud'wingk), vt. To blind by covering the eyes; deceive.
**hopper** (hop'er), n. Part of a mill.
**hopple** (hop'l), vt. To tie the feet.
**horal** (hor'al), a. Relating to an hour.
**horde** (hord), n. A migratory tribe.
**horehound** (hor'hound), n. A bitter medicinal plant.
**horizon** (ho-ri'zun), n. The line that bounds the sight.
**horizontal** (hor-e-zon'tal), a. Parallel to the horizon; level.
**horology** (hor-ol'o-je), n. Art of measuring time.
**horoscope** (hor'os-kop), n. Aspect of planets at the hour of birth.
**horrible** (hor're-bl), a. Tending to excite horror; frightful; awful.
**horrid** (hor'rid), a. Dreadful; hideous.
**horror** (hor'rer), n. A shuddering with fear; terror.
**horse-power** (hors'pow-er), n. Power of a horse or its equivalent; power which will raise 33,000 pounds avoirdupois one foot per minute—used to express the power of a steam engine.
**hortation** (hor-ta'shun), n. Advice. [**hortative**]
**horticulturist** (hor-te-kul'-tur-ist), n. One skilled in gardening.
**hosanna** (ho-zan'na), n. Praise to God.
**hosier** (ho'zhe-er), n. One who deals in stockings. [**hosiery**]
**hospitable** (hos'pit-a-bl), a. Kind to strangers or guests.
**hospital** (hos'pit-al), n. A building for the sick or insane.
**hostage** (host'aj), n. A person given as a pledge for the performance of certain conditions.
**hostile** (hos'til), a. Unfriendly; opposite. [**hostility**]
**hottentot** (hot'n-tot), n. A native of South Africa.
**hound** (hound), n. A dog for hunting.
**hour** (our), n. Twenty-fourth of a day; a particular time.
**hovel** (hov'el), n. A small or mean dwelling.
**hover** (hov'er), vi. To remain aloft flapping the wings; to wait in suspense; to move about near.
**howl** (howl), vi. To yell or cry, as a wolf or dog; to utter a long, loud, whining sound; to wail; to roar.
**huckleberry** (huk'l-ber'ri), n. A North American shrub and its fruit, a bluish berry.
**huckster** (huk'ster), n. A retailer of small wares, a hawker or peddler; a mean, trickish fellow.
**huddle** (hud'l), vi. To put up things confusedly; to hurry in disorder; to crowd.
**hue** (hu), n. Appearance; color; tint; dye; n. A

shouting. **hue and cry**, a loud clamor about something.

**huge** (huj), a. Having great dimensions.

**human** (hu'man), a. Belonging or pertaining to man or mankind; having the qualities of man.

**humanist** (hu'man-ist), n. A student of polite literature; a student of human nature.

**humanitarian** (hu-man'i-ta'ri-an), n. One who denies Christ's divinity; a philanthropist.

**humanity** (hu'man'it-i), n. The nature peculiar to a human being; the kind feelings of man; benevolence; tenderness; mankind collectively.

**humble** (hum'bl), a. Low; meek; modest.

**humeral** (hu'mer-al), a. Belonging to the shoulder.

**humid** (hu'mid), a. Moist; damp; rather wet.

**humiliate** (hu-mil'i-at), vt. To make humble; to depress; to lower in condition.

**humility** (hu-mil'i-ti), n. The state or quality of being humble; lowliness of mind; modesty.

**humming** (hum'ing), n. A low, murmuring sound, like that made by bees.

**hummock** (hum'uk), n. A hillock; pile or ridge (of ice).

**humor** (hu'mer), n. The moisture or fluids of animal bodies; state of mind; disposition; caprice; a mental quality which delights in ludicrous and mirthful ideas; playful fancy.

**hunger** (hung'ger), n. Desire for food; strong desire for anything.

**hunk** (hungk), n. A lump, hunch.

**hurdle** (hur'd'l). n. A texture of twigs or sticks; a crate; a sledge.

**hurl**, vt. & i. To throw violently.

**hurra** (hur-ra'), **hurrah** interj. A shout of joy or exultation.

**hurricane** (hur'ri-kan), n. A violent storm, with high wind.

**hurry** (hur'ry), vt. & i. To move hastily; to hasten. n. Haste; speed; urgency; bustle.

**hurt**, vt. To wound; to injure; to harm; to grieve.

**hush**, vt. To still; to silence; to calm.

**husk**, n. The external covering of certain fruits or seeds of plants.

**husking** (husk'ing), n. Act of stripping off husks.

**hussy** (huz'zy), n. An ill-behaved woman; a pert girl; a jade; a housewife, or bag containing thread, needles, etc.

**hustings** (hus'tingz), n. pl. The place where the election of a member of Parliament is held; the platform on which candidates stand.

**hustle** (hus''l), vt. To shake together; to handle roughly.

**hutch** (huch), n. A chest, box, etc., for storing things or confining animals.

**huzza** (huz-za'), interj. Hurrah; an expression of joy, exultation, of encouragement.

**hyacinth** (hi'a-sinth), n. A flowering plant; a gem, the red zircon.

**hybrid** (hi'brid), n. An animal or plant produced from mixture of two species.

**hydrant** (hi'drant), n. A pipe for discharging water from an aqueduct; a water-plug.

**hydraulic** (hi-dra'lik), a.

**hydraulics.** Pertaining to hydraulics. [hydrau'lics]

**hydrogen** (hi'dro-jen), n. An abundant gaseous element, colorless, tasteless, and odorless, and the lightest known substance.

**hydrophobia** (hi'dro-fo'bi-a), n. A preternatural dread of water; a disease caused by inoculation with saliva of a rabid dog.

**hydrostatics** (hi-dro-stat'iks), n. Science treating of fluids at rest.

**hyena** (hi-e'na), n. Fierce wild beast of the dog kind.

**hygiene** (hi'ji-en), n. Science treating of the preservation of health.

**hymen** (hi'men), n. The god of marriage; marriage.

**hymeneal** (hi-men-e'al), a. Pertaining to marriage; nuptial.

**hymn** (him), n. A song of praise, esp. to God.

**hyperbola** (hi-per'bo-la), n. A section of a cone formed by a plane cutting the base at a greater angle than does the side.

**hyperbole** (hi-per'bo-le), n. Rhetorical exaggeration.

**hyperborean** (hi-per-bor'e-an), a. Pertaining to the extreme north.

**hypercritic** (hi-per-krit'ik), n. One who is over-critical.

**hyphen** (hi-fen), n. The mark (-) used to join the parts of a word.

**hypnotism** (hip'no-tizm), n. Artificial sleep or trance.

**hypochondria** (hip-o-kon'dri-a), n. The abdomen; morbid lowness of spirits.

**hypocrisy** (hip-ok'ri-si), n. Simulation of virtue or piety; dissimulation. [hypocrite]

**hypotenuse** (hi-pot'e-nus), n. Longest side of a right-angled triangle.

**hypothecate** (hi-poth'e-kat) vt. To pledge as security; mortgage.

**hypothesis** (hi-poth'e-sis), n. Something assumed as the foundation of an argument; supposition.

**hysteria** (his-ter'i-a), n. Morbid state marked by nervous excitement or convulsion. [hysteric, hysterical]

# I

**iconoclast** (i-kon'o-klast), n. A destroyer of idols or images.

**icy** (i'si), a. Abounding in, or like, ice; cold.

**idea** (i-de'a), n. Mental image; notion; opinion.

**ideal** (i-de'al), a. Existing in idea; mental; imaginative. [idealism]

**idealist** (i-de'al-ist), n. One who aspires to, or depicts, ideal conditions.

**identity** (i-den'ti-ti), n. Sameness.

**idiom** (id'i-om), n. Mode of expression peculiar to a language.

**idiosyncrasy** (id-i-o-sin'kra-si), n. Peculiarity of bodily or mental constitution.

**idiot** (id'i-ot), n. An imbecile or foolish person.

**idle** (i'dl), a. Of no account; useless; inactive; lazy.

**idol** (i'dol), n. An image; image of a false god; object of worship; deceitful image; phantom; person or thing greatly loved. [idol'ater]

**idyl** (i'dil), **idyll**, n. A short pastoral poem; a narrative poem, written in an elevated style.

**igneous** (ig'ne-us), a. Consisting of, containing, or resulting from, the action of fire.

**ignite** (ig-nit'), vt. & i. To kindle; to light.

**ignoble** (ig-no'b'l), a. Of low birth; base; shameful; scandalous; infamous.

**ignominy** (ig'no-min-y), n. Public disgrace; dishonor; shame; infamy.

**ignoramus** (ig'no-ra'mus), n. An ignorant person; a vain pretender to knowledge.

**ignorant** (ig'no-rant), a. Destitute of knowledge; unconscious; unaware. [**ig'norance**]

**ignore** (ig-nor'), vt. To be or profess to be ignorant of; to refuse to notice; to leave out of consideration.

**illegal** (il-le'gal), a. Contrary to law; unlawful.

**illegible** (il-lej'i-b'l), a. Incapable of being read; not readable.

**illicit** (il-lis'it), a. Not allowed; unlawful.

**illimitable** (il-lim'it-a-b'l), a. Incapable of being limited or bounded; immeasurable; infinite; vast.

**illiterate** (il-lit'er-at), a. Ignorant of letters or books; untaught; unlearned.

**illogical** (il-loj'i-kal), a. Ignorant or negligent of logic; contrary to the rules of logic or sound reason.

**illude** (il-lud'), vt. To deceive; to mock.

**illume** (il-lum'), vt. To make light or bright; to illuminate.

**illusion** (il-lu'zhun), n. False appearance.

**illusive** (il-lu'siv), a. Deceiving by false show.

**illustrate** (il-lus'trat), v. To explain by picture; to make clear; to elucidate.

**illustrious** (il-lus'tri-us), a. Conspicuous for greatness or splendor.

**image** (im'aj), n. A likeness; statue; idol; idea. [**imagery**]

**imaginable** (im-aj'in-a-bl), a. That may be conceived. [**imaginary**]

**imagination** (im-aj-in-a'shun), n. The forming of mental images; conception; idea. [**imagine**]

**imbecile** (im'be-sil), a. Feeble in mind or body. [**imbecility**]

**imbricated** (im'bri-ka-ted), a. Overlapping; laid one over another, as tiles.

**imbroglio** (im-brol'yo), n. Intricacy; a complicated plot.

**imbrue** (im-bro'), v. To steep; to wet.

**imbue** (im-bu'), v. To tincture deeply; to imbibe.

**imitate** (im'i-tat), v. To follow; to copy. [**imitation**]

**immaculate** (im-mak'u-lat), a. Spotless; pure; undefiled.

**immanent** (im'a-nent), a. Remaining within; inherent.

**immaterial** (im-a-te'ri-al), a. Not consisting of matter; incorporeal; unimportant.

**immature** (im-a-tur'), a. Not ripe; not perfect; come before the natural time.

**immediate** (im-me'di-at), a. With nothing between; not acting by second causes; direct; present; without delay.

**immemorial** (im-me-mor'i-al), a. Beyond the reach of memory.

**immense** (im-mens'), a.

**immerse** (im-mers'), vt. To plunge into; to dip; to baptize by dipping the whole body; to engage deeply; to overwhelm.

**immigrate** (im'i-grat), vi. To migrate or remove into a country.

**imminent** (im'i-nent), a. Near at hand; threatening; impending.

**immobility** (im-mo-bil'i-ti), n. The character of being immovable.

**immoderate** (im-mod'er-at), a. Exceeding proper bounds; extravagant.

**immodest** (im-mod'est), a. Wanting restraint; impudent; forward; wanting shame or delicacy.

**immolate** (im'o-lat), vt. To offer in sacrifice.

**immortal** (im-mor'tal), a. Exempt from death; imperishable; never to be forgotten (as a name, poem, etc.)

**immune** (im-mun'), a. Free from obligation; not liable to infection.

**immure** (im-mur'), vt. To wall in; to shut up; to imprison.

**immutable** (im-mut'a-bl), a. Unchangeable.

**impact** (im-pakt'), vt. To press firmly together; to drive close.

**impair** (im-par'), vt. To diminish in quantity, value, or strength; to injure.

**impale** (im-pal'), vt. To fence in with stakes; to shut in; to put to death by spitting on a stake.

**impalpable** (im-pal'pa-bl), a. Not perceivable by touch; not coarse; not easily understood.

**impanel** (im-pan'el), vt. To enter upon a list, or swear in, for jury service. Also **empanel**.

**impart** (im-part'), vt. To bestow a part of; to give; to communicate; to make known.

**impartial** (im-par'shal), a. Not favoring one more than another; just.

**impassable** (im-pas'a-bl), a. That can not be passed.

**impassible** (im-pas'e-bl), a. Incapable of passion or pain.

**impassionate** (im-pash'un-at), vt. To affect powerfully.

**impassive** (im-pas'iv), a. Exempt from suffering or pain.

**impeach** (im-pech'), v. To accuse and try before a public body. [**impeachment**]

**impeccable** (im-pek'a-bl), a. Not liable or subject to sin.

**impede** (im-ped'), v. To hinder; to obstruct; to stop. [**impediment**]

**impellant** (im-pel'lant), n. A power that drives forward.

**impend** (im-pend'), v. To hang over; to threaten.

**impenetrable** (im-pen'e-tra-bl), a. That cannot be penetrated.

**imperative** (im-per'a-tiv), a. Commanding; authoritative.

**imperceptible** (im-per-sep'ti-bl), a. Not to be perceived.

**imperial** (im-pe'ri-al), a. Pertaining to an empire or an emperor; royal; supreme. [**imperialism**]

**imperious** (im-pe'ri-us), a. Haughty; arrogant.

**impertinence** (im-per'ti-nens), n. Rudeness. intrusion.

**imperturbable** (im-per-turb'a-bl), a. That cannot be disturbed or agitated.

**impervious** (im-per'vi-us), a. Not penetrable.

**impetuous** (im-pet'u-us), a. Violent; furious; passionate.

**impetus** (im'pe-tus), n. Force or quantity of motion.

**impiety** (im-pi'e-ti), n. Ungodliness; profaneness; irreligion.

**impinge** (im-pinj'), v. To strike or dash against.

**impious** (im'pi-us), a. Irreverent toward God; profane.

**implacable** (im-pla'ka-bl), a. Not to be appeased.

**implement** (im'ple-ment), n. A tool or instrument.

**implicate** (im'pli-kat), v. To involve; to entangle.

**implicit** (im-plis'it), a. Implied; trusting to another.

**implore** (im-plor'), v. To beg or entreat earnestly; to beseech.

**imply** (im-pli'), v. To include in reality; to signify; to mean.

**impolite** (im-po-lit'), a. Rude in manners; uncivil.

**impolitic** (im-pol'i-tik), a. Not wise or prudent.

**imponderable** (im-pon'der-a-bl), a. That cannot be weighed.

**import** (im-port'), v. To bring from another country or port; to signify.

**import** (im'port), n. A thing imported; meaning; signification; tendency.

**importance** (im-part'ans), n. Weight; consequence. [important]

**importation** (im-por-ta'shun), n. Act of bringing from abroad; the articles imported.

**importunate** (im-par'tu-nat), a. Urgent solicitation.

**impose** (im-poz'), v. To place or lay on; to deceive. [imposition]

**impossible** (im-pos'si-bl), a. That cannot be done.

**impost** (im'post), n. A tax; a duty; a top part of a pillar.

**impostor** (im-pos'tur), n. A cheat; a deceiver.

**impotent** (im'po-tent), a. Weak; powerless; unable imbecile.

**impoverish** (im-pov'er-ish) v. To make poor; to exhaust.

**impracticable** (im-prak'ti-ka-bl), a. That cannot be done; impossible.

**imprecate** (im'pre-kat), v. To invoke, as an evil or curse on any one.

**impregnable** (im-preg'na-bl), a. That cannot be taken; invincible.

**impregnate** (im-preg'nat), v. To fertilize; to infuse.

**impress** (im-pres'), v. To stamp; to print; to compel into service.

**impress** (im'pres), n. Mark; stamp; device.

**impressive** (im-pres'siv), a. Tending to effect; susceptible.

**impressment** (im-pres'ment), n. The act of forcing men into warlike service.

**imprimis,** adv. In the first place.

**imprint,** vt. To make by pressure; stamp; impress.

**imprison** (im-priz'n), vt. To put in prison; confine.

**improbable** (im-prob'a-bl), a. Not likely.

**impromptu** (im-prom'tu), a. Without study; off-hand.

**improve** (im-proev'), vt. To make better; use to advantage. [improvement]

**improvident** (im-prov'i-dent), a. Not provident or prudent.

**improvise** (im-pro-viz'), vt. and vi. To compose without preparation; devise or do off-hand.

**imprudent** (im-pru'dent), a. Not prudent; indiscreet.

**impudent** (im'pyu-dent), a. Wanting modesty; insolent; pert.

**impure** (im-pur'), a. Not pure; unholy; unchaste.

**imputation** (im-pu-ta'shun), n. Act of imputing charge; censure.

**impugn** (im-pun'), vt. To attack; call in question.

**impulse** (im'puls), n. Force communicated; instigation; sudden feeling.

**impunity** (im-pun'i-ti), n. Exemption from punishment or injury.

**inadvertent** (in-ad-vert'ent), a. Not attentive; heedless. n. **inadvertence**.

**inalienable** (in-al'yen-a-bl), a. That cannot be lost or transferred.

**inane** (in-an'), a. Empty; void; senseless.

**inanition** (in-a-nish'un), n. Exhaustion from want of food.

**inapposite** (in-ap'o-zit), a. Not apposite; irrelevant.

**inaugural** (in-a'gyu-ral), a. Pertaining to an inauguration.

**inaugurate** (in-a'gyu-rat), vt. To induct into an office; cause to begin.

**incandescent** (in-kan-des'ent), a. Glowing with heat.

**incantation** (in-kan-ta'shun), n. A charm; spell; magic rite.

**incapacitate** (in-ka-pas'i-tat), vi. To make incapable; disqualify.

**incarcerate** (in-kar'ser-at), vt. To imprison.

**incarnate** (in-kar'nat), a. Embodied in flesh. [**incarnation**]

**incautious** (in-kau'shus), a. Not cautious; imprudent.

**incendiary** (in-sen'di-a-ri), n. One who maliciously burns a house, or foments strife. [**incendiarism**]

**incense** (in'sens), n. Perfume of burning aromatics; the aromatics themselves; perfume; fulsome praise.

**incense** (in-sens'), vt. To inflame with anger.

**incentive** (in-sen'tiv), a. Inciting; encouraging.

**inception** (in-sep'shun), n. A beginning.

**incessant** (in-ses'ant), a. Unceasing.

**inchoate** (in'ko-at), a. Recently begun; incomplete.

**incident** (in'si-dent), a. Falling upon; casual; naturally belonging.

**incinerate** (in-sin'er-at), vt. To reduce to ashes.

**incipient** (in-sip'i-ent), a. Beginning.

**incise** (in-siz'), vt. To cut into; engrave.

**incision** (in-sizh'un), n. A cut; gash.

**incisor** (in-siz'or), n. A fore-tooth.

**incite** (in-sit'), vt. To rouse; encourage; impel.

**incivility** (in-si-vil'i-ti), n. Lack of civility; rudeness.

**inclement** (in-klem'ent), a. Unmerciful; severe.

**inclination** (in-kli-na'shun), n. A leaning; tendency; disposition.

**incline** (in-klin'), vt. or i. To lean; bend; dispose; feel disposed.

**inclose** (in-kloz'), vt. To surround; put in a case or envelope. [**inclosure**]

**include** (in-klood'), vt. To comprehend; comprise. [**inclusion**]

**inclusive** (in-kloo'siv), a. Comprehending; enclosing.

**incognisable** (in-kog'ni-za-bl, in-kon'i-za-bl), a. That cannot be recognized, known, or distinguished.

**incognito** (in-kog'ni-to), a. or ad. In disguise; in private.

**incoherence** (in-ko-her'ens), n. Want of connection.

**incombustible** (in-kum-bus'ti-bl), a. That will not burn.

**income** (in'kum), n. Rent; revenue; profits, interest, etc.

**incommensurable** (in-ku-men'su-ra-bl), a. Having no common standard of comparison.

**incommode** (in-ku-mod'), vt. To give inconvenience to. [incommodious]

**incommunicable** (in-ku-mu'ni-ka-bl), a. Not transferable; unspeakable.

**incomparable** (in-kom'pa-ra-bl), a. That admits no comparison; matchless.

**incompatibility** (in-kum-pat-i-bil'i-ti), n. Inconsistency; inherent difference.

**incompetence** (in-kom'pe-tens), n. Inability; want of means or of legal power; incapability.

**incomprehensible** (in-kom-pre-hen'si-bl), a. That cannot be understood.

**incompressible** (in-kum-pres'i-bl), a. That cannot be reduced into a smaller compass.

**incomputable** (in-kum-pu'ta-bl), a. That cannot be reckoned; incalculable.

**inconceivable** (in-kun-se'va-bl), a. That cannot be conceived.

**incongruent** (in-kong'groo-ent), a. Inconsistent. [incongruity, incongruous]

**inconsiderate** (in-kun-sid'er-at), a. Thoughtless; careless.

**inconsistency** (in-kun-sis'ten-si), n. Want of agreement; incongruity.

**inconsolable** (in-kun-so'la-bl), a. Not admitting comfort.

**inconspicuous** (in-kun-spik'u-us), a. Not conspicuous.

**inconstancy** (in-kon'stan-si), n. Changeableness in temper or affection.

**inconstant** (in-kon'stant), a. Subject to change of opinion or purpose; not uniform; variable; fickle.

**incontestable** (in-kun-tes'ta-bl), a. That cannot be disputed.

**incontinence** (in-kon'ti-nens), n. Want of restraint; unchastity.

**inconvenience** (in-kun-ven'yens), n. Want of convenience; anything unsuitable or annoying.

**incorporate** (in-kor'po-rat), vt. or i. To form into a body; unite. [incorporation]

**incorporeal** (in-kor-po're-al) a. Not consisting of matter; not material.

**incorrigible** (in-kor'i-ji-bl), a. That cannot be corrected.

**increase** (in'kres), n. Augmentation; produce.

**increment** (in'kre-ment), n. Increase.

**incriminate** (in-krim'i-nat), vt. To charge with a crime or fault.

**incrust** (in-krust'), vt. To cover with a crust or hard coat.

**incubate** (in'ku-bat), vi. To sit on, as eggs.

**incubus** (in'ku-bus), n. The nightmare.

**inculcate** (in-kul'kat), vt. To enforce or urge.

**inculpate** (in-kul'pat), vt. To censure.

**incumbent** (in-kum'bent), n. One who has a benefice or an office.

**incur** (in-kur'), vt. To become liable to.

**indecision** (in-de-sizh'un), n. Want of decision.

**indecorum** (in-de-ko'rum), n. Impropriety of conduct.

**indefatigable** (in-de-fat'i-ga-bl), a. Not yielding to fatigue; unremitting.

**indefensible** (in-de-fen'si-bl), a. That cannot be defended.

**indefinable** (in-de-fi'na-bl), a. That cannot be defined

**indefinite** (in-def'i-nit), a. Not precise; unlimited; uncertain.

**indelible** (in-del'i-bl), a. That cannot be blotted out.

**indelicate** (in-del'i-kat), a. Offensive to purity.

**indemnify** (in-dem'ni-fi), vt. To secure against loss; make good.

**indemnity** (in-dem'ni-ti), n. Security against loss or penalty; compensation.

**indent** (in-dent'), vt. To notch; bind to service.

**indentation** (in-den-ta'shun) n. A cut; notch.

**indenture** (in-den'tur), n. A written contract or agreement.

**independence** (in-de-pen'dens), n. Exemption from control. **[independent]**

**index** (in'deks), n. Something that points; table of contents. pl. **indexes** or **indices**.

**indicate** (in'di-kat), vt. To show; point to.

**indicative** (in-dik'a-tiv), a. Pointing out.

**indict** (in-dit'), vt. To charge and summon for trial.

**indictable** (in-di'ta-bl), a. Subject to indictment.

**indictment** (in-dit'ment), n. Accusation by a grand jury; any formal charge.

**indifferent** (in-dif'e-rent), a. Impartial; not good; middling; neutral; unconcerned.

**indigens** (in'di-jens), n. State of destitution; poverty; want; need.

**indigenous** (in-dij'e-nus), a. Native to a country.

**indigent** (in'di-jent), a. Needy; poor.

**indigestible** (in-di-jes'ti-bl), a. That cannot be digested. **[indigestion]**

**indignant** (in-dig'nant), a. Affected with anger; feeling wrath and scorn.

**indignity** (in-dig'ni-ti), n. Insult; contemptuous conduct.

**indiscernible** (in-diz-zern'i-bl), a. That is not visible.

**indiscreet** (in-dis-kret'), a. Injudicious; incautious. **[indiscretion]**

**indiscriminate** (in-dis-krim'i-nat), a. Confused; not making a distinction.

**indispensable** (in-dis-pen'sa-bl), a. Needful; not to be dispensed with.

**indispose** (in-dis-poz'), v. To make unfit or averse to.

**indisputable** (in-dis'pu-ta-b'l), a. Not disputable; unquestionable; certain.

**indissoluble** (in-dis'so-lu-b'l), a. Not capable of being dissolved; perpetually obligatory.

**indite** (in-dit'), vt. To direct what is to be uttered; to compose; to write; to be author of.

**individual** (in-di-vid'u-al), a. Not divided; single; one; peculiar to a single person or thing; distinctive.

**indolent** (in'do-lent), a. Indulging in ease; lazy; sluggish; inactive.

**indomitable** (in-dom'i-ta-b'l), a. Not to be subdued or tamed; invincible.

**indorse** (in-dors'), vt. To write upon the back of; to write one's name upon the back of (a paper) to transfer it, or to secure payment of a note, draft, etc.; to give one's name or support to; to sanction.

**indubitable** (in-du'bi-ta-b'l), a. Not dubitable; too plain to admit of doubt; evident.

**induce** (in-dus'), vt. To lead in; to prevail on; to impel; to press; to cause. **[induce'ment]**

**induct** (in-dukt'), vt. To bring in; to introduce; to put in possession (of a benefice or office). [**induc'tion**]

**inductile** (in-duk'til), a. Not ductile; incapable of being drawn into threads.

**indue** (in-du'), vt. To put on; to clothe; to invest; to supply.

**indulge** (in-dulj'), vt. To yield to the desire of; to gratify; to humor; to allow; to favor. [**indul'gence**]

**indurate** (in'du-rat), vi. & t. To harden.

**industry** (in'dus-try), n. Habitual diligence; assiduousness; laboriousness.

**inebriate** (in-e'bri-at), vt. To make drunk; to stupefy; to exhilarate.

**ineffable** (in-ef'fa-b'l), a. Incapable of being expressed in words; unspeakable; unutterable.

**inept** (in-ept'), a. Not suitable; foolish.

**inert** (in-ert'), a. Dull; inactive; powerless.

**inertia** (in-er'sha), n. Property of matter by which it tends to remain in motion or at rest.

**inestimable** (in-es'ti-ma-bl), a. Not to be valued; priceless.

**inevitable** (in-ev'i-ta-bl), a. That cannot be avoided.

**inexplicable** (in-eks'pli-ka-bl), a. That cannot be explained.

**infallible** (in-fal'i-bl), a. Incapable of error; certain.

**infamous** (in'fa-mus), a. Publicly disgraced; notoriously vile; detestable. [**infamy**]

**infancy** (in'fan-si), n. State or time of being an infant; first beginning. [**infant**]

**infanticide** (in-fant'i-sid), n. Murder or murderer of a child.

**infantile** (in'fant-il), a. Pertaining to infancy or an infant.

**infantry** (in'fant-ri), n. Foot-soldiers.

**infatuate** (in-fat'yu-at), vt. To make foolish; deprive of judgment.

**infect** (in-fekt'), vt. To taint with disease; corrupt; render offensive.

**infection** (in-fek'shun), n. Act of infecting; that which infects.

**infelicity** (in-fe-lis'i-ti), n. Unhappiness.

**infer** (in-fer'), vt. and vi. To deduce.

**inference** (in'fer-ens), n. Deduction; conclusion.

**inferential** (in-fer-en'shal), a. Deduced by inference.

**inferior** (in-fe'ri-or), a. Lower in any respect; less.

**infernal** (in-fer'nal), a. Pertaining to hell; devilish.

**infest** (in-fest'), vt. To molest; overrun.

**infidel** (in'fi-del), n. Unbelieving; not believing Christianity. [**infidelity**]

**infiltrate** (in-fil'trat), vt. To enter by pores.

**infinite** (in-fin'it), a. Boundless; unlimited.

**infinitesimal** (in-fin-i-tes'i-mal), a. Infinitely small.

**infirm** (in-ferm'), Feeble; sick. [**infirmity**]

**inflammation** (in-flam-a'shun), n. Act of setting on fire; heat with pain and swelling.

**inflammatory** (in-flam'a-to-ri), a. Inflaming; exciting.

**inflate** (in-flat'), vt. To swell with air; puff up.

**inflect** (in-flekt'), vt. To bend; modulate; in grammar vary in terminations.

**inflexible** (in-fleks'i-bl), a. That cannot be bent.

**inflict** (in-flikt'), vt. To lay on; impose.

**influence** (in'flu-ens), n. Operating power; authority. [**influential**]

**influenza** (in-flu-en'za), n. Severe epidemic catarrh.

**influx** (in'fluks), n. A flowing in.

**informal** (in-form'al), a. Not formal; irregular.

**informant** (in-form'ant), n. One who gives intelligence.

**information** (in-for-ma'-shun), n. Knowledge; accusation. [**informatory**]

**infraction** (in-frak'shun), n. Breach; violation.

**infrangible** (in-franj'i-bl), a. That cannot be broken.

**infuriate** (in-fu'ri-at), vt. To enrage; madden.

**infuse** (in-fuz'), vt. To pour into; inspire with; steep in a liquid without boiling. [**infusion**]

**infusoria** (in-fu-zo'ri-a), n. pl. Minute animal organisms.

**ingenious** (in-jen'yus), a. Naturally intelligent; skilful in contriving; adroit; clever.

**ingenuity** (in-je-nu'i-ti), n. Power of contriving; dexterity; skill.

**ingenuous** (in-jen'yu-us), a. Honorable; candid; sincere.

**ingot** (in'got), n. Mass of metal poured into a mould.

**ingraft** (in-graft'), vt. To insert, as a graft in a stock; fix deeply.

**ingrate** (in'grat), n. An ungrateful person.

**ingratiate** (in-gra'shi-at), vt. To get into favor.

**ingratitude** (in-grat'i-tud), n. Unthankfulness.

**ingredient** (in-gred'i-ent), n. A component part.

**ingress** (in'gres), n. Entrance.

**inhabitable** (in-hab'i-ta-bl), a. That may be inhabited. [**inhabitant**]

**inhale** (in-hal'), vt. To breathe in; draw into the lungs.

**inherent** (in-her'ent), n. Existing firmly in.

**inherit** (in-her'it), vt. To acquire as an heir. [**inheritance**]

**inhibit** (in-hib'it), vt. To restrain; forbid.

**inimical** (in-im'i-kal), a. Not friendly; repugnant; antagonistic.

**inimitable** (in-im'it-a-bl), a. That which cannot be imitated.

**iniquity** (in-ik'wi-ti), n. Injustice; crime; [**iniquitous**]

**initial** (in-ish'al), a. Commencing.

**initiate** (in-ish'i-at), vt. Make a beginning; instruct in principles; introduce. [**initia'tion**]

**inject** (in-jekt'), vt. Throw into.

**injudicious** (in-jo-dish'us), a. Wanting in judgment.

**injunction** (in-jungk'shun), n. Writ of prohibition; mandate; order.

**injure** (in'jor), vt. Do injury to; wrong; damage. [**injurious**]

**injustice** (in-jus'tis), n. Violation or withholding of another's rights.

**inn** (in), n. House for the lodging and entertainment of travelers; hotel; tavern.

**innate** (in'at or in-nat'), a. Inborn; natural.

**innocent** (in'o-sent), a. Harmless; pure. [**in'nocence**]

**innovate** (in'o-vat), vi. To make changes.

**innuendo** (in-nu-en'do), n. Hint.

**inoculate** (in-ok'u-lat), vt. To insert (a bud) in another plant; communicate (a disease) by inserting matter under the skin. [**inocula'tion**]

**inordinate** (in-ar'din-at), a.

| INQUEST | 115 | INSUPPORTABLE |

Beyond usual bounds; immoderate.
**inquest** (in'kwest), n. Judicial inquiry.
**inquire** (in-kwīr'), vt. and vi. Ask; investigate. **[inquiry]**
**inquisition** (in-kwi-zish'un), n. Searching; judicial inquiry; ecclesiastical tribunal for punishing heretics.
**inroad** (in'rōd), n. Invasion.
**insane** (in-sān'), n. Not sound of mind. **[insanity]**
**insatiable** (in-sā'shi-a-bl), a. That cannot be satiated.
**inscribe** (in-skrīb'), vt. Write; engrave; address; dedicate. **[inscrip'tion]**
**inscrutable** (in-skrō'ta-bl), a. That cannot be understood.
**insect** (in'sekt), n. Small animal, with a body divided into sections. **[insectiv'orous]**
**insecure** (in-sē-kūr'), a. Not safe.
**insensate** (in-sen'sāt), a. Void of sense.
**insensible** (in-sen'si-bl), a. Not having feeling; unconscious.
**insert** (in-sert'), vt. Introduce; put in or among. **[inser'tion]**
**insert** (in'sert), n. Thing inserted.
**insidious** (in-sid'i-us), a. Treacherous.
**insignia** (in-sig'ni-a), n. pl. Badge or mark of office, rank or honor.
**insignificant** (in-sig-nif'i-kant), a. Unimportant.
**insincere** (in-sin-sēr'), a. Deceitful. **[insincerity]**
**insinuate** (in-sin'ū-āt), vt. Introduce artfully; hint.
**insipid** (in-sip'id), a. Tasteless; dull. **[insipid'ity]**
**insist** (in-sist'), vi. Dwell (on) in discourse; persist in pressing. **[insist'ence]**

**insnare** (in-snār'), vt. Entrap.
**insolent** (in'sō-lent), a. Haughty and insulting. **[in'solence]**
**insoluble** (in-sol'ū-bl), a. Not to be dissolved or solved.
**insolvent** (in-sol'vent), a. Not able to pay one's debts.
**insomnia** (in-som'ni-a), n. Sleeplessness.
**inspect** (in-spekt'), vt. Examine.
**inspire** (in-spīr'), vt. Breathe into; infuse into the mind by divine influence. **[inspira'tion]**
**install** (in-stal'), vt. Establish. **[installa'tion]**
**instead** (in-sted'), adv. In place (of.)
**instigate** (in'sti-gāt), vt. Incite.
**instill** (in-stil'), vt. Infuse slowly into the mind.
**instinct** (in'stingkt), n. Natural impulse.
**instinct** (in-stingkt'), a. Alive.
**institute** (in'sti-tūt), vt. Establish; appoint to office.
**instruct** (in-strukt'), vt. Inform; teach; order; direct. **[instruct'or]**
**instrument** (in'stro-ment), n. Tool; utensil; musical device; written contract.
**insubordinate** (in-sub-ar'din-at), a. Disobedient; mutinous.
**insufferable** (in-suf'er-a-bl), a. Unbearable.
**insular** (in'sū-lar), a. Belonging to, or like, an island.
**insulate** (in'sū-lāt), vt. Place in a detached situation; separate by a non-conductor.
**insult** (in'sult), n. Insolent attack.
**insuperable** (in-sū'per-a-bl), a. Insurmountable.
**insupportable** (in-sup-port'-

**insufferable** (a-bl), n. Unbearable; insufferable.
**insure** (in-shor'), vt. Make sure; secure against loss. [insur'ance]
**insurgent** (in-sur'jent), a. Rebellious. [insurrection]
**intact** (in-takt'), a. Uninjured; entire.
**integer** (in'te-jer), n. Whole.
**integrity**, n. Uprightness of character; probity.
**integument** (in-teg'yument), n. Any natural outer covering, as the skin of an animal.
**intellect** (in'tel-lect), n. The faculty of perception or thought; mind.
**intend** (in-tend'), vt. To set the mind upon as something to be done; purpose; design.
**intense** (in-tens'), a. Strained or exerted to a high degree; putting forth strenuous effort; extreme.
**intent** (in-tent'), a. Having the mind earnestly fixed; eager; earnest.
**intercede**, vi. To mediate between persons.
**intercept** (in-ter-sept'), vt. Stop and seize on its passage; obstruct.
**intercession** (in-ter-sesh'-un), n. An interceding or pleading for another.
**intercostal** (in-ter-kos'tal), a. Lying between the ribs.
**intercourse** (in'ter-kors), n. Mutual dealings or communication; communion.
**interdict** (in-ter-dikt'), vt. To forbid; to exclude from communion.
**interest** (in'ter-est), vt. To engage, as the attention; to awaken concern in; move; affect.
**interfere** (in-ter-fer'), vi. To interpose; to come in collision; to act reciprocally, said of waves, rays of light, &c.
**interim** (in'ter-im), n. The mean or intervening time.
**interior** (in-te'ri-ur), a. Internal; inland.
**interject** (in-ter-jekt'), vt. Throw between; insert. [interjec'tion]
**interlace** (in-ter-las'), vt. Lace together; entwine.
**interlard** (in-ter-lard'), vt. Insert between.
**interline** (in-ter-lin'), vt. Write between lines.
**interlude** (in'ter-lod), n. Piece of music between the acts of a drama, or verses of a hymn; entertainment between acts of a play.
**intermarry** (in-ter-mar'i), vi. Become connected by marriage, as two families or tribes.
**intermediate** (in-ter-me'di-at), a. In the middle; between; intervening.
**interment** (in-ter'ment), n. Burial.
**interminable** (in-ter'min-a-bl), a. Endless.
**intermission** (in-ter-mish'-un), n. Interval; pause; cessation.
**intermit** (in-ter-mit'), vt. Cause to cease for a time; interrupt. [intermit'tent]
**internal** (in-ter'nal), a. Interior; inward; inner.
**interpolate** (in-ter'po-lat), vt. Alter (a text) by inserting a spurious word or passage.
**interpose** (in-ter-poz'), vt. and vi. Place or come between; thrust in.
**interpret** (in-ter'pret), vt. Explain the meaning of. [interpreta'tion, inter'-preter]
**interrogate** (in-ter'o-gat), vt. Question. [interroga'tion]
**interrupt** (in-ter-rupt'), vt. Break in; stop; hinder.
**intersect** (in-ter-sekt'), vt. and vi. Cut or cross each other. [intersec'tion]

# INTERSPERSE 117 INVETERATE

**intersperse** (in-ter-spers'), vt. Scatter in between.
**interstate** (in'ter-stat), a. Pertaining to relations between states.
**interstice** (in-ter'stis), n. Crevice; chink. [**intersti'tial**]
**interval** (in'ter-val), n. Time between.
**intervene** (in-ter-ven'), vi. Come or be between; interpose. [**interven'tion**]
**interview** (in'ter-vu), n. Meeting; conference.
**intestate** (in-tes'tat), a. Without having made a valid will.
**intestine** (in-tes'tin), a. Contained in the animal body.
**inthrall** (in-thral'), vt. Enslave.
**intimate** (in'ti-mat), a. Innermost; familiar. [**in'timacy**]
**intimate** (in'ti-mat), vt. Hint; announce. [**intima'tion**]
**intimidate** (in-tim'i-dat), vt. Make timid. [**intimida'tion**]
**intolerable** (in-tol'er-a-bl), a. That which cannot be endured.
**intolerant** (in-tol'er-ant), a. Not enduring difference of opinion; illiberal. [**intol'erance**]
**intoxicate** (in-toks'i-kat), vt. Make drunk. [**intoxica'tion**]
**intractable** (in-trak'ta-bl), a. Unmanageable; obstinate.
**intransitive** (in-tran'si-tiv), a. Not taking a direct object.
**intrench** (in-trench'), vt. Dig a trench around; fortify.
**intrepid** (in-trep'id), a. Undaunted; brave. [**intrepid'ity**]
**intricate** (in'tri-kat), a. Involved; perplexing. [**in'tricacy**]

**intrigue** (in-treg'), n. Complex plot.
**intrinsic** (in-trin'sik), a. Inward; essential; inherent.
**introduce** (in-tro-dus'), vt. Formally made known. [**introduc'tion**]
**intrude** (in-trod'), vi. Enter uninvited or unwelcome. [**intru'sion, intru'sive**]
**intuition** (in-tu-ish'un), n. Direct cognition (without reasoning.)
**inundate** (in-un'dat), vt. Flow upon or over.
**inure** (in-ur'), vt. To accustom.
**invade** (in-vad'), vt. Enter as an enemy.
**invalid** (in'va-lid), a. Not strong; sick.
**invalid** (in-val'id), a. Without value; null. [**inval'idate**]
**invasion** (in-va'zhun), n. Act of invading.
**invective** (in-vek'tiv), n. Severe expression.
**inveigh** (in-va'), vt. Rail; revile.
**inveigle** (in-ve'gl), vt. Entice.
**invent** (in-vent'), Original contrivance.
**inventory** (in'ven-to'ri), n. A detailed account or schedule, as of the property of a deceased person.
**invert** (in-vert'), vt. To turn inside out or upside down.
**invest** (in-vest'), vt. To lay out (money) in purchase for permanent use; to clothe; dress; to endow, as with office; to beleaguer.
**investigate** (in-ves'ti-get), vt. To inquire into systematically.
**inveterate** (in-vet'er-et), a. Firmly established by long continuance; deep-rooted; confirmed in a particular character or habit.

**invidious** (in-vid'i-us), a. Unjustly discriminating; provoking.

**invigorate** (in-vig'or-et), vt. To give vigor and energy to; animate.

**invincible**, a. Not to be overcome; unconquerable.

**inviolate** (in-vai'o-let), a. Not violated; unprofaned; unbroken.

**invite** (in-vait'), v. To ask to do some act or go to some place; to allure; entice.

**invocation** (in'vo-ke'shun), n. The act of invoking; a judicial order; a form of prayer, as at the opening of a service.

**invoice** (in'vois'), n. A list sent to a purchaser, etc.; goods listed.

**invoke** (in-vok'), vt. To address, as in prayer; to call for, as in supplication.

**involuntary** (in-vol'un-te-ri), a. Contrary to one's will or wish; not under the control of the will.

**involve** (in-volv'), vt. To draw into entanglement; embroil; complicate.

**irascible** (ai-ras'i-bl), a. Prone to anger; choleric.

**irate** (ai-ret'), a. Moved to anger; wrathful.

**ire** (air), n. Strong resentment; wrath; anger.

**iridescent** (ir'i-des'ent), a. Exhibiting changing rainbow colors.

**iris**, n. The colored circle that surrounds the pupil of the eye; the rainbow; any similar iridescent appearance.

**irony** (ai'ro-ni), n. Ridicule under cover of praise or compliment; covert sarcasm or satire.

**irradiate**, vt. & vi. To make luminous; illuminate; shine.

**irrational** (ir-rash'un-al), a. Not possessed of or not exercising reasoning powers.

**irrefragable** (ir-ref'ra-ga-bl), a. That can not be refuted or disproved.

**irrelevant** (ir-rel'e-vant), a. Not relevant or apposite; impertinent.

**irrevocable** (ir-rev'o-ca-bl), a. Incapable of being revoked or repealed; unalterable.

**irrigate** (ir'i-gat), vt. Cause water to flow upon. [**irriga'tion**]

**irritable** (ir'i-ta-bl), a. Easily provoked.

**irritate** (ir'i-tat), vt. Make angry.

**irruption** (ir-rup'shun), n. Sudden invasion.

**island** (i'land), n. Land surrounded with water.

**isle** (il), n. Island. [**isl'et**]

**isolate** (i'so-lat), vt. Detach; insulate.

**isosceles** (i-sos'e-lez), a. Having two equal sides or legs, as a triangle.

**issue** (ish'u), vi. Go, flow, or come out.

**isthmus** (is'mus), n. Neck of land connecting two larger portions of land.

**itch** (ich), n. Eruptive disease of the skin; craving.

**iterate** (it'er-at), vt. Repeat.

**ivory** (i'vo-ri), n. Substance composing the tusks of the elephant, walrus, etc.

# J

**January** (jan'u-ar-i), n. First month of the year.

**Japanese** (jap-a-nez'), a. Of or pertaining to Japan or its inhabitants.

**jargon** (jar'gun), n. Con-

**fused**, unintelligible talk.

**jaundice** (jan'dis), n. Disease characterized by a yellowness of the eyes, skin, etc.

**jaunt** (jant), vi. Go from place to place.

**javelin** (jav'lin), n. Light spear.

**jealous** (jel'us), a. Suspicious of or incensed at, rivalry; exacting. [jealousy]

**jean** (jan) n. Twilled cotton cloth. pl. Garments made of jean.

**jeer** (jer), vt. and vi. Make sport of.

**Jehovah** (je-ho'va), n. Scriptural name for the Supreme Being.

**jelly** (jel'i), n. Anything gelatinous.

**jeopard** (jep'ard), n. Danger; peril; hazard.

**jerk** (jerk), vt. Throw with a quick effort.

**Jesuit** (jez'u-it), n. One of the Society of Jesus.

**Jew** (jo) n. Hebrew; Israelite.

**jewel** (jo'el), n. Precious stone.

**jocose** (jo-cos'), a. Of the nature of a joke.

**join**, vt. To set or bring together; connect; combine; to associate with; effect a junction with.

**jostle** (jos'l), vt. & vi. To push or crowd against.

**journal** (jur'nal) n. A daily record or register; diary; a newspaper; that part of a shaft or axle which rotates in or against a bearing.

**journey** (jur'ne), n. Passage from one place to another, especially by land.

**jovial** (jo'vi-al), a. Possessing or expressive of good-natured mirth or gaiety; jolly.

**jowl** (jol), n. The cheek or jaw.

**jubilant** (ju'bi-lant), a. Manifesting great joy; exultingly glad; expressing triumph.

**judge** (juj), vt. To come to a conclusion regarding; to decide authoritatively.

**judicature** (ju'di-ca-chur), n. The power of administering justice; the jurisdiction of a court; a court of justice.

**judicial** (ju-dish'al), a. Pertaining to the administration of justice.

**judicious** (ju-dish'us), a. According to sound judgment; discreet.

**juggle** (jug'l), vt and vi. Play tricks by sleight-of-hand; deceive.

**jugular** (jo'gu-lar), n. One of the two large veins of the neck.

**juice** (jos), n. Sap of vegetables.

**July** (jo-li'), n. Seventh month of year.

**jumble** (jum'bl), vt. and vi. Mix confusedly.

**junction** (jungk'shun), n. A joining; place or point of union.

**juncture** (jungk'tur), n. Joining; critical point of time.

**June** (jon), n. Sixth month of the year.

**jungle** (jung'gl), n. Dense tangle of vegetation.

**junior** (jo'ni-ur), a. Younger; lower in rank.

**junk** (jungk), n. Scraps of old iron, glass, etc.

**junket** (jung'ket), n. Picnic; excursion.

**junta** (jun'ta), n. Spanish grand council of State; a council.

**Jupiter** (jo'pi-ter), n. Largest of planets.

**jurisdiction** (jo-ris-dik'-shun), n. Judicial authority.

**jurist** (jo'rist), n. One versed in law.

**juror** (jo'rur), n. One who serves on a jury.
**justice** (jus'tis), n. Impartiality; retribution.
**justify** (jus'ti-fi), vt. Prove to be just or right; vindicate; exonerate.
**juvenile** (ju've-nil), a. Pertaining to youth.

# K

**kaleidoscope** (ka-li'do-skop), n. An optical instrument which exhibits objects in endless varieties of colors.
**keel** (kel), n. The lower timber of a ship.
**keen** (ken), a. Prompt; eager; sharp; piercing; severe; acute of mind; penetrating.
**keepsake** (kep'sak), n. A token of remembrance; gift.
**keg** (keg), n. A small cask.
**kennel** (ken'el), n. A cot for dogs; a pack of hounds; the hole of a fox, &c.
**kerchief** (ker'chif), n. Any loose cloth used in dress.
**kernel** (kern'el), n. The seed of a pulpy fruit; anything in a husk or shell; heart.
**kettle** (ket'l), n. A metal vessel for boiling water.
**kidnap** (kid'nap), vt. Carry off a human being clandestinely.
**kidney** (kid'ni), n. One of two glands which secrete the urine.
**kiln** (kil), n. Oven in which bricks are dried, lime burned, etc.
**kilt** (kilt), n. Short skirt worn by the Highlanders.
**kimono** (ki-mo'no), n. Japanese garment, somewhat like a lady's dressing gown.
**kindergarten** (kin'der-gar-ten), n. School for young children.
**kindle** (kin'dl), vt. Set fire to; excite.

**kindred** (kin'dred), n. pl. Relatives.
**kine** (kin), n. pl. Cows.
**kinetoscope** (ki-ne'to-skop), n. Apparatus for exhibiting pictures of objects in motion.
**kink** (kingk), n. Sharp bend in a rope, etc.
**kinsfolk** (kinz'fok), n. Relatives.
**kismet** (kis'met), n. Fate; destiny.
**knave**, n. A dishonest person; rogue.
**knead**, vt. To mix and work into a homogeneous mass.
**knee** (ni), n. The joint between the thigh and the leg in man.
**kneel**, vi. To make obeisance; support the body on the bent knee or knees.
**knell** (nel), vt. and vi. [Poet] To summon by a knell; sound a knell; give a sad or warning sound.
**knife** (naif), n. A blade, commonly set in a handle, for cutting.
**knight** (nait), n. In medieval times, a gentleman bred to the profession of arms; a title next below that of baronet.
**knit** (nit), vt. and vi. To form (a fabric or garment) by a series of interlocked loops of yarn or thread.
**knives**, n. Plural of knife.
**knob** (nob), n. A rounded protuberance, bunch, or boss; a rounded handle, as of a door.

**knock** (noc), vt. and vi. To give a blow to; strike a blow with; rap, as on a door, for admittance; collide or cause to collide.

**knoll** (nol), n. Round hillock; top or crown of a hill; mound; knob.

**knot** (not), n. Interlacement of parts of a cord.

**know** (no), vt. Be informed or assured of; recognize.

**knowledge** (nol'ej), n. Clear perception; instruction; enlightenment; skill.

**knuckle** (nuk'l), n. Projecting joint of the fingers.

**kodak** (ko'dak), n. Portable, photographic camera.

**Koran** (ko'ran or ko-ran'), n. Mohammedan Bible.

**kraal** (kral), n. Hottentot village or hut.

**kumiss** (ko'mis), n. Carbonated or fermented liquor made from milk.

# L

**label** (la'bel), n. Small slip of writing or printing affixed to anything to denote its contents, ownership, etc.

**labial** (la'bi-al), a. Pertaining to the lips; formed by the lips.

**labor** (la'bur), n. Toil; work. **[laboratory]**

**labyrinth** (lab'i-rinth), n. The internal ear; place of intricate windings; bewilderment.

**lace** (las), n. Fabric of fine thread.

**lacerate** (las'er-at), vt. Tear; wound.

**lachrymal** (lak'ri-mal), a. Pertaining to, or secreting, tears.

**lackey** (lak'i), n. Footman.

**laconic** (la-kon'ik), a. Expressing much in few words.

**lactation** (lak-ta'shun), n. The secretion of milk by mammary glands.

**lacteal** (lak'te-al), a. Pertaining to or resembling milk; conveying chyle.

**ladder** (lad'er), n. Frame with steps between two upright pieces.

**ladle** (la'dl), n. Large spoon.

**lagoon** (la-gon'), n. Shallow pond bordering on the sea.

**laid** (lad), pa. t. and pa. p. of **lay**.

**lain** (lan), pa. p. of **lie** (rest).

**lair** (lar), n. Den of a wild beast.

**laity** (la'i-ti), n. The people as distinct from the clergy.

**lam** (lam), vt. **[lam'ming, lammed]** Beat severely.

**lamb** (lam), n. Young of a sheep.

**lambent** (lam'bent), a. Moving about like a tongue; flickering.

**lambkin** (lam'kin), n. Little lamb.

**lament** (la-ment'), vi. and vt. Utter or feel grief; deplore. **[lamentable]**

**lamp** (lamp), n. Vessel for burning oil with a wick.

**lampoon** (lam-pon'), n. Personal satire.

**lance** (lans), n. Long spear.

**lancet** (lan'set), n. Surgical instrument for opening veins, etc.

**landscape** (land'skap), n. Aspect of a country.

**lane** (lan), n. Narrow road.

**language** (lang'gwaj), n. Speech or any method of expressing ideas.

**languid** (lang'gwid), a. Spiritless. [**lan'guor**]

**lank** (langk), a. Long and loosely built.

**lantern** (lant'ern), n. Case for holding and enclosing a light.

**lapel** (la-pel'), n. The part of a coat which laps over.

**lapidary** (lap'i-dar-i), n. A dealer in precious stones.

**lappet** (lap'et), n. A little lap or flap.

**lapse** (laps), v. To slip or glide; to fall to another.

**larboard** (lar'bord), n. Left side of a vessel, looking from the stern.

**larceny** (lar'se-ni), n. Theft.

**larder** (lar'der), n. A place where meats, etc., are kept.

**largely** (larj'li), ad. Extensively; abundantly.

**largess** (lar'jes), n. A gift or donation; liberality.

**lariat** (lar'i-at), n. A lasso.

**larva** (lar'va), n. An insect in a caterpillar or grub state.

**larynx** (lar'ingks), n. Upper part of the windpipe.

**lash** (lash), n. The flexible part of a whip; hair on eyelid.

**lass** (las), n. A young girl.

**lassitude** (las'si-tud), n. Languor; weakness; weariness.

**lasso** (las'so), n. A rope with a noose.

**latch** (lach), n. The fastening for a door.

**latchet** (lach'et), n. The string for fastening a shoe.

**latent** (la'tent), a. Concealed; hid; secret; unseen.

**lateral** (lat'er-al), a. Proceeding from or inclined to the side.

**lath** (lath), n. A strip of wood used in plastering, etc.

**lathe** (lath), n. A machine for turning and shaping articles of wood, iron, etc.

**lather** (lath'er), n. A foam from soap and water.

**latitude** (lat'i-tud), n. Breadth; freedom from restraint; distance from the equator.

**latitudinarian** (lat-i-tu-di-na'ri-an), n. One who departs from orthodoxy.

**latter** (lat'ter), a. Coming or existing after; the last.

**lattice** (lat'is), n. A framework of cross-bars.

**laudable** (la'da-bl), a. Praiseworthy; commendable.

**laudatory** (lad'a-tor-i), a. Containing praise.

**laugh** (laf), v. To manifest mirth.

**laughable** (laf'a-bl), a. That may excite laughter.

**launch** (lanch), vt. To send forth; cause to slide into water.

**launder** (lan'der), vt. To wash and iron.

**laundress** (lan'dres), n. A washerwoman.

**laundry** (lan'dri), n. Place where clothes are washed.

**laureate** (la're-at), a. Crowned with laurel. n. Title of honor conferred upon a poet.

**laurel** (lar'el), n. An evergreen tree or shrub.

**lava** (la'va), n. Melted rock ejected by a volcano.

**lavatory** (lav'a-to-ri), n. A place for washing.

**lave** (lav), vt. and vi. To wash; bathe.

**lavender** (lav'en-der), n. A fragrant plant; a pale purple color.

**laver** (lav'er), n. A vessel for washing.

**lavish** (lav'ish), vt. To expend profusely.

**lawful** (la'ful), a. Accord-

**LAWN**     123     **LEGEND**

**ing** to law; rightful; permitted by law.
**lawn** (lan), n. An open, grassy space; kind of fine linen.
**lawyer** (la'yer), n. One who is versed in, or practises, law.
**laxative** (laks'a-tiv), a. Having the power to relieve costiveness.
**layman** (la'man), n. One of the laity.
**lazar** (laz'ar, la'-), n. One covered with sores.
**lazaretto** (laz-a-ret'o), n. Hospital of persons with infectious diseases.
**lea** (le), n. A meadow.
**leach** (lech), vt. To wash out an alkali, as from ashes.
**lead** (led), vt. To go before, as a guide; conduct; precede. p. t. and p. p. **led.**
**league** (leg), n. An alliance; confederacy.
**league** (leg), n. A distance of three miles.
**leak** (lek), n. Crack or hole that allows fluid to pass.
**leakage** (lek'aj), n. A leaking; allowance for leaking.
**lean** (len), a. wanting flesh or fat; meagre.
**lean** (len), vi. To incline; bend.
**leap** (lep), vi. To spring; jump; rush forward.
**leap-year** (lep'yer), n. Every fourth year, in which February has 29 days.
**learn** (lern), vt. To acquire knowledge of, or skill in.
**lease** (les), n. A letting of lands or tenements; contract of such letting.
**leasehold** (les'hold), a. Held by a lease.
**leash** (lesh), n. Line for holding a hound; three of a kind.
**least** (lest), a. Smallest.

**leather** (leth'er), n. Prepared hide of an animal.
**leathery** (leth'er-i), a. Like leather; tough.
**leave** (lev), n. Permission; formal parting.
**leaven** (lev'n), a. Fermenting dough.
**leaves** (levz), n. pl. of **leaf.**
**lecture** (lekt'yur), n. A discourse; reading; formal reproof.
**led** (led), p.t. and p.p. of **lead.**
**ledge** (lej), n. A shelf; ridge.
**ledger** (lej'er), n. Principal book in bookkeeping.
**lee,** (le), n. Sheltered side; side which the wind reaches last. a. On the lee side.
**leech** (lech), n. A bloodsucking aquatic worm.
**leech** (lech), n. Edge of a sail.
**leek** (lek), n. A kind of onion.
**leer** (ler), n. An oblique glance.
**lees** (lez), n. pl. Dregs; sediment.
**leeward** (le'ward, lu'ard), adv. Toward the lee side.
**leeway** (le'wa), n. Drift of a ship to leeward of her course.
**legacy** (leg'a-si), n. A bequest.
**legal** (le'gal), a. According to law. [**legal'ity**]
**legality** (le-gal'i-ti), n. Lawfulness; observance of the letter of the law. Also **legalism.**
**legate** (leg'at), n. Ambassador of the pope; deputy.
**legatee** (leg-a-te'), n. One who has a legacy.
**legation** (le-ga'shun) n. An embassy; suit of an ambassador.
**legend** (lej'end), n. An ancient tale or tradition; any marvelous story;

motto or inscription. **[legendary]**

**legerdemain** (lej-er-de-man'), n. Sleight of hand.

**legibility** (lej-i-bil'i-ti), n. Quality or state of being easily read. Also **legibleness**

**legible** (lej'i-bl), a. That can be read.

**legion** (le'jun), n. A body of soldiers; a great number. **[legionary]**

**legislate** (lej'is-lat), vt. To make laws. **[legislation]**

**legislative** (lej'is-la-tiv), a. Passing laws. **[legislator, legislature]**

**legitimacy** (le-jit'i-ma-si), n. Lawfulness of birth; genuineness; logical sequence.

**leisure** (lezh'ur, le'zhur), n. Freedom from occupation; spare time; convenience.

**lemma** (lem'a), n. A previous or assumed proposition.

**lemon** (lem'un), n. An acid fruit of the orange sort; the tree that produces lemons. **[lemonade]**

**lemur** (le'mur), n. An animal of the monkey kind.

**lender** (len'der), n. One who lends money on interest.

**length** (length), n. Extent from end to end; extension; reach; long duration.

**lengthen** (leng'thn), vt. To make longer. vi. To grow longer.

**lengthy** (leng'thi), a. Somewhat long.

**leniency** (len'yen-si), n. Mildness; clemency.

**lenient** (len'yent), a. Softening; mild.

**lenitive** (len'i-tiv), a. Assuasive; easing; softening.

**lenity** (len'i-ti), n. Mildness; mercy.

**lens** (lenz), n. A glass by which rays of light are refracted and objects are magnified and diminished.

**lentil** (len'til), n. An annual plant allied to the bean.

**Leo** (le'o), n. The lion; fifth sign of the zodiac.

**leonine** (le'u-nin), a. Having the qualities of a lion.

**leopard** (lep'ard), n. A spotted beast of prey.

**leper** (lep'er), n. One infected with leprosy.

**leprosy** (lep'ru-si), n. A cutaneous disease.

**leprous** (lep'rus), a. Affected with leprosy.

**lesion** (le'zhun), n. Hurting; wound; injury.

**lessee** (le-se'), n. One to whom a lease is made.

**lessen** (les'n), vt. or i. To make or become less in any sense.

**lesser** (les'er), a. Smaller of two; inferior.

**lesson** (les'n), n. A portion of a book to be read or learned; a doctrine inculcated.

**lessor** (les-er'), n. He who grants a lease.

**lest** (lest), con. For fear that.

**lethal** (le'thal), a. Mortal; deadly.

**lethargic** (le-thar'jik), a. Sleepy; drowsy.

**lethargy** (leth'ar-ji), n. Morbid drowsiness; dullness.

**lethe** (le'the), n. Oblivion; death.

**lettered** (let'erd), a. Learned; docqueted; stamped with name or title.

**lettuce** (let'is), n. A garden plant eaten as a salad.

**Levant** (le-vant'), n. The

**eastern** countries along the Mediterranean.

**levee** (lev'e), n. Assembly of people on a morning or evening visit to a great personage; a bank of earth.

**level** (lev'el), a. Even; flat; plain.

**leveller** (lev'el-er), n. One who levels.

**lever** (le'ver), n. A bar, turning on a prop, for raising weights.

**leverage** (le'ver-ij), n. Mechanical power or purchase of a lever.

**leveret** (lev'er-et), n. A young hare.

**leviable** (lev'i-a-bl), a. That may be levied.

**leviathan** (le-vi'a-than), n. A large sea animal.

**Levite** (le'vit), n. One of the tribe of Levi.

**Leviticus** (le-vit'i-kus), n. The third book of the Old Testament scriptures.

**levity** (lev'i-ti), n. Want of weight; lightness; thoughtlessness; trifling disposition; frivolity.

**levy** (lev'i), To raise; collect. n. The act of raising money or troops; the amount or number raised.

**lewd** (lud), a. Given to the indulgence of lust; licentious; lascivious.

**lexical** (lek'si-kal), a. Pertaining to a lexicon.

**lexicographer** (lek-si-kog'-ra-fer), n. The writer of a dictionary.

**lexicography** (lek-si-kog'-ra-fi), n. The art of composing dictionaries.

**lexicon** (lek'si-kun), n. A dictionary.

**liability** (li-a-bil'i-ti), n. A state of being liable; responsibility; tendency.

**liar** (li'ar), n. One who utters falsehood.

**libation** (li-ba'shun), n. An offering of wine.

**libel** (li'bel), n. A defamatory writing; a lampoon. vt. To defame by writing.

**libeller** (li'bel-er), n. One who libels.

**libellous** (li'bel-us), a. Defamatory.

**liberal** (lib'e-ral), a. Free in giving; enlarged; candid.

**liberalise** (lib'e-ral'iz), vt. To free from narrow views.

**liberality** (lib-e-ral'i-ti), n. Generosity; largeness of mind; impartiality. [**liberation, liberator**]

**libertine** (lib'er-tin), n. A dissolute man. a. Licentious.

**libertinism** (lib'er-tin-izm), n. Licentiousness of doctrine or life.

**liberty** (lib'er-ti), n. Freedom; permission; immunity.

**libidinous** (li-bid'in-us), a. Lustful; lewd; licentious.

**Libra** (li'bra), n. The balance; seventh sign of the zodiac.

**librarian** (li-bra'ri-an), n. One who has charge of a library.

**librate** (li'brat), vt. or i. To balance; poise.

**libration** (li-bra'shun), n. Act of balancing.

**libretto** (li-bret'o), n. A book of the words of an opera.

**lice** (lis), pl. of louse.

**licence** (li'sens), n. Leave; grant of permission to practise or deal in; the document itself; excess or abuse of freedom.

**licentiate** (li-sen'shi-at), n. One who has a licence.

**licentious** (li-sen'shus), a. Loose in morals; dissolute.

**lichen** (li'ken), n. A cellular flowerless plant.
**lick** (lik), vt. To pass the tongue over.
**licorice** (lik'or-is), n. A plant with a sweetish root; extract prepared from its root.
**lie** (li), n. An intentional falsehood; deception.
**lie** (li), vi. To rest horizontally; lean; be situated; consist. p.t. **lay**. p.p. **lain**.
**lief** (lef), adv. Willingly.
**liege** (lej), a. Feudally subject; sovereign.
**lien** (len or le'en), n. Right in property of another to pay a claim.
**lieu** (lu), n. Place; stead.
**lieutenant** (lu-ten'ant), n. Officer next below a captain.
**ligament** (lig'a-ment), n. Anything that binds; band of tissue.
**ligation** (li-ga'shun), n. Bond.
**ligature** (lig'a-tur), n. Bandage; cord for tying blood vessels.
**lighter** (lit'er), n. Large boat used in unloading ships.
**lighthouse** (lit'hows), n. Structure with a light at the top to guide mariners.
**lightning** (lit'ning), n. Electric flash from the sky.
**lights** (lits), n. pl. Lungs of animals.
**lignite** (lig'nit), n. Coal retaining the texture of wood.
**lilac** (li'lak), n. Flowering shrub; pale purple.
**lily** (lil'i), n. Bulbous plant with showy flowers.
**limb** (lim), n. Jointed part in animals, as the leg, etc.
**limber** (lim'ber), a. Flexible; pliant.
**lime** (lim), n. Any slimy or gluey material; earth from limestone, used with sand to make mortar.
**lime** (lim) n. Kind of lemon tree and its fruit.
**limekiln** (lim'kil), n. Furnace in which limestone is burned.
**limit** (lim'it), n. Utmost extent.
**limp** (limp), a. Wanting stiffness; flexible; flaccid; weak.
**limpet** (lim'pet), n. Small shell-fish.
**limpid** (lim'pid), a. Clear; pure.
**linchpin** (linch'pin), n. Pin holding the wheel on the axle.
**linden** (lin'den), n. Tree with heart shaped leaves.
**lineage** (lin'e-aj), n. A race; descent.
**lineal** (lin'e-al), a. Composed of lines; being in a direct line.
**lineament** (lin'e-a-ment), n. Outline; feature.
**linear** (lin'e-er), a. Like a line. [**lineation**]
**linen** (lin'en), a. Made of flax or hemp.
**linendraper** (lin'en-drap-er), n. One who deals in linen.
**liner** (lin'er) n. A vessel of a regular line of packets.
**linger** (ling'ger), vi. To remain long; to delay.
**lingering** (ling'ger-ing), a. Slow; tardy.
**lingual** (ling'gwal), a. Pertaining to the tongue.
**linguist** (ling'gwist), n. One skilled in languages.
**liniment** (lin'e-ment), n. A soft ointment.
**link** (lingk), n. Part of a chain; torch.
**linnet** (lin'et), n. A small singing bird.
**lint** (lint), n. Soft scrapings of linen.
**lintel** (lin'tel), n. The upper part of a door-frame.
**lipogram** (lip'o-gram), n. A

writing in which a particular letter is omitted.
**lipped** (lipt), a. Having lips;
**liquefaction** (lik-we-fak'-shun), n. Act of melting.
**liquefiable** (lik'we-fi-a-bl), a. That may be melted.
**liquefier** (lik'we-fi-er), n. That which dissolves.
**liquescent** (le-kwes'ent), a. Dissolving.
**liquid** (lik'wid), a. That flows.
**liquidate** (lik'wid-at), vt. To adjust. **[liquidation]**
**liquor** (lik'er), n. A liquid; strong drink.
**liquorice** (lik'or-is), n. A sweet root from which the article called Spanish juice is extracted; also written licorice.
**listen** (lis'n), vi. To hear watchfully; to attend to.
**listless** (list'les), a. Heedless; indifferent.
**Litany** (lit'a-ne), n. A solemn form of supplication and prayer.
**literal** (lit'er-al), a. Word for word.
**literary** (lit'er-ar-e), a. Relating to literature.
**Literati** (lit-er-a'ti), n. pl. Men of letters.
**literature** (lit'er-a-tur), n. Acquaintance with books.
**lithe** (lith), a. Pliant; flexible; limber.
**litheness** (lith'nes), n. Flexibility.
**lithographic** (lith-o-graf'-ik), a. Pertaining to lithography.
**lithography** (le-thog'ra-fe), n. The art of tracing letters &c., on stone, and of transferring them to paper by impression.
**lithology** (le-thol'o-je), n. The natural history of stones.
**litigant** (lit'e-gant), n. One engaged in a lawsuit.

**litigate** (lit'e-gat), vi. or t. To contest by lawsuit. **[litigation]**
**litigious** (le-tij'e-us), a. Inclined to go to law.
**litter** (lit'er), vt. To bring forth; to strew with scraps.
**liturgical** (le-tur'jik-al), a. Pertaining to a liturgy.
**liturgy** (lit'ur-je), n. A formulary of prayers.
**livelihood** (liv'li-hud), n. Means of living.
**livelong** (liv'long), a. Lasting long.
**lively** (liv'li), a. Vigorous; brisk; vivid.
**live-oak** (liv'ok), n. An American tree with very durable wood.
**liver** (liv'er), n. One who lives; gland which secretes the bile.
**livery** (liv'er-i), n. Delivery of possessions; uniform worn by servants; keeping of horses for money.
**livid** (liv'id), n. Of a leaden or purplish color.
**lizard** (liz'ard), n. Genus of four-footed scaly reptiles.
**llama** (la'ma, lya'ma), n. S. American animal of the camel kind.
**loaf** (lof), n. Mass of bread. pl. **loaves.**
**loam** (lom), n. Rich, crumbly soil.
**loan** (lon), n. Act of lending; anything lent.
**loathe** (loth), vt. To abhor; to be disgusted with.
**loathsome** (loth'sum), a. Exciting abhorrence; detestable; disgusting.
**lobby** (lob'i), n. A waiting-room; passage.
**lobe** (lob), n. A rounded part or division.
**lobster** (lob'ster), n. Crustaceous marine animal with large claws and a tail.

**local** (lo'kal), a. Pertaining, or restricted, to a place.
**locality** (lo-kal'i-ti), n. State of being local; place.
**locate** (lo'kat), vt. To place; assign the place of. [**location**]
**loch** (lokh), n. Lake; arm of the sea.
**locket** (lok'et), n. Clasp; trinket containing a small picture, etc.
**locket** (lok'et), n. Small ornamental cases of gold or silver.
**locust** (lo'kust), n. Insect like the grasshopper; name of several trees.
**lode** (lod), n. Vein of metallic ore.
**lodge** (loj), n. A small house; a den; a meeting or club.
**lodger** (loj'er), n. One who hires a lodging. [**lodgment**]
**loft** (laft), n. A room near the roof.
**lofty** (laf'ti), a. High; proud; stately; haughty.
**logarithm** (log'a-rithm), n. A series of artificial numbers in arithmetical progression.
**log-book** (log'bok), n. Register of a ship's way.
**loggerhead** (log'er-hed), n. A dunce; a blockhead.
**logic** (loj'ik), n. The art of reasoning correctly. [**logician**]
**log-line** (log'lin), n. A line to measure a ship's speed.
**logwood** (log'wod), n. A dye wood.
**loin** (loin), n. The back of an animal; reins.
**loiter** (loi'ter), v. To linger; to saunter.
**loll** (lol), v. To lounge; to hang from the mouth.
**loneliness** (lon'li-nes), n. Want of company. [**lonesome**]

**longevity** (lan-jev'i-ti), n. Length of life; old age.
**longing** (lang'ing), n. An earnest desire; continual wish.
**longitude** (lan'ji-tud), n. Distance east or west.
**loom** (lom), n. A weaver's frame. v. To appear elevated.
**loon** (lon), n. A simple fellow; a fowl.
**loop** (lop), n. A noose or double in a rope or string.
**loose** (los), v. To untie or unbind; to release; to open.
**loquacious** (lo-kwa'shus), a. Talkative; garrulous.
**lore** (lor), n. Learning; instruction; erudition.
**lorn** (larn), a. Forsaken; lost; lonely.
**lose** (loz), v. To suffer loss; to miss; to let slip; to forfeit.
**loss** (las), n. Forfeiture; destruction, or ruin; waste.
**lotion** (lo'shun), n. A medicinal wash.
**lottery** (lot'er-i), n. A distribution of prizes and blanks by lot or chance.
**loud** (lowd), a. High sounding.
**lounge** (lownj), v. To spend time lazily.
**louse** (lows), n. An insect.
**lout** (lowt), n. An awkward person; a bumpkin.
**lovable** (luv'a-bl), a. Worthy of love; amiable.
**lowly** (lo'li), a. Humble; meek; mean. ad. Humbly; meekly.
**lowness** (lo'nes), n. Depression; dejection; meanness.
**loyal** (loi'al), a. Faithful to a prince, to plighted love, or duty. [**loyalist, loyally, loyalty**]
**lozenge** (loz'enj), n. A rhomb; a small cake of sugar.
**lubber** (lub'er), n. A heavy, idle fellow.

**lubricant** (loo'bri-kant), n. Any oily or greasy substance.

**lubricate** (loo'bri-kat), vt. To make slippery.

**lubricity** (loo-bris'i-ti), n. Smoothness; instability; lewdness.

**lucid** (loo'sid), a. Clear; transparent; easily understood; intellectually bright.

**lucidity** (loo-sid'it-i), n. Clearness of statement or exposition.

**lucifer** (loo'si-fer), n. The planet of Venus; Satan; a combustible match lighted by friction.

**luckily** (luk'i-li), ad. By good chance.

**lucky** (luk'i), a. Fortunate; successful by chance.

**lucrative** (loo'kra-tiv), a. Profitable; gainful.

**lucre** (loo'ker) n. Profit; gain.

**ludicrous** (loo'di-krus), a. Exciting laughter; funny; ridiculous.

**luff** (luf), n. The part toward the wind.

**luggage** (lug'ij), n. Baggage.

**lugubrious** (loo-gu'bri-us), a. Mournful.

**lukewarm** (look'wawrm), a. Moderately warm; indifferent.

**lull** (lul), vt. or i. To soothe; compose; subside. n. A season of calm.

**lullaby** (lul'a-bi), n. A song to quiet infants.

**lumbaginous** (lum-baj'i-nus), a. Pertaining to lumbago.

**lumbago** (lum-ba'go), n. A rheumatic pain in the small of the back.

**lumbar** (lum'bar), a. Pertaining to or near the loins.

**lumber** (lum'ber), n. Anything useless or cumbersome; rough timber. vt. To heap carelessly together. vi. To move heavily.

**luminary** (loo'mi-na-ri), n. Any body that gives light.

**luminous** (loo'mi-nus), a. Giving light; shining; clear; lucid.

**lumpish** (lum'pish), a. Heavy; dull.

**lumpy** (lum-pi), a. Full of lumps.

**lunacy** (loo'na-si), n. Mental derangement; madness in general.

**lunar** (loo'nar), a. Pertaining to the moon.

**lunarian** (loo-na'ri-an), n. Inhabitant of the moon.

**lunatic** (loo'na-tik), a. Affected with lunacy. n. A madman.

**lunch** (lunsh), n. Food taken between breakfast and dinner. Also **luncheon**.

**lunette** (loo-net'), n. A detached bastion; a kind of lens; a watch glass flattened in the centre.

**lunge** (lunj), n. A sudden push or thrust with a sword.

**lunular** (loo'nu-lar), a. Shaped like a new moon.

**lurch** (lurch), n. A sudden roll of a ship; deserted condition.

**lure** (lur), n. That which allures. vt. To entice.

**lurid** (lu'rid) a. Ghastly pale; gloomy; dismal.

**lurk** (lurk), vt. To lie in wait; lie close or out of sight.

**luscious** (lush'us), a. Sweet or rich, so as to cloy.

**lustful** (lust'fool), a. Having irregular or evil desires.

**lustily** (lus'ti-li), ad. Stoutly; boldly.

**lustral** (lus'tral), a. Used in purification.

**lustrate** (lus'trat), vt. To purify; survey.

**lustre** (lus'ter), n. Brightness; a kind of lamp.

**lustring** (lus'tring), n. A glossy silk.

**lustrous** (lus'trus), a. Bright; luminous; shining.

**lustrum** (lus'trum), n. A period of five years.

**lusty** (lus'ti), a. Vigorous; robust; stout; hearty.

**lute** (loot), n. Instrument of music.

**Lutheran** (loo'ther-an), a. Pertaining to Luther.

**luxate** (luk'sat), vt. To put out of joint; dislocate.

**luxuriance** (lug-zhoo'ri-ans) n. Rank growth; exuberance. [luxuriant, luxuriate]

**luxurious** (lug-zhoo'ri-us), a. Given to luxury; furnished with luxuries; enervating by pleasure.

**luxury** (luk'zhu-ri), n. Excess in eating, dress, or equipage, any expensive habit or article.

**lyceum** (li-se'um), n. A literary association, or the place where they meet.

**lye** (li), n. A solution of alkaline salt.

**lying** (li'ing), n. The vice of falsehood.

**lymph** (limf), n. A colourless animal fluid.

**lynch** (linsh), vt. To punish, as a criminal without legal trial.

**lynx** (lingks), n. A wild animal of the cat kind, noted for its keen sight.

**lyre** (lir), n. Instrument of music; a kind of harp, much used by the ancients.

# M

**macadamise** (ma-kad'am-iz), vt. To form or cover a road with small broken stones.

**macaroni** (mak-a-ro'ni), n. A finical fellow; a food made of wheaten paste formed into long slender tubes.

**mace** (mas), n. A club; a cue; an ensign of authority; a spice.

**macerate** (mas'e-rat), vt. To make lean.

**machiavelian** (mak-i-a-ve'li-an), a. Politically cunning; crafty.

**machinate** (mak'i-nat), vt. To plot; contrive. [machination]

**machine** (ma-shen'), n. An engine; any mechanical contrivance to produce or regulate force; a mere tool.

**machinist** (ma-she'nist), n. Constructor of machines.

**mackerel** (mak'e-rel), n. A small sea fish spotted with blue.

**maculate** (mak'u-lat), vt. To spot; defile.

**madam** (mad'am), n. Complimentary address to a woman.

**madden** (mad'n), vt. or i. To make or become mad.

**madonna** (ma-don'a), n. Virgin Mary.

**maelstrom** (mal'strom), n. Whirlpool.

**magazine** (mag-a-zen'), n. Store-house; gunpowder room.

**maggot** (mag'ut), n. Footless worm. [mag'goty]

**magi** (ma'ji), n. pl. Priestly caste in ancient Persia; sages.

**magic** (maj'ik), n. Sorcery. [magician]

**magistracy** (maj'is-tra-si), n. Office or body of magistrates.

**magnanimous** (mag-nan'-

imus), a. Nobly unselfish. [**magnanim'ity**]

**magnate** (mag'nat), n. Person of distinction.

**magnet** (mag'net), n. The loadstone which attracts iron. [**magnetism**]

**magnetize** (mag'net-iz), v. To render magnetic; to attract.

**magnific** (mag-nif'ik), a. Great; illustrious; noble. [**magnificence, magnificent**]

**magnifier** (mag'ni-fi-er), n. One who magnifies; a glass which increases the size of a body to the eye.

**magnify** (mag'ni-fi), v. To enlarge; to extol; to praise.

**magniloquence** (mag-nil'o-kwens), n. Lofty speech.

**magnitude** (mag'ni-tud), n. Extent; size.

**mahogany** (ma-hog'a-ne), n. A beautiful hard wood used in making furniture.

**maid** (mad), n. A young unmarried woman.

**maiden** (mad'n), n. A young unmarried woman.

**maidenly** (mad'n-le), a. Modest.

**maim** (mam), vt. To disable a limb.

**main** (man), a. Chief; principal.

**mainland** (man'land), n. A continent.

**mainly** (man'le), ad. Chiefly; principally.

**mainmast** (man'mast), n. The chief or middle mast.

**mainsail** (man'sal), n. The principal sail.

**maintain** (men-tan'), vt. To keep; to preserve; to support with food; to uphold.

**maintainable** (men-tan'a-bl), a. That may be maintained.

**maintenance** (man'ten-ans), n. Sustenance.

**maize** (maz), n. Indian corn.

**majestic** (ma-jes'tik), a. Stately; grand.

**majesty** (maj'es-te), n. Dignity; grandeur; a title.

**major** (ma'jer), a. Greater; elder. n. A military officer next above a captain.

**majordomo** (ma-jer-do'mo), n. A steward.

**majority** (ma-jor'e-te), n. The greater number; full age; rank of a major.

**maladministration** (mal-ad-min-is-tra'shun), n. Bad management of affairs.

**malady** (mal'a-de), n. Sickness; disease; bodily ailment.

**malapert** (mal'a-pert), a. Bold; saucy.

**malaria** (ma-la're-a), n. Noxious exhalation.

**malcontent** (mal'kon-tent), a. Discontented.

**male** (mal), a. Belonging to the male sex.

**malediction** (mal-e-dik'-shun), n. A curse.

**malefactor** (mal-e-fak'ter), n. Criminal; culprit.

**malevolent** (mal-ev'o-lent), a. Wishing evil; malignant. [**malevolence**]

**malfeasance** (mal-fe'zans, -fa'), n. Evil-doing.

**malformation** (mal-for-ma'shun), n. Defective formation; deformity.

**malice** (mal'is), n. Ill-will; spite. [**mali'cious**]

**malign** (ma-lin'), a. Malicious; unfavorable.

**malignant** (ma-lig'nant), a. Malicious; bitterly hostile; dangerous to life. [**malignity**]

**malinger** (ma-ling'ger), vi. To feign inability or sickness. [**malingerer**]

**malison** (mal'i-zon), n. A curse.

**mall** (mal), n. A heavy wooden hammer; a beetle.

**mall** (mal, mel), n. A public walk.

**mallard** (mal'ard), n. A drake; species of waterfowl.

**malleable** (mal'e-a-bl), a. That may be extended by

hammering. **[malleabil'ity]**
**mallet** (mal'et), n. A wooden hammer.
**mallow** (mal'o), n. A plant with downy leaves.
**malodorous** (mal-o'dor-us), a. Having an offensive odor.
**malpractice** (mal-prak'tis), n. Improper or criminal practice.
**malt** (malt), n. Grain partially germinated, for use in brewing.
**maltreat** (mal-tret'), vt. To treat ill; abuse. **[maltreatment]**
**malversation** (mal-ver-sa'-shun), n. Evil conduct; corruption in office.
**mama, mamma** (ma-ma'), n. Mother; a word used by children.
**mammal** (mam'al), n. An animal that suckles its young.
**mammalia** (ma-ma'li-a), n. pl. The whole class of mammals.
**mammon** (mam'on), n. Riches.
**mammoth** (mam'oth), n. An extinct species of elephant.
**manacle** (man'a-kl), n. A shackle for the wrist.
**manage** (man'aj), vt. To conduct; control; contrive. vi. To conduct affairs; contrive. **[manageable, management]**
**manatee** (man-a-te'), n. A sea-cow.
**mandamus** (man-da'mus), n. A writ to compel performance.
**mandarin** (man'da-ren), n. A Chinese governor.
**mandate** (man'dat), n. An order; official command. **[mandatory]**
**mandible** (man'di-bl), n. A jaw.
**mandolin** (man'do-lin), n. A kind of small lute strung with wires.
**mane** (man), n. Long hair on the neck of a quadruped.
**manes** (ma'nez), n. Departed souls.
**manganese** (man'gan-es), n. A grayish white metal.
**mange** (manj), n. The itch on animals.
**manger** (man'jer), n. Eating-trough for horses and cattle.
**mangle** (mang'gl), vt. To cut to pieces; tear in cutting; mutilate; to smooth with a mangle.
**mangrove** (man'grov), n. A tropical tree growing in swamps.
**mania** (ma'ni-a), n. Madness; inordinate fondness.
**maniac** (ma'ni-ak), n. A madman. **[maniacal]**
**manifest** (man'i-fest), a. Apparent; evident. **[manifestation]**
**manifesto** (man-i-fest'o), n. Public declaration of intentions.
**manifold** (man'i-fold), a. Many; various.
**manikin** (man'i-kin), n. A dwarf; model of the human body.
**manipulate** (man-ip'yu-lat), vt. To handle; work with the hands. **[manipula'tion]**
**manly** (man'li), a. Like, or befitting, a man; courageous; noble.
**manna** (man'a), n. Food miraculously supplied to the Hebrews; sweetish excretion from various trees.
**manner** (man'er), n. Mode; style; custom; in pl. behavior.
**mannerism** (man'er-izm), n. Peculiar, artificial mode or style.
**manœuvre** (ma-nu'ver), n. Stratagem; device; adroit military movement.
**manor** (man'or), n. Landed estate of a nobleman; domain. **[mano'rial]**
**manse** (mans), n. A parsonage-house.

**mansion** (man'shun), n. Large dwelling-house.

**manslaughter** (man'sla'ter), n. Killing of a person without premeditation.

**mantel** (man'tl), **mantelpiece** n. Shelf above a fireplace.

**mantilla** (man-til'a), n. A woman's light cloak.

**mantis** (man'tis), n. An insect allied to the grasshopper.

**mantle** (man'tl), n. A loose garment; cloak.

**manual** (man'u-al), a. Performed by the hand. n. A small book; keyboard of an organ.

**manufactory** (man-u-fak'tur-i), n. A place where goods are made.

**manufacture** (man-u-fak'tur), n. Anything made by the hand. [**manufacturer**]

**manumission** (man-u-mish'un), n. Act of freeing slaves.

**manumit** (man-u-mit'), vt. To release from slavery.

**manure** (ma-nur'), n. Anything that fertilises land.

**manx** (mangks), a. Denoting the Isle of Man, its people, or its language.

**manuscript** (man'u-skript), n. Any writing done by hand.

**maori** (mou'ri), n. A native of New Zealand.

**maple** (ma'pl), n. A tree of several species.

**mar** (mar), vt. To hurt; impair; disfigure.

**maraud** (ma-rad'), vi. To rove in quest of plunder. [**marauder**]

**marble** (mar'bl), n. Kind of fine hard limestone; anything made of marble; small ball used as a plaything.

**March** (march), n. Third month of the year.

**march** (march), vi. To move in order, as soldiers.

**marchioness** (mar'shun-es), n. fem. of marquis.

**mare** (mar), n. Female of the horse.

**margin** (mar'jin), n. Edge; border. a. marginal.

**marguerite** (mar-ge-ret'), n. A daisy.

**marine** (ma-ren'), a. Pertaining to the sea. [**mariner**]

**marital** (mar'i-tal), a. Pertaining to a husband.

**maritime** (mar'i-tim), a. Pertaining to the sea or naval affairs; near the sea.

**marketable** (mar'ket-a-bl), a. Fit for sale.

**marl** (marl), n. Decomposed fossils used for manure

**marline-spike** (mar'lin-spik), n. Pointed iron tool for splicing, etc.

**marmalade** (mar'ma-lad), n. A jam or preserve of fruit boiled with sugar.

**marmoset** (mar-mo-zet'), n. A small squirrel-like species of monkey.

**marmot** (mar'mot), n. A burrowing rodent animal.

**maroon** (ma-roon'), a. Brownish crimson.

**maroon** (ma-roon'), vt. To put on shore on a desolate island.

**maroon** (ma-roon'), n. Fugitive slave in the mountains of the West Indies.

**marque** (mark), n. License to capture an enemy's ships.

**marquee** (mar-ke'), n. A large field-tent.

**marquetry** (mar'ket-ri), n. Inlaid work on wood.

**marquis** (mar'kwis), n. Nobleman next in rank below a duke. fem. **marchioness**.

**marquisate** (mar'kwiz-at), n. Rank or lordship of a marquis.

**marriageable** (mar'ij-a-bl), a. Of a suitable age for marrying.

**marrow** (mar'o), n. Fatty substance in a bone.

**marry** (mar'i), vt. To take as a husband or wife; unite in matrimony.

**marsh** (marsh), n. A swamp; low, wet ground.

**marshal** (mar'shal), n. A chief military commander; a civil officer; master of ceremonies.

**marsupial** (mar-su'pi-al), a. Having a pouch to shelter the young, as the opossum.

**mart** (mart), n. A market; place of trade.

**marten** (mart'en), n. A species of weasel.

**martial** (mar'shal), a. War-like; brave.

**martin** (mart'in), n. A bird of the swallow kind.

**martinet** (mar-ti-net'), n. A rigid disciplinarian.

**martingale** (mart'in-gal), n. Strap to hold down the head of a horse; spar under a ship's bowsprit.

**martlet** (mart'let), n. A martin.

**martyr** (mar'ter), n. One who suffers death for his belief; a sufferer. [**martyrdom**]

**marvel** (mar'vel), n. A wonder. [**marvellous, marvelous**]

**masculine** (mas'kyu-lin), a. Male; manly; like a man.

**masonic** (ma-son'ik), a. Relating to freemasonry.

**masonry** (ma'sn-ri), n. Trade of a mason; stone work; freemasonry.

**masquerade** (mas-ker-ad'), n. An assembly of persons in disguise.

**mass** (mas), n. A body; a lump; an assemblage; the celebration of the Eucharist in the Roman Catholic Church.

**massacre** (mas'a-ker), n. Great slaughter.

**massage** (ma-sazh'), n. Treatment by manipulation of surface and of muscles.

**masseur** (mas-ser), n. Male who practices massage; fem. **masseuse** (mas-sez).

**massive** (mas'siv), a. Bulky; solid; ponderous; weighty.

**mast** (mast), n. The elevated beam of a vessel which supports the yards, sails and rigging; fruit of beech and oak.

**masterly** (mas'ter-li), n. Superiority over; victory.

**masticate** (mas'ti-kat), v. To chew, as food. [**mastication**]

**mastiff** (mas'tif), n. A large, strong species of dog.

**matadore** (mat-a-dor), n. A bull-fighter.

**match** (mach), n. A game; a contest; an equal; marriage; something to take fire.

**material** (ma-te'ri-al), a. Consisting of matter; essential.

**maternal** (ma-ter'nal), a. Belonging to a mother. [**maternity**]

**mathematic** (math-e-mat'ik), **mathematical**, a. Pertaining to or done by mathematics; very accurate. [**mathematician**]

**matin** (mat'in), a. Used in the morning.

**matinee** (mat-i-na'), n. Entertainment in the afternoon.

**matriculate** (ma-trik'u-lat), vt. and vi. Admit or be admitted to membership, esp. in a college. [**matricula'tion**]

**matrimony** (mat'ri-mon-i), n. Union of husband and wife. [**matrimo'nial**]

**matrix** (ma'triks or mat'-riks), n. pl. **matrices**. A mold or die.

**matron** (ma'trun), n. Married, elderly, or motherly woman.

**matter** (mat'er), n. Substance; subject; type set.

**mattock** (mat'uk), n. Kind

**of** pick-axe with broad ends.

**mattress** (mat'res), n. Quilted bed stuffed with horsehair, etc.

**maturate** (mat'u-rat), vt. Promote the suppuration or maturity of.

**mature** (ma-tur'), a. Fully developed; ripe. [**maturity**]

**matutinal** (mat-u-ti'nal), a. Pertaining to the morning; early.

**maudlin** (mad'lin), a. Weeping; silly; drunken.

**maul, mall** (mal), n. Heavy wooden hammer.

**mausoleum** (ma-so-le'um), n. Magnificent tomb.

**mauve** (mov), n. Delicate purple, lilac or violet color.

**maw** (ma), n. Stomach; craw.

**mawkish** (mak'ish), a. Disgusting.

**maxillar** (maks'il-ar), **maxillary**, a. Pertaining to the jaw.

**maxim** (maks'im), n. Moral truth.

**maximum** (maks'i-mum), a. Greatest.

**mayhem** (ma'hem), n. Crime of violently crippling a person.

**mayonnaise** (ma-on-az'), n. A sauce of eggs beaten up with salad oil; a dish dressed with this sauce.

**mayor** (ma'or), n. Chief magistrate of a city or borough. [**mayoralty**]

**maze** (maz), n. A labyrinth; perplexity.

**mazurka** (ma-zur'ka), n. A Polish dance or the music for it.

**mead** (med), n. Beverage of honey and water fermented.

**mead** (med), n. A meadow.

**meagre** (me'ger), a. Lean; poor; scanty.

**meal** (mel), n. Grain ground but not bolted.

**meal** (mel), n. Food taken at one time; a repast.

**mean** (men), a. Middle; average; low; humble; base; sordid. [**meanness**]

**mean** (men), vt. To intend; signify.

**meander** (me-an'der), n. A winding course.

**meaning** (men'ing), n. Intention; signification.

**means** (menz), n. pl. Instrument; income; estate.

**meantime** (men'tim), **meanwhile** (men'whil), adv. In the intervening time.

**measles** (mez'lz), n. An eruptive disease.

**measurable** (mezh'ur-a-bl), a. That may be measured; moderate.

**measure** (mezh'ur), n. Expression, or standard, of extent; extent; stated quantity; degree; moderation; metre; musical time; means to an end. [**measurement**]

**meat** (met), n. Food; flesh for food.

**mechanic** (me-kan'ik), n. An artisan. [**mechanician**]

**medal** (med'al), n. Piece of metal like a coin, bearing a device.

**medallion** (me-dal'yun), n. Large medal; circular tablet with figures.

**medallist** (medal-ist), n. One skilled in medals; one who has gained a medal.

**meddle** (med'l), vi. To interfere; have to do.

**mediæval, medieval** (me-die'val), a. Pertaining to the middle ages.

**medial** (me'di-al), a. Middle; noting a mean.

**mediate** (me'di-at), vi. To interpose amicably.

**mediator** (me'di-a-tor), n. One who mediates; intercessor.

**medical** (med'i-kal), a. Pertaining to medicine or healing.

**medicate** (med'i-kat), vt. To treat with medicine;

render medicinal. [**medicine**]

**mediocrity** (me-di-ok'ri-ti), n. A middle state or condition.

**meditate** (med'i-tat), vt. and vi. To consider thoughtfully; to purpose. [**meditation**]

**medium** (me'di-um), n. Middle place or degree; anything which intervenes or transmits; means; substance in which a body exists. pl. **media, mediums**.

**medley** (med'li), n. Confused mixture; miscellany.

**medullar** (me-dul'ar), a. Of, or resembling, marrow or pith.

**meed** (med), n. A reward; recompense.

**meekly** (mek'li), ad. Mildly; softly.

**meerschaum** (mer'shawm), n. Sea-scum; a mineral; a kind of tobacco-pipe.

**meeting** (me'ting), n. An assembly; an interview.

**melancholy** (mel'an-kol-i), a. Dejected. n. Dejection of spirits.

**melee** (ma-la'), n. A confused fight; scuffle.

**meliorate** (mel'yu-rat), vt. To make better. [**melioration**]

**melliferous** (me-lif'e-rus), a. Producing honey. [**mellifluous**]

**mellow** (mel'o), a. Soft with ripeness.

**melodeon** (me-lo'de-un), n. An organ with metallic reeds.

**melodious** (me-lo'di-us), a. Sounding sweetly; harmonious.

**melody** (mel'u-di), n. An agreeable succession of sounds; air; tune.

**melon** (mel'un), n. A plant and its edible fruit.

**member** (mem'ber), n. A limb of the body; one of a society or legislature.

**membrane** (mem'bran), n. A thin animal or vegetable tissue which covers the organs or parts.

**memento** (me-men'to), n. That which reminds. pl. **mementoes**.

**memoir** (mem'wor, mem'oir), n. A written account of personal recollections or the transactions of a society; short sketch.

**memorabilia** (mem-u-ra-bil'i-a), n. pl. Things to be remembered.

**memorable** (mem'u-ra-bl), a. Worthy of remembrance.

**memorandum** (mem-u-ran'dum), n. A note to help the memory. pl. **memoranda**.

**memorial** (me-mo'ri-al), a. Preserving remembrance.

**memorialise** (me-mo'ri-al-iz) vt. To present a memorial to. [**memorialist**]

**memorise** (mem'u-riz), vt. To cause to be remembered.

**memory** (mem'u-ri), n. The faculty by which ideas are retained in the mind; recollection.

**menace** (men'as), vt. To threaten. n. A threat.

**menacingly** (men'as-ing-li), ad. In a threatening way.

**menage** (me-nazh'), n. Housekeeping; a household; training of horses.

**menagerie** (me-naj'e-ri), n. A collection of wild or exotic animals.

**mendacious** (men-da'shus), a. Given to deception; lying; false. [**mendacity**]

**mender** (men'der), n. One who repairs.

**mendicant** (men'di-kant), n. A beggar.

**mendicity** (men-dis'i-ti), n. State of beggary; life of a beggar.

**menial** (men'yal), a. Ser-

vile; mean. n. An inferior servant; a mean-spirited fellow.
**menstrual** (men'stroo-al), a. Monthly.
**mensurable** (men'shu-ra-bl), a. Measurable. [**mensuration**]
**mental** (men'tal), a. Belonging to the mind.
**mention** (men'shun), n. Notice; remark. [**mentionable**]
**mentor** (men'ter), n. A wise adviser or monitor.
**menu** (men'u), n. A bill of fare.
**mephitis** (me-fi'tis), n. A poisonous exhalation arising from the ground or from decaying animal or vegetable matter.
**mercantile** (mer'kan-til), a. Commercial.
**mercenary** (mer'se-nar-i), a. That may be hired; greedy of gain; venal.
**mercer** (mer'ser), n. One who deals in silks.
**merchandise** (mer'chan-diz), n. Goods for sale; trade. [**merchant**]
**merciful** (mer'si-fool), a. Compassionate; forgiving; tender.
**mercurial** (mer-ku'ri-al), a. Composed of quicksilver; spirited; active. [**mercury**]
**meretricious** (mer-e-trish'-us), a. Lewd; gaudy, showy, and deceitful.
**merge** (merj), vt. or i. To immerse; be lost in.
**meridian** (me-rid'i-an), n. Noon; highest point; great circle passing through the poles.
**meridional** (me-rid'i-on-al), a. Southern.
**merino** (me-re'no), n. Variety of sheep with very fine wool; fabric made of this wool.
**merit** (mer'it), n. Desert; worth. [**meritorious**]
**mermaid** (mer'mad), n. A fabulous creature, part woman and part fish. masc. **merman**.
**merriment** (mer'i-ment), n. Mirth; hilarity.
**merry** (mer'i), a. Gay; sportive; lively.
**merry-andrew** (mer-i-an'-dru), n. A buffoon.
**mesentery** (mes'en-ter-i), n. Membrane attached to the intestines.
**mesh** (mesh), n. Opening between the threads of a net.
**mesmerism** (mez'mer-izm), n. A system which connects animal life with a supposed magnetic fluid. a. **mesmer'ic**.
**message** (mes'aj), n. Communication; errand.
**messenger** (mes'en-jer), n. One who bears a message.
**Messiah** (mes-si'a), n. The Anointed; Christ.
**messmate** (mes'mat), n. A companion at a mess.
**messuage** (mes'waj), n. House with adjoining grounds.
**metal** (met'al), n. A simple, fixed, opaque body, fusible by heat. [**metal'lic**]
**metalliferous** (met-al-lif'-er-us), a. Producing metal. [**metallurgy**]
**metamorphosis** (met-a-morf'o-sis), n. Transformation.
**metaphor** (met'a-for), n. A trope; giving one object the sense of another.
**metaphysician** (met-a-fi-zish'an), n. One versed in metaphysics. [**metaphysics**]
**meteor** (me'te-or), n. A luminous or opaque body in the atmosphere. [**meteorolite**]
**meter, metre** (me'ter), Measure of 39.37 inches.
**method** (meth'od), n. Orderly procedure; manner;

system. [**method'ic, method'ical**]

**Methodist** (meth'od-ist), n. Member of a religious denomination founded by John Wesley.

**metonymy** (me-ton'i-mi), n. Figure of speech in which one word is put for another.

**metre** (me'ter), n. Poetical arrangement of syllables; verse. [**met'rical**]

**metric system** (met'rik sis'tem), n. A decimal system of weights and measures, founded on the meter as the standard unit.

**metronome** (met'ro-nom), n. Instrument for measuring musical time.

**metropolis** (me-trop'o-lis), n. Chief city; capital. [**metropol'itan**]

**mezzanine** (mez'an-in), n. In arch. a low storey between high storeys.

**mezzotint** (mez'o-tint), **mezzotinto** (med-zo-tin'to, met-), n. Kind of engraving on copper.

**miasm** (mi'azm), **miasma** (mi-az'ma), n. Noxious effluvia.

**mica** (mi'ka), n. A mineral which cleaves into thin transparent plates.

**Michaelmas** (mik'l-mas), n. The feast of St. Michael. September 29th.

**microbe** (mi'krob), n. A microscopic organism.

**microcosm** (mi'kro-kozm, mik'-), n. A little world; man.

**micrometer** (mi-krom'e-ter), n. Instrument for measuring very small dimensions.

**microphone** (mi'kro-fon), n. Instrument for rendering faint sounds audible.

**microscope** (mi'kro-skop), n. Optical instrument for viewing very small objects.

**middling** (mid'ling), a. Of moderate size, quality, degree, etc.

**midge** (mij), n. A small fly; gnat.

**midget** (mij'et), n. Very small creature.

**midland** (mid'land), a. Inland.

**midnight** (mid'nit), n. Twelve o'clock at night.

**midrib** (mid'rib), n. Middle rib of a leaf.

**midriff** (mid'rif), n. Diaphragm.

**mien** (men), n. Appearance, esp. of the face.

**miff** (mif), vt. Displease; offend.

**migrate** (mi'grat), vi. Remove from one country to another. [**migra'tion, mi'gratory**]

**mikado** (mi-ka'do), n. Title of the Emperor of Japan.

**mildew** (mil'du), n. Fungi on plants.

**mile** (mil), n. 1760 yards.

**militant** (mil'i-tant), a. Fighting.

**military** (mil'i-tar-i), a. Pertaining to soldiers. [**mil'itarism**]

**militia** (mi-lish'a), n. Citizens enrolled and drilled as soldiers.

**millennium** (mil-len'i-um), n. Thousand years during which, as some believe, Christ will reign on earth.

**milleped** (mil'e-ped), n. Worm with an immense number of legs.

**miller** (mil'er), n. One who runs a mill; kind of moth.

**milliard** (mil'yard), n. Thousand millions.

**milliner** (mil'in-er), n. One who makes head-dresses for women. [**millinery**]

**million** (mil'yun), n. Thousand thousands (1,000,000). [**millionaire**]

**millrace** (mil'ras), n. Current of water that turns a mill wheel.

**millstone** (mil'ston), n. Stone used in a mill for grinding grain.

**millwright** (mil'rit), n. One who builds and repairs mills.

**milt** (milt), n. Spleen.

**mimic** (mim'ik), a. Consisting of ludicrous imitation.

**minaret** (min'a-ret), n. Turret on a Mohammedan mosque.

**mince** (mins), vt. Chop fine; pronounce only partly.

**mincemeat**, n. Mixture of chopped meat, suet, fruit, etc., used for pie.

**mineral** (min'er-al), n. Inorganic substance, neither animal nor vegetable.

**mingle** (ming'gl), vt. and vi. Mix.

**miniature** (min'i-a-tur), n. Painting on small scale.

**minim** (min'im), n. Smallest liquid measure, =1/60 dram. [min'imize, min'imum]

**minion** (min'yun), n. Servile favorite; size of type between nonpareil and brevier (7-point).

**minister** (min'is-ter), n. Clergyman; one intrusted with the management of state affairs.

**ministration** (min-is-tra'shun), n. Office of a minister; agency; act of ministering.

**ministrative** (min'is-trativ), a. Affording service.

**mink** (mingk), n. A small animal with valuable fur.

**minor** (mi'nur), n. A person under age of twenty-one. [minority]

**minster** (min'ster), n. A monastery or cathedral.

**minstrel** (min'strel), n. A singer and player of music; a reciter of lyric poetry. [minstrelsy]

**mint** (mint), n. An aromatic herb.

**mintage** (mint'aj), n. That which is coined or stamped.

**minuend** (min'u-end), n. The number from which another is to be subtracted.

**minuet** (min'u-et), n. A graceful dance.

**minus** (mi'nus), a. An algebraic term denoting subtraction; less.

**minute** (min'it), n. The sixtieth part of an hour; short note or sketch.

**minute** (mi-nut'), a. Very small; of little consequence.

**minx** (mingks), n. A pert, wanton girl.

**miracle** (mir'a-kl), n. An act or event beyond human power. [miraculous]

**mirage** (me-razh'), n. An optical illusion, presenting an image of water in sandy deserts, or elevating objects in the air.

**mire** (mir), n. Soft, wet earth; mud.

**mirror** (mir'er), n. A looking-glass.

**mirth** (merth), n. Noisy gaiety.

**miry** (mir'e), a. Full of mire.

**misanthropic** (mis-anthrop'ik), a. Hating mankind. [misanthropist]

**miscellaneous** mis-sel-la'ne-us), a. Mixed; consisting of several kinds. [mis'cellany]

**mischief** (mis'chief), n. Evil; damage; disposition to do harm. [mischievous]

**misconceive** (mis-kon-sev'), vt. Conceive wrongly; mistake. [misconcep'tion]

**misconstrue** (mis-kon'stro), vt. Construe or interpret wrongly. [misconstruc'tion]

**miscreant** (mis'kre-ant), n. A vile, unprincipled wretch.

**misdeed** (mis-ded'), n. An evil action; fault; crime.

**misdemeanor** (mis-de-me′-nur), n. Bad conduct.

**miser** (mi′zer), n. An extremely covetous person.

**miserable** (miz′er-a-bl), a. Wretched; very unhappy.

**miserly** (mi′zer-li), a. Very covetous; sordid; niggardly.

**misery** (miz′er-i), n. Great unhappiness; distress; calamity.

**misform** (mis-farm′), v. To make of an ill form.

**misfortune** (mis-far′tun), n. Adversity; disaster; calamity.

**misgovern** (mis-guv′ern), v. To govern ill. [**misgovernment**]

**misguidance** (mis-gid′ans), n. False direction.

**misinterpret** (mis-in-ter′pret), v. To understand or explain in a wrong sense.

**misle** (miz′l), v. To rain in very fine drops.

**misnomer** (mis-no′mer), n. A wrong name; a misnaming.

**mispronounce** (mis-pronowns′), v. To utter words incorrectly. [**mispronunciation**]

**missile** (mis′il), n. A weapon to be thrown.

**mission** (mish′un), n. Act of sending; persons sent on certain duties, esp. to propagate religion; embassy; appointed duty. [**missionary**]

**missive** (mis′iv), a. Sent; to be sent or thrown.

**mistake** (mis-tak′), vt. To take in error; understand wrongly. [**mistaken**]

**mistletoe** (miz′l-to), n. A parasitic evergreen plant.

**mistress** (mis′tres), n. A woman in authority; female head or ruler; woman skilled in anything; title of address to a married woman (usually written **Mrs.**).

**mistrust** (mis-trust′), n. Want of confidence.

**misty** (mist′i), a. Full of mist; dim; obscure.

**mite** (mit), n. Anything very small; particle; a minute insect.

**mitigate** (mit′i-gat), vt. To lessen; soften; alleviate. [**mitiga′tion**]

**mitre** (mi′ter), n. A bishop's crown; junction of mouldings with an angle of 45°.

**mitten** (mit′n), n. A glove without fingers, or without separate fingers.

**mixture** (miks′tyur), n. Act of mixing; mingled mass.

**mnemonic** (ne-mon′ik), a. Assisting the memory. [**mnemonics**]

**moan** (mon), vi. To make a low sound of grief or pain.

**moat** (mot), n. Trench round a castle, etc.

**mobile** (mo′bil), a. That can be moved.

**moccasin** (mok′a-sin), n. Indian shoe of soft leather; venomous American snake.

**mock** (mok), vt. To deride; mimic; frustrate; deceive. [**mockery**]

**model** (mod′el), n. Pattern; copy.

**moderate** (mod′er-at), vt. To lessen in intensity; repress.

**moderator** (mod′er-a-tor), n. One who presides at a meeting.

**modern** (mod′ern), a. Of recent time; not ancient.

**modest** (mod′est), a. Diffident; chaste; not forward; moderate. [**modesty**]

**modicum** (mod′i-kum), n. A small portion.

**modify** (mod′i-fi), vt. To change the form of. [**modifica′tion**]

**modulate** (mod′yu-lat), vt. To regulate; vary, as

**sounds**; in mus. to change the key. [**modula'tion**]

**Mohammedan** (mo-ham'e-dan), a. Pertaining to, or holding, the religion of Mohammed.

**moiety** (moi'e-ti), n. Half.

**moil** (moil), vi. To toil; drudge.

**moist** (moist), a. Somewhat wet; damp.

**molar** (mo'lar), a. Adapted to grind.

**molasses** (mu-las'ez), n. The syrup which drains from sugar; treacle.

**mole** (mol), n. A natural spot on the skin; a pier; a mound; a little animal.

**molecular** (mo-lek'u-lar), a. Pertaining to molecule.

**molecule** (mol'e-kul), n. A very minute particle of matter.

**molehill** (mol'hil), n. A hillock raised by a mole.

**moleskin** (mol'skin), n. A strong twilled fustian.

**molest** (mu-lest'), vt. To render uneasy; annoy.

**molestation** (mol-es-ta'shun), n. Annoyance.

**mollify** (mol'i-fi), vt. To soften; assuage.

**mollusc** (mol'usk), n. An animal with a fleshy, inarticulate body, as the snail, oyster, etc.

**molten** (molt'n), a. Melted, or made of melted metal.

**moment** (mo'ment), n. A portion of time; importance; weight. [**momentary, momentous**]

**momentum** (mo-men'tum), n. Force of a moving body. pl. **momenta**.

**monachism** (mon'a-kizm), n. Monastic life.

**monad** (mon'ad), n. An atom.

**monarch** (mon'ark), n. A sole supreme ruler; hereditary sovereign; the chief of its kind. [**monarchical, monarchist**]

**monastery** (mon'as-te-ri), n. A house of religious retirement; convent; nunnery.

**Monday** (mun'da), n. Second day of the week.

**monetary** (mun'e-ta-ri), a. Relating to or consisting of money.

**monger** (mung'ger), n. A trader; a seller.

**mongoose** (mong'gos), n. A weasel-like animal common in India.

**mongrel** (mung'grel), a. Of a mixed breed.

**monition** (mon-ish'un), n. Warning; instruction.

**monitor** (mon'i-tur), n. One who warns; a subordinate in a school. [**monitory**]

**monk** (mungk), n. One who lives in a monastery.

**monkey** (mungk'i), n. An animal like the ape.

**monocracy** (mon-ok'ra-si), n. Government by one person.

**monocular** (mon-ok'u-lar), a. One-eyed.

**monody** (mon'o-di), n. Song by one person.

**monogamy** (mon-og'a-mi), n. Marriage to one woman only.

**monogram** (mon'o-gram), n. A character or cipher composed of several letters interwoven.

**monolith** (mon'o-lith), n. A column of a single stone.

**monologue** (mon'o-log), n. A speech by a person alone.

**monomania** (mon-o-ma'ni-a), n. Madness confined to one particular subject.

**monopoly** (mo-nop'o-li), n. Entire control or appropriation.

**monosyllable** (mon-o-sil'la-bl), n. A word of one syllable.

**monotheism** (mon'o-the-izm), n. The belief in the

**existence** of one God only.

**monotone** (mon'o-ton), n. With dull uniformity. [**monotonous, monotony**]

**monsoon** (mon-son'), n. A periodical wind.

**monster** (mon'ster), n. Anything out of the usual course of nature.

**monstrosity** (mon-stros'-i-ti), n. An unnatural production. [**monstrous**]

**month** (munth), n. The twelfth part of a year.

**monument** (mon'u-ment), n. A tomb; a record.

**moor** (mor), n. A black man; a marsh.

**moorings** (mor'ingz), n. pl. Anchors, buoys, etc., to fasten a ship.

**moose** (mos), n. The largest of the deer kind.

**moot** (mot), v. To plead or argue; to discuss or debate.

**mope** (mop), v. To be dull or spiritless. [**mopish**]

**moral** (mor'al), a. Pertaining to the practices or conduct of men with reference to right and wrong; virtuous; mental.

**morale** (mo-ral'), n. Moral condition, as of a body of men.

**moralist** (mor'al-ist), n. One who teaches morals.

**moralize** (mor'al-iz), v. To speak or write on moral subjects; to apply to a moral purpose.

**morass** (mo-ras'), n. A marsh; low, wet ground.

**morbid** (mar'bid), a. Diseased; not sound or healthy.

**morgue** (marg), n. A place for dead bodies.

**moribund** (mor'i-bund), a. In a state of dying.

**Mormon** (mar'mun), n. One of a sect founded by Joseph Smith. [**Mormonism**]

**morocco** (mo-rok'o), n. A fine kind of grained leather of goat or sheepskin, dressed.

**morose** (mo-ros'), a. Sullen; sour; peevish; gloomy.

**Morpheus** (mar'fe-us or mar'fus), n. The god of dreams.

**morphia** (mar'fi-a), n. A vegetable alkaloid extracted from opium.

**morsel** (mar'sel), n. A bite; a mouthful; small piece.

**mortal** (mar'tal), a. Subject to death; deadly; human. [**mortality**]

**mortar** (mar'tar), n. A cement used in building; a vessel for pounding substances with a pestle; a bomb-cannon.

**mortage** (mar'gaj), n. A pledge of houses and land for debt.

**mortgagee** (mar-ga-je'). One to whom an estate is mortgaged.

**mortgager** (mar'ga-jer),
**mortgagor** (mar'ga-jar), One who gives a mortgage.

**mortification** (mor-ti-fi-ka'-shun), n. Loss of vitality; humiliation; ascetic austerities.

**mortify** (mor'ti-fi), vt. To humble; render ashamed.

**mortise** (mor'tis), n. Cavity made to receive a tenon.

**mortuary** (mort'yu-a-ri), a. Pertaining to death or burial.

**Mosaic** (mo-za'ik), a. Pertaining to Moses or the Jewish law.

**mosaic** (mo-za'ik), n. Work in which objects are represented by small pieces of colored stone, etc., cemented to a ground.

**Moslem** (moz'lem), n. A Mohammedan.

**mosque** (mosk), n. Mohammedan house of worship.

**mosquito** (mos-ke'to), n. A blood-sucking gnat.

**mote** (mot), n. A particle; speck.

**moth** (moth), n. A winged insect resembling the butterfly; an insect larva injurious to woolen fabrics or furs.

**motion** (mo'shun), n. Act or state of moving; proposal.

**motive** (mo'tiv), a. Causing movement.

**motley** (mot'li), a. Particolored; diversified.

**motor** (mo'tor), n. A moving power; device for obtaining motion from an electric current.

**motto** (mot'o), n. Sentence prefixed to anything; phrase attached to a device.

**mould, mold** (mold), n. Rich soil.

**moulder, molder** (mold'er), vi. To waste away.

**moulding, molding** (mold'ing), n. Ornamental ridge or projection.

**moult** (molt), vi. To shed the feathers, etc., as birds.

**mound** (mound), n. A raised bank; hillock.

**mount** (mount), n. A hill; elevation. [mountain, mountaineer, mountainous]

**mountebank** (mount'e-bangk), n. A boastful quack; buffoon.

**mourn** (morn), vi. To grieve; lament.

**mouse** (mous), n. The smallest mammal, a little gnawing quadruped. pl. mice.

**movable** (moov'a-bl), a. That may be moved. [movables]

**Mr.** (mis'ter), n. Master; title of address to a man.

**Mrs.** (mis'is), n. Mistress; title of address to a married woman.

**mucilage** (mu'sil-aj), n. A slimy fluid.

**mucus** (mu'kus), n. A slimy animal fluid.

**muddle** (mud'l), vt. To render muddy or confused.

**muddy** (mud'i), a. Defiled with mud; covered with mud; turbid.

**muff** (muf), n. Warm soft cover for the hands.

**muffin** (muf'in), n. A light kind of cake.

**muffle** (muf'l), vt. To wrap up; cover; blindfold.

**muffler** (muf'ler), n. A covering for the head and face.

**muggy** (mug'i), a. Foggy; damp and close.

**mulatto** (mu-lat'o), n. Child of one white and one negro parent.

**mulberry** (mul'ber-i), n. A tree and its fruit.

**mulct** (mulkt), n. A fine.

**muleteer** (mu-le-ter'), n. A mule-driver.

**mulish** (mul'ish), a. Like a mule; obstinate.

**mullein** (mul'in), n. A plant with downy leaves and yellow flowers.

**mullion** (mul'yun), n. Upright bar in a Gothic window.

**multifarious** (mul-ti-fa'ri-us), a. Having great variety; manifold.

**multiple** (mul'ti-pl), n. A number or quantity exactly divisible by another.

**multitude** (mul'ti-tud), n. Great number; crowd. [multitu'dinous]

**mum** (mum), a. Silent.

**mumble** (mum'bl), vi. and vt. Speak or eat with the lips closed.

**mummy** (mum'i), n. Dead body preserved.

**mumpish** (mum'pish), a. Dull; sullen.

**mumps** (mumps), n. Swelling of the glands of the neck.

**munch** (munch), vt. and vi. Chew; masticate.

**mundane** (mun'dan), a. Earthly.

**municipal** (mu-nis'i-pal), a. Pertaining to a city. [**municipal'ity**]

**munificence** (mu-nif'i-sens), n. Bountifulness.

**munition** (mu-nish'un), n. Materials used in war, as powder, etc.

**murky** (mur'ki), a. Gloomy; dark.

**murmur** (mur'mur), n. Low, indistinct sound, like that of running water.

**murrain** (mur'in), n. Cattle plague; foot and mouth disease.

**muscle** (mus'l), n. Fleshy part in an animal body, the contraction of which produces motion. [**muscular**]

**muscle, mussel** (mus'l), n. Marine bivalve shell-fish, used for food.

**muse** (muz), vi. and vt. Study in silence.

**museum** (mu-ze'um), n. Collection of curiosities or works of art.

**musk** (musk), n. Strong perfume, obtained from the male muskdeer.

**musket** (mus'ket), n. Former hand-gun of soldiers. [**musketeer**]

**muslin** (muz'lin), n. Thin white cotton cloth or fabric.

**muss** (mus), n. Disturbance; disorder.

**Mussulman** (mus'ul-man), n. Mohammedan. pl. **Mus'sulmans**.

**mustache** (mus-tash'), n. Hair on the upper lip.

**mustang** (mus'tang), n. A wild horse.

**mustard** (mus'tard), n. A plant; condiment made from its seeds.

**muster** (mus'ter), v. To assemble.

**musty** (mus'ti), a. Moldy.

**mutability** (mu-ta-bil'i-ti), n. Change of mind; instability. [**mutable, mutation**]

**mute** (mut), a. Incapable of speaking; silent.

**mutilate** (mu'ti-lat), v. To cut off; to maim. [**mutilation**]

**mutineer** (mu-ti-ner'), n. One guilty of mutiny.

**mutinous** (mu'ti-nus), a. Disposed to mutiny; seditious.

**mutter** (mut'er), v. To speak low; to grumble.

**mutton** (mut'n), n. The flesh of sheep.

**mutual** (mu'tu-al), a. Given and received; acting in return.

**muzzle** (muz'l), v. To restrain from biting; to restrain from speech.

**myopic** (mi-op'ik), a. Short-sighted.

**myriad** (mir'i-ad), n. Ten thousand; any large number.

**myrrh** (mer), n. Medicinal, aromatic, gum resin.

**myrtle** (mer'tl), n. A shrub.

**mysterious** (mis-te'ri-us), a. Obscure; secret; incomprehensible. [**mystery**]

**mystic** (mis'tik), n. A believer in the mystical. [**mystical, mysticism**]

**myth** (mith), n. A fable.

**mythology** (mi-thol'o-ji), n. System of myths; a nation's legends pertaining to its gods.

# N

**nabob** (na'bob), n. A European who has enriched himself in the East; any man of great wealth.

**nacre** (na'kr), n. A white brilliant matter which forms the interior of several shells; mother of pearl.

**nadir** (na'der), n. Point opposite the zenith.

**naiad** (na'yad), n. A water-nymph; a shell-fish.

**nail** (nal), n. A claw; A horny substance on the fingers and toes; an iron pin; a boss; two and a quarter inches.

**naive** (na'ev), a. Artless; ingenuous.

**naivete** (na-ev-ta'), n. Native simplicity.

**nape** (nap), n. The joint of the neck behind.

**naphtha** (nap'tha), n. A volatile, bituminous, and inflammable liquid.

**napkin** (nap'kin), n. Cloth or small towel to wipe the hands.

**narcissus** (nar-sis'us), n. A genus of bulbous flowering plants.

**narcotic** (nar-kot'ik), a. Inducing sleep.

**narcotine** (nar'ko-tin), n. The active principle in opium.

**narrate** (na-rat'), vt. To tell; relate. [**narration**]

**narrative** (nar'a-tiv), n. Recital of particulars; a story.

**narrows** (nar'oz), n. pl. A narrow passage.

**nasal** (na'zal), a. Pertaining to the nose. n. A sound uttered through the nose.

**nascent** (nas'ent) a. Beginning to exist.

**nasty** (nas'ti), a. Dirty; filthy.

**natal** (na'tal), a. Relating to nativity.

**natant** (na'tant), a. Floating.

**nation** (na'shun), n. A people living under one government; race; great number. [**national**]

**nationality** (nash-un-al'i-ti), n. Love of one's nation; national character or bias.

**native** (na'tiv), a. Produced by nature; pertaining to the place of one's birth; original.

**nativity** (na-tiv'i-ti), n. Birth; time, place, or manner of birth.

**natty** (nat'i), a. Trim; neat; tidy; spruce.

**natural** (nat'u-ral), a. Pertaining to nature; inborn; normal; not revealed; not artificial; illegitimate.

**naturalisation** (nat-u-ral-i-za'shun), n. Admission to native privileges.

**naturalism** (nat'u-ral-izm), n. Mere state of nature; natural religion; denial of supernatural agency.

**naturalist** (nat'u-ral-ist) n. One versed in natural history.

**naturally** (nat'u-ral-i), ad. According to nature.

**nature** (na'tur), n. Whatever is made; essential qualities; constitution; regular course; natural affection; sort; kind.

**naught** (nawt), n. Nothing.

**naughtiness** (naw'ti-nes), n. Slight wickedness; bad behaviour. [**naughty**]

**nausea** (naw'sha, naw'she-a), n. Sickness at the stomach; loathing.

**nauseate** (naw'she-at), vt. or i. To affect with disgust; loathe.

**nauseous** (naw'shus), a. Loathsome; disgusting.

**nautical** (naw'ti-kal), a. Pertaining to seamen or navigation.

**naval** (na'val), a. Belonging to ships.

**nave** (nav), n. The central piece, or hub, from which the spokes of a wheel radiate; the body of a church, from the choir to the entrance.

**navel** (na'vl) n. The middle of the abdomen.

**navigable** (nav'i-ga-bl), a. Passable for ships.

**navigate** (nav'i-gat), vt. or i. To pass on water with ships; sail. [**navigation**]

**navigator** (nav'i-ga-ter), n. One who directs the course of a ship.

**navvy** (nav'i), n. A labourer employed in cutting railways, etc.

**navy** (na'vi), n. A fleet of ships.

**neap** (nep), a. Low, as a tide.

**near** (ner), a. Not far; close; intimate.

**neat** (net), a. Tidy; clean; pure. [**neatness**]

**nebula** (neb'yu-la) n. Misty luminous spot in the heavens. pl. **nebulæ**.

**nebular** (neb'yu-lar), a. Pertaning to nebulæ.

**nebulous** (neb'yu-lus), a. Cloudy; misty; relating to, or like, a nebula.

**necessary** (nes'es-a-ri), a. Indispensable; unavoidable.

**necessitate** (ne-ses'i-tat), vt. To render necessary; compel.

**necessitous** (ne-ses'i-tus), a. Needy; destitute.

**necessity** (ne-ses'i-ti), n. That which must be; compulsion; need; poverty.

**necklace** (nek'las), n. A string of beads, etc., for the neck.

**necrology** (ne-krol'o-ji), n. The register of deaths; accounts of the dead.

**necromancer** (nek'ro-manser), n. A sorcerer; wizard. [**necromancy**]

**necropolis** (ne-krop'o-lis), n. A cemetery.

**nectarine** (nek'ta-rin), n. A smooth variety of the peach.

**nectary** (nek'ta-ri), n. Part of a flower which contains the honey.

**needle** (ne'dl), n. Pointed instrument for sewing; magnetic bar of a compass; slender crystal.

**needless** (ned'les), a. Unnecessary.

**needy** (ned'i), a. In need; poor.

**nefarious** (ne-fa'ri-us), a. Impious; villainous.

**negation** (ne-ga'shun), n. Denial.

**negative** (neg'a-tiv), a. Denying; implying absence.

**neglect** (neg-lekt'), vt. To leave uncared for; disregard; carelessly omit. n. Disregard; omission.

**negligent** (neg'li-jent), a. Neglecting; careless.

**negotiable** (ne-go'shi-a-bl), a. That may be negotiated.

**negotiate** (ne-go'shi-at), vi. To bargain; treat with. [**negotia'tion**]

**negro** (ne'gro), n. One of the black race. fem. **negress**.

**neigh** (na), vi. To cry as a horse.

**neighbor** (na'bor), n. One who lives near another.

**neighborly** (na'bor-li), a. Befitting a neighbor; social; friendly.

**neither** (ne'ther), pron. Not either. conj. Not; nor.

**nemesis** (nem'e-sis), n. A retributive or avenging power; retribution.

**neology** (ne-ol'o-ji), n. Introduction of new words or doctrines.

**neophyte** (ne'o-fit), a. A new convert; novice.

**nepenthe** (ne-pen'the), n. A drink supposed to dispel sorrow.

**nephew** (nev'u, nef'u), n. Son of a brother or sister.

**nepotism** (nep'o-tizm), n.

**NEREID** 147 **NOMAD**

Favoritism to one's relations.
**nereid** (ne're-id), n. A sea-nymph.
**nerve** (nerv), n. Organ which transmits sensations to, or impulses from, the brain; firmness; courage.
**nervous** (nerv'us), a. Strong; vigorous; having weak or irritable nerves.
**nether** (neth'er), a. Lower. [neth'ermost]
**nettle** (net'l), n. Plant covered with stinging hairs.
**neuralgia** (nu-ral'ji-a), n. Pain in the nerves.
**neuter** (nu'ter), a. Taking no part with either side; neither masculine nor feminine; intransitive.
**newsmonger** (nuz'munger), n. Gossip.
**newt** (nut), n. An aquatic animal, similar to a lizard.
**nibble** (nib'l), vt. and vi. Eat by small, dainty bites.
**nice** (nis) a. Fastidious; exact; delicate; dainty; agreeable. [nicety]
**niche** (nich), n. Recess in a wall.
**nick** (nik), n. Notch.
**nidus** (ni'dus), n. A nest or hatching-place.
**niece** (nes), n. A daughter of a brother or sister.
**niggard** (nig'ard), n. A stingy, covetous person. a. Miserly; meanly covetous.
**nigh** (ni), a. Near; allied closely.
**night** (nit), n. Time when the sun is beneath the horizon.
**nightingale** (nit'in-gal), n. A small bird that sings at night.
**nightly** (nit'li), a. Done by night.
**nightmare** (nit'mar), n. Sensation of weight about the breast in dreams.
**nihil** (ni'hil), n. Nothing.
**nihilism** (ni'hil-izm), n. Nothingness; the doctrine that nothing can be known; a name given to Russian radicalism and communism. [nihilist]
**nimble** (nim'bl), a. Brisk; quick in motion.
**nimbus** (nim'bus) n. Circle of rays around heads on medals and pictures.
**ninny** (nin'ni), n. A simpleton; a fool.
**nippers** (nip'perz), n. pl. Small pinchers.
**nipple** (nip'l), n. A teat; a part of a gun.
**nit** (nit), n. The egg of insects.
**niter** (ni'ter), n. Nitrate of potassa; saltpeter. [nitric]
**nitrogen** (ni'tro-jen), n. Element of niter; azote.
**niveous** (niv'e-us), a. Snowy; resembling snow.
**nobility** (no-bil'i-ti), n. Dignity of mind; distinction of family or rank; peerage.
**noble** (no'bl), a. Worthy; elevated; liberal.
**nobody** (no'bod-i), n. Not any person.
**nocent** (no'sent), a. Guilty; mischievous; hurtful.
**nocturnal** (nok-tur'nal), a. Nightly; done at night.
**node** (nod), n. Point where the orbit of a planet intersects the ecliptic.
**nodule** (nod'ul), n. A small knot or lump.
**noggin** (nog'in), n. Wooden cup or mug.
**noise** (noiz), n. Sound; din; rumor.
**noisome** (noi'sum), a. Offensive; noxious.
**noisy** (noi'zi), a. Clamorous; turbulent.
**nomad** (nom'ad), n. One

who leads a wandering pastoral life. [**nomadic**]

**nomenclature** (no′men′kla-tur), n. The technical names used in any art or science.

**nominal** (nom′i-nal), a. Existing in name only; not real.

**nominate** (nom′in-at), v. To name; to propose. [**nomination**]

**nominative** (nom′i-na-tiv), a. The name which precedes a verb.

**nominee** (nom′i-ne), n. One named by another.

**non** (non), a. Prefix meaning not.

**nonage** (non′aj), n. Minority, or under age.

**nonagenarian** (non-a-jen-a′ri-an), n. One who is ninety years old.

**nonchalant** (non′sha-lant′) a. Careless; indifferent.

**nondescript** (non′de-skript) a. Not yet described; new and strange.

**none** (nun) a. and pron. Not one; not any.

**nonentity** (non-en′ti-ti), n. Want of being; thing not existing; utterly insignificant person.

**nones** (nonz), n. pl. In the ancient Roman calendar, the 7th of March, May, July, and October, and the 5th of the other months.

**nonpareil** (non-pa-rel′), n. A person or thing unrivalled; a small size of type.

**nonplus** (non′plus), n. Great difficulty; perplexity.

**nonsense** (non′sens), n. Words without meaning; absurdity; trifles.

**nonsuit** (non′sut), n. Stopping of a suit at law.

**noose** (noos), n. A running knot.

**normal** (nor′mal), a. Regular; analogical; serving as a standard.

**north** (north), n. Point or region opposite the sun at noon.

**nosology** (no-sol′o-ji), n. Classification of diseases.

**nostril** (nos′tril), n. One of the openings of the nose.

**nostrum** (nos′trum), n. A secret remedy; quack medicine.

**notable** (no′ta-bl), a. Remarkable; notorious.

**notary** (no′ta-ri), n. An officer who attests writings.

**notation** (no-ta′shun), n. Act of noting; system of characters.

**notch** (noch), n. A cut or nick.

**notice** (no′tis), n. Attention; observation; information; warning.

**noticeable** (no′tis-a-bl), a. Worthy of notice.

**notify** (no′ti-fi) vt. To give notice of; declare. [**notification**]

**notion** (no′shun), n. Conception; opinion; judgment.

**notional** (no′shun-al), a. Ideal; fanciful; crotchety.

**notorious** (no-to′ri-us), a. Publicly known (in a bad sense); infamous. [**notori′ety**]

**nought** (nat), n. Nothing.

**noun** (nown), n. Name of anything; substantive.

**nourish** (nur′ish), vt. Feed; encourage. [**nourishment**]

**novel** (nov′el), a. New; unusual; strange. [**novelist, nov′elty**]

**November** (no-vem′ber), n. The eleventh month of the year.

**novice** (nov′is), n. Beginner. [**novitiate**]

**noxious** (nok'shus), a. Injurious; poisonous.

**nozzle** (noz'l), n. Spout; projecting mouth-piece.

**nucleus** (nu'kle-us), n. [pl. **nuclei**.] Central mass; kernel; core.

**nude** (nud), a. Naked; bare; undraped. [**nu'dity**]

**nudge** (nuj), n. Gentle jog.

**nugatory** (nu'ga-to-ri), a. Trifling; vain; inoperative; null; void.

**nugget** (nug'et), n. Lump.

**nuisance** (nu'sans), n. That which annoys or harms or is offensive.

**null** (nul), a. Of no force; void. [**nul'lify**]

**numb** (num), a. Deprived of sensation or motion.

**numeral** (nu'mer-al), a. Pertaining to or consisting of numbers.

**numerate** (nu'mer-at), vt. Point off and read, as figures. [**numera'tion**]

**numerator** (nu'mer-a-tur), n. One who numbers; upper number of a vulgar fraction, or after a decimal, which expresses the number of fractional parts taken.

**numismatic** (nu-mis-mat'ik), a. Pertaining to money, coins, or medals. [**numismat'ics**]

**nuncio** (nun'shi-o), n. Ambassador of the Pope.

**nuncupative** (nun-ku'pa-tiv), a. Verbal; not written.

**nunnery** (nun'er-i), n. A convent of nuns.

**nuptial** (nup'shal), a. Pertaining to marriage. [**nuptials**]

**nurse** (nurs), n. One who nourishes or tends a child or sick person.

**nursling** (nurs'ling), n. One who is nursed; an infant.

**nurture** (nurt'yur), n. Nourishment; education.

**nutation** (nu-ta'shun), n. Vibratory motion of the earth's axis.

**nutmeg** (nut'meg), n. Spicy nut of an E. Indian tree.

**nutrient** (nu'tri-ent), a. Nourishing.

**nutriment** (nu'tri-ment), n. That which nourishes; food. [**nutrition**]

**nutritious** (nu-trish'us), a. Nourishing.

**nymph** (nimf), n. A maiden; one of the minor goddesses.

# O

**oak** (ok) n. Genus of timber trees.

**oakum** (ok'um), n. Old ropes pulled to pieces, used for calking ships' seams.

**oar** (or), n. Instrument to row boats.

**oasis** (o-a'sis), n. A fertile spot in a desert.

**oat** (ot), n. A plant and its seed.

**oaten** (o'ten), a. Pertaining to oats.

**oath** (oth), n. A solemn affirmation with an appeal to God for its truth.

**oatmeal** (ot'mel), n. Meal made of oats.

**obduracy** (ob'du-ra-si), n. Hardness of heart.

**obdurate** (ob'du-rat), a. Hardened in heart or feelings; stubborn.

**obedience** (o-bed'yens), n. Compliance with a command. [**obedient**]

**obeisance** (o-ba'sans), n. Act of reverence or respect; a bow.

**obelisk** (ob'e-lisk), n. A quadrangular pillar or pyramid.

**obese** (o-bes'), a. Fat; fleshy.

**obesity** (o-bes'i-ti), n. Fatness; corpulence.

**obey** (o-ba'), vt. To comply with; yield to; do as told.

**obit** (o'bit, ob'it), n. Death; decease.

**obituary** (o-bit'u-ar-i), n. A register of deaths.

**object** (ob'jekt), n. Anything set before the mind or senses; thing sought for; aim; design; end in view.

**object** (ob-jekt'), vt. or i. To oppose by words or reasons; urge against. [**objection**]

**objective** (ob-jekt'iv), a. Contained in the object.

**objector** (ob-jek'ter), n. One who objects.

**objurgate** (ob-jur'gat), vt. To chide; reprove. [**objurgation**]

**oblate** (ob'lat), a. Broad or flattened at the poles.

**oblation** (ob-la'shun), n. Anything offered in divine worship; sacrifice.

**obligate** (ob'li-gat), vt. To bind over by contract or duty. [**obligation**]

**obligatory** (ob'li-ga-tur-i), a. Imposing an obligation; binding.

**oblige** (o-blij'), vt. To constrain; bind; gratify.

**obligee** (ob-li-je'), n. The person obliged, or to whom a bond is given.

**oblique** (ob-lek'), a. Deviating from a right line; not parallel; indirect.

**obliquity** (ob-lik'wi-ti), n. Deviation from a right line, or from moral rectitude.

**obliterate** (ob-lit'e-rat), vt. To blot out; efface. [**obliteration**]

**oblivion** (ob-liv'i-un), n. Forgetting; state of being forgotten; general pardon.

**oblivious** (ob-liv'i-us), a. Causing forgetfulness; forgetful.

**oblong** (ob'long), a. Longer than broad.

**obloquy** (ob'lu-kui), n. Censorious language; calumny; abuse.

**obnoxious** (ob-nok'shus), a. Liable; exposed; offensive; odious.

**oboe** (o'boi), n. A musical wind instrument sounded by a reed.

**obscene** (ob-sen'), a. Grossly indelicate and disgusting; lewd; licentious. [**obscenity**]

**obscure** (ob-skur'), a. Darkened. [**obscuration, obscurity**]

**obsequies** (ob'se-kwiz), n. pl. Funeral solemnities or ceremonies.

**obsequious** (ob-se'kwi-us), a. Meanly servile.

**observance** (ob-zer'vans), n. Attention; rite. [**observant, observa'tion**]

**obsolescent** (ob-so-les'ent), a. Going out of use.

**obsolete** (ob'so-let), a. Antiquated.

**obstacle** (ob'sta-kl), n. Anything that stands in the way.

**obstinate** (ob'sti-nat), a. Blindly or exceedingly firm. [**ob'stinacy**]

**obstreperous** (ob-strep'er-us), a. Clamorous.

**obstruct** (ob-strukt'), vt. Block; retard. [**obstruc'tion**]

**obtain** (ob-tan'), vt. Get; procure.

**obtrude** (ob-trod'), vt. and vi. Thrust in, or enter, when not wanted. [**obtru'sion**]

**obtuse** (ob-tus'), a. Blunt; stupid; greater than a right angle.

**obverse** (ob-vers'), a. Bearing the face.

**obverse** (ob'vers), n. Side of coin showing the principal symbol.

**obviate** (ob'vi-at), vt. Avoid.

**obvious** (ob'vi-us), a. Manifest.

**occasion** (ok-ka'zhun), n. Occurrence; opportunity; cause; necessity.

**occident** (ok'si-dent), n. West.

**occiput** (ok'si-put), n. Back part of the skull.

**occlude** (ok-klod'), vt. Absorb.

**occult** (ok-kult'), a. Hidden; mysterious. [**occult'ism**]

**occupy** (ok'u-pi), vt. Seize or hold possession of; fill; employ. [**oc'cupancy**]

**occur** (ok-kur'), v. To come to the mind; to happen.

**occurrence** (ok-kur'ens), n. Any event that happens.

**ocean** (o'shan), n. A vast expanse of salt water. [**oceanic**]

**ochre** (o'ker), n. Yellow clay, used as a pigment.

**octagon** (ok'ta-gon), n. A figure of eight sides and angles.

**octahedron** (ok-ta-he'dron), n. A solid figure, with eight equal equilateral triangles.

**octave** (ok'tav), a. Denoting eight.

**octavo** (ok-ta'vo), a. Having eight leaves to a sheet.

**October** (ok-to'ber), n. The tenth month of the year.

**octogenarian** (ok-to-je-na'ri-an), n. One who is eighty years of age.

**octopus** (ok-to'pus or ok'-to-pus), n. The devil-fish.

**octuple** (ok'tu-pl), a. Eightfold.

**ocular** (ok'u-lar), a. Known by, or relating to, the eye. [**oculist**]

**odd** (od), a. Uneven in number; strange; not mated.

**Oddfellows** (od'fel-loz), n. A benevolent society, having secret signs.

**oddity** (od'di-ti), n. Singularity; queerness.

**oddly** (od'li), ad. Strangely.

**odds** (odz), n. pl. Dispute; inequality; excess; advantage.

**ode** (od), n. A song; a poem.

**odious** (o'di-us), a. Very offensive; detestable.

**odium** (o'di-um), n. Enmity; provoking hate.

**odor** (o'dur), n. Scent; perfume; fragrance.

**odoriferous** (o-dur-if'er-us), a. Fragrant; sweet-scented. [**odorous**]

**offal** (of'al), n. Refuse.

**offend** (of-fend'), v. To displease; to disgust.

**offense** (of-fens'), n. Displeasure; anger; sin. [**offensive**]

**offer** (of'fer), v. To present; to propose; to exhibit; to bid.

**offertory** (of'er-to-ri), n. Words sung or said while a collection is made in church.

**officer** (of'fi-ser), n. One who holds an office.

**official** (of-fish'al), a. Pertaining to an office; done by authority.

**officiate** (of-fish'i-at), v. To act by virtue of an office.

**officinal** (of-fis'i-nal), a. Denoting an approved medicine kept in stores.

**officious** (of-fish'us), a. Forward in offering services.

**offing** (af'fing), n. A sea-term for the open sea.

**offscouring** (af'skowr-ing), n. That which is rejected.

**offset** (af'set), n. A shoot or sprout; a sum or account placed as an equivalent for another.

**often** (af'n), ad. Frequently.

**ogle** (o'gl), v. To view with side glances.

**ogre** (o'ger), n. A monster.

**ohm** (om), n. Unit of resistance of 1000 ft. copper wire 1-10" thick.

**oily** (oil'i), a. Containing or like oil; smooth.

**ointment** (oint'ment), n. Oily substance for wounds.

**oleaginous** (o-le-aj'i-nus), a. Like oil; oily.

**oleander** (o-le-an'der), n. An evergreen shrub with beautiful flowers.

**oleiferous** (o-le-if'er-us), a. Producing oil, as seeds.

**oleomargarine** (o-le-o-mar'ga-rin), n. Artificial butter.

**olfactory** (ol-fak'tor-i), a. Having the sense of smelling.

**oligarchy** (ol'i-gar-ki), n. Government in the hands of a few; rule by aristocracy.

**olio** (o'li-o), n. A medley.

**olympiad** (o-lim'pi-ad), n. In ancient Greece, a period of four years.

**omega** (o-me'ga), n. The last letter of the Greek alphabet; the last.

**omelet** (om'e-let). Eggs beaten, sweetened and fried.

**omen** (o'men), n. A prognostic; a good or bad sign.

**ominous** (om'i-nus), a. Foreboding ill.

**omission** (o-mish'un), n. A leaving out; neglect or failure to do.

**omit** (o-mit'), v. To pass by; to neglect; to leave out.

**omnibus** (om'ni-bus), n. A large carriage for conveying passengers.

**omniferous** (om-nif'er-us), a. Bearing or producing all kinds.

**omnific** (om-nif'ik), a. All-creating.

**omnipotence** (om-nip'o-tens), n. Infinite power. [**omnipotent**]

**omnipresence** (om-ni-prez'-ens), n. Presence everywhere. [**omnipresent**]

**omniscience** (om-nish'ens), n. Knowledge unbounded, or infinite. [**omniscient**]

**omnivorous** (om-niv'o-rus), a. All-devouring; feeding on both animal and vegetable food.

**once** (wuns), adv. At one time; a single time.

**one** (wun), a. Single; undivided; the same.

**onerous** (on'er-us), a. Burdensome.

**onion** (un'yun), n. Plant with a bulbous root used for food.

**onset** (on'set), n. An assault.

**onslaught** (on'slat), n. Violent attack; assault.

**ontology** (on-tol'o-ji), n. Science which treats of the nature and existence of beings.

**onward** (on'ward), a. Advanced; advancing.

**onyx** (on'iks), n. A precious stone.

**ooze** (ooz), n. Soft mud.

**opal** (o'pal), n. A precious stone of changeable colors.

**opalescent** (o-pal-es'ent), a. Like an opal.

**opaque** (o-pak'), a. Not transparent.

**opera** (op'er-a), n. A musical drama.

**operate** (op'er-at), vi. To exert power; produce effect; act. [**operation**]

**operative** (op'er-a-tiv), a. Acting; producing effects. [**operator**]

**operose** (op'er-os), a. Requiring labor; toilsome.

**ophthalmia** (of-thal'mi-a), n. Inflammation of the eye.

**opiate** (o'pi-at), n. Medicine containing opium; narcotic.

**opinion** (o-pin'yun), n. Mental judgment; notion.

**opium** (o'pi-um), n. Narcotic juice of the poppy.

**opossum** (o-pos'um), n. A pouch-bearing quadruped.

**opponent** (op-po'nent), a. Opposing. n. An opposer; antagonist.

**opportune** (op-por-tun'), a. Timely; seasonable. [**opportunist.**]

**opportunity** (op-por-tun'i-ti), n. Fit or convenient time; occasion.

**oppose** (op-poz'), vt. To set against; resist; compete with.

**opposite** (op'po-zit), a. Facing; adverse; contrary.

**opposition** (op-po-zish'un), n. State of being opposite; resistance; repugnance; contrariety; obstacle; party opposed to the existing administration.

**oppress** (op-pres'), vt. To burden; rule with severity. [**oppression**]

**oppressive** (op-pres'iv), a. Burdensome; heavy; tyrannical.

**oppressor** (op-pres'or), n. One who oppresses; tyrant.

**opprobrious** (op-pro'bri-us), a. Disgraceful; infamous; expressing opprobrium. [**opprobrium**]

**oppugn** (op-pun'), vt. To oppose; combat.

**optative** (op'ta-tiv), a. Expressing desire.

**optic** (op'tik, -al), a. Pertaining to vision or optics.

**optician** (op-tish'an), n. One who makes or sells optical instruments.

**optics** (op'tiks), n. Science of the laws of vision and light.

**optimism** (op'ti-mizm), n. Doctrine that all things are ordered for the best. [**optimist**]

**option** (op'shun), n. Act or power of choosing; choice.

**opulent** (op'yu-lent), a. Wealthy. [**opulence**]

**oracle** (or'a-kl), n. Answer given by a divinity; place where such answers are delivered; very wise person. n. pl. Prophetic revelations.

**oral** (o'ral), a. Uttered by the mouth; spoken.

**orange** (or'anj), n. A tree bearing a gold-colored fruit; its fruit; a color between yellow and red.

**oration** (o-ra'shun), n. An elaborate public address.

**orator** (or'a-tor), n. A public speaker; eloquent person; in law, a petitioner.

**oratorio** (or-a-to'ri-o), n. A musical drama on a religious theme.

**oratory** (or'a-to-ri), n. A place of prayer; art of public speaking.

**orbit** (orb'it), n. Circular course; path of a heavenly body; cavity of the eye.

**orchard** (or'chard), n. An inclosure of fruit trees.

**orchestra** (or'kes-tra), n. Part of a theatre appropriated to the musicians; the musicians.

**orchid** (or'kid), **orchis** (or'kis), n. A genus of flowering plants.

**ordain** (or-dan'), vt. To appoint; establish; decree; invest with sacerdotal functions. [**ordina'tion**]

**ordeal** (or'de-al), n. Ancient form of trial by appealing to the judgment of God; any severe trial.

**orderly** (or'der-li), a. In order; regular; quiet.

**ordinal** (or'di-nal), a. Showing order or succession.

**ordinance** (or'di-nans), n. Law; established rule.

**ordinary** (or'di-na-ri), a. Usual; common; inferior.

**ordnance** (ord'nans), n. Heavy guns; artillery.

**ordure** (ord'yur), n. Dirt; dung.

**organic** (or-gan'ik), a. Containing, or pertaining to, organs; derived from animals or vegetables; pertaining to construction.

**organist** (or'gan-ist), n. One who plays on the organ.

**organize** (or'gan-iz), vt. To form, as an organic body; to furnish with officers and rules, as a meeting or society; arrange. [**organiza'tion**]

**orgy** (or'ji), n. A wild or drunken revel.

**oriel** (o'ri-el), n. A large projecting window.

**orient** (o'ri-ent), a. Rising, as the sun; eastern; bright. [**orient'al**]

**Orient** (o'ri-ent), n. The East.

**orifice** (or'i-fis), n. A hole; opening.

**origin** (or'i-jin), n. Beginning; source; cause.

**original** (o-rij'i-nal), a. First; primitive; not copied. [**originality**]

**originate** (o-rij'i-nat), v. To bring into existence; to cause to be; to begin.

**orison** (or'i-zun), n. A prayer or supplication.

**ornament** (ar'na-ment), n. Decoration. [**ornamental, ornamentation**]

**ornate** (ar'nat), a. Ornamented; adorned; decorated.

**ornithologist** (ar-ni-thol'o-jist), n. One skilled in the science of birds. [**ornithology**]

**orotund** (o'ro-tund), a. Said of the utterance of letters or words with fulness, clearness, and strength.

**orphan** (ar'fan), n. A fatherless or motherless child. [**orphanage**]

**orrery** (or'er-i), n. An instrument for exhibiting the motions, etc., of the planets.

**orthodox** (ar'tho-doks), a. Sound in the Christian faith; not heretical.

**orthoepist** (ar'tho-e-pist), n. One skilled in pronunciation. [**orthoepy**]

**orthographer** (ar-thog'ra-fer), n. A correct speller of words. [**orthography**]

**oscillate** (os'sil-lat), v. To move backward and forward.

**osculate** (os'ku-lat), v. To kiss.

**osier** (o'zher), n. A willow.

**osseous** (os'se-us), a. Bony; of or resembling bone.

**ossific** (os-sif'ik), a. Having power to ossify. [**ossification**]

**ossify** (os'si-fi), v. To become bone.

**ostensible** (os-ten'si-bl), a. Apparent; declared; manifest.

**ostentation** (os-ten-ta'shun), n. Proud display. [**ostentatious**]

**osteology** (os-te-ol'o-ji), n. Description of bones. [**osteopath, osteopathy**]

**ostracism** (os'tra-sizm), n. Banishment; expulsion. [**ostracize.**]

**ostrich** (os'trich), n. A large bird prized for its plumes.

**ottar** (ot'tar), n. Essential oil of roses.

**otter** (ot'ter), n. An amphibious quadruped.

**ottoman** (ot'to-man), n. A

**ought** (at), v. To be necessary; to be obliged.

**ounce** (owns), n. A weight, 12th of a pound troy, and 16th of a pound avoirdupois.

**ours** (owrz), pron. Noting what belongs to us.

**oust** (owst), v. To expel.

**outcast** (owt'kast), n. One cast out or expelled.

**outcry** (owt'kri), n. Clamor; noisy opposition.

**outcrop** (owt'krop), n. Exposure of strata at the surface.

**outer** (owt'er), a. That is without.

**outface** (owt-fas'), v. To bear or stare down.

**outlandish** (owt-land'ish), a. Foreign; strange; rustic.

**outlast** (owt-last'), v. To surpass in duration.

**outlaw** (owt'la), n. One proscribed from the benefit of the law. [outlawry]

**outlay** (owt'la), n. A laying out or expending.

**outlet** (owt'let), n. A passage outward; egress.

**outline** (owt'lin), n. The first sketch of a figure.

**outlook** (owt'lok), n. A vigilant watch; a view.

**outmost** (owt'most), a. Furthest outward.

**outpost** (owt'post), n. A station at a distance.

**outpour** (owt-por'), v. To send forth in a stream.

**outrage** (owt'raj), v. To insult. n. Excessive abuse. [outrageous]

**oval** (o'val), a. Of the form of an egg; oblong. n. A body shaped like an egg.

**ovarious** (o-va'ri-us), a. Consisting of eggs. [ovary]

**ovate** (o'vat), a. Egg-shaped, as a leaf.

**ovation** (o-va'shun), n. A lesser triumph; any expression of popular applause.

**oven** (uv'n), n. An arched cavity for baking, heating, drying, etc.

**overact** (o-ver-akt'), vt. To perform to excess.

**overalls** (o'ver-awlz), n. A kind of long, loose trousers.

**overawe** (o-ver-aw'), vt. To restrain by awe.

**overdue** (o'ver-du), a. Past time of payment.

**overhaul** (o-ver-hawl'), vt. To turn over and examine; overtake.

**overseer** (o-ver-ser'), n. A supervisor.

**overt** (o'vert), a. Open; public.

**overture** (o'ver-tur), n. An opening; proposal; an introductory piece of music.

**overweening** (o-ver-we'ning), a. Self-conceited; arrogant.

**overwhelm** (o-ver-whelm'), vt. To spread over and crush; immerse and bear down.

**oviform** (o'vi-form), a. Egg-shaped.

**oviparous** (o-vip'a-rus), a. Producing eggs.

**ovule** (o'vul), n. Rudiment of a seed.

**owe** (o), vt. or i. To possess; be indebted to; be obliged for.

**owing** (o'ing), ppr. or a. Due; imputable to.

**owl** (owl), n. A bird that flies at night.

**own** (on), a. Belonging to. v. To acknowledge; to confess. [owner]

**oxalic** (oks-al'ik), a. Relating to an acid and to sorrel.

**oxygen** (oks'i-jen), n. A kind of gas which generates acids; the vital part of air.

**oyer** (o'yer), n. A hearing or trial of criminal cases.

**oyster** (ois'ter), n. A bivalvular shell-fish.

**ozone** (o'zon), n. A peculiar modification of oxygen, nearly always present in the atmosphere.

# P

**pabulum** (pab'u-lum), n. Nourishment; food; fuel.

**pace** (pas), n. A step; manner of walking; measure of five feet.

**pacer** (pa'ser), n. A horse that paces.

**pacha** (pa-sha'), n. A Turkish viceroy.

**Pacific** (pa-sif'ik), a. Appeasing; conciliatory; calm. [pacify]

**package** (pak'aj), n. A bundle or bale of goods.

**packet** (pak'et), n. A small parcel; a vessel plying regularly between ports.

**pad** (pad), n. A flat cushion; a robber.

**paddle** (pad'dl), v. To play in water; to propel by an oar or paddle.

**padlock** (pad'lok), n. A kind of portable lock.

**pæan** (pe'an), n. A song of triumph.

**pagan** (pa'gan), n. A heathen. [paganism]

**pageant** (paj'ant), n. A showy exhibition; brilliant display. [pageantry]

**pagoda** (pa-go'da), n. An East Indian temple, or idol.

**pail** (pal), n. Open vessel for liquids; bucket.

**pain** (pan), n. Mental or bodily suffering; in pl. labor; care.

**painter** (pant'er), n. One who paints; artist. [painting]

**pair** (par), n. Two things suited to each other, or used together; a couple; man and wife.

**pajamas** (pa-jam'az), n. pl. Loose garment for chamber-wear.

**palace** (pal'as), n. A royal house; a splendid mansion. [pala'tial]

**paladin** (pal'a-din), n. One of Charlemagne's peers; a hero.

**palæontology** (pal-e-on-tol'-o-ji), n. Science which treats of fossils.

**palatable** (pal'a-ta-bl), a. Pleasing to the taste.

**palate** (pal'at), n. Roof of the mouth; taste.

**palatine** (pal'a-tin), n. A prince or noble having almost royal power.

**palaver** (pa-lav'er), n. Idle or cajoling talk.

**pale** (pal), a. Not brightly colored; wan.

**pale** (pal), n. A stake in a fence or stockade; inclosure.

**palette** (pal'et), n. Tablet on which a painter mixes his colors.

**palfrey** (pal'fri, pal'-), n. A saddle-horse.

**palimpsest** (pal'imp-sest), n. Manuscript from which the first writing has been erased to make room for a second.

**paling** (pal'ing), n. A fence of pales.

**palisade** (pal-i-sad'), n. Fence of stakes.

**pall** (pal), n. A cloth over a coffin.

**pall** (pal), vi. To become vapid.

**palladium** (pal-la'di-um), n. A statue of Pallas; a safeguard; a light rare metal.

**pallet** (pal'let), n. A small low bed.

**palliate** (pal'li-at), vt. To excuse; extenuate; mitigate. [**pallia'tion**]

**pallid** (pal'lid), a. Pale; wan.

**pallium** (pal'i-um), n. An archbishop's vestment.

**palm** (pam), n. Inner part of the hand; tropical tree, or its branch; a symbol of victory.

**palmate** (pal'mat), a. Shaped like the open hand; webbed, as feet.

**palmetto** (pal-met'o), n. Small species of palm-tree.

**palmistry** (pal'mis-tri), n. Art of telling fortunes from the lines in the palm of the hand.

**Palm-Sunday** (pam-sun'da) n. Sunday before Easter.

**palmy** (pam'i), a. Flourishing; prosperous.

**palpable** (pal'pa-bl), a. That may be felt; manifest.

**palpitate** (pal'pi-tat), vi. To throb; beat rapidly. [**palpita'tion**]

**palsy** (pal'zi), n. Paralysis.

**palter** (pal'ter), vi. To act insincerely; trifle. [**paltry**]

**pamper** (pam'per), vt. To feed luxuriously; indulge excessively.

**pamphlet** (pam'flet), n. Small unbound book of stitched sheets.

**pamphleteer** (pam-flet-er'), n. A writer of pamphlets.

**panacea** (pan-a-se'a), n. A universal remedy.

**pandemonium** (pan-de-mo'ni-um), n. The hall of demons; place of crime or uproar.

**pander** (pan'der), n. One who procures vicious gratification for another.

**pane** (pan), n. A plate of glass.

**panegyric** (pan-e-jir'ik), n. A discourse in praise of some person or event.

**panel** (pan'el), n. A compartment in a frame.

**panel** (pan'el), n. A list of jurymen.

**pang** (pang), n. Sudden pain; agony.

**panic** (pan'ik), n. Sudden or causeless fright.

**pannier** (pan'yer), n. Basket borne by a horse.

**panoply** (pan'o-pli), n. Complete defensive armor for the body.

**panorama** (pan-o-ra'ma), n. A picture presenting many objects at one view.

**pant** (pant), v. To gasp rapidly.

**pantaloons** (pan-ta-lonz'), pl. Trousers.

**pantheism** (pan'the-izm), n. The doctrine identifying Nature with God.

**pantheon** (pan'the-on), n. A temple dedicated to all the gods.

**panther** (pan'ther), n. A spotted wild beast.

**pantology** (pan-tol'o-ji), n. A dictionary of universal knowledge.

**pantomime** (pan'to-mim), n. A representation by gesture in dumb show. [**pantomimist**]

**pantry** (pan'tri), n. A storeroom for provisions.

**papacy** (pa'pa-si), n. Office or dignity of the Pope.

**papal** (pa'pal), a. Belonging to the Pope.

**papoose** (pap-pos'), n. A North American Indian baby.

**papyrus** (pa-pi'rus), n. An Egyptian plant, and the paper made from it.

**par** (par), n. State of equality; equal value.

**parable** (par'a-bl), n. A fable; a similitude.

**parabola** (pa-rab'o-la), n. One of the conic sections.

**parachute** (par'a-shot), n. An instrument to prevent rapidity of descent from a balloon.

**parade** (pa-rad'), n. A pompous military display.

**paradigm** (par'a-dim), n. An example; a model.

**paradise** (par'a-dis), n. Eden; a place of bliss.

**paradox** (par'a-doks), n. A truth seemingly absurd.

**paragon** (par'a-gon), n. Pattern of great excellence.

**paragraph** (par'a-graf), n. A distinct part of a discourse; a section.

**parallel** (par'al-lel), a. Equally distant.

**paralysis** (pa-ral'i-sis), n. Palsy; loss of motion.

**paralytic** (par-a-lit'ik), a. Having lost the power of muscular motion. [**paralyze**]

**paramount** (par'a-mount), a. Chief; supreme.

**parapet** (par'a-pet), n. A wall or rampart breast-high.

**paraphernalia** (par'a-ferna'li-a), n. pl. Personal ornaments and apparel of a wife.

**paraphrase** (par'a-fraz), n. A free version or re-statement.

**parasite** (par'a-sit), n. A hanger-on; plant or animal nourished by the juices of another.

**parasol** (par'a-sol), n. Small umbrella used as a screen from the sun.

**parboil** (par'boil), vt. To boil partially.

**parcel** (par'sel), n. A portion; package.

**parch** (parch), vt. To scorch.

**parchment** (parch'ment), n. Skin of a sheep or goat prepared for writing on.

**pardon** (par'don), vt. To forgive; remit the penalty of. [**pardonable**]

**pare** (par), vt. To shave off; cut away the surface of.

**paregoric** (par-e-gor'ik), n. A soothing medicine; camphorated tincture of opium.

**parentage** (par'ent-aj), n. Birth; extraction. [**parental**]

**parenthesis** (pa-ren'the-sis), n. Something inserted in a sentence otherwise complete. pl. **parentheses**, the marks () indicating a parenthesis. [**parenthet'ic**]

**parhelion** (par-he'li-on), n. A mock sun produced by atmospheric refraction.

**pariah** (pa'ri-a), n. A Hindu of the lowest caste; outcast.

**Parian** (pa'ri-an), a. Pertaining to the island of Paros; denoting a kind of white unglazed porcelain.

**parish** (par'ish), n. District under one pastor; district.

**parishioner** (par-ish'un-er), n. One belonging to a parish.

**parity** (par'i-ti), n. Equality; analogy.

**parlance** (par'lans), n. Talk; forms of speech.

**parley** (par'li), vi. To speak; confer.

**parliament** (par'li-ment), n. A meeting for consultation.

**Parliament** (par'li-ment), n. The national legislature of Great Britain. [**parliamentary**]

**parlor** (par'lor), n. A sitting-room; drawing-room.
**parochial** (pa-ro'ki-al), a. Pertaining to a parish.
**parody** (par'o-di), n. Poem closely imitating another.
**parol** (par'ol), n. Oral declaration in law.
**parole** (pa-rol'), n. Word; word of honor; pass-word.
**parotid** (pa-rot'id), a. Denoting a gland situated below the ear.
**paroxysm** (par'oks-izm), n. Sudden fit of pain or passion.
**parquet** (par-ka'), n. Floor; lowest range of seats in a theatre.
**parricide** (par'i-sid), n. The murder, or murderer, of a parent.
**parrot** (par'ot), n. A tropical fruit-eating bird.
**parry** (par'i), vt. To ward off.
**parse** (pars), vt. To analyze grammatically.
**parsimony** (par'si-mon-i), n. Frugality.
**parsley** (pars'li), n. Herb used for seasoning.
**parson** (par'son), n. The clergyman of a parish. [**parsonage**]
**partake** (par-tak'), vt. and vi. To have a part; share.
**parterre** (par-tar'), n. An ornamental plot of ground.
**partial** (par'shal), a. Relating to a part; not total; inclined to favor one party. [**partial'ity**]
**participant** (par-tis'i-pant), a. Sharing; partaking.
**participate** (par-tis'i-pat), vi. To partake; have a share. [**participa'tion**]
**participle** (par'ti-si-pl), n. Form of a verb partaking of the nature of both adjective and verb.
**particle** (par'ti-kl), n. A minute portion; atom; small uninflected part of speech.
**particular** (par-tik'yu-lar), a. Pertaining to a single person or thing; special; exact.
**particularity** (par-tik-yu-lar'i-ti), n. Quality of being particular; peculiarity. [**particularize**]
**partisan** (par'te-zan), n. An adherent to a party.
**partition** (par-tish'un), n. That which separates.
**partitive** (par'te-tiv), a. Distributive
**partner** (part'ner), n. Associate in business; a sharer. [**partnership**]
**partridge** (par'trij), n. A well known bird of game.
**parts** (parts), n. pl. Faculties; region.
**parturient** (par-tu're-ent), a. Giving birth to young. [**parturition**]
**paschal** (pas'kal), a. Pertaining to the passover.
**passable** (pas'a-bl), a. That may be passed; tolerable.
**passage** (pas'aj), n. Act of passing; way; incident; clause or portion of a book.
**passenger** (pas'en-jer), n. One that travels in some public conveyance.
**passibility** (pas-e-bil'e-te), n. Capacity of receiving impressions.
**passible** (pas'e-bl), a. Susceptible of impressions.
**passim** (pas'im), ad. Everywhere.
**passion** (pash'un), n. That which is suffered; any strong emotion.
**passionate** (pash'un-at), a. Easily excited.
**passive** (pas'iv), a. Receiving impressions; unresisting.
**Passover** (pas'o-ver), n. Feast of the Jews, com-

memorating the escape of the Hebrews.

**passport** (pas'port), n. A permission to pass; a license.

**paste** (past), n. An adhesive mixture. vt. To unite with paste.

**pastern** (pas'tern), n. Joint of a horse next the foot.

**pastille** (pas-tel'), n. A roll of paste; a kind of perfume.

**pastime** (pas'tim), n. Diversion; sport.

**pastor** (pas'tor), n. A shepherd; minister of a church.

**pastoral** (pas'tor-al), a. rural; relating to a pastor.

**pastorate** (pas'tor-at), n. The office of a pastor.

**pastry** (pas'tri), n. Pies; tarts; cake.

**pasturable** (pas'tur-a-bl), a. Fit for pasture.

**pasturage** (pas'tur-aj), n. Lands grazed by cattle; grass for cattle.

**pasture** (pas'tur), n. Land for grazing.

**pasty** (pas'te), a. Like paste or dough.

**patch** (pach), n. A piece of cloth.

**patchwork** (pach'wurk), n. Bits of cloth sewed together; bungling work.

**pate** (pat), n. The head; skin of a calf's head.

**patent** (pat'ent), a. Open; manifest; protected by a patent.

**patentee** (pat-en-te'), n. One who holds a patent.

**paternal** (pa-ter'nal), a. Fatherly; derived from a father.

**paternity** (pa-ter'ni-ti), n. Relation of a father to his child.

**Paternoster** (pat'er-nos'-ter), n. The Lord's prayer.

**pathetic** (pa-thet'ik), a. Exciting pity; touching.

**pathology** (pa-thol'o-ji), n. The science of disease.

**pathos** (pa'thos), n. That which excites pity or tender feeling.

**patient** (pa'shent), a. Sustaining pain, wrong, or toil without complaint; meek; resigned; calmly expectant. [patience]

**patriarch** (pat'ri-ark), n. Head of a family; dignitary in the Greek Church.

**patrimony** (pat'ri-mo-ni), n. Hereditary estate.

**patriot** (pa'tri-ot), n. A lover of his native land. [patriotism]

**patrol** (pa-trol'), vi. To go the rounds, as a guard.

**patron** (pa'tron), n. A protector; one who countenances.

**patronage** (pat'ron-aj), n. Countenance; support; aid.

**patronize** (pat'ron-iz), vt. To act as patron to; countenance; support.

**patronymic** (pat-ro-nim'ik), n. Name derived from an ancestor.

**patten** (pat'en), n. Kind of shoe standing on an iron ring; base of a column.

**pattern** (pat'ern), n. A model; example.

**patty** (pat'i), n. A little pie.

**paucity** (pa'si-ti), n. Fewness; smallness of quantity.

**paunch** (panch, -a), n. The belly; first stomach of ruminants.

**pauper** (pa'per), n. A poor person; one supported by charity.

**pauperism** (pa'per-izm), n. State of being a pauper; destitution.

**pause** (paz), n. A stop; cessation; suspense.

**pavement** (pav'ment), a. A paved surface.

**pavilion** (pa-vil'yun), n. A large tent; ornamented building.

**paw** (pa), n. The foot of a beast with claws.

**pawl** (pal), n. Catch falling into the teeth of a wheel or rack.

**pawn** (pan), n. A pledge deposited as security.

**pawn** (pan), n. The smallest piece in chess.

**pawnbroker** (pan'brok'er), n. One who lends money on pledges.

**payable** (pa'a-bl), a. Due; that may or should be paid.

**payee** (pa-e'), n. One to whom money is paid or to be paid.

**payment** (pa'ment), n. Act of paying; anything paid.

**pea** (pe), n. A vine and its edible seeds.

**peace** (pes), n. Quiet; freedom from war or disturbance; friendliness; silence.

**peaceable** (pes'a-bl), a. Disposed to peace; tranquil.

**peaceful** (pes'ful), a. Quiet; tranquil; calm.

**peach** (pech), n. A tree; its stone-fruit.

**peacock** (pe'kok), n. Large fowl with splendid plumage.

**peak** (pek), n. Pointed end of anything; sharp top of a mountain.

**peaked** (pekt), a. Pointed; having a peak.

**peal** (pel), n. A loud sound; set of bells.

**peanut** (pe'nut), n. The ground-nut.

**pear** (par), n. A tree and its fruit.

**pearl** (perl), n. Beautiful white concretion found in shell-fish; anything precious, or like a pearl.

**peasant** (pez'ant), n. A countryman; rustic; rural laborer. [peasantry]

**pease** (pez), n. pl. Peas in quantity or bulk.

**peat** (pet), n. Fossil vegetable matter used as fuel.

**pebble** (peb'l), n. Small roundish stone.

**pecan** (pe-kan'), n. A nut-tree of the hickory kind, and its fruit.

**peccadillo** (pek-a-dil'o), n. A petty fault.

**peccary** (pek'a-ri), n. A hog-like American quadruped.

**peck** (pek), n. Measure of eight quarts, or one-fourth of a bushel.

**pectoral** (pek'to-ral), a. Pertaining to the breast or chest.

**peculate** (pek'yu-lat), vi. To steal; embezzle. [pecula'tion]

**peculiar** (pe-kul'yar), a. One's own; special; strange. [peculiar'ity]

**pecuniary** (pe-kun'i-ar-i), a. Relating to money.

**pedagogue** (ped'a-gog), n. A schoolmaster.

**pedal** (ped'al), n. Lever moved by the foot.

**pedant** (ped'ant), n. One who makes a useless or uncalled-for display of learning. [pedant'ic]

**pedantry** (ped'ant-ri), n. Vain or useless display of learning.

**peddle** (ped'l), vi. and vt. To travel and retail small wares.

**pedestal** (ped'es-tal), n. The base of a column.

**pedestrian** (pe-des'tri-an), a. On foot. [pedestrianism]

**pedicel** (ped'i-sel), n. A short stem or foot-stalk.

**pedigree** (ped'i-gre), n. Genealogy; lineage.

**pediment** (ped'i-ment), n. A

**peddler** triangular ornamental facing over porticoes, windows, etc.

**peddler** (ped'lar), n. A travelling trader in small wares.

**pedometer** (pe-dom'e-ter), n. An instrument to measure the distance traversed in walking.

**peduncle** (pe-dung'kl), n. The stem of the flower or of the fruit of a plant.

**peel** (pel), vt. or i. To strip off skin or rind; pare; come off, as skin.

**peer** (per), n. An equal; a nobleman. **[peerage]**

**peeress** (per'es), n. A peer's lady.

**peerless** (per'les), a. Without an equal.

**peevish** (pev'ish), a. Easily vexed.

**peevishness** (pev'ish-nes), n. Fretfulness.

**pegasus** (peg'a-sus), n. A winged horse; a northern star-cluster.

**pelf** (pelf), n. Money, in an odious sense.

**pelisse** (pe-les'), n. A silk habit for a female.

**pell** (pel), n. A skin; a hide.

**pellet** (pel'et), n. A little ball.

**pellicle** (pel'e-kl), n. Thin external skin; film.

**pellucid** (pel-lu'sid), a. Clear; transparent; not opaque.

**pelt** (pelt), n. A raw hide; a skin.

**peltry** (pelt're), n. Skins; furs.

**pelvis** (pel'vis), n. The bony cavity which forms the lower part of the belly.

**penal** (pe'nal), a. Denouncing or incurring punishment.

**penalty** (pen'al-te), n. Punishment attached to the commission of a crime.

**penance** (pen'ans), n. Suffering inflicted or self-imposed for sin.

**pence** (pens), n. pl. of penny.

**penchant** (pan-shan'), n. Inclination.

**pencil** (pen'sil), n. A brush used in drawing, writing, or painting.

**pendant** (pen'dant), n. A jewel; a flag.

**pendent** (pen'dent), a. Hanging.

**pendulous** (pend'u-lus), a. Swinging.

**pendulum** (pend'u-lum), n. A body suspended and vibrating.

**penetrable** (pen'e-tra-bl), a. That may be penetrated.

**penetrate** (pen'e-trat), vt. To pierce; to enter; to feel deeply. **[penetration]**

**peninsula** (pen-in'su-la), n. Land nearly surrounded by water.

**peninsular** (pen-in'su-lar), a. In the form of a peninsula.

**peninsulate** (pen-in'su-lat), vt. To form a peninsula.

**penitence** (pen'e-tens), n. Sorrow of heart for sin; contrition.

**penitent** (pen'e-tent), a. Suffering sorrow for sin. n. One sorrowful for sin.

**penitential** (pen-e-ten'she-al), a. Expressing penitence.

**penitentiary** (pen-e-ten'she-ar-e), n. A house of correction; prison.

**penmanship** (pen'man-ship) n. Manner of writing; use of the pen.

**pennant** (pen'ant), n. A small flag or streamer; a tackle for hoisting.

**pennate** (pen'nat), a. Winged.

**penniless** (pen'e-les), a. Having no money.

**pennyweight** (pen'ni-wat), n. 24 grains of troy weight.

**pennywise** (pen'i-wiz), a. Saving small sums at the hazard of losing larger ones.

**pension** (pen'shun), n. A stated allowance for past services. [**pensioner**]

**pensive** (pen'siv), a. Thoughtful; reflective; sad.

**pensiveness** (pen'siv-nes), n. Melancholy; thoughtfulness.

**pent** (pent), a. Closely confined; crowded in narrow space.

**pentagon** (pen'ta-gon), n. A figure of five angles.

**pentangular** (pen'tang-gu-lar), a. Having five angles.

**Pentateuch** (pen'ta-tuk), n. The first five books of the Old Testament.

**Pentecost** (pen'te-kost), n. A Jewish festival.

**penult** (pe-nult' or pe'nult), n. Last syllable but one.

**penultimate** (pe-nul'ti-mat) a. Denoting last syllable but one.

**penumbra** (pen-um'bra), n. A partial shadow in an eclipse.

**penurious** (pe-nu'ri-us), a. Niggardly; sordid.

**penury** (pen'u-ri), n. Poverty; indigence.

**peony** (pe'o-ni), n. A perennial plant and flower.

**people** (pe'pl), n. A nation; inhabitants; population.

**pepper** (pep'per), n. A plant and its seed. v. To sprinkle with pepper.

**pepsin** (pep'sin), n. Active principle in gastric juice.

**peradventure** (per-ad-ven'tur), ad. By chance.

**perambulate** (per-am'bu-lat), v. To walk round.

**perceive** (per-sev'), v. To see; to feel; to discern.

**percentage** (per-sent'aj), n. The rate per hundred.

**perception** (per-sep'shun), n. The act of perceiving.

**perch** (perch), n. A fish; a pole; a roost; a rod.

**perchance** (per-chans'), ad. Perhaps; peradventure.

**percolate** (per'ko-lat), v. To stream through; to filter.

**percussion** (per-kush'un), n. The act of striking; the shock produced.

**perdition** (per-dish'un), n. Ruin; loss; death.

**peregrination** (per-e-grin-a'shun), n. A traveling; a wandering about.

**peremptory** (per'emp-tor-i), a. Positive; absolute.

**perennial** (per-en'ni-al), a. Lasting through the year; durable; perpetual.

**perfect** (per'fekt), a. Complete; finished. [**perfection**]

**perfidious** (per-fid'i-us), a. False to trust; base.

**perforate** (per'fo-rat), vt. To bore through; pierce. [**perfora'tion**]

**perforce** (per-fors'), adv. By force; of necessity.

**perform** (per-form'), vt. To do thoroughly; execute; act. [**performance**]

**perfume** (per'fum), n. A sweet odor; fragrant substance.

**perfume** (per-fum'), vt. To scent. [**perfumery**]

**perfunctory** (per-fungk'to-ri), a. Done to get rid of the duty; negligent.

**perhaps** (per-haps'), adv. By chance; possibly.

**Peri** (pe'ri), n. A fairy in Persian mythology.

**pericardium** (per-i-kard'i-um), n. Membranous bag surrounding the heart

**perigee** (per'i-je), n. Point of the moon's orbit nearest the earth.

**perihelion** (per-i-he'li-on), n. Point in a planet's orbit nearest the sun.

**peril** (per'il), n. Danger; risk.

**perilous** (per'il-us), a. Dangerous.

**perimeter** (pe-rim'e-ter), n. Measure around a figure.

**period** (pe'ri-od), n. A circuit; time in which anything is performed; portion of time; date; elaborate sentence.

**periodic** (pe-ri-od'ik), a. Returning at regular intervals.

**periphery** (per-if'er-e), n. Circumference of a circle.

**periphrase** (per'e-fraz), n. A round-about mode of expression.

**perishable** (per'ish-a-bl), a. Liable to perish.

**perispheric** (per-e-sfer'ik), a. Having the form of a ball.

**peristaltic** (per-e-stal'tik), a. Spiral; worm-like.

**peristyle** (per'e-stil), n. A range of columns round an edifice.

**periwig** (per'e-wig), n. A small wig.

**periwinkle** (per'e-wingk-l), n. A small shell-fish.

**perjure** (per'joor), vt. To take a false oath wilfully.

**perjury** (per'joor-e), n. The act of wilfully taking a false oath.

**perk** (perk), a. Lively.

**permanence** (per'ma-nens), n. Continuance; fixedness.

**permanent** (per'ma-nent), a. Durable; lasting; without change.

**permeable** (per'me-a-bl), a. That may be passed through.

**permeate** (per'me-at), vt. To pass through the interstices or pores. [permeation]

**permiscible** (per-mis'e-bl), a. That may be mixed.

**permissible** (per-mis'e-bl), a. That may be allowed.

**permission** (per-mish'un), n. Act of permitting.

**permit** (per-mit'), vt. To give leave; to license.

**permit** (per'mit), n. A warrant in writing.

**pernicious** (per-nish'us), a. Tending to injure.

**peroration** (per-o-ra'shun), n. The closing part of an oration.

**perpendicular** (per-pen-dik'u-ler), a. Upright; crossing at right angles.

**perpetration** (per-pe-tra'shun), n. Commission of something wrong.

**perpetrator** (per'pe-trat-er), n. One who perpetrates a crime.

**perpetual** (per-pet'u-al), a. Never ceasing.

**perpetuate** (per-pet'u-at), vt. To make perpetual.

**perpetuity** (per-pe-tu'e-te), n. Endless duration.

**perplexing** (per-pleks'ing), a. Embarrassing. [perplexity]

**perquisite** (per'kwe-zit), n. A fee.

**persecute** (per'se-kut), vt. To pursue with malignity; to harass. [persecution]

**persecutor** (per'se-kut-er), n. One who persecutes.

**perseverance** (per-se-ver'-ans), n. A persisting in what is undertaken.

**persevere** (per-se-ver'), vi. To persist.

**persist** (per-sist'), vi. To persevere steadily and firmly. [persistence]

**persistive** (per-sist'iv), a. Persevering.

**personage** (per'sun-aj), n. A person of distinction.

**personal** (per'sun-al), a. Belonging to a person; movable. [personality]

**personalty** (per'sun-al-te), n. Personal estate.

**personate** (per'sun-at), vt. To represent a person. [personation]

**personator** (per'sun-at-er), n. One who assumes another's character.

**personification** (per-son-e-fe-ka'shun), n. A representation of inanimate things as living beings.

**personify** (per-son'e-fi), vt. To speak of inanimate beings, &c., as though they were persons.

**perspective** (per-spekt'iv), a. Relating to vision.

**perspicacious** (per-spe-ka'she-us), a. Quick-sighted; discerning. [perspicacity]

**perspicuity** (per-spe-ku'e-te), n. Clearness. [perspicuous]

**perspirable** (per-spir'a-bl), a. That may be perspired. [perspiration]

**perspire** (per-spir'), vt. or i. To emit fluid matter through the pores; to sweat.

**persuade** (per-swad'), vt. To induce by argument or entreaty.

**persuasible** (per-swa'ze-bl), a. That may be persuaded.

**persuasive** (per-swa'siv), a. Tending to persuade.

**pert** (pert), a. Smart; brisk; saucy.

**pertain** (per-tan'), vi. To belong; to relate.

**pertinacious** (per-te-na'she-us), a. Holding firmly to any opinion or purpose.

**pertinacity** (per-te-nas'e-te), n. Obstinacy in adherence.

**pertinent** (per'ti-nent), a. Adapted to the case; relevant.

**perturb** (per-turb'), v. To disturb the mind; to agitate.

**perusal** (pe-ro'zal), n. Act of reading or examining.

**peruse** (pe-roz'), v. To read with attention.

**pervade** (per-vad'), v. To permeate; to pass through.

**perverse** (per-vers'), a. Obstinate; in the wrong; petulant.

**perversion** (per-ver'shun), n. A diverting from the true intent or object.

**perversity** (per-ver'si-ti), n. Disposition to thwart or cross.

**pervert** (per-vert'), v. To turn from true use, end or purpose; to corrupt.

**pervious** (per'vi-us), a. That may be penetrated.

**pessimist** (pes'i-mist), n. One who complains that everything is for the worst.

**pest** (pest), n. Plague; pestilence; a scourge.

**pester** (pes'ter), v. To disturb; to perplex; to harass.

**pestiferous** (pes-tif'er-us), a. Pestilential; malignant.

**pestilence** (pes'ti-lens), n. Any contagious disease.

**pestilent** (pes'ti-lent), a. Producing disease and injury.

**pestilential** (pes-ti-len'shal), a. Producing pestilence; infectious; pernicious.

**pestle** (pes'l), n. An instrument for pounding things in a mortar.

**pet** (pet), n. A fit of peevishness; any creature petted.

**petal** (pet'al), n. A flower-leaf.

**petard** (pe-tard'), n. A piece

of ordnance for bombarding.

**petit** (pet'i), a. Small; diminutive; mean.

**petition** (pe-tish'un), n. Request; prayer. [**petitioner**]

**petrifaction** (pet-ri-fak'shun), n. Change into stone; anything petrified.

**petrifactive** (pet-ri-fak'tiv) a. Having the power to change into stone.

**petroleum** (pe-tro'le-um), n. An inflammable bituminous liquid found in the earth.

**petrology** (pet-rol'o-ji), n. The science of rocks.

**petticoat** (pet'i-kot), n. A woman's underskirt.

**pettifogger** (pet'i-fog-er), n. Paltry lawyer.

**petty** (pet'i), n. Small; trifling; contemptible.

**petulant** (pet'yu-lant), a. Saucy; peevish. [**petulance**]

**petunia** (pe-tu'ni-a), n. Genus of flowering plants.

**pew** (pu), n. An inclosed seat in a church.

**pewit** (pe'wit), n. A European bird; the lapwing.

**pewter** (pu'ter), n. Alloy of tin and lead.

**phaeton** (fa'e-ton), n. An open four-wheeled carriage.

**phalanx** (fal'angks, fa'-), n. A compact body of soldiers. pl. **phalan'ges.**

**phantasm** (fan'tazm), n. A fancied vision; illusion; spectre.

**phantasmagoria** (fan-taz-ma-go'ri-a), n. Exhibition of figures by a magic lantern.

**phantom** (fan'tom), n. An apparition; illusion.

**Pharisee** (far'i-se), n. One of a Jewish sect very strict in the observance of religious ordinances.

**pharmacopœia** (far-ma-ko-pe'ya), n. Book containing instructions in pharmacy.

**pharmacy** (far'ma-si), n. Art of preparing and mixing medicines.

**pharos** (fa'ros), n. A lighthouse.

**pharynx** (far'ingks), n. Upper expansion of the gullet.

**phase** (faz), n. Appearance; one of a series of changes.

**pheasant** (fez'ant), n. A genus of gallinaceous birds.

**phenomenon** (fe-nom'e-non), n. An appearance; anything observed; something unusual. pl. **phenomena.** [**phenomenal**]

**phial** (fi'al), n. A small bottle.

**philanthropist** (fil-an'thro-pist), n. A lover of mankind; person of abstract benevolence.

**philanthropy** (fil-an'thro-pi), n. Love of mankind in general. [**philanthrop'ic**]

**philatelist** (fil-at'e-list), n. One who collects postage stamps.

**philology** (fil-ol'o-ji), n. Science of language. [**philol'ogist**]

**philopena** (fil-o-pe'na), n. Present made as a forfeit in a game.

**philosopher** (fil-os'o-fer), n. One versed in philosophy. [**philosophy**]

**phlegm** (flem), n. Mucus; sluggishness. [**phlegmat'ic**]

**phlox** (floks), n. American garden plant with showy flowers.

**phone** (fon), n. Common abbreviation of telephone.

**phonetic** (fo-net'ik), **phonic** (fon'ik), a. Pertaining to the sound of the voice. [phonet'ics, phon'ics]

**phonograph** (fo'no-graf), n. An instrument for recording and reproducing sounds.

**phonography** (fo-nog'ra-fi), n. A system of shorthand.

**phosphorescent** (fos-fo-res'ent), a. Shining with a faint light, without heat. [phosphorescence]

**phosphorus** (fos'fo-rus), n. An elementary combustible substance; faintly luminous in the dark.

**photograph** (fo'to-graf), n. A picture produced by photography. [photographer, photography]

**photophone** (fo'to-fon), n. An instrument by which light-vibrations are made to produce, or reproduce, sound.

**photosphere** (fo'to-sfer), n. The solid body of the sun.

**phrase** (fraz), n. Part of a sentence; short expression; form of speech.

**phraseology** (fra-ze-ol'o-ji), n. Style or manner of expression.

**phrenology** (fren-ol'o-ji), n. Doctrine of a special connection between certain parts of the brain and certain functions of the mind.

**phthisical** (tiz'i-kal), a. Consumptive; breathing hard.

**phthisis** (thi'sis, tis'-, ti'-) n. Consumption of the lungs.

**phylactery** (fi-lak'ter-i), n. A strip of parchment inscribed with passages from the Hebrew Scriptures.

**physic** (fiz'ik), n. Medicine; the art of healing.

**physical** (fiz'i-kal), a. Pertaining to nature or material things; corporeal. [physician]

**physics** (fiz'iks), n. The science of nature or natural objects.

**physiognomy** (fiz-i-og'no-mi), n. Art of discerning character from the features; the countenance.

**physiography** (fiz-i-og'ra-fi), n. The science which treats of the earth's physical features and changes.

**physiology** (fiz-i-ol'o-ji), n. Science of the functions of living bodies.

**physique** (fi-zek'), n. Bodily constitution or conformation.

**pianist** (pi-a'nist), n. A performer on the pianoforte.

**piazza** (pi-az'a), n. A covered walk; porch.

**picaresco** (pik-a-res'ko), a. Denoting a kind of fiction in which the principal personage is a shifty knave.

**pickerel** (pik'er-el), n. Fresh-water fish of the pike family.

**picket** (pik'et), n. Pointed stake; outpost of soldiers.

**pickle** (pik'l), n. Brine; spiced vinegar; anything pickled.

**picnic** (pik'nik), n. A pleasure party in which each one furnishes refreshment.

**pictorial** (pik-to're-al), a Pertaining to or illustrated by pictures.

**picture** (pik'tur), n. A resemblance in colours.

**picturesque** (pik-tu-resk') a. Like a picture; romantic.

**pie** (pi), n. Baked fruit or meat in crusts; mixed type.

**piebald** (pi'bald), a. Diver-

**piece** (pes), n. A part; a play; a patch.

**pied** (pid), a. Spotted.

**pier** (per), n. Support of an arch; a projection into the sea; a wharf.

**pierce** (pers), v. To penetrate; to enter; to force a way into; to touch, as the passions.

**piety** (pi'e-ti), n. Reverence for the Deity; filial duty.

**pigeon** (pij'un), n. A dove.

**pigment** (pig'ment), n. A color for painting; a paint.

**pigmy** (pig'mi), n. A dwarf. Also written **pygmy**.

**pike** (pik), n. A lance; a fish.

**piked** (pikt), a. Sharp-pointed.

**pilaster** (pi-las'ter), n. A square pillar or column.

**pile** (pil), n. A large stake; a heap; an edifice.

**piles** (pilz), n. pl. A disease.

**pilfer** (pil'fer), v. To steal trifling things; to rob.

**pilgrim** (pil'grim), n. One who travels to sacred places; a wanderer. [**pilgrimage**]

**pillage** (pil'aj), n. Plunder; spoil.

**pillar** (pil'ar), n. A column; anything that supports.

**pillory** (pil'lu-ri), n. A frame to confine criminals by the neck, head, or hands.

**pilot** (pi'lut), n. One who conducts a ship; a guide. v. To steer; to direct; to guide.

**pilotage** (pi'lut-aj), n. The fee of a pilot; act of piloting.

**pinafore** (pin'a-for), n. A little apron; a gown for children.

**pinch** (pinch), v. To nip; to squeeze.

**pinchbeck** (pinch'bek), n. An alloy of copper and zinc.

**pinchers** (pinch'erz), n. An instrument for drawing.

**pine** (pin), n. A forest tree. v. To languish.

**pinion** (pin'yun), n. A wing; a small toothed wheel; a fetter.

**pink** (pingk), n. A flower; a small eye; a reddish color; to work in eyelet holes; to cut in small scollops or angles.

**pinnacle** (pin'na-kl), n. A turret; highest point.

**pint** (pint), n. Half a quart.

**pioneer** (pi-o-ner'), n. One who goes before to clear the way.

**pious** (pi'us), a. Religious; godly; holy; devout.

**pipe** (pip), n. A tube; a musical instrument; a cask.

**pippin** (pip'in), n. A species of apple.

**piquant** (pe'kant), a. Tart; sharp; pungent.

**pique** (peq), n. Offense taken. v. To offend; to nettle; to wound one's pride.

**piquet** (pi-ket'), n. A game at cards.

**piracy** (pi'ra-si), n. Robbery on the seas; literary theft. [**pirate**]

**pirogue** (pi-rog'), n. Canoe from a hollow log.

**piscatory** (pis'ka-to-ri), a. Relating to fishes.

**pistil** (pis'til), n. The seed-bearing organ of a plant.

**pistol** (pis'tul), n. The smallest of firearms.

**piston** (pis'tun), n. A short, solid cylinder, fitted to a hollow one, within which it moves.

**pitcher** (pich'er), n. A

**water-pot** with a handle and a spout.

**pitchfork** (pich'fark), n. A fork to throw hay, straw, etc.

**piteous** (pit'e-us), a. That may excite pity; sorrowful.

**pitfall** (pit'fal), n. A pit covered as a trap.

**pith** (pith), n. Soft substance in plant stems; strength or force.

**pittance** (pit'tans), n. A trifle; a small allowance of money.

**pivot** (piv-ut), n. A pin on which anything turns.

**placard** (pla-kard'), n. A written or printed paper posted in a public place.

**placer** (plas'er), n. Deposits of valuable minerals in particles in alluvial soil, etc.

**placid** (plas'id), a. Calm; quiet; mild; tranquil. [placidity]

**plagiarist** (pla'ji-a-rist), n. One who steals the writings of another. [plagiarize]

**plague** (plag), n. A contagious disease; vexatious.

**plaid** (plad), n. Scottish garment of variegated woolen cloth; goods of checked pattern.

**plain** (plan), a. Flat; evident; homely.

**plaintiff** (plan'tif), n. One who begins a lawsuit.

**plaintive** (plan'tiv), a. Mournful; touching; sad.

**plait** (plat), n. A fold; a braid.

**plane** (plan), n. A level surface; a joiner's tool.

**planet** (plan'et), n. A celestial body revolving about another larger body.

**planetary** (plan'et-ar-i), a. Pertaining to planets.

**planetoid** (plan'et-oid), n. Small planet; asteroid.

**plank** (plangk), n. A thick board.

**plano-concave** (pla'no-kon'-kav), a. Flat on one side and concave on the other.

**plano-convex** (pla'no-kon'-veks), a. Flat on one side and convex on the other.

**plantain** (plan'tan), n. A tropical plant and its fruit; a weed.

**plantation** (plan-ta'shun), n. Act of planting; a place planted with trees; cultivated estate.

**planter** (plant'er), n. One who plants; one who owns a plantation.

**plantigrade** (plant'i-grad), a. Walking on the sole of the foot, as bears.

**plaque** (plak), n. A decorated plate or saucer used as an ornament.

**plash** (plash), vt. To splash.

**plaster** (plas'ter), n. Kind of mortar for overlaying walls; gypsum; drugs spread on cloth for external use.

**plastic** (plas'tik), a. Forming; moulding; that may be moulded. [plasti'city]

**plate** (plat), n. Thin piece of metal; wrought gold and silver; small dish; engraved plate of metal; engraving.

**plateau** (pla-to'), n. High plain; tableland.

**platform** (plat'form), n. Floor of boards; terrace; formal declaration of principles.

**platinum** (plat'i-num), n. A heavy metal resembling silver.

**platitude** (plat'i-tud), n. Flatness; a commonplace or empty remark.

**platonic** (pla-ton'ik), a. Pertaining to Plato or his doctrines; purely spiritual, as love.

**platoon** (pla-toon'), n. Part of a company of soldiers.

**platter** (plat'er), n. A broad shallow dish.

**plaudit** (pla'dit), n. Expression of applause.

**plausible** (plaz'i-bl), a. Superficially pleasing; apparently right. [**plausibil'ity**]

**plea** (ple), n. Act of pleading; excuse; entreaty.

**plead** (pled), vt. To offer in excuse or defense; defend, as a cause.

**pleasant** (plez'ant), a. Agreeable; cheerful. [**pleasantry**]

**please** (plez), vt. To give pleasure to; gratify.

**pleasurable** (plezh'ur-a-bl), a. Giving pleasure.

**pleasure** (plezh'ur), n. Gratification; choice of the will.

**plebeian** (ple-be'yan), a. Pertaining to the common people; vulgar.

**pledge** (plej), n. Anything offered as security; solemn promise.

**plenary** (ple'na-ri), a. Full; complete.

**plenipotentiary** (plen-i-po-ten'shi-a-ri), n. Envoy with full powers for a special service.

**plenitude** (plen'i-tud), n. Fulness.

**plenteous** (plen'te-us), a. Copious; abundant.

**plenty** (plen'ti), n. Full supply; abundance.

**pleonasm** (ple'o-nazm), n. Redundancy of words.

**plethora** (pleth'o-ra), n. Overfulness of blood; repletion.

**pleurisy** (plu'ri-si), n. Inflammation of the membrane covering the lungs.

**pliable** (pli'a-bl), a. Easily bent; flexible; yielding.

**pliant** (pli'ant), a. Flexible; yielding. n. **pliancy**.

**pliers** (pli'erz), n. pl. Small pincers.

**plight** (plit), vt. To pledge.

**plinth** (plinth), n. Square block at the base of a column.

**plodder** (plod'er), n. A dull, laborious person.

**plow** (plou), n. Instrument for turning up the soil.

**pluck** (pluk), vt. To pull; snatch.

**plumage** (plum'aj), n. Feathers of a bird.

**plumb** (plum), n. A leaden weight on a line.

**plumber** (plum'er), n. One who works in lead.

**plumbline** (plum'lin), n. A perpendicular line.

**plume** (plum), n. A feather; token of honour; pride.

**plumiped** (plum'e-ped), n. A bird that has feathers on its feet.

**plummet** (plum'et), n. A piece of lead for sounding, or to draw lines with.

**plump** (plump), a. Fat; sleek; full; round.

**plunder** (plun'der), vt. To take by pillage or open force. [**plunderer**]

**plunge** (plunj), vt. To put suddenly into water.

**plural** (plu'ral), a. Expressing more than one.

**plurality** (plu-ral'e-te), n. A number greater than any other, and less than half.

**Plutonian** (plu-to'ne-an), n. One who holds that the world was formed by the action of fire.

**pluvial** (plu've-al), a. Rainy; wet.

**pneumatic** (nu-mat'ik), a. Consisting of air. [**pneumatics**]

**pneumonia** (nu-mo'ne-a), n. Inflammation of the lungs.

**poach** (poch), vt. To boil

**POACHY**     171     **POMACE**

slightly; to steal game. [poacher]

**poachy** (poch'e), a. Soft; wet.

**podded** (pod'ed), a. Having pods formed.

**poem** (po'em), n. A composition in verse.

**poesy** (po'e-se), n. Art of writing poems.

**poetical** (po-et'ik-al), a. Written in verse; suitable to poetry.

**poet-laureate** (po'et-law're-at), n. A poet whose office is to celebrate the birthdays, &c., of a prince.

**poetry** (po'et-re), n. The compositions of poets; language of excited imagination.

**poignancy** (poin'an-se), n. Sharpness; point.

**poignant** (poin'ant), a. Sharp; satirical; severe; painful.

**poise** (poiz), n. A balancing weight; gravity.

**poison** (poi'zn), n. Anything having an injurious or deadly effect; venom.

**poke** (pok), n. A pocket; a machine to check cattle from leaping fences; a thrust.

**poker** (po'ker), n. An iron rod to stir a fire.

**polar** (po'lar), a. Pertaining to the poles.

**polemic** (po-lem'ik), n. A disputant. [polemics]

**pole-star** (pol'star), n. Polaris; north-star.

**police** (po-les'), n. Civil officers or government of a town for preserving order.

**policy** (pol'i-si), n. Art or manner of government; prudence; cunning; contract of insurance.

**polish** (pol'ish), v. To make smooth or glossy; to refine. n. Artificial gloss; refinement.

**polite** (po-lit'), a. Polished; refined; well-bred; obliging.

**politic** (pol'i-tik), a. Pertaining to polity; prudent.

**politician** (pol-i-tish'an), n. One skilled in politics.

**politics** (pol'i-tiks), n. pl. The art of government; management of political parties.

**polity** (pol'i-ti), n. Constitution of civil government.

**poll** (pol), n. The head; a register of persons.

**pollen** (pol'len), n. The fecundating powder of plants.

**poll-tax** (pol'taks), n. A tax levied by the head.

**pollute** (pol-lut'), v. To make foul or unclean; to defile.

**polonaise** (pol-o-naz'), n. The Polish language; a kind of dress; a dance.

**poltroon** (pol-tron), n. A coward; a dastard.

**polygamy** (po-lig'a-mi), n. Plurality of wives.

**polyglot** (pol'i-glot), a. Having or containing many languages.

**polygon** (pol'i-gon), n. A figure of many sides and angles.

**polyhedron** (pol-i-he'dron), n. Solid body having many sides.

**polypus** (pol'i-pus), n. An animal with many feet; a tumor in the nose, etc.

**polysyllable** (pol'i-sil'a-bl), n. Word of more than 3 syllables.

**polytechnic** (pol-i-tek'nik), a. Comprehending many arts.

**polytheism** (pol'i-the-izm), n. The doctrine of a plurality of gods.

**pomace** (pum'as), n. Refuse of cider-grindings.

**pomade** (po-mad'), n. An unguent for the hair.

**pomegranate** (pum'gran-at), n. An Oriental tree; its fruit.

**pommel** (pum'el), n. A knob; a protuberance.

**pomology** (po-mol'o-ji), n. The science of raising fruit.

**pompadour** (pom'pa-dor), n. A mode of dressing women's hair.

**pomposity** (pom-pos'i-ti), n. Ostentation; boastfulness.

**ponderable** (pon'der-a-bl), a. That may be weighed.

**ponderous** (pon'der-us), a. Heavy; massive.

**poniard** (pon'yard), n. A small dagger.

**pontiff** (pon'tif), n. A high priest; the Pope.

**pontoon** (pon-ton'), n. Hollow float for making bridges.

**poodle** (pod'dl), n. A lapdog.

**Pope** (pop), n. The Bishop of Rome, head of the R.C. Church.

**popinjay** (pop'in-ja), n. A parrot; a woodpecker; a fop; a coxcomb.

**poplin** (pop'lin), n. A stuff of silk and worsted.

**poppy** (pop'pi), n. A soporific plant and flower.

**populace** (pop'u-las), n. The people; the multitude.

**popular** (pop'u-lar), a. Pleasing to the people; prevailing; general. [**popularity**]

**populate** (pop'u-lat), v. To people; to furnish with inhabitants. [**population**]

**populous** (pop'u-lus), a. Full of people.

**porcelain** (pars'lan), n. A fine semi-transparent species of earthenware.

**porch** (porch), n. A covered entrance to a building; a portico.

**porcine** (par'sin), a. Relating to swine.

**pore** (por), n. A passage in the skin.

**porosity** (po-ros'i-ti), n. The quality of having pores.

**porous** (por'us), a. Having pores; light and spongy.

**porpoise** (par'pus), n. A cetaceous fish; a dolphin.

**porridge** (por'ij), n. A mixture of meal and water boiled; a thick broth.

**porrinjer** (por'in-jer), n. A small metal vessel.

**portable** (port'a-bl), a. That may be carried.

**portage** (port'aj), n. Price of carriage; carrying place.

**portal** (port'al), n. An imposing gate or entrance.

**Porte** (port), n. The Ottoman court.

**portend** (por-tend'), vt. To foretoken.

**portent** (por-tent'), n. An omen of ill.

**portentous** (por-tent'us), a. Ominous.

**porter** (por'ter), n. A doorkeeper; a carrier; a kind of malt liquor.

**porterage** (por'ter-aj), n. Money for carriage.

**portfolio** (port-fo'le-o), n. A portable case for papers.

**porthole** (port'hol), n. An opening in a ship's side for cannon.

**portico** (por'te-ko), n. A piazza or covered walk. pl. **porticos**.

**portion** (por'shun), vt. To divide; to allot; to endow.

**portliness** (port'le-nes), n. Dignity of mien; largeness of person.

**portmanteau** (port-man'to), n. A bag to carry clothes in.

**portrait** (por'trat), n. A picture from life.

**portray** (por-tra'), vt. To paint the likeness of; to describe.

**portrayer** (por-tra'er), n. One who paints or describes.

**poser** (poz'er), n. One who poses; that which puzzles.

**position** (po-zish'un), n. Situation; principle laid down.

**positive** (poz'it-iv), a. Certain; real; confident; absolute.

**possess** (poz-zes'), vt. To have or hold one's own. [possession]

**possessive** (poz-zes'iv), a. Denoting possession.

**posset** (pos'et), n. Milk curdled with wine or other liquors.

**possibility** (pos-e-bil'e-te), n. The power of being or doing.

**postal** (post'al), a. Belonging to the post-office.

**postdiluvian** (post-de-lu've-an), a. Being after the deluge.

**posterior** (pos-te're-or), a. Later in time or order; subsequent.

**posteriors** (pos-te're-orz), n. pl. The hinder parts of an animal.

**posterity** (pos-ter'e-te), n. Descendants.

**postern** (post'ern), n. A small back gate.

**posthumous** (post'hum-us), a. Being after one's decease.

**postil** (pos'til), n. A marginal note.

**postillion** (pos-til'yun), n. One who rides a coach horse.

**postman** (post'man), n. A letter-carrier.

**postmark** (post'mark), n. The post-master's stamp.

**postmeridian** (post-me-rid'e-an), a. Being in the afternoon.

**postpone** (post-pon'), vt. To put off; to delay. [postponement]

**postscript** (post'skript), n. A part added to a writing.

**postulate** (pos'tu-lat), n. Any thing assumed without proof.

**posture** (pos'tur), n. Attitude; position; situation.

**posy** (po'ze), n. A motto on a ring; a nosegay. pl. posies.

**potash** (pot'ash), n. An alkaline salt from the ashes of plants.

**potation** (po-ta'shun), n. A drinking; excessive draught.

**potato** (po-ta'to), n. An esculent root.

**potency** (po'ten-se), n. Relative power, strength, or efficacy.

**potent** (po'tent), a. Having great power or authority.

**potentate** (po'tent-at), n. A monarch.

**potential** (po-ten'she-al), a. Having power.

**potently** (po'tent-le), ad. Powerfully.

**pother** (poth'er), n. Confusion; stir.

**potion** (po-shun), n. A draught; a liquid medicine.

**potsherd** (pot'sherd), n. A piece of broken pot.

**pottage** (pot'aj), n. Porridge.

**potter** (pot'er), n. One who makes earthen vessels. [pottery]

**pouch** (pouch), n. A small bag. vt. To pocket.

**poultice** (pol'tis), n. A soothing application for sores.

**poultry** (pol'tre), n. Domestic fowls.

**pounce** (pouns), n. The claw of a bird; a fine powder.

**pound** (pound), n. Weight of 16 ounces avoirdupois, or 12 of troy; a pinfold; twenty shillings. vt. To beat; to confine in a pen.

**pour** (por), vt. To throw out in a continuous stream.

**pout** (pout), n. A sullen look; a fish.

**poverty** (pov'er-te), n. Want of riches.

**powerful** (pow'er-fool), a. Having power; strong.

**practicable** (prak'te-ka-bl), a. That can be done.

**practical** (prak'tik-al), a. Relating to practice.

**practice** (prak'tis), n. Customary use; habit; performance.

**practise** (prak'tis), vt. To do frequently or habitually. [**practitioner**]

**pragmatical** (prag-mat'ik-al), a. Very positive or dictatorial.

**prairie** (pra're), n. An extensive tract of land with few trees.

**praise** (praz), n. Commendation; object or ground of praise.

**prance** (prans), vi. To spring; to leap.

**prank** (prangk), vt. To adorn.

**prate** (prat), vi. To utter foolishly.

**pratique** (prat'ek), n. A license to trade after performing quarantine.

**prattle** (prat'l), n. Childish talk.

**prawn** (prawn), n. A small crustaceous fish.

**preamble** (pre'am-bl), n. An introductory writing; something previous.

**prebend** (preb'end), n. A stipend in a cathedral church.

**prebendary** (preb'en-dar-e), n. The stipendiary of a cathedral.

**precarious** (pre-ka're-us), a. Held by a doubtful tenure.

**precaution** (pre-ka'shun), n. Previous care. [**precautionary, precautious**]

**precede** (pre-sed'), v. To go before. [**precedence**]

**precedent** (pre-se'dent), a. Former; going before; anterior.

**precedent** (pres'e-dent), n. A previous example or rule.

**precept** (pre'sept), n. A command, rule, or maxim. [**preceptor**]

**precession** (pre-sesh'un), n. A going before.

**precinct** (pre'sinkgt), n. An outward limit; a boundary; territorial district.

**precious** (presh'us), a. Of great price or worth; highly esteemed.

**precipice** (pres'i-pis), n. Any steep descent.

**precipitate** (pre-sip'i-tat), v. To throw headlong; to hasten; to fall or cast to the bottom of a vessel. [**precipitation**]

**precipitous** (pre-sip'i-tus), a. Very steep; abrupt.

**precise** (pre-sis'), a. Exact; strict; nice; stiff.

**precision** (pre-sizh'un), n. Exactness; accuracy.

**preclude** (pre-klod'), v. To hinder; to prevent.

**precocity** (pre-kos'i-ti), n. Premature development.

**preconceive** (pre-kon-sev'), v. To conceive beforehand.

**precursor** (pre-kur'sur), n. One who, or that which, precedes or indicates an event. [**precursory**]

**predatory** (pred'a-to-ri), a. Plundering; rapacious.

**predecessor** (pre-de-ses'ur), n. One gone before.

**predestine** (pre-des'tin), v. To decree beforehand.

**predetermine** (pre-de-ter'min), v. To determine beforehand.

**predicable** (pred'i-ka-bl), a. That may be affirmed of or attributed to.

**predicament** (pre-dik'a-ment), n. Class; state; particular condition.

**predicate** (pred'i-kat), n. What is affirmed or denied.

**predict** (pre-dikt'), v. To foretell; to prophesy. [prediction]

**predilection** (pre-di-lek'shun), n. Previous liking.

**predispose** (pre-dis-poz'), v. Previously liable.

**predominate** (pre-dom'i-nat), v. To prevail; to be superior; to rule over.

**pre-eminent** (pre-em'i-nent), a. Surpassing others.

**pre-emption** (pre-emp'shun), n. Act or right of buying before another.

**preface** (pref'as), n. Something introductory, spoken or written.

**prefatory** (pref'a-tor-i), a. Introductory.

**prefect** (pre'fekt), n. A governor or chief officer.

**prefer** (pre-fer'), v. To regard more highly; to offer; to present.

**preferable** (pref'er-a-bl), a. Eligible to go before another. [preference]

**prefigure** (pre-fig'ur) v. Represent beforehand; foreshow.

**prefix** (pre-fiks'), v. To settle beforehand; to place before.

**pregnant** (preg'nant), a. Fruitful; full of promise.

**prehensible** (pre-hen'si-bl), a. That may be seized.

**prehensile** (pre-hen'sil), a. Adapted for seizing or holding.

**prejudge** (pre-juj'), v. To decide beforehand.

**prejudicate** (pre-jo'di-kat), v. To form a judgment beforehand.

**prejudice** (prej'u-dis), n. Previous judgment; bent or bias; injury. [prejudicial]

**prelate** (prel'at), n. An ecclesiastical official.

**preliminary** (pre-lim'i-nari), a. That precedes; introductory.

**prelude** (prel'ud), n. A flourish of music, or brief act; something introductory.

**prelude** (pre-lud'), v. To play before, as introducing.

**premature** (pre-ma-tur'), a. Ripe too soon; too early; too hasty.

**premeditate** (pre-med'i-tat), v. To meditate or contrive beforehand.

**premier** (pre'mi-er), n. First minister or secretary of state; a diplomat.

**premise** (prem'is), n. A first or antecedent proposition.

**premise** (pre-miz'), v. To lay down premises.

**premises** (prem'is-ez), n. pl. Propositions admitted; a house or land, with its adjuncts.

**premium** (pre'mi-um), n. Reward; advance; profit.

**premonition** (pre-mo-nish'un), n. Previous admonition or warning. [premonitory]

**preparative** (pre-par'a-tiv), a. Adapted to prepare.

**prepare** (pre-par'), v. To make fit or ready; to qualify.

**prepense** (pre-pens'), a. Premeditated.

**preponderate** (pre-pon'der-at), vi. To outweigh; incline; exceed in influence.

**preposition** (prep-o-zish'un), n. Part of speech

**prepossess** (pre-poz-zes'), vt. To preoccupy; bias favorably. [**prepossession**]

**preposterous** (pre-pos'ter-us), a. Irrational; absurd.

**prerogative** (pre-rog'a-tiv), n. Peculiar privilege.

**presage** (pre-saj'), vt. To forebode; predict.

**presage** (pres'aj), n. Prognostic; token; omen.

**presbyter** (prez'bi-ter), n. A church-elder.

**prescient** (pre'shi-ent), a. Foreknowing. [**prescience**]

**prescribe** (pre-skrib'), vt. and vi. To direct; lay down rules; give directions for a remedy. [**prescription**]

**prescript** (pre'skript), n. Prescribed rule or model.

**prescription** (pre-skrip'-shun), n. Act of prescribing; written direction of remedies; custom or use long continued.

**prescriptive** (pre-skrip'tiv), a. Acquired by custom or continued use.

**presence** (prez'ens), n. State of being present; nearness; personal appearance; readiness, as of mind.

**present** (prez'ent), a. In a certain place; being now or here; immediate.

**present** (pre-zent'), vt. To set before; introduce; offer; give; indict. [**presentation**]

**presentiment** (pre-sent'i-ment), n. Previous opinion; foreboding.

**presentment** (pre-zent'-ment), n. Presenting; representation; accusation by a grand jury.

**preservative** (pre-zerv'a-tiv), a. Having power to preserve.

**preserve** (pre-zerv'), vt. To rescue; keep from injury; keep; prepare for keeping. [**preservation**]

**preserve** (pre-zerv'), n. Fruit, etc., prepared by boiling in sirup; place where game is preserved.

**preside** (pre-zid'), vi. To govern; direct; superintend.

**presidency** (prez'i-den-si), n. Office, jurisdiction, or term of office, of a president. [**president**]

**pressure** (presh'yur), n. Act of pressing; state of being pressed; urgency; force.

**prestige** (prest'ij), n. Influence due to past success or eminence.

**presumable** (pre-zum'a-bl), a. That may be presumed.

**presume** (pre-zum'), vt. To take for granted.

**presumption** (pre-sump'-shun), n. Act of presuming; supposition; probability; confidence; forward conduct. [**presumptive**]

**presumptuous** (pre-zump'-tyu-us), a. Bold and confident.

**pretend** (pre-tend'), vt. and vi. To hold out an appearance of; feign; put in a claim.

**pretender** (pre-tend'er), n. One who pretends; a claimant.

**pretense** (pre-tens'), n. Anything pretended; pretext; assumption; show.

**pretentious** (pre-ten'shus), a. Full of assumption; showy.

**pretermit** (pre-ter-mit'), vt. To omit. [**pretermission**]

**preternatural** (pre-ter-nat'-yur-al), a. Beyond what is natural; extraordinary.

# PRETEXT — PROBOSCIS

**pretext** (pre'tekst), n. An excuse; pretense.

**pretty** (pret'i), a. Handsome; neat; pleasing.

**prevail** (pre-val'), vt. To have influence; overcome; be in force; be general.

**prevalent** (prev'a-lent), a. Powerful; victorious; general. [prevalence]

**prevaricate** (pre-var'i-kat), vi. To evade the truth; quibble. [prevarica'tion]

**prevent** (pre-vent'), vt. To hinder. [prevention]

**previous** (pre'vi-us), a. Earlier in time; former.

**prevision** (pre-vizh'un), n. Foresight.

**priest** (prest), n. A man in orders; a clergyman. [priestcraft]

**primacy** (pri'ma-se), n. Office or dignity of an archbishop.

**primarily** (pri'ma-re-le), ad. Originally.

**primary** (pri'ma-re), a. Original; first in time, meaning, or rank.

**primate** (pri'mat), n. An archbishop.

**primeval** (prim-e'val), a. Belonging to the earliest age.

**primitive** (prim'i-tiv), a. Original; ancient.

**primogeniture** (pri-mo-jen'-i-tur), n. State of being born first; right of inheritance of the eldest child.

**primordial** (prim-ord'i-al), a. Original; earliest.

**prince** (prins), n. A sovereign; son of a king; high noble; chief.

**principal** (prin'si-pal), a. Chief. n. A chief person; head; money on which interest is paid.

**principality** (prin-si-pal'i-ti), n. Territory of a prince.

**principle** (prin'si-pl), n Fundamental doctrine; rule of conduct; faculty of the mind; constituent part.

**prior** (pri'or), a. Previous; former.

**priority** (pri-or'i-ti), n. State of being first.

**prism** (prizm), n. A solid, whose ends and bases are similar, equal, parallel, and whose sides are parallelograms.

**prismatic** (priz-mat'ik), a. Formed by prisms.

**prison** (priz'n), n. A jail. [prisoner]

**pristine** (pris'tin), a. Former; ancient; original.

**privacy** (pri'va-si), n. Seclusion; retreat; retirement; secrecy.

**private** (pri'vat), a. Peculiar to one's self; not public; alone.

**privateer** (pri-va-ter'), n. A private ship of war commissioned to seize enemy's ships.

**privation** (pri-va'shun), n. Act of depriving; destitution; absence; loss.

**privilege** (priv'i-lej), v. To grant exemption or peculiar rights.

**privily** (priv'i-li), ad. Secretly.

**privy** (priv'i), a. Knowing secretly and consenting.

**probability** (prob-a-bil'i-ti), n. Appearance of truth; likelihood; chance. [probable]

**probate** (pro'bat), n. Proof of a will. [probation]

**probationary** (pro-ba'shun-a-ri), a. Serving for trial. [probationer]

**probe** (prob), n. A surgeon's instrument.

**probity** (prob'i-ti), n. Uprightness; integrity; honesty.

**problem** (prob'lem), n. A question for solution.

**proboscis** (pro-bos'is), n.

The snout or trunk of an elephant, etc.

**procedure** (pro-se'dur), n. Act or manner of proceeding; progress.

**proceed** (pro-sed'), v. To go forward.

**proceeds** (pro'sedz), n. pl. Issues; rents.

**process** (pros'es), n. A proceeding; method; operation. [procession]

**proclaim** (pro-klam'), v. To promulgate; to publish. [proclamation]

**proclivity** (pro-kliv'i-ti), n. Natural inclination; steep descent; proneness; tendency.

**procrastinate** (pro-kras'ti-nat), v. To put off from day to day; to postpone. [procrastination]

**procure** (pro-kur'), v. To obtain; to acquire; to attract.

**prodigal** (prod'i-gal), a. Lavish; wasteful; profuse. [prodigality]

**prodigious** (pro-dij'us), a. Enormous; astonishing.

**prodigy** (prod'i-ji), n. Anything extraordinary; a wonder.

**produce** (pro-dus'), v. To bring forth; to yield.

**produce** (prod'us), n. That which is produced; profit.

**product** (prod'ukt), n. Thing produced; performance; effect; result; sum. [production]

**productive** (pro-duk'tiv), a. Having the power to produce.

**profanation** (prof-a-na'shun), n. Act of profaning; desecration. [profane]

**profanity** (pro-fan'i-ti), n. Quality of being profane; irreverence.

**profess** (pro-fes'), v. To declare; to avow; to own. [profession]

**professor** (pro-fes'ur), n. One who declares his faith; a teacher of learning.

**proffer** (prof'fer), v. To propose; to tender.

**proficiency** (pro-fish'en-si), n. Progress in learning. [proficient]

**profile** (pro'fel or pro'fil), n. Outline; side face.

**profit** (prof'it), n. Gain; advantage.

**profligacy** (prof'li-ga-si), n. A vicious course of life.

**profligate** (prof'li-gat), a. Lost to virtue.

**profound** (pro-fownd'), a. Deep; thorough; learned.

**profundity** (pro-fun'di-ti), n. Depth of knowledge or skill.

**profuse** (pro-fus'), a. Lavish; extravagant. [profusion]

**progenitor** (pro-jen'i-tur), n. An ancestor; a forefather.

**progeny** (proj'e-ni), n. Offspring; race; descendants.

**prognosticate** (prog-nos'ti-kat), v. To predict.

**program** (pro'gram), n. Preliminary sketch; public notice; outline of a public performance.

**progress** (prog'res), n. Advance onward; improvement.

**progress** (pro-gres'), v. To advance; to improve. [progressive]

**prohibit** (pro-hib'it), v. To forbid; to hinder; to debar. [prohibition]

**prohibitive** (pro-hib'i-tiv), a. Forbidding.

**project** (pro-jekt'), v. To jut; to form a plan; to contrive.

**project** (proj'ekt), n. A plan; scheme; contrivance.

**projectile** (pro-jek'til), a. Impelling forward.

**projection** (pro-jek'shun), n. Act of projecting; plan; delineation.

**proletarian** (pro-le-ta'ri-an), a. Plebeian.

**prolific** (pro-lif'ik), a. Fruitful; productive.

**prolix** (pro-liks'), a. Long; tedious; protracted; diffused. [prolixity]

**prologue** (pro'log), n. A preface to a play.

**prolong** (pro-lang'), v. To lengthen out; to extend. [prolongation]

**prolusion** (pro-lu'zhun), n. A preliminary or slight treatise.

**promenade** (prom-e-nad'), n. A walk; place for walking.

**prominence** (prom'i-nens), n. State of being prominent; a projection; elevation.

**promiscuous** (pro-mis'kyuus), a. Mixed; confused; indiscriminate.

**promissory** (prom'i-so-ri), a. Containing a promise.

**promontory** (prom'on-to-ri), n. A headland; high cape.

**promote** (pro-mot'), vt. To forward; further; elevate. [promotion, promoter]

**prompt** (promt), a. Ready; quick.

**promulgate** (pro-mul'gat), vt. To make publicly known.

**prone** (pron), a. With the face downward; headlong; disposed.

**pronoun** (pro'noun), n. Word used in place of a noun.

**pronounce** (pro-nouns'), a. To utter; speak. [pronuncia'tion]

**propagandist** (prop-a-gand'-ist), n. One who propagates opinions.

**propagate** (prop'a-gat), vt. To produce; multiply; spread.

**propel** (pro-pel'), vt. To drive forward.

**propeller** (pro-pel'er), n. One who, or that which, propels; screw to propel a steamboat; boat so propelled.

**propensity** (pro-pen'si-ti), n. Inclination; disposition.

**proper** (prop'er), a. One's own; fit; correct; belonging.

**property** (prop'er-ti), a. Inherent quality; something owned; estate; ownership.

**prophecy** (prof'e-si), n. Prediction.

**prophesy** (prof'e-si), vt. and vi. To predict; foretell.

**prophet** (prof'et), n. One who prophesies.

**prophylactic** (pro-fil-ak'tik), a. Preventive of disease.

**propinquity** (pro-pin'kwi-ti), n. Nearness.

**propitiate** (pro-pish'i-at), vi. To render favorable.

**propitious** (pro-pish'us), a. Favorably disposed.

**proportion** (pro-por'shun), n. Relation of one thing to another; fitness of parts; just share; similarity of ratios.

**proportional** (pro-por'shun-al), a. Having, or relating to, proportion.

**proposal** (pro-poz'al), n. Anything proposed; conditions offered.

**propose** (pro-poz'), vt. To offer for consideration.

**proposition** (prop-o-zish'un), n. Anything proposed; offer of terms; statement to be proved.

**propound** (pro-pound'), vt. To propose; declare.

**proprietary** (pro-pri'e-ta-ri), a. Belonging to a proprietor. [**proprietor**]

**propriety** (pro-pri'e-ti), n. Fitness; suitableness; decorum.

**propulsion** (pro-pul'shun), n. Act of driving forward.

**prorogue** (pro-rog'), vt. To continue to another session.

**proscenium** (pro-se'ni-um), n. Front of the stage.

**proscribe** (pro-skrib'), vt. To denounce and condemn; interdict. [**proscription**]

**proscriptive** (pro-skrip'tiv), a. Pertaining to proscription.

**prosecute** (pros'e-kut), vt. To pursue; follow; pursue by law. [**prosecution**]

**prosecutor** (pros-e-kut'or), n. One who prosecutes.

**proselyte** (pros'e-lit), n. A convert.

**prosody** (pros'o-di), n. Part of grammar which treats of quantity, accent, and versification.

**prospect** (pros'pekt), n. A view; outlook; expectation.

**prospective** (pro-spek'tiv), a. Looking forward; in the future.

**prospectus** (pro-spek'tus), n. Plan, esp. of a literary work.

**prosper** (pros'per), vi. To thrive; be successful.

**prosperity** (pros-per'i-ti), n. Success; good fortune. [**prosperous**]

**prostitute** (pros'ti-tut), vt. To devote to a bad or infamous use.

**prostrate** (pros'trat), a. Lying at length; overthrown.

**prostrate** (pros'trat), vt. To throw down; overthrow; reduce to extreme weakness. [**prostration**]

**protean** (pro'te-an, pro'te-), a. Assuming various shapes.

**protect** (pro-tekt'), vt. To defend; shelter. [**protection**]

**protection** (pro-tek'shun), n. Defence from injury or danger. [**protective, protector**]

**protege** (pro-ta-zha'), n. One patronized.

**protest** (pro-test'), vi. To affirm solemnly.

**protest** (pro'test), n. A formal declaration.

**Protestant** (prot'est-ant), n. One who protests against popery. [**Protestantism**]

**protestation** (pro-test-a'shun), n. Solemn declaration.

**prothonotary** (pro-thon'o-tar-e), n. Clerk of a court.

**protocol** (pro'to-kol), n. A registry or record.

**prototype** (pro'to-tip), n. An original model.

**protract** (pro-trakt'), v. To lengthen; to prolong. [**protraction**]

**protrude** (pro-trod'), v. To extend forward; to thrust out.

**protuberance** (pro-tu'ber-ans), n. Prominence.

**proud** (prowd), a. Elated; arrogant; haughty.

**provender** (prov'en-der), n. Food for beasts.

**proverb** (prov'erb), n. A maxim of wisdom; a byword; an adage. [**proverbial**]

**provide** (pro-vid'), v. To procure beforehand; to prepare.

**providence** (prov'i-dens), n. Foresight; God's care; prudence.

**provident** (prov'i-dent), a. Providing for the future; frugal. [**providential**]

**province** (prov'ins), n. A subject country, governed by a delegate; sphere; duty.

**provincial** (pro-vin'shal), n. An inhabitant of a province. a. Belonging to a province.

**provision** (pro-vizh' un), n. Stipulation; something provided; food. [**provisional**]

**proviso** (pro-vi'zo), n. Any conditional stipulation.

**provocation** (prov-o-ka'shun), n. A cause of anger.

**provocative** (pro-vok'a-tiv), a. That excites.

**provost** (prov'ust), n. A chief officer of any body; an army or navy official.

**prow** (prow), n. Fore part of a ship.

**prowess** (prow'es), n. Bravery; valor; boldness.

**prowl** (prowl), v. To rove for prey.

**proximate** (proks'i-mat), a. Nearest; next; closest.

**proximity** (proks-im'i-ti), n. Immediate nearness.

**proxy** (proks'i), n. A substitute or deputy.

**prude** (prod), n. A woman who is over-affected.

**prudence** (pro'dens), n. Wisdom; discretion.

**prudent** (pro'dent), a. Practically wise; provident.

**prudential** (pro-den'shal) a. Proceeding from or dictated by prudence.

**prudery** (prod'er-i), n. Affected reserve.

**prune** (pron), n. A dried plum.

**prurient** (pro'ri-ent), a. Uneasy with longing.

**pruriency** (pro'ri-en-si), n. An itching; a longing desire for anything.

**Prussian** (prush'an), a. From or relating to Prussia.

**psalm** (sam), n. A sacred song or hymn.

**pseudonym** (su'do-nim), n. A false name.

**psychical** (si'ki-kal), a. Relating to the soul or spirit.

**psychologic** (si-ko-loj'ik), a. Relating to psychology.

**psychology** (si-kol'o-ji), n. The science of the mind or soul.

**public** (pub'lik), a. Pertaining to a community; common; open.

**publican** (pub'li-kan), n. An innkeeper; a collector of toll or taxes.

**publication** (pub-li-ka'shun) n. The act of publishing; thing published.

**publicist** (pub'li-sist), n. One skilled in the laws and rights of nations.

**publicity** (pub-lis'i-ti), n. State of being public.

**publicly** (pub'lik-li), ad. Openly.

**publish** (pub'lish), v. To make known; to announce.

**Puck** (puk), n. A celebrated fairy.

**pucker** (puk'er), v. To plait; to fold; to wrinkle.

**pudding** (pod'ing), n. A food made with meal, eggs, fruit, flour, etc.

**puddle** (pud'dl), n. A pool of muddy water.

**puerile** (pu'er-il), a. Childish; boyish; trifling. [**puerility**]

**puffery** (puf'fer-i), n. Extravagant praise.

**puffy** (puf'fi), a. Swelled up; windy; bombastic.

**pugh** (po), interj. A word of contempt or disdain.

**pugilism** (pu'jil-izm), n. Art of fighting with the fists. [**pugilist**]

**pugilistic** (pu-jil-is'tik), a. Pertaining to boxing.

**pugnacious** (pug-na'shus),

a. Fond of fighting; quarrelsome.
**pugnacity** (pug-nas'i-ti), n. Inclination to fight.
**pule** (pul), v. To whine like a child, or chicken.
**pullet** (pol'let), n. A young hen; a chicken.
**pulley** (pol'li), n. A small wheel in a block, for a running cord or rope.
**pulmonary** (pul'mon-ar-i) a. Relating to or affecting the lungs. [pulmonic]
**pulp** (pulp), n. The soft part of fruit.
**pulpit** (pol'pit), n. An elevated desk for a preacher.
**pulsate** (pul'sat), v. To beat or throb, as an artery. [pulsation]
**pulse** (puls), n. The beating of arteries; peas, etc.
**pulverize** (pul'ver-iz), v. To reduce to powder.
**puma** (pu'ma), n. The American lion.
**pumice** (pum'is), n. A hard, light, spongy, volcanic mineral.
**pump** (pump), n. A machine for raising water.
**pumpkin** (pump'kin), n. A plant and its fruit.
**punch** (punch), n. A tool; a blow; a beverage.
**puncheon** (punch'un), n. A tool; a cask.
**punctilious** (pungk-til'i-us), a. Exact in ceremony or behavior; nice.
**punctual** (pungk'tu-al), a. Exact in time; punctilious.
**punctuality** (pungk-tu-al'i-ti), n. Scrupulous exactness as to time.
**punctuate** (pungk'tyu-at), vt. To mark with points. [punctua'tion]
**puncture** (pungk'tyur), n. Small hole made with a point.
**pungent** (pun'jent), a. Sharp; acrid; stinging.

**pungy** (pun'gi), n. A long narrow sail-boat.
**punish** (pun'ish), vt. To exact a penalty from; inflict pain or loss for ill-doing.
**punishment** (pun'ish-ment), n. Penalty inflicted for offense.
**punitive** (pu'ni-tiv), a. Punishing.
**punk** (pungk), n. Decayed wood used as tinder.
**punster** (pun'ster), n. One addicted to punning.
**punt** (punt), n. A flat-boat.
**puny** (pu'ni), a. Small; weak.
**pupa** (pu'pa), n. A larva undergoing its final change.
**pupil** (pu'pil), n. A scholar; Central spot of the eye.
**puppet** (pup'et), n. Small figure moved by wires.
**puppy** (pup'i), n. A young dog; coxcomb.
**purblind** (pur'blind), a. Dim-sighted; near-sighted.
**purchase** (pur'chas), vt. To obtain by paying; buy.
**purfle** (pur'fl), vt. To decorate with a border.
**purgation** (pur-ga'shun), n. Act of purging; act of clearing from a charge.
**purgative** (pur'ga-tiv), a. Cleansing; cathartic.
**purgatory** (pur'ga-to-ri), n. A place where, according to some creeds, the souls of the dead are purified.
**purge** (purj), vt. To cleanse; clear; purify.
**purify** (pu'ri-fi), vt. and vi. To make or become pure.
**purism** (pu'rizm), n. Purity of style.
**Puritan** (pu'ri-tan), n. One of a sect of dissenters in the 16th and 17th centuries.
**purity** (pu'ri-ti), n. State of being pure.
**purl** (purl), n. A soft sound as of flowing water; waved

**edging;** stitch in knitting; spiced malt liquor.
**purlieu** (pur'lu), n. Environs.
**purloin** (pur-loin'), vt. To steal.
**purple** (pur'pl), n. Color composed of red and blue; a purple robe.
**purport** (pur'port), n. Meaning; design. vi. To mean.
**purpose** (pur'pus), n. Aim; intention; effect.
**purr** (pur), n. Murmur uttered by cats.
**purse** (purs), n. A small bag for money; treasury.
**pursuance** (pur-su'ans), n. Act of following; process; continuance.
**pursuant** (pur-su'ant), a. Following; agreeable.
**pursue** (pur-su'), vt. To follow; chase; seek; continue.
**pursuit** (pur-sut'), n. Act of pursuing; endeavor to attain; occupation.
**pursuivant** (pur'swi-vant), n. A herald of subordinate rank; state messenger.
**pursy** (pur'si), a. Fat; short-breathed.
**purulent** (pur'yu-lent), a. Of, or containing, pus.
**purvey** (pur-va'), vt. To provide; procure.
**purview** (pur'vu), n. Scope; extent.
**pus** (pus), n. Creamy liquid formed on a sore; matter.
**pusillanimous** (pu-sil-an'i-mus), a. Mean-spirited; cowardly.

**pustule** (pus'tyul), n. Pimple containing pus.
**putative** (put'a-tiv), a. Supposed.
**putrefactive** (pu-tre-fak'tiv) a. Pertaining to, or producing, putrefaction.
**putrefy** (pu'tre-fi), vi. and vt. To become, or make, putrid or rotten. [**putrefac'tion**]
**putrescent** (pu-tres'ent), a. Becoming putrid.
**putrid** (pu-trid), a. Rotten; corrupt. n. **putrid'ity**.
**puzzle** (puz'l), vt. To perplex.
**pyæmia** (pi-e'mi-a), n. Morbid state caused by the absorption of purulent matter into the blood.
**pygmy** (pig'mi), n. A dwarf. a. **pygmy, pygme'an.**
**pyramid** (pir'a-mid), n. A solid with rectilinear base and triangular sides meeting at an apex.
**pyre** (pir), n. A funeral pile for burning.
**pyrites** (pir-i'tez), n. A native sulphide of iron, copper, etc.
**pyrometer** (pir-om'e-ter), n. An instrument for measuring high degrees of heat.
**pyrotechnic** (pir'o-tek-nik), a. Pertaining to fireworks. [**pyrotechnics**]
**pyx** (piks), n. Box in which the consecrated host is kept.

# Q

**quackery** (kwak'er-i), n. The pretensions or practice of a quack.
**Quadragesima** (kwod-ra-jes'i-ma), n. Lent.
**quadrangle** (kwod'rang-gl), n. Plane figure of four equal sides and angles.
**quadrant** (kwod'rant), n. Quarter of a circle; arc of 90°; instrument for taking altitudes.
**quadratic** (kwod-rat'ik), a. Pertaining to a square.
**quadrature** (kwod'ra-tur), n. A square; the act of squaring.
**quadrille** (ka-dril', kwa-dril')

n. A set dance; game at cards.

**quadruped** (kwod'roo-ped), n. An animal having four feet.

**quadruple** (kwod'roo-pl), a. Fourfold.

**quaff** (kwaf), vt. To drink largely.

**quagmire** (kwag'mir), n. A bog that shakes under the feet.

**quail** (kwal), n. A bird of the grouse kind.

**quaintly** (kwant'le), ad. Nicely; prettily; oddly.

**quake** (kwak), vi. To shake.

**Quaker** (kwak'er), n. One of the society of Friends.

**qualifiable** (kwol'e-fi-a-bl), a. That may be abated or modified. [qualification]

**quality** (kwol'i-ti), n. An attribute; character; rank.

**qualm** (kwam), n. Scruple; nausea.

**quandary** (kwon'da-ri), n. Perplexity; uncertainty.

**quantity** (kwon'ti-ti), n. Bulk; extent, number, or portion.

**quarantine** (kwor'an-ten), n. Prohibition of a vessel's intercourse with the shore.

**quarrel** (kwor'rel), n. A breach of amity; a noisy dispute. v. To dispute; to find fault.

**quarry** (kwor'ri), n. A pit from which stones are dug.

**quart** (kwart), n. The fourth part of a gallon; two pints.

**quarter** (kwar'ter), n. A fourth part of anything; 3 months; 8 bushels; mercy granted.

**quarterly** (kwar'ter-li), a. Occurring every three months.

**quartermaster** (kwar'ter-mas-ter), n. An officer who regulates the quarters, forage, food, etc., of an army.

**quartette** (kwar-tet'), n. Music in four parts; four persons performing together.

**quarto** (kwar'to), n. Book in which each leaf is a quarter of a sheet.

**quash** (kwash), v. To annul; to crush; to subdue.

**quasi** (kwa'si), ad. As if; just as if; almost.

**quatrain** (kwot'ran), n. A stanza of four lines.

**quaver** (kwa'ver), v. To vibrate; to shake the voice.

**quay** (ke), n. A wharf; a mole, or bank.

**queen** (kwen), n. The wife of a king; a female sovereign.

**queer** (kwer), a. Odd; quaint.

**quell** (kwel), v. To crush; to allay; to appease.

**quench** (kwench), v. To extinguish; to allay.

**querist** (kwe'rist), n. One who inquires or questions.

**querulous** (kwer'u-lus), a. Habitually complaining.

**query** (kwe'ri), n. A question. v. To ask questions.

**quest** (kwest), n. Act of seeking; search; request.

**question** (kwes'chun), n. Act of asking; inquiry; doubt. v. To ask; to interrogate; to doubt.

**queue** (ku), n. A tie of hair.

**quibble** (kwib'l), n. An evasion; a pun.

**quick** (kwik), a. Done with speed; living.

**quicklime** (kwik'lim), n. Lime unslacked.

**quicksand** (kwik'sand), n. Sand easily moved, and yielding to pressure; anything deceptive, treacherous, or dangerous.

**quicksilver** (kwik'sil-ver), n. Mercury.

**quiddity** (kwid'i-ti), n. A trifling nicety; a cavil.

**quidnunc** (kwid'nungk), n.

**quiescent** (kwi-es'ent), a. Quiet; at rest; silent.

**quiet** (kwi'et), a. Calm; gentle; peaceable.

**quietude** (kwi'e-tud), n. Repose; rest; tranquility.

**quietus** (kwi-e'tus), n. Final discharge; death.

**quill** (kwil), n. A strong feather; a piece of reed.

**quilt** (kwilt), n. A cover of a bed.

**quince** (kwins), n. A tree and its acid fruit.

**quinine** (kwi'nin), n. An alkaloid obtained from Peruvian bark.

**quinsy** (kwin'zi), n. Inflammation and soreness of the throat.

**quintal** (kwin'tal), n. A weight of 100 or 112 pounds.

**quintessence** (kwin-tes'ens), n. Pure essence of anything.

**quintuple** (kwin'tu-pl), a. Fivefold.

**quip** (kwip), n. A sarcastic jest.

**quire** (kwir), n. 24 sheets of paper.

**quirk** (kwerk), n. An artful or smart retort; a quibble.

**quit** (kwit), v. To leave; to discharge. a. Released; free; absolved.

**quite** (kwit), ad. Entirely; wholly; perfectly; very.

**quittance** (kwit'tans), n. Discharge from a debt.

**quixotic** (kwiks-ot'ik), a. Absurdly romantic.

**quiz** (kwiz), n. A riddle; puzzle; v. To banter; to puzzle.

**quoin** (koin, kwoin), n. A corner; external angle; wedge.

**quoit** (kwoit), n. A heavy flat ring for pitching.

**quondam** (kwon'dam), Having been formerly.

**quorum** (kwo'rum), n. A number of the members of any body sufficient to transact business.

**quota** (kwo'ta), n. The part or share assigned to each.

**quotation** (kwo-ta'shun), n. That which is quoted.

**quote** (kwot), v. To repeat the words of any one.

**quotient** (kwo'shent), n. The number of times one number is contained in another.

# R

**rabbi** (rab'bi), n. A Jewish doctor or expounder of the law. [rabbinical]

**rabbit** (rab'bit), n. A small, long-eared quadruped.

**rabble** (rab'l), n. A crowd of low people; a mob.

**rabid** (rab'id), a. Raving; furious; mad.

**raccoon** (rak-kon'), n. A badger-like quadruped.

**race** (ras), n. A running; a breed, or variety; family.

**rack** (rak), n. An engine of torture; extreme pain; a grating for hay; frame holding articles.

**racket** (rak'et), n. A clattering noise; a framed net.

**racy** (ra'si), a. Pungent; rich; piquant; flavorous; strong.

**radiant** (ra'di-ant), a. Emitting, or issuing in, rays; shining. [radiance]

**radiate** (ra'di-at), vi. To emit rays; proceed in straight lines from any point. [radiator]

**radical** (rad'i-kal), a. Original; rooted; implanted by nature; reaching to the principles; pertaining to radicals.

**radicle** (rad'i-kl), n. Part of a seed which becomes the root.

**radio** (ra'di-o), n. Aerial receiver or apparatus to broadcast or radiocast.

**radius** (ra'di-us), n. A line from the centre to the circumference of a circle; the outer bone of the fore-arm. pl. **radii**.

**raffle** (raf'l), n. A kind of lottery.

**ragged** (rag'ed), a. Torn into rags; covered with rags; having a rough edge or surface.

**ragout** (ra-goo'), n. A highly-seasoned dish.

**raid** (rad), n. A hostile incursion; foray.

**rail** (ral), n. A wooden bar; iron bar on which cars run.

**raillery** (ral'er-i, ral'), n. Banter; playful mockery.

**raiment** (ra'ment), n. Clothing; apparel.

**raise** (raz), vt. To lift; erect; elevate.

**raisin** (ra'zin), n. A dried grape.

**rake** (rak), vt. To scrape with something toothed; search in or over; sweep with guns.

**rake** (rak), n. A libertine.

**rally** (ral'i), vt. To collect and re-form, as troops; recover.

**ramie** (ra-me'), n. A nettle-like plant, yielding fibres which are used in weaving.

**ramify** (ram'i-fi), vi. To branch out. [ramifica'tion]

**ramp** (ramp), vi. To rear up; act violently.

**rampant** (ram'pant), a. Unrestrained; wild.

**rampart** (ram'part), n. Mound or wall surrounding a fortified place.

**ramrod** (ram'rod), n. Rod used in loading a gun.

**ranch** (ranch), n. A stock-farm (in the Western States).

**rancid** (ran'sid), a. Strong; rank, as old oil.

**rancor** (rang'kor), n. An old grudge; inveterate enmity; bitterness. [rancorous]

**random** (ran'dum), n. Want of direction.

**rankle** (rangk'l), vi. To become inflamed or violent.

**rankness** (rangk'nes), n. A strong scent.

**ransack** (ran'sak), vt. To search narrowly; to pillage.

**ransom** (ran'sum), n. The price paid to redeem a person or goods from an enemy.

**rant** (rant), n. Extravagant language. vi. To rave. [ranter]

**rapacious** (ra-pa'she-us), a. Inclined to plunder; greedy.

**rapacity** (ra-pas'e-te), n. Disposition to plunder.

**rape** (rap), n. A seizing by violence; carnal knowledge by force; a plant.

**rapid** (rap'id), a. Swift; quick. [rapidity]

**rapids** (rap'idz), n. pl. The part of a river where the bed descends rapidly.

**rapier** (ra'pe-er), n. A small sword.

**rapine** (rap'in), n. Act of plundering by violence.

**rapt** (rapt), a. Transported in ecstasy.

**rapture** (rapt'yur), n. Extreme delight; transport. [rapturous]

**rare** (rar), a. Thin; uncommon; excellent.

**rarefy** (rar'e-fi), vt. To make less dense; expand. [rarefac'tion]

**rarity** (rar'i-ti), n. State of being rare; something uncommon.

**rascal** (ras'kal), n. A rogue; knave.

**rase** (raz), vt. To cancel; demolish.

**rash** (rash), a. Hasty; overbold.

**raspberry** (raz'ber-i), n. A garden shrub, and its fruit.

**rasure** (ra'zhur), n. Erasure; demolition.

**ratchet** (rach'et), n. A bar falling into the teeth of a wheel or rack; pawl.

**rate** (rat), n. Allowance; price; degree; movement; tax.

**rather** (ra'ther), adv. Sooner; more willingly; more so; somewhat.

**ratify** (rat'i-fi), vt. To approve and sanction. [**ratifica'tion**]

**ratio** (ra'sho), n. Proportion; relation.

**ratiocination** (rash-i-os-i-na'shun), n. Act of reasoning.

**ration** (ra'shun), n. Allowance of provisions.

**rational** (rash'un-al), a. Endowed with reason; agreeable to reason; intelligent.

**rationale** (rash-un-a'li), n. An account with reasons. [**rationalism, rationalist**]

**ratsbane** (rats'ban), n. Arsenic.

**rattan** (rat-tan'), n. Genus of climbing palms with very slender stems; a stem or stick of rattan.

**ravage** (rav'aj), vt. To pillage; lay waste. n. Plunder; devastation.

**ravel** (rav'l), vt. To untwist or unweave.

**ravine** (ra-ven'), n. A long deep hollow; narrow pass.

**ravish** (rav'ish), vt. To carry away by force; to fill with ecstasy; to know carnally by force.

**raze** (raz), vt. To erase; to efface; to demolish; to ruin.

**razor** (ra'zer), n. An instrument for removing the beard or hair.

**razure** (ra'zhur), n. An erasing or effacing.

**reach** (rech), vt. To extend; to stretch; to hand over; to attain or obtain by stretching forth the hand; to extend to; to arrive at; to gain.

**ready** (red'y), a. Prepared; not behindhand or backward; prompt; apt; skillful; handy; easy; willing; cheerful.

**real** (re'al), a. Actually being or existing; not artificial, counterfeit, or factitious; true; genuine; authentic. [**re'ally, real'ity**]

**realizable** (re'al-i'za-b'l), a. Capable of being realized. [**re'aliza'tion**]

**realm** (relm), n. A royal jurisdiction; kingdom; region; department.

**realty** (re'alty), n. Real property.

**ream** (rem), n. A package of twenty quires of paper.

**reap** (rep), vt. & i. To cut (grain) with a sickle; to gather; to obtain.

**rear** (rer), n. The hinder troop, class, or part.

**reason** (re'zn), n. The faculty of the mind which judges and distinguishes; motive. [**reasonable**]

**reassure** (re-a-shur'), v. To assure again.

**rebate** (re-bat'), v. To deduct from; to refund as a drawback.

**rebel** (reb'el), n. One who opposes lawful authority. a. Acting in revolt.

**rebel** (re-bel'), v. To rise against lawful rule. [**rebellion**]

**rebellious** (re-bel'yus), a. Disobedient; resisting.

**rebound** (re-bownd'), v. To spring back.

**rebuff** (re-buf'), n. A sudden check.

**rebuke** (re-buk'), v. To reprove.

**rebus** (re'bus), n. A riddle.

**rebut** (re-but'), v. To oppose by argument; to repel.

**recalcitrant** (re-kal'si-trant) a. Kicking back; showing repugnance.

**recant** (re-kant'), v. To retract an opinion; to unsay.

**recapitulate** (re-ka-pit'u-lat), v. To repeat in the way of a summary.

**recast** (re-kast'), v. To cast or throw again.

**recede** (re-sed'), v. To draw back; to desist.

**receipt** (re-set'), n. Reception; a writing that something has been received.

**receive** (re-sev'), v. To take what is offered; to accept.

**recent** (re'sent), a. New; late; fresh; modern.

**receptacle** (re-sep'ta-kl), n. A place to receive things in.

**reception** (re-sep'shun), n. Act of receiving; entertainment.

**receptive** (re-sep'tiv), a. Having the quality of receiving or admitting.

**recess** (re-ses'), n. Privacy; retirement, or suspension.

**recession** (re-sesh'un), n. Act of ceding back.

**recherche** (re-sher-sha') a. Exquisite; well finished; sought out with care.

**recipe** (res'i-pe), n. Medical prescription; a formula.

**recipient** (re-sip'i-ent), n. One who receives.

**reciprocal** (re-sip'ro-kal), a. Mutual; acting in return.

**reciprocate** (re-sip'ro-kat), v. To give and receive mutually. [reciprocity]

**recital** (re-si'tal), n. Act of reciting; rehearsal. [recitation]

**recite** (re-sit'), v. To repeat aloud; to narrate.

**reckless** (rek'les), a. Careless of effect; heedless.

**reckon** (rek'n), v. To count; to calculate; to esteem. [reckoning]

**reclaim** (re-klam'), v. To recall; to reform; to recover or regain. [reclamation]

**recline** (re-klin'), v. To lean; to rest, or repose.

**recluse** (re-klos'), a. Secluded; retired; solitary.

**recognition** (rek-og-nish'un), n. Renewed or revived acknowledgement; avowal.

**recognizance** (re-kog'ni-zans), n. A legal obligation; a profession; recognition.

**recognize** (rek'og-niz), v. To know again; to recollect; to acknowledge.

**recoil** (re-koil'), v. To move back.

**recollect** (rek-ol-lekt'), v. To recall or bring to memory.

**re-collect** (re-kol-lekt'), v. To collect again. [recollection]

**recommend** (rek-om-mend'), v. To commend to another; to advise. [recommendation]

**recompense** (rek'om-pens), n. Reward.

**reconcile** (rek'on-sil), v. To reunite; to make agreeable.

**recondite** (rek'on-dit), a. Abstruse; profound; secret.

**reconnaissance** (re-kon'na-sans), n. A survey or examination of a country for warlike purposes.

**reconnoiter** (rek-on-noi'ter), v. To examine or

**reconsider** (re-kon-sid'er), v. To consider again.

**reconstruct** (re-kon-strukt'), v. To construct anew.

**record** (re-kard'), v. To register; to enroll; to imprint.

**record** (rek'urd), n. Authentic or official register.

**recourse** (re-kors'), n. A going to for aid or protection.

**recover** (re-kuv'er), v. To regain what was lost; to cure; to revive; to restore. [recovery]

**recreant** (rek're-ant), a. False; apostate.

**recreate** (rek're-at), v. To revive or refreshen after toil, to amuse; to cheer.

**recreate** (re-kre-at), v. To create anew. [recreation]

**recrimination** (re-krim-i-na'shun), n. Accusation retorted.

**recruit** (re-krot'), v. To obtain fresh supplies; to enlist new soldiers.

**rectangle** (rek'tang-gl), n. A four-sided figure with right angles.

**rectification** (rek-ti-fi-ka'shun), n. Act of correcting.

**rectify** (rek'ti-fi), v. To correct; to refine by distillation. [rectitude]

**rector** (rek'tur), n. A clergyman of a parish; a governor. [rectory]

**rectum** (rek'tum), n. Last part of the large intestines.

**recumbent** (re-kum'bent), a. Leaning; reclining; idle.

**recuperation** (re-ku-per-a'shun), n. Recovery.

**recur** (re-kur'), v. To resort; to return to the mind.

**recurrent** (re-kur'ent), a. Returning; running.

**recusant** (rek'yu-zant), a. Refusing to conform.

**redeem** (re-dem'), vt. To buy back; ransom; rescue; fulfill, as a promise. [redeemer]

**redemption** (re-demp'shun), n. Act of redeeming; repurchase; deliverance.

**redintegration** (red-in-ti-gra'shun), n. Restoration; renewal.

**redolent** (red'o-lent), a. Fragrant; odorous.

**redoubt** (re-dout'), n. A fortified work within another work. [redoubtable]

**redound** (re-dound'), vi. To roll back; result.

**redress** (re-dres'), vt. To set right; make amends for.

**reduce** (re-dus'), vt. To bring back; lessen; lower; change into equivalent values. [reducible, reduction]

**redundant** (re-dun'dant), a. Overflowing; excessive; superfluous. [redundance]

**reduplicate** (re-du'pli-kat), vt. To redouble; repeat. [reduplica'tion]

**refection** (re-fek'shun), n. Refreshment; a repast.

**refectory** (re-fek'to-ri), n. Eating-hall.

**refer** (re-fer'), vt. To take or send back; submit to another; assign.

**referee** (ref-er-e'), n. One to whom something is referred.

**reference** (ref'er-ens), n. Act of referring, relation; person or thing referred to.

**referendum** (ref-er-en'dum), n. Submission of a law or measure to popular vote.

**refine** (re-fin'), vt. To purify; polish. [refinement]

**refinery** (re-fin'er-i), n. Place for refining or purifying

**reflect** (re-flekt'), vt. To bend or throw back from a surface. [**reflection, reflective, reflector**]

**reflex** (re'fleks), a. Thrown back; reflected. n. Reflection.

**reflux** (re'fluks), n. A backward flow; ebb.

**reformation** (ref-or-ma'shun), n. Act of reforming; amendment; improvement. [**reformative, reformatory**]

**refract** (re-frakt'), vt. To bend from the direct course, as light. [**refraction**]

**refrain** (re-fran'), vi. To abstain; forbear. n. Recurrent phrase or burden of a song.

**refrangible** (re-fran'ji-bl), a. That may be refracted.

**refrigerant** (re-frij'er-ant), a. Cooling.

**refrigerate** (re-frij'er-at), vt. To cool. [**refrigerator**]

**refuge** (ref'uj), n. A shelter; asylum; retreat; resource.

**refugee** (ref'yu-je), n. One who takes refuge in another country.

**refulgent** (re-ful'jent), a. Brilliant; radiant. [**refulgence**]

**refund** (re-fund'), vt. To repay; restore.

**refusal** (re-fuz'al), n. Act of refusing; rejection; right of prior acceptance.

**refuse** (re-fuz'), vt. and vi. To deny; reject; decline; to accept or comply.

**refuse** (ref'us), a. Rejected; worthless.

**refutable** (re-fut'a-bl), a. That may be refuted.

**refute** (re-fut'), vt. To disprove; confute.

**regal** (re'gal), a. Kingly; royal.

**regale** (re-gal'), vt. To refresh; entertain.

**regalia** (re-gal'i-a), n. pl. Insignia or badges of royalty, as crown, sceptre, etc.; insignia of an office or order.

**regality** (re-gal'i-ti), n. Royalty.

**regard** (re-gard'), vt. To observe; consider; esteem.

**regatta** (re-gat'a), n. A boat-race; sailing-match.

**regency** (re'jen-si), n. Office of, or government by, a regent; body of regents.

**regenerate** (re-jen'er-at), vt. To produce anew; purify the heart. [**regeneration**]

**regent** (re'jent), n. One who rules in the place of a king; a ruler.

**regicide** (rej'i-sid), n. The killing, or the slayer, of a king.

**regime** (ra-zhem'), n. Form of government; administration.

**regimen** (rej'i-men), n. Prescribed rule; rule of diet and living.

**regiment** (rej'i-ment), n. Body of soldiers commanded by a colonel.

**region** (re'jun), n. A tract of land; country.

**register** (rej'is-ter), n. A written record; list; damper of a stove or flue; stop of an organ.

**registrar** (rej'is-trar), n. One who keeps a register; keeper of public records. [**registration**]

**registry** (rej'is-tri), n. Registration; place where a record is kept.

**regnant** (reg'nant), a. Reigning.

**regress** (re'gres), n. Return; passage back. [**regression**]

**regret** (re-gret'), vt. To grieve at; remember with sorrow.

**regular** (reg'yu-lar), a. According to rule; uniform; orderly; belonging to the standing army. [**regularity**]

**regulate** (reg'yu-lat), vt. To adjust by rule; put in order. [**regulation, regulator**]

**regurgitate** (re-gur'ji-tat), vi. To rush or flow back.

**rehabilitate** (re-ha-bil'i-tat), vt. To restore; reinstate. [**rehabilita'tion**]

**rehearsal** (re-hers'al), n. Act of rehearsing; preliminary recitation.

**rehearse** (re-hers), vt. To repeat; recite; recite or practise before exhibition.

**reign** (ran), n. Rule, or time of rule, of a sovereign; influence; control.

**reimburse** (re-im-burs'), vt. To repay.

**rein** (ran), n. The strap of a bridle; restraint.

**reindeer** (ran'der), n. Species of deer inhabiting cold climates.

**reinforce** (re-in-fors'), vt. To add new strength to; supply with additional troops. [**reinforcement**]

**reins** (ranz), n. pl. The kidneys; the loins.

**reinstate** (re-in-stat'), vt. To place in a former state; replace in possession.

**reiterate** (re-it'er-at), vt. To repeat.

**reject** (re-jekt'), vt. To throw away; discard; refuse. [**rejec'tion**]

**rejoice** (re-jois'), vi. To feel or express joy.

**rejoin** (re-join'), vt. To join again.

**rejoinder** (re-join'der), n. An answer; answer to a reply.

**rejuvenate** (re-ju'ven-at), vt. To make young again. [**rejuvena'tion**]

**relapse** (re-laps'), vi. To fall back; return to a former state.

**relate** (re-lat'), vt. To tell; recite.

**related** (re-lat'ed), a. Allied by blood.

**relative** (rel'a-tiv), a. Having relation.

**relax** (re-laks'), v. To slacken; to abate; to divert. [**relaxation**]

**relay** (re-la'), n. A supply of horses to relieve others.

**release** (re-les'), v. To free from obligation or penalty; to let go; to quit claim.

**relegate** (rel'e-gat), v. To dispatch; to banish.

**relent** (re-lent'), v. To soften in temper; to grow tender.

**relevant** (rel'e-vant), a. Relieving; suitable; pertinent.

**reliable** (re-li'a-bl), a. That may be relied on or trusted.

**reliance** (re-li'ans), n. Trusty confidence; dependence. [**reliant**]

**relic** (rel'ik), n. Remains.

**relict** (rel ikt), n. A widow.

**relief** (re-lef'), n. Help; succor; aid; alleviation; prominence in sculpture.

**relieve** (re-lev'), v. To alleviate; to ease; to help; to release.

**relievo** (re-le'vo), n. The projection of a figure in sculpture.

**religion** (re-lij'un), n. Any system of faith and worship; piety; godliness. [**religious**]

**relinquish** (re-ling'kwish), v. To abandon; to give up.

**reliquary** (rel'i-kwar-i), n. A depository for relics.

**relish** (rel'ish), n. An agreeable taste; flavor; sauce.

**reluctance** (re-luk'tans), n. Unwillingness; aversion. [**reluctant**]

**rely** (re-li'), v. To rest or

repose in; to depend on.
**remain** (re-man'), v. To continue; to stay; to be left.
**remains** (re-manz'), n. pl. A dead body; relics; remnants.
**remand** (re-mand'), v. To order or send back.
**remarkable** (re-mark'a-bl), a. Worthy of particular notice; wonderful; famous; notable.
**remedial** (re-me'di-al), a. Tending to remedy.
**remedy** (rem'e-di), n. That which cures or restores; that which counteracts an evil.
**remembrance** (re-mem'brans), n. Keeping in mind.
**remind** (re-mind'), v. To put in remembrance.
**reminiscence** (rem-i-nis'ens), n. Recollection.
**remiss** (re-mis'), a. Slack; slothful; negligent; careless. [remission]
**remit** (re-mit'), v. To send money; to forgive; to relax. [remittance]
**remonstrance** (re-mon'strans), n. Expostulation.
**remonstrate** (re-mon'strat), v. To expostulate.
**remorse** (re-mars'), n. Pain from a guilty conscience.
**remote** (re-mot'), a. Distant; not immediate or proximate; foreign.
**remove** (re-mov'), v. To change place; to take or carry away.
**remunerate** (re-mu'ner-at), v. To reward; to repay.
**rencounter** (ren-kown'ter), n. A sudden combat. v. To meet with.
**render** (ren'der), v. To return; to translate.
**rendezvous** (ren'de-vo), n. A place of meeting.
**rendition** (ren-dish'un), n. Act of yielding; surrender.

**renegade** (ren'e-gad), n. An apostate; a deserter.
**renewal** (re-nu'al), n. Act of renewing; renovation.
**renounce** (re-nowns'), v. To disown; to disclaim.
**renovate** (ren'o-vat), v. To renew; to restore; to refresh. [renovation]
**rental** (rent'al), n. An account of rents; rent.
**renunciation** (re-nun-si-a'shun), n. Act of renouncing.
**reorganize** (re-or'gan-iz) vt. To organize anew.
**repair** (re-par'), vt. To restore; mend; make amends for.
**repair** (re-par'), vi. To betake one's self to.
**reparation** (rep-a-ra'shun), n. Act of repairing; amends.
**repartee** (rep-ar-te'), n. A smart reply.
**repast** (re-past'), n. A meal; food.
**repeal** (re-pel'), vt. To recall; annul.
**repeat** (re-pet'), vt. To do or say again; quote from memory.
**repeater** (re-pet'er), n. One who repeats; watch that strikes the hour; one who fraudulently votes more than once.
**repel** (re-pel'), vt. To drive back; resist.
**repellent** (re-pel'ent), a. Tending to repel.
**repent** (re-pent'), vt. and vi. To feel sorrow for something done. [repentance]
**repercussion** (re-per-kush'un), n. A striking or driving back; reverberation.
**repertory** (rep'er-to-ri), n. A storehouse; treasury; magazine.
**repetition** (rep-e-tish'un), n. Act of repeating.
**repine** (re-pin'), vi. To be

**REPLACE** 193 **REQUIEM**

discontented or fretful; to envy.

**replace** (re-plas'), vt. To restore to its place; provide a substitute for; take the place of.

**replenish** (re-plen'ish), vt. To fill again; stock.

**replete** (re-plet'), a. Full; completely filled. [**reple'tion**]

**replevin** (re-plev'in), n. Action or writ for replevying goods.

**replevy** (re-plev'i), vt. To recover by law, goods wrongfully detained.

**replication** (rep-li-ka'shun), n. Answer; answer to a defendant's plea.

**repose** (re-poz'), vt. To lay at rest.

**reposit** (re-poz'it), vt. To lodge for safety. [**repository**]

**reprehensible** (rep-re-hen'si-bl), a. Deserving blame or reproof.

**reprehensive** (rep-re-hen'siv), a. Containing reproof.

**represent** (rep-re-zent'), vt. To exhibit the image of; stand for; act the part of; stand in the place of; bring before the mind; describe. [**representation**]

**repress** (re-pres'), vt. To check; restrain. [**repression**]

**reprieve** (re-prev'), vt. To delay the punishment of; give a respite to.

**reprimand** (rep'ri-mand), n. Sharp reproof.

**reprint** (re-print'), vt. To print again, esp. in another country.

**reprisal** (re-pri'zal), n. Seizure in retaliation; retaliation.

**reproach** (re-proch'), vt. To censure; upbraid; revile.

**reproachful** (re-proch'ful), a. Conveying reproach.

**reprobate** (rep'ro-bat), a. Lost to virtue; depraved.

**reproduction** (re-pro-duk'shun), n. A producing anew.

**reproductive** (re-pro-duk'tiv), a. Producing again.

**reproof** (re-proof'), n. Censure expressed.

**reprovable** (re-proov'bl), a. Worthy of reproof; culpable.

**reproval** (re-proov'al), n. Reproof.

**reprove** (re-proov'), vt. To censure to the face.

**reptile** (rep'til), a. Creeping; grovelling. n. A creeping animal.

**reptilian** (rep-til'e-an), a. Pertaining to reptiles.

**republic** (re-pub'lik), n. A state governed by representatives elected by the citizens.

**republican** (re-pub'lik-an), a. Pertaining to, or consistent with, a republic.

**republication** (re-pub-leka'shun), n. A new publication.

**repudiate** (re-pu'de-at), vt. To divorce; to reject; to disclaim. [**repudiation**]

**repugnance** (re-pug'nans), n. Unwillingness.

**repugnant** (re-pug'nant), a. Unwilling; inconsistent.

**repulse** (re-puls'), n. A check in advancing; refusal. [**repulsion**]

**repulsive** (re-puls'iv), a. Forbidding; cold; reserved.

**reputable** (rep'ut-a-bl), a. Of good repute.

**reputation** (rep-ut-a'shun), n. General estimation; good name; honour derived from public esteem.

**repute** (re-put'), vt. To hold in estimation; to think.

**request** (re-kwest'), n. Expression of desire; a petition.

**requiem** (re'kwe-em), n.

hymn or prayer for the dead.
**requirable** (re-kwir'a-bl), a. That may be required.
**require** (re-kwir'), vt. To make necessary; to ask as a right. [requirement]
**requisite** (rek'we-zit), a. Required; necessary.
**requisition** (rek-we-zish'-un), n. Claim made.
**requital** (re-kwit'al), n. Recompense.
**requite** (re-kwit'), vt. To recompense.
**rescind** (re-sind'), vt. To repeal.
**rescission** (re-sizh'un), n. Act of abrogating.
**rescript** (re'skript), n. Edict of an emperor.
**rescue** (res'ku), vt. To deliver from danger or confinement.
**research** (re-serch'), n. Diligent inquiry.
**reseize** (re-sez'), vt. To seize again.
**resemblance** (re-zem'blans), n. Likeness.
**resemble** (re-zem'bl), vt. To be like.
**resent** (re-zent'), vt. To be angry at.
**reservation** (rez-er-va'shun), n. Act of reserving; something reserved.
**reserve** (re-zerv'), vt. To keep back; retain. n. Something reserved; want of frankness or cordiality.
**reservoir** (rez'er-vwor), n. A place for collecting and storing water, or other substances.
**residence** (rez'i-dens), n. Abode; dwelling. [resident]
**residual** (re-zid'yu-al), a. Remaining as residue. [residuary]
**residue** (rez'i-du), n. Remainder; what is left.
**residuum** (re-zid'yu-um), n. Residue; substance remaining.

**resign** (re-zin'), vt. To yield up. vr. To submit patiently. [resignation]
**resigned** (re-zind'), a. Patiently submissive.
**resilient** (re-sil'i-ent, -zil'i-) a. Recoiling; rebounding. [resilience]
**resin** (rez'in), n. Inflammable substance produced by the pine, etc.
**resist** (re-zist'), vt. To oppose; withstand. [resistance]
**resolute** (rez'o-lut), a. Determined; firm.
**resolution** (rez-o-lu'shun), n. Act of resolving; solution; determination; formal proposal or declaration.
**resolve** (re-zolv'), v. To separate into parts; to analyze; to explain; to determine.
**resolvent** (re-zolv'ent), a. Having the power to dissolve.
**resonance** (rez'o-nans), n. The returning of sound. [resonant]
**resort** (re-zart'), v. To apply; to frequent; to repair; to go.
**resound** (re-zownd'), v. To send back sound; to echo; to praise; to celebrate with sound.
**resource** (re-sors'), n. Means of supply.
**respect** (re-spekt'), v. To esteem for merit; to relate to. n. Regard; deference. [respectability]
**respective** (re-spekt'iv), a. Having reference to; relative.
**respiration** (res-pi-ra'shun), n. The act of breathing.
**respire** (re-spir'), v. To breathe; to breathe out; to rest.
**respite** (res'pit), n. Delay; suspension of punishment.
**resplendent** (re-splen'dent), a. Bright; splendid.

**respond** (re-spond'), v. To rejoin; to answer; to reply.

**response** (re-spons'), n. An answer; reply; rejoinder. [**responsibility**]

**responsible** (re-spon'si-bl), a. Answerable; amenable.

**responsive** (re-spon'siv), a. Answering; corresponding.

**restaurant** (res'to-rant), n. A place for refreshment.

**restitution** (res-ti-tu'shun), n. Act of restoring; amends.

**restive** (res'tiv), a. Unwilling to stir; stubborn; uneasy.

**restore** (re-stor'), v. To return; to replace; to heal; revive.

**restrain** (re-stran'), v. To curb; to repress; to hold back. [**restraint**]

**restrict** (re-strikt'), v. To limit; to confine; to repress.

**result** (re-zult'), v. To fly back; to arise or proceed as a consequence; to issue.

**resume** (re-zum'), v. To take back; to begin again.

**resume** (ra-zo-ma'), n. A summing up; a recapitulation.

**resumption** (re-zump'shun), n. Act of resuming.

**resurrection** (rez-ur-rek'-shun), n. Rising from the dead.

**resuscitate** (re-sus'i-tat), v. To revive; to revivify.

**retail** (re-tal'), v. To sell in small quantities.

**retail** (re'tal), n. The sale of goods in small quantities.

**retain** (re-tan'), v. To keep; to hire; to continue. [**retainer**]

**retaliate** (re-tal'i-at), v. To return like for like.

**retard** (re-tard'), v. To hinder; to delay.

**retch** (rech), v. To strain in the effort to vomit.

**retention** (re-ten'shun), n. Act of retaining; restraint. [**retentive**]

**reticence** (ret'i-sens), n. Concealment by silence.

**reticent** (ret'i-sent), a. Silent; reserved; taciturn.

**reticule** (ret'i-kul), n. A small net or bag.

**retina** (ret'i-na), n. Innermost coat of eye; receives all ocular impressions.

**retinue** (ret'i-nu), n. A train of attendants.

**retire** (re-tir'), v. To retreat; to withdraw. [**retirement**]

**retort** (re-tart'), n. Censure returned; a vessel for distilling.

**retrace** (re-tras'), v. To trace back; to renew the outline.

**retract** (re-trakt'), v. To take back; to recall; to recant.

**retreat** (re-tret'), n. A retiring; place of seclusion. v. To withdraw.

**retrench** (re-trench'), v. To cut off; to lessen. [**retrenchment**]

**retribution** (ret-ri-bu'shun), n. Repayment; requital. [**retributive**]

**retrieve** (re-trev'), v. To recover; to regain. [**retriever**]

**retroaction** (re-tro-ak'shun), n. Action opposed to past decisions or acts.

**retrocession** (re-tro-sesh'-un), n. Act of going back, or of ceding back.

**retroflex** (ret'ro-fleks), a. Bent backward.

**retrograde** (ret'ro-grad), a. Going backward. [**retrogression**]

**retrospect** (ret'ro-spekt), n. A view of things past. [**retrospective**]

**reunion** (re-un'yun), n. Act of reuniting or rejoining.

**reveal** (re-vel'), v. To make known; to disclose.

**reveille** (ra-val'ya, or rev-

**c-le'),** n. The morning call to awaken soldiers by drum or bugle.

**revel** (rev'el), v. To carouse. n. A disorderly feast.

**revelation** (rev-e-la'shun), n. Act of revealing; sacred communication.

**revelry** (rev'el-ri), n. Loose or noisy jollity; festive mirth.

**revenge** (re-venj'), n. Spiteful return of an injury.

**revenue** (rev'e-nu), n. Income of a state or an individual; annual profits.

**reverberate** (re-ver'ber-at), v. To resound; to echo. [reverberatory]

**revere** (re-ver'), v. To regard with reverence.

**reverence** (rev'er-ens), n. Veneration; respect; v. To regard with much respect. [reverend]

**reverie** (rev'er-i), n. Loose or irregular thought; meditation.

**reverse** (re-vers'), v. To change; to invert; to make void.

**reversion** (re-ver'shun), n. Returning; the right to future possession; atavism.

**revert** (re-vert'), v. To return; to fall or refer back.

**review** (re-vu'), v. To reconsider; to inspect.

**reviewer** (re-vu'er), n. One who reviews; a critic.

**revile** (re-vil'), v. To abuse; to calumniate; to vilify.

**revise** (re-viz'), v. To review.

**revival** (re-viv'al), n. Act of reviving; recovery from neglect, etc.; religious awakening.

**revivify** (re-viv'i-fi), vt. To restore to life.

**revocable** (rev'o-ka-bl), a. That may be revoked.

**revocation** (rev-o-ka'shun), n. Act of revoking; repeal.

**revoke** (re-vok'), vt. To recall; repeal; reverse.

**revolt** (re-volt'), vi. To renounce allegiance; rebel; be shocked.

**revolution** (rev-o-lu'shun), n. Motion round a centre; rotation; entire change in government; revolt. [revolutionary, revolutionize]

**revolve** (re-volv'), vi. To move round a centre; reflect.

**revulsion** (re-vul'shun), n. Reversal of feeling; repugnance. a. **revulsive**.

**reward** (re-ward'), n. Recompense; retribution. vt. To recompense; requite.

**reynard** (ren'ard), n. A name given to the fox in fables, etc.

**rhapsody** (rap'so-di), n. A disconnected, wild, or extravagant composition.

**rhapsodist** (rap'so-dist), n. A composer or reciter of rhapsodies.

**rheostat** (re'o-stat), n. An instrument for measuring the strength of an electric current.

**rhetoric** (ret'o-rik), n. Art of speaking with eloquence and force.

**rhetorician** (ret-o-rish'an), n. One versed in rhetoric; an orator.

**rheum** (rum), n. Mucus; phlegm; watery secretion.

**rheumatism** (rum'a-tizm), a. Painful inflammation or neuralgia of the joints or fibrous tissues.

**rhinoceros** (ri-nos'er-os), n. Large African quadruped with one horn, or two, on the nose.

**rhomb** (romb), **rhombus**, (rom'bus), n. Figure of four equal sides, with its angles not right angles.

**rhomboid** (rom'boid), n. An oblique-angled parallelogram, having only the

**rhubarb** (ru'barb), n. A plant, and its medicinal root.
**rhyme** (rim), n. Correspondence in sound of words; verses.
**rhythm** (rithm), n. Ordered succession of motions, accents, etc.
**ribald** (rib'ald), n. A loose, scurrilous fellow. [**ribaldry**]
**ribbon** (rib'on), n. A fillet of silk; narrow strip.
**rickets** (rik'ets), n. sing. Disease of children marked by softness of the bones. [**rickety**]
**ricochet** (rik-o-sha'), vi. To bound along the surface of the ground or water.
**riddance** (rid'ans), n. Act of ridding; deliverance.
**riddle** (rid'l), n. An enigma; puzzle.
**ridge** (rij), n. Top of the back or of a slope.
**ridicule** (rid'i-kul), n. Laughter with contempt. [**ridiculous**]
**rife** (rif), a. Prevalent.
**rift** (rift), n. A cleft; a breach. v. To cleave; to burst.
**rigging** (rig'ing), n. The ropes and tackling supporting sails and masts.
**rightangle** (rit'ang-gl), n. An angle of ninety degrees.
**righteous** (ri'chus), a. Just; virtuous; honest; free of sin.
**rigid** (rij'id), a. Stiff; strict; exact; severe.
**rigor** (rig'ur), n. Strictness; severity; stiffness. [**rigorous**]
**ringlet** (ring'let), n. A little ring; a curl of hair.
**rinse** (rins), v. To cleanse with clean water.
**riot** (ri'ot), n. Uproar; tumult.

**riparian** (ri-pa'ri-an), a. Pertaining to the bank of a stream.
**ripple** (rip'l), v. To ruffle the surface. [**rippling**]
**rise** (riz), v. To get up; to attain greater height; to increase.
**risibility** (riz-i-bil'i-ti), n. Proneness to laugh.
**risible** (riz'i-bl), a. Exciting laughter; prone to laugh.
**rite** (rit), n. A religious usage or ceremony.
**ritual** (rit'u-al), n. A book of services.
**rival** (ri'val), n. One in pursuit of the same object as another.
**robust** (ro-bust'), a. Strong; vigorous.
**rodeo** (ro'de-o), n. Sporting event with cattle, roundup.
**rodomontade** (rod-o-montad'), n. Vain boasting; swagger.
**roe** (ro), n. A species of deer.
**roe** (ro), n. The eggs of a fish.
**roebuck** (ro'buk), n. Male of a small species of deer.
**rogation** (ro-ga'shun), n. Supplication.
**rogue** (rog), n. A dishonest person; knave; frolicsome person.
**roguery** (rog'er-i), n. Knavish tricks; fraud; mischievousness. [**roguish**]
**roller** (rol'er), n. Cylinder used for rolling; long bandage; long wave.
**Roman** (ro'man), a. Pertaining to Rome or its inhabitants, or to Roman Catholics; aquiline, as a nose; erect letters (as opposed to italics); indicated by letters, not figures, as numerals.
**Romance** (ro-mans'), a. Denoting, or pertaining to, the languages of Latin origin.

**romance** (ro-mans'), n. Fictitious and wonderful tale. [**romancer**]

**romantic** (ro-man'tik), a. Pertaining to, or befitting, romance; wild; picturesque. [**romanticism**]

**rondeau** (ron-do'), n. A poem of which the initial line or phrase is repeated as a refrain.

**rope** (rop), n. Thick, twisted cord.

**rosary** (ro'za-ri), n. A garland of roses; a series of prayers; a string of beads to count them.

**rosin** (roz'in), n. Thickened turpentine.

**rostrum** (ros'trum), n. A platform to speak or sing from.

**rotary** (ro'tar-i), a. Turning on an axis, as a wheel.

**rotate** (ro'tat), v. To move on an axis. a. Wheel-shaped. [**rotation**]

**rotatory** (ro'ta-to-ri), a. Going in a circle; turning.

**rote** (rot), n. Mere repetition of words by memory.

**rotund** (ro-tund'), a. Round; circular; spherical.

**rotunda** (ro-tun'da), n. A Round; building; circular hall.

**rouge** (rozh), n. A delicate red paint; a cosmetic.

**rough** (ruf), a. Not smooth; harsh; coarse.

**roulette** (rol-et'), n. A gambling game.

**round** (rownd), a. Globular; circular.

**rouse** (rowz), v. To stir; to excite; to wake up.

**rout** (rowt), n. A defeat; a multitude; fashionable company.

**route** (rot), n. A course or way; road; journey.

**routine** (ro-ten'), n. Regular course of duties.

**royalist** (roi'al-ist), n. An adherent to a king.

**rubber** (rub'ber), v. Caoutchouc; eraser; one who rubs; a round at cards; overshoe.

**rubbish** (rub'ish), n. Waste matter; ruins; nonsense.

**rubefacient** (ro'be-fa'shent) a. Making red.

**rubicund** (ro'bi-kund), a. Inclined to redness.

**rubric** (ro'brik), n. Directions for service in prayer-books; an ecclesiastical injunction.

**ruby** (ro'bi), n. A precious stone of a red color.

**rudder** (rud'der), n. That which directs the course of a ship.

**rudiment** (rood'e-ment), n. First principle; first part of education.

**rudimental** (rood-e-ment'-al), a. Pertaining to elements; initial.

**rue** (roo), n. A very bitter plant.

**rueful** (roo'fool), a. Sorrowful.

**ruffian** (ruf'e-an), n. A boisterous, brutal fellow; a cut-throat. [**ruffianism**]

**ruffle** (ruf'l), vt. To wrinkle; to vex; to disturb.

**rugged** (rug'ed), a. Rough; harsh; shaggy.

**ruin** (roo'in), n. Overthrow; destruction; remains of buildings, &c. [**ruinous**]

**rumble** (rum'bl), vi. To make a low continued noise.

**ruminant** (roo'me-nant), a. Chewing the cud. [**ruminate, rumination**]

**rummage** (rum'aj), n. A close search.

**rumor** (roo'mur), n. A flying or popular report.

**rumple** (rum'pl), vt. To wrinkle.

**rupture** (rup'tur), n. A breach; a burst; hernia.

**rural** (roor'al), a. Belonging to the country.

**russet** (rus'et), a. Of a reddish brown colour. n.

Rustic dress; an apple of a russet colour.

**rustic** (rus'tik), a. Rural.

**rusticate** (rus'ti-kat), vt. To banish to the country.

**rustle** (rus'l), vi. To make a soft whispering sound, as dry leaves, etc.

**rusty** (rust'i), a. Covered with rust; dull from inaction.

**rye** (ri), n. A kind of grain.

# S

**Sabbath** (sab'ath), n. The seventh day of the week, devoted by the Jewish law to rest and worship.

**sable** (sa'bl), n. Animal of the weasel kind, and its fine black fur. a. Made of sable; dark; black.

**sabre** (sa'br), n. A broad sword with curved blade.

**sac** (sak), n. Small bag or receptacle in animals or vegetables.

**saccharine** (sak'a-rin), a. Pertaining to, containing, or like, sugar.

**sacerdotal** (sas-er-do'tal), a. Priestly.

**sachem** (sa'chem), n. Am. Indian chief.

**sacrament** (sak'ra-ment), n. A solemn religious ordinance, esp. the Lord's Supper.

**sacred** (sa'kred), a. Pertaining to God; holy; inviolable.

**sacrifice** (sak'ri-fis), vt. To offer up; destroy or give up; devote with loss; kill.

**sacrilege** (sak'ri-lej), n. Profanation of sacred things or places. [sacrile'gious]

**sacristy** (sak'ris-ti), n. Room in a church where the vessels, etc., are kept.

**saddle** (sad'l), n. Seat for a horse's back, etc.; the two loins of venison, etc.

**Sadducee** (sad'yu-se), n. One of a Jewish sect that denied the resurrection and the existence of angels.

**saffron** (saf'ron), n. Bulbous plant with orange flowers; dye prepared from these.

**sagacious** (sa-ga'shus), a. Of keen perception; shrewd; wise.

**sage** (saj), a. Wise.

**sago** (sa'go), n. Kind of starch from the stem of certain palmtrees.

**sailer** (sal'er), n. That which sails.

**sailor** (sal'or), n. A seaman; mariner.

**saint** (sant), n. A holy person.

**salaam** (sa-lam'), n. An Eastern salutation.

**salable** (sal'a-bl), a. That may be sold.

**salad** (sal'ad), n. Raw herbs cut up and seasoned.

**salamander** (sal-a-man'der), n. Small reptile, once thought to be able to live in fire.

**salaried** (sal'a-rid), a. Receiving a salary.

**salary** (sal'a-ri), n. Stated allowance for services.

**saleratus** (sal-e-ra'tus), n. Bicarbonate of potash.

**salesman** (salz'man), n. One employed to sell goods.

**Salic** (sal'ik), a. Denoting a Frankish law by virtue of which females were excluded from the throne of France.

**salient** (sal'i-ent), a. Shooting out; projecting.

**saline** (sa-lin', sa'lin), a. Containing, or having the qualities of, salt.

**saliva** (sa-li'va), n. The

moisture of the mouth; spittle. [**salivary**]

**salivate** (sal'i-vat), vt. To produce an excessive flow of saliva. [**saliva'tion**]

**sally** (sal'i), n. A sudden breaking forth; outbreak of wit or gaiety.

**salmon** (sam'un), n. A fish highly valued for food.

**saloon** (sa-lon'), n. A spacious hall; a main cabin.

**salsify** (sal'si-fi), n. The oyster-plant.

**saltpeter** (salt-pe'ter), n. A salt composed of nitric acid and potash; niter.

**salubrious** (sa-lo'bri-us), a. Healthful; promoting health. [**salubrity**]

**salutary** (sal'u-tar-i), a. Promotive of health or safety. [**salutation**]

**salutatory** (sa-lu'ta-tor-i), a. Containing congratulations.

**salute** (sa-lot'), v. To greet; to kiss; to honor.

**salvage** (sal'vaj), n. Reward for saving a ship or goods.

**salvation** (sal-va'shun), n. Preservation; saving from eternal misery; deliverance.

**salve** (sav), n. An ointment; anything to cure sores.

**salver** (sal'ver), n. A plate on which anything is presented.

**salvo** (sal'vo), n. A military salute; reservation.

**sample** (sam'pl), n. A specimen; an example.

**sanatory** (san'a-tor-i), a. Healing; conducive to health.

**sanctification** (sangk-ti-fi-ka' shun), n. Act of making holy.

**sanctify** (sangk'ti-fi), v. To make pure or holy.

**sanctimonious** (sangk'ti-mo'ni-us), a. Holy; devout; affecting holiness.

**sanction** (sangk'shun), n. A confirming; ratification.

**sanctity** (sangk'ti-ti), n. Holiness; purity; inviolability.

**sanctum** (sangk'tum), n. A private retreat or room.

**sandal** (san'dal), n. A loose kind of shoe; a loose slipper.

**sandwich** (sand'wich), n. Two slices of bread with a slice of meat between.

**sanguinary** (sang'gwin-ar-i) a. Bloody; bloodthirsty.

**sanguine** (sang'gwin), a. Ardent; hopeful; confident.

**sanguineous** (sang-gwin'e-us), a. Resembling or abounding with blood.

**sanitarium** (san-i-ta'ri-um), n. A hospital; health station. [**sanitary**]

**sanity** (san'i-ti), n. Soundness of mind or body.

**Sanskrit** (san'skrit), n. The ancient language of Hindostan.

**sapid** (sap'id), a. Well-tasted; savory; palatable.

**sapient** (sa'pi-ent), a. Wise; discerning; sagacious.

**sapling** (sap'ling), n. A young tree.

**saponaceous** (sap-o-na'shus) a. Soapy; soap-like.

**saponify** (sa-pon'i-fy), v. To convert into soap.

**sapphire** (saf'fir), n. A highly brilliant, blue, precious stone.

**sarcasm** (sar'kazm), n. Keen reproach; a bitter sneer. [**sarcastic**]

**sarcophagus** (sar'kof'a-gus), n. A stone coffin or tomb.

**sardine** (sar-den'), n. A small fish.

**sardonic** (sar-don'ik), a. Forced; heartless; fiendish.

**sardonyx** (sar'don-iks), n. A yellowish red precious stone.

**sarsaparilla** (sar-sa-pa-ril'-la), n. A medicinal plant.

**sassafras** (sas'a-fras), n. A kind of tree used in medicine.

**Satan** (sa'tan), n. The enemy of man; the devil.

**satchel** (sach'el), n. A small sack or bag.

**sate** (sat), v. To satisfy.

**satellite** (sat'el-lit), n. A small planet which revolves around a larger; an obsequious follower.

**satiate** (sa'shi-at), v. To gratify fully; to glut.

**satiety** (sa-ti'e-ti), n. Fulness; surfeit; repletion.

**satin** (sat'in), n. A glossy silk.

**satire** (sat'ir), n. A censorious discourse or poem; ridicule.

**satisfaction** (sat-is-fak'shun), n. Content; that which satisfies; gratification. [satisfactory]

**satisfy** (sat'is-fi), v. To content; to recompense.

**satrap** (sa'trap), n. A kind of viceroy.

**saturate** (sat'u-rat), v. To fill to excess.

**Saturday** (sat'ur-da), n. The last day of the week.

**Saturn** (sat'urn), n. One of the planets.

**Satyr** (sat'er, sa'ter), n. A sylvan deity—half man, half goat, and very wanton.

**sauce** (sas), n. A liquid seasoning for food; a relish; impudence.

**saucer** (sas'er), n. A vessel for a tea-cup.

**saucy** (sa'si), a. Impudent.

**sauerkraut** (sowr'krowt), n. A kind of pickled cabbage.

**saunter** (san'ter), v. To wander idly; to loiter.

**sausage** (sas-aj), n. A roll of minced meat in a skin.

**savage** (sav'aj), a. Wild; fierce; uncivilized.

**savannah** (sa-van'na), n. A grassy plain.

**savant** (sa-vang'), n. A man of learning.

**Savior** (sav'yur), n. One who saves or preserves; Jesus Christ; the Redeemer.

**savor** (sa'vur), n. Taste; odor; smell; relish. [savory]

**Saxon** (saks'un), a. Pertaining to the Saxons or their language.

**scabbard** (skab'ard), n. Sheath of a sword.

**scabbed** (skab'ed), a. Covered with scabs; paltry.

**scabious** (ska'be-us), a. Consisting of scabs.

**scabrous** (ska'brus), a. Rough; rugged.

**scaffold** (skaf'old), n. A staging for workmen; a stage for the execution of a criminal.

**scalable** (skal'a-bl), a. That may be scaled.

**scald** (skawld), vt. To burn by a hot liquid.

**scale** (skal), n. Dish of a balance; crusty covering of a fish; gradation; gamut.

**scalene** (ska-len'), a. Having three sides and angles unequal.

**scaliness** (skal'e-nes), n. Quality of being scaly.

**scallop** (skol'up), n. A genus of shell-fish; a curved indentation on the edge.

**scalp** (skalp), n. Skin of the top of the head.

**scalpel** (skal'pel), n. A surgeon's knife.

**scaly** (skal'e), a. Full of scales; rough.

**scamp** (skamp), n. A knavish fellow.

**scan** (skan), vt. To examine closely; to measure by counting the poetic feet.

**scandal** (skan'dal), n. Of-

# SCANDALIZE — SCORCH

**fence**; disgrace; defamatory speech.

**scandalize** (skan'dal-iz), vt. To offend; to defame. [**scandalous**]

**scansorial** (skan-so're-al), a. Adapted to climbing.

**scant** (skant), vt. To limit; to straiten; to restrain.

**scanty** (skant'e), a. Narrow; small.

**scape** (skap), n. A stem bearing the fructification without leaves.

**scapula** (skap'u-la), n. The shoulder-bone.

**scapular** (skap'u-lar), a. Belonging to the shoulder.

**scar** (skar), n. Mark of a wound.

**scarce** (skars), a. Uncommon; rare. [**scarcity**]

**scare** (skar), vt. To terrify.

**scarf** (skarf), n. A loose covering of cloth. pl. scarfs.

**scarification** (skar-e-fe-ka'shun), n. A slight incision of the skin.

**scarify** (skar'e-fi), vt. To scratch and cut the skin.

**scarlatina** (skar-la-ti'na), n. Scarlet fever.

**scarlet** (skar'let), n. A deeply red colour.

**scarp** (skarp), n. The interior slope of a ditch.

**scathless** (skath'les), a. Without harm.

**scatter** (skat'er), vt. To spread thin; to disperse.

**scavenger** (skav'en-jer), n. One employed to clean streets.

**scene** (sen), n. A stage; exhibition; place of exhibition. [**scenery**]

**scenical** (sen'ik-al), a. Dramatic; theatrical.

**scent** (sent), n. Odour; smell.

**sceptic** (skep'tik), n. One who doubts of all things, especially divine truth; an infidel; also written skeptic. [**scepticism**]

**sceptre** (sep'ter), n. Ensign of royalty.

**schedule** (sed'ul), n. An inventory of property, debts, &c.

**scheme** (skem), n. A plan; project; contrivance.

**schemer** (skem'er), n. A projector; a contriver.

**schism** (sizm), n. Division or separation in a church. [**schismatic**]

**scholar** (skol'ar), n. A learner; man of letters.

**scholium** (sko'le-um), n. An explanatory observation.

**schooner** (skoon'er), n. A vessel with two masts.

**sciatic** (si-at'ik), a. Affecting the hip.

**sciatica** (si-at'ik-a), n. Rheumatism in the hip.

**science** (si'ens), n. Knowledge.

**scimetar** (sim'e-tar), n. An Eastern sword with curved blade.

**scintillate** (sin'ti-lat), vi. To sparkle. [**scintillation**]

**sciolism** (si'o-lizm), n. Superficial knowledge.

**sciolist** (si'o-list), n. A smatterer; pretender to knowledge.

**scion** (si'on), n. A young shoot; twig for grafting.

**scirrhous** (skir'us), a. Hardened by disease, as a gland.

**scissors** (siz'orz), n. pl. Cutting instrument of two blades joined by a pivot.

**scoff** (skof), vt. To mock; jeer.

**scoop** (skoop), vt. To ladle up; dig out; make hollow.

**scope** (skop), n. Range of vision or mind; space for action; intention.

**scorbutic** (skor-bu'tik), a. Pertaining to, or diseased with, scurvy.

**scorch** (skorch), vt. To burn slightly or on the surface.

**score** (skor), n. Notch; mark for counting; twenty; a reckoning; account; musical composition with all the parts.

**scornful** (skorn'ful), a. Disdainful.

**scorpion** (skor'pi-on), n. Articulate animal with a sting in the tail; the sign Scorpio in the zodiac.

**Scotch** (skoch), **Scottish** (skot'ish), a. Pertaining to Scotland, its language or people.

**scour** (skour), vt. To clean by rubbing with something rough; cleanse from grease, etc.; range; traverse rapidly.

**scourge** (skurj), n. A heavy whip; punishment.

**scout** (skout), n. One sent to observe the enemy, bring information, etc.

**scow** (skou), n. A flatboat; lighter.

**scowl** (skoul), vi. To look angrily; frown.

**scrag** (skrag), n. Something lean; bony part of the neck.

**scramble** (skram'bl), vi. To move on hands and knees; climb with difficulty; struggle to seize something in a crowd of competitors.

**scrap** (skrap), n. A small piece; fragment.

**scrape** (skrap), vt. To rub or abrade with something sharp; grate; collect laboriously.

**scratch** (skrach), vt. and vi. To mark or scrape with something pointed; tear with the claws; scrape with the nails.

**scrawl** (skral), vt. and vi. To write or mark clumsily.

**scream** (skrem), vi. To utter a sudden piercing cry.

**screech** (skrech), vi. To scream; shriek.

**screen** (skren), n. A partition; something to shelter or interpose; a long coarse sieve.

**screw** (skru), n. A cylinder grooved spirally, used for various purposes.

**scribble** (skrib'l), vt. To write carelessly; cover with careless or worthless writing.

**scribe** (skrib), n. A writer; clerk; Jewish writer of the law.

**Scripture** (skrip'tyur), n. Sacred writings; the Bible.

**scrivener** (skriv'n-er), n. Public writer; copyist.

**scrofula** (skrof'yu-la), n. Disease marked by swelling of the glands. [**scrofulous**]

**scroll** (skrol), n. Roll of paper or parchment; roll of writing; curling ornament.

**scruple** (skru'pl), n. Weight of twenty grains; doubt; hesitation.

**scrupulous** (skrup'yu-lus), a. Having doubts; conscientious; exact.

**scrutinize, -ise** (skru'ti-niz), vt. To examine minutely. [**scrutiny**]

**scud** (skud), vt. To run quickly; run before the wind.

**scuffle** (skuf'l), vi. To struggle; fight confusedly.

**scull** (skul), n. A short light oar.

**scullery** (skul'er-i), n. Place for kitchen utensils.

**scullion** (skul'yun), n. Servant that cleans kitchen vessels, etc.

**sculptor** (skulp'tor), n. One who carves figures.

**sculpture** (skulp'tyur), n. Art of carving figures in stone or wood; carved figures.

**scurrility** (skur-ril'i-ti), n. Vulgar, abusive language. [**scurrilous**]

**scurvy** (skur'vi), n. A distemper.

**scythe** (sith), n. An instrument to mow grass, etc.

**seal** (sel), n. A marine animal; a stamp.

**seam** (sem), n. The joining of two edges; the line or space between edges; a vein of mineral.

**seaman** (se'man), n. A sailor.

**seamstress** (sem'stres), n. A woman who sews.

**seaport** (se'port), n. A harbor for vessels.

**sear** (ser), v. To scorch or burn; to cauterize; to render callous.

**search** (serch), v. To examine; to probe; to seek for; to look; to inquire.

**searchlight** (serch'lit), n. Powerful movable electric light backed by reflectors.

**season** (se'zn), n. Suitable time; division of the year. [seasonable]

**seat** (set), n. A chair; bench; place of sitting; mansion.

**secede** (se-sed'), v. To withdraw from fellowship. [secession]

**seclusion** (se-klo'zhun), n. Retirement; privacy.

**second** (sek'und), a. Next to the first; inferior.

**secrecy** (se'kre-si), n. Close privacy; silence; solitude.

**secret** (se'kret), a. Concealed; unseen.

**secretary** (sek're-tar-i), n. A writer; an officer; a piece of furniture.

**secrete** (se-kret'), v. To hide; to conceal; to separate. [secretion]

**sectarian** (sek-ta'ri-an), n. One of a sect.

**section** (sek'shun), n. The act of cutting; division; part.

**secular** (sek'u-lar), a. Worldly; not spiritual.

**secure** (se-kur'), a. Free from fear or danger; safe. [security]

**sedan** (se-dan'), n. A covered portable carriage.

**sedate** (se-dat'), a. Calm; undisturbed.

**sedative** (sed'a-tiv), n. That which relieves and composes.

**sedentary** (sed'en-tar-i), a. Sitting much; inactive.

**sediment** (sed'i-ment), n. That which settles at the bottom; lees; dregs.

**sedition** (se-dish'un), n. Tumult; insurrection. [seditious]

**seduce** (se-dus'), v. To entice; to mislead; to corrupt.

**seduction** (se-duk'shun), n. Act of seducing; corruption. [seductive]

**sedulous** (sed'u-lus), a. Diligent; persevering; laborious.

**seer** (ser), n. A prophet.

**seethe** (seth), v. To boil; to decoct; to be hot.

**segment** (seg'ment), n. A part cut off, or divided.

**segregate** (seg're-gat), v. To separate from others.

**seine** (sen), n. A fishing net.

**seismic** (sis'mik), a. Pertaining to earthquakes.

**seize** (sez), v. To take suddenly; to snatch; to arrest. [seizure]

**seldom** (sel'dum), ad. Rarely; not often; unfrequently.

**select** (se-lekt'), v. To choose; to cull; to pick out.

**selvage** (sel'vaj), n. The edge of cloth; also written selvedge.

**semblance** (sem'blans), n. Likeness.

**semi** (sem'e). Used in compound words, signifies half.

**seminal** (sem'in-al), a. Pertaining to seed; original; radical.

**seminary** (sem'in-ar-e), n.

**SENARY**     205     **SERGEANT**

A place of education; a college; academy.

**senary** (sen'ar-e), a. Containing six.

**senate** (sen'at), n. A legislative body. [**senator**]

**senescence** (se-nes'ens), n. A growing old.

**senile** (se'nil), a. Belonging to old age.

**senility** (se-nil'e-te), n. Old age.

**senior** (se'ne-or), n. One older than another.

**seniority** (se-ne-or'e-te), n. Priority in age or office.

**sensate** (sens'at), a. Perceived by the senses.

**sensation** (sens-a'shun), n. Perception by the senses.

**sense** (sens), n. Faculty by which external objects are perceived.

**sensibility** (sens-e-bil'e-te), n. Capability of sensation; acuteness of perception.

**sensible** (sens'e-bl), a. Capable of perceptions; perceptible by the senses.

**sensitive** (sens'it-iv), a. Having sense or feeling.

**sensorial** (sen-so're-al), a. Pertaining to the sensorium.

**sensorium** (sen-so're-um), n. The organ of sense, supposed to be in the brain.

**sensual** (sens'u-al), a. Affecting the senses; carnal. [**sensualism, sensuality**]

**sentient** (sen'she-ent), a. Having the faculty of perception.

**sentiment** (sen'te-ment), n. A thought prompted by feeling; sensibility; opinion. [**sentimental**]

**sentimentality** (sen-te-ment-al'e-te), n. Affectation of sensibility.

**sentinel** (sen'te-nel), n. A soldier on guard.

**separable** (sep'ar-a-bl), a. That may be separated.

**separate** (sep'ar-at), vt. or i. To disunite; to withdraw.

**sepoy** (se'poy), n. A native of India in the military service of Europeans.

**septangular** (sept-ang'gu-lar), a. Having seven angles.

**September** (sep-tem'ber), n. The 9th month.

**septuagenarian** (sep-tu-a-je-na'ri-an), **septuagenary** (sep-tu-aj'e-na-ri), n. Person seventy years old.

**Septuagint** (sep'tu-a-jint), n. The Alexandrian Greek version of the Old Testament.

**sepulchre** (sep'ul-ker), n. A grave; tomb. [**sepulchral**]

**sequel** (se'kwel), n. Following part; consequence; event.

**sequence** (se'kwens), n. Order of following; series; consequence.

**sequester** (se-kwes'ter), vt. To withdraw; set apart; hold for a time.

**sequoia** (se-kwoi'a), n. A genus of gigantic pines.

**seraglio** (se-ral'yo), n. Palace of the Sultan; harem.

**seraph** (ser'af), n. A celestial being; angel. pl. **seraphs, seraphim.**

**serenade** (ser-e-nad'), n. Music performed in the open air at night to compliment some one.

**sere** (ser), a. Dry; withered.

**serene** (se-ren'), a. Clear; calm; unclouded. [**serenity**]

**serfdom** (serf'dom), n. Condition of a serf; system under which serfs exist.

**serge** (serj), n. A thin woollen stuff.

**sergeant** (sar'jant), n. A non-commissioned officer; lawyer of the highest rank.

**serial** (se'ri-al), a. Pertaining to a series.

**series** (se'ri-ez), n. Order; succession. sing. and pl.

**serious** (se'ri-us), a. Grave; solemn; important; dangerous.

**serpent** (ser'pent), n. A footless reptile; snake; wind-instrument. [serpentine]

**serrate** (ser'at), a. Notched like a saw; jagged.

**serum** (se'rum), n. Whey; watery part of the blood.

**serviceable** (serv'is-a-bl), a. Fit for service; useful; diligent.

**servile** (serv'il), a. Slavish; obsequious; menial. [servil'ity]

**servitude** (serv'i-tud), n. Slavery; servile dependence.

**session** (sesh'un), n. Meeting of a public body, or the time it sits.

**settee** (set-e'), n. A long seat with a back.

**setter** (set'er), n. A dog which crouches at sight of game.

**sever** (sev'er), vt. To divide; separate. [severance]

**several** (sev'er-al), a. Distinct; separate; various; sundry.

**severe** (se-ver'), a. Strict; austere; grave; distressing; harsh; cruel; inclement. [sever'ity]

**sewage** (su'aj), n. Water carried off by sewers.

**sewerage** (su'er-aj), n. Drainage by sewers.

**sextant** (seks'tant), n. Sixth part of a circle; instrument for measuring angular distances.

**sexton** (seks'ton), n. Officer who has charge of a church, digs graves, etc.

**sexual** (seks'yu-al), a. Pertaining to sex.

**shackle** (shak'l), vt. To fetter; restrain. n. Open link closed with a bolt.

**shaggy** (shag'i), a. Covered with long wool or hair.

**Shah** (sha), n. A Persian king.

**shaker** (sha'ker), n. One that shakes; one of a religious sect.

**shammy** (sham'mi), n. A kind of soft leather.

**shampoo** (sham-po'), v. To knead the body after a hot bath; to wash the head.

**shamrock** (sham'rok), n. A kind of clover; the national emblem of Ireland.

**shank** (shangk), n. The bone of the leg; long part of an instrument.

**shanty** (shan'ti), n. A rude temporary building.

**shawl** (shal), n. A covering for the shoulders.

**sheaf** (shef), n. A bundle of stalks; any bundle or collection.

**shear** (sher), v. To clip from the surface; to reap.

**shears** (sherz), n. pl. An instrument for cutting; a machine for raising heavy weights.

**sheath** (sheth), n. A scabbard.

**sheathe** (sheth), v. To put in a case; to cover.

**sheave** (shev), n. The wheel of a block or pulley.

**sheer** (sher), a. Clear; unmingled; perpendicular.

**sheet** (shet), n. A cloth for a bed; a piece of paper.

**sheeting** (shet'ing), n. A cloth used for bed-sheets.

**shelter** (shel'ter), n. A protection; a refuge. v. To cover; to protect; to defend.

**shelve** (shelv), v. To slope; to furnish with shelves; to put aside.

**shepherd** (shep'erd), n. One who tends sheep.

**sheriff** (sher'if), n. An ofcer who executes the law in each county.

**shibboleth** (shib'bo-leth), n. Test or watchword of a party.

**shield** (sheld), n. Defensive armor.

**shift** (shift), v. To transfer; to find some expedient; to dress; to scheme.

**shingle** (shing'gl), n. A thin board; loose pebbles. v. To cover with shingles.

**shire** (shir), n. A county.

**shirk** (sherk), v. To avoid, slink, or get off from duty.

**shirt** (shert), n. An undergarment worn by men.

**shiver** (shiver), v. To break in pieces; to shake; to shatter.

**shoal** (shol), n. A large number of fishes; a sandbank.

**shoat** (shot), n. A young swine.

**shoddy** (shod'di), n. An inferior woolen cloth.

**shoe** (sho), n. A covering for the foot of man or beast. v. To put on shoes.

**shoulder** (shol'der), n. The joint that connects the arm with the body.

**shout** (shout), vi. To cry aloud.

**shovel** (shuv'l), n. A utensil for throwing earth, &c.

**shrew** (shroo), n. An ill-tempered woman.

**shrewd** (shrood), a. Sagacious; sly.

**shriek** (shrek), vi. To utter a shrill cry.

**shrimp** (shrimp), n. A shellfish.

**shrine** (shrin), n. A case or box, as for sacred relics.

**shrivel** (shriv'l), vt. or i. To contract into wrinkles.

**shroud** (shroud), n. A cover; a winding sheet.

**Shrovetide** (shrov'tid), n. Confession time; Tuesday before Lent.

**shrub** (shrub), n. A bush; a small woody plant; a drink. [**shrubbery**]

**shrug** (shrug), vt. To contract, as the shoulders.

**shudder** (shud'er), n. A tremor as with horror.

**shuffle** (shuf'l), vt. To change the position of cards.

**shunt** (shunt), n. A siding on a main-line of railway.

**shuttle** (shut'l), n. A weaver's instrument to shoot the threads.

**shyly** (shi'le), ad. In a timid manner.

**sibilant** (sib'e-lant), a. Hissing. [**sibilation**]

**siccative** (sik'a-tiv), a. Drying.

**sickle** (sik'l), n. A reaping-hook.

**sickly** (sik'le), a. Unhealthy; faint.

**siege** (sej), n. A besetting a fortified place.

**siesta** (si-es'ta), n. A short sleep in the afternoon.

**sieve** (sev), n. A small utensil for sifting.

**sigh** (si), vi. To emit breath audibly; to lament.

**sightly** (sit'li), a. Pleasing to the sight.

**sign** (sin), n. Token; mark; gesture conveying meaning; omen; something set up as a public indication; one of the twelve divisions of the zodiac.

**signalize** (sig'nal-iz), vt. To make signal or eminent.

**signature** (sig'na-tyur), n. A person's name written by himself; characters indicating the key in music; folded sheet of a book.

**signet** (sig'net), n. A seal; privy-seal.

**significance** (sig-nif'i-kans), n. Quality of being significant; meaning; importance. [**significant**]

**signify** (sig'ni-fi), vt. To

# SILENCE 203 SLAKE

make known; mean; have consequence.

**silence** (si-lens), n. Stillness; quiet; absence of sound or speech.

**silhouette** (sil-oo-et'), n. A flat black portrait in profile.

**silt** (silt), n. Deposit from water.

**silvan** (sil'van), a. Pertaining to, or inhabiting, woods; woody.

**silvery** (sil'ver-i), a. Like silver; white and shining; clear in tone.

**similar** (sim'i-lar), a. Like; resembling. [**similar'ity**]

**simile** (sim'i-le), n. A comparison.

**similitude** (sim-il'i-tud), n. Resemblance; comparison.

**simious** (sim'i-us), a. Pertaining to monkeys; monkey-like.

**simony** (sim'o-ni), n. Offense of buying or selling church preferment.

**simoom** (si-moom'), n. A hot wind from the Arabian desert.

**simpleton** (sim'pl-ton), n. A foolish person.

**simplicity** (sim-plis'i-ti), n. Singleness; plainness; artlessness; folly. [**simplify**]

**simulate** (sim'u-lat), v. To counterfeit; to assume.

**simultaneous** (sim-ul-ta'ne-us), a. Existing or happening at the same time.

**sincere** (sin-ser'), a. True; pure; genuine; honest. [**sincerity**]

**sinecure** (si'ne-kur), n. Office with pay but no work.

**sinew** (sin'u), n. A tendon; nerve; muscle.

**singular** (sing'gu-lar), a. Not plural; only one; rare; odd. [**singularity**]

**sinister** (sin'is-ter), a. Left; evil; unfair; unlucky.

**sinuous** (sin'u-us), a. Winding in and out; **undulating**.

**siphon** (si'fun), n. A bent pipe or tube for drawing and transferring liquids.

**siren** (si'ren), n. A mermaid. a. Enticing; alluring.

**sirloin** (ser'loin), n. The loin of beef.

**site** (sit), n. A situation; local position; ground-plot.

**situation** (sit-u-a'shun), n. Position; condition; state.

**skedaddle** (ske-dad'l), v. To run away from a post of duty or danger; to flee.

**skein** (skan), n. A knot of threads of cotton, silk, yarn.

**skeleton** (skel'e-tun), n. The bones of an animal; an outline or framework.

**skeptic** (skep'tik), n. One who doubts; an infidel.

**sketch** (skech), n. An outline; a rough draught.

**skewer** (sku'er), n. A pin to fasten meat.

**ski** (ske), n. A wooden runner used for traveling over snow and ice.

**skid** (skid), n. Device used in loading or unloading a truck.

**skiff** (skif), n. A light boat.

**skillet** (skil'let), n. A small long-handled cooking vessel.

**skirmish** (sker'mish), n. A small battle.

**skittish** (skit'tish), a. Shy; easily frightened; unsteady.

**skulk** (skulk), v. To lurk in fear or shame; to hide.

**skull** (skul), n. Spherical bony covering of the brain.

**skunk** (skungk), n. An animal of the weasel kind.

**slag** (slag), n. Dross or refuse of metal; scoriæ of a volcano.

**slake** (slak), v. To quench, as thirst; to extinguish;

**slander** to disintegrate by mixing with water, as lime.
**slander** (slan'der), v. To censure falsely; to defame.
**slattern** (slat'tern), n. A woman negligent of neatness.
**slaughter** (sla'ter), n. Great destruction of life.
**slavery** (slav'er-i), n. Bondage; servitude; drudgery. [slavish]
**sledding** (sled'ing), n. The act of sledding; snow enough for sleds.
**sledge** (slej), n. A large hammer; a sled.
**sleeve** (slev), n. Covering of the arm.
**sleigh** (sla), n. A vehicle for travelling on snow.
**sleight** (slit), n. An artful trick; dexterity.
**slender** (slen'der), a. Thin and long.
**slice** (slis), n. A thin piece cut off.
**slily** (sli'le), ad. In a sly manner.
**slimy** (slim'e), a. Viscous; clammy.
**slipper** (slip'er), n. A loose shoe.
**slippery** (slip'er-e), a. Smooth; glib.
**sloping** (slop'ing), a. Oblique; inclined.
**sloppy** (slop'e), a. Wet and dirty.
**sloth** (sloth), n. Sluggishness; a slow-moving animal.
**slouch** (slouch), n. A hanging down.
**slough** (slou), n. A miry place.
**slough** (sluf), n. The cast skin of a serpent.
**sloven** (sluv'en), n. A man careless of dress and neatness. [slovenly]
**sluggard** (slug'ard), n. A person habitually lazy.
**sluggish** (slug'ish), a. Habitually lazy.

**sluice** (slus), n. A stream of water issuing through a floodgate; a floodgate.
**sluicy** (slus'e), a. Falling, as from a sluice.
**slur** (slur), vt. To soil; to sully; to perform in a smooth, gliding manner.
**slut** (slut), n. A woman who neglects dress and neatness.
**smartly** (smart'le), ad. Briskly; wittily.
**smatter** (smat'er), vi. To talk superficially.
**smear** (smer), vt. To daub; to soil; to pay over.
**smelt** (smelt), vt. To melt ore.
**smelter** (smelt'er), n. One that smelts.
**smerk** (smerk), vi. To smile affectedly.
**smicker** (smik'er), vi. To smerk.
**smooth** (smooth), a. Even on the surface. vt. To make even.
**smother** (smuth'er), vt. To stifle or suffocate.
**smouldering** (smol'der-ing), a. Burning and smoking without vent.
**smuggle** (smug'l), vt. To import without paying duties; to convey privately.
**smut** (smut), n. Soot; foul mucus.
**smutch** (smuch), vt. To blacken with smoke.
**smutty** (smut'e), a. Soiled; obscene.
**snack** (snak), n. A share; repast.
**snaggy** (snag'e), a. Full of knots or sharp points.
**snail** (snal), n. A slimy reptile.
**snare** (snar), n. Any thing which entraps; a noose.
**snarl** (snarl), vt. To entangle.
**snatch** (snach), vt. To seize hastily.

**sneak** (snek), vi. To creep slily; to behave meanly; to hide.

**sneer** (sner), vi. To show contempt by laughing or by a look.

**sneeze** (snez), vi. To eject air suddenly through the nose.

**snob** (snob), n. One who apes gentility.

**snooze** (snoz), v. To slumber; to doze.

**snore** (snor), v. To breathe roughly and hoarsely in sleep.

**snuffle** (snuf'fl), v. To speak or breathe through the nose.

**soak** (sok), v. To steep in a liquid; to drench; to wet.

**soap** (sop), n. A compound of oil and fat and alkali.

**soar** (sor), v. To fly aloft.

**sober** (so'ber), a. Serious; not intoxicated.

**sobriety** (so-bri'e-ti), n. Temperance; calmness; gravity.

**sociable** (so'sha-bl), a. Conversable; familiar; friendly.

**social** (so'shal), a. Pertaining to society; festive; convivial. **[socialism]**

**society** (so-si'e-ti), n. Union of many in one interest; fellowship; a religious body.

**soda** (so'da), n. Fixed mineral alkali, the basis of common salt.

**sofa** (so'fa), n. An ornamental long seat, stuffed.

**soften** (saf'n), v. To make or grow soft.

**soggy** (sog'i), a. Soaked with water.

**soil** (soil), v. To daub; to stain; to pollute.

**sojourn** (so'jurn), v. To tarry for a time.

**sol** (sol), n. A note in music.

**solace** (sol'as), v. To cheer; to comfort.

**solar** (so'lar), a. Relating to the sun.

**solder** (sod'er), v. To unite by fusion with a metallic cement.

**soldier** (sol'jer), n. A man in military service; a warrior.

**sole** (sol), n. Bottom of the foot, or of a boot or shoe; a fish.

**solecism** (sol'e-sizm), n. Misuse of language; bad manners.

**solemn** (sol'em), a. Religiously grave; awful; devout. **[solemnity]**

**solemnize** (sol'em-niz), v. To celebrate; to make serious.

**solicit** (so-lis'it), v. To ask earnestly; to entreat; to petition. **[solicitor]**

**solicitude** (so-lis'i-tud), n. Anxiety; carefulness; trouble.

**solid** (sol'id), a. Firm; compact; sound. A solid substance. **[solidarity]**

**soliloquy** (so-lil'o-kwi), n. A talking to one's self alone.

**solitaire** (sol-i-tar'), n. A hermit; single gem; a game.

**solitary** (sol'i-tar-i), a. Lonely; retired; gloomy.

**solitude** (sol'i-tud), n. Loneliness; a lonely place or desert.

**solo** (so'lo), n. Music by one person or one instrument.

**solstice** (sol'stis), n. The point where the sun ceases to recede from the equator.

**soluble** (sol'u-bl), a. Capable of being dissolved.

**solution** (so-lu'shun), n. Matter dissolved; that which contains anything dissolved; removal of a

## SOLVE — SPECIALIZE

**doubt or difficulty; explanation.**

**solve** (solv), v. To explain; to clear up; to remove.

**solvent** (sol'vent), a. Able to pay all debts; dissolving. n. A fluid which dissolves.

**somber** (som'ber), a. Dusky; dark; gloomy; melancholy.

**somersault** (sum'er-salt), n. A spring or leap with heels over head.

**somnambulist** (som-nam'bu-list), n. A sleep-walker.

**somnolent** (som'no-lent), a. Sleepy, or inclined to sleep.

**sonata** (so-na'ta), n. A musical composition consisting of three or more movements.

**sonnet** (son'net), n. A poem of 14 lines.

**sonorous** (so-no'rus), a. Sounding when struck.

**sooth** (soth), n. Reality; truth.

**soothe** (soth), v. To calm.

**sophism** (sof'izm), n. A fallacious argument; a fallacy. [**sophist**]

**sophisticate** (so-fis'ti-kat), v. To adulterate; to debase.

**soprano** (so-pra'no), n. The highest female voice; the treble.

**sorcery** (sar'ser-i), n. Magic; enchantment; witchcraft.

**sordid** (sar'did), a. Covetous; mean; vile; base; filthy.

**sore** (sor), n. Tender or painful flesh; a wound. a. Tender to the touch; painful.

**sororicide** (so-ror'i-sid), n. Murder or murderer of a sister.

**sorosis** (so-ro'sis), n. A woman's club.

**soup** (soop), n. Liquid food prepared by boiling eatable substances esp. meat.

**sour** (sour), a. Acid; tart; crabbed.

**source** (sors), n. Origin; spring; that which supplies.

**souse** (sous), n. Ears, feet, etc., of swine, pickled.

**souse** (sous), vt. To plunge into a liquid.

**southerly** (suth'er-li), a. Lying toward, or coming from, the south.

**southern** (suth'ern), a. Situated at the south.

**southron** (suth'ron), n. A native of the south.

**souvenir** (soov'ner), n. A remembrance; keepsake.

**sovereign** (suv'ren), a. Supreme; having supreme authority. [**sovereignty**]

**spacious** (spa'shus), a. Extensive; roomy.

**Spaniard** (span'yard), n. A native of Spain.

**spaniel** (span'yel), n. A kind of small water-dog.

**spare** (spar), vt. To use frugally; do without; save from anything; grant.

**sparing** (spar'ing), a. Scanty; saving.

**sparse** (spars), a. Thinly scattered. n. **sparseness**.

**Spartan** (spar'tan), a. Of, or pertaining to, Sparta or its natives; hardy; austere.

**spasm** (spazm), n. Convulsive action of the muscles; convulsive fit; sudden pang.

**spawn** (span), n. Eggs of fish or frogs.

**spear** (sper), n. Weapon consisting of a pole pointed with iron.

**special** (spesh'al), a. Designating a species; distinctive; particular; specific. [**speciality**]

**specialize** (spesh'al-iz), vt. To make special; to indi-

**SPECIE** 212 **SPLICE**

cate particularly. [**specialty**]

**specie** (spe'shi), n. Gold and silver coin.

**species** (spe'shez), n. Group agreeing in certain distinctive characteristics; sort; kind. pl. **species**.

**specific** (spe-sif'ik), a. Pertaining to, or designating, a species; peculiar.

**specification** (spes-i-fi-ka'shun), n. Act of specifying; statement of particulars.

**specimen** (spes'i-men), n. A sample.

**specious** (spe'shus), a. Looking well; plausible.

**spectacle** (spek'ta-kl), n. A show; sight; exhibition.

**spectacles** (spek'ta-klz), n. pl. Glasses to assist the sight.

**spectator** (spek-ta'tor), n. A beholder; a looker-on.

**spectre** (spek'ter), n. An apparition; phantom; ghost.

**spectrum** (spek'trum), n. Figure of colored light formed by the dispersion of a beam of light by means of a prism, etc.

**speculate** (spek'yu-lat), vi. To consider; theorize; conjecture; deal in with the expectation of future profit. [**specula'tion**]

**speculator** (spek'yu-la-tor), n. One who speculates.

**spermaceti** (sper-ma-se'ti), n. Crystalline fatty matter from the head of the sperm-whale.

**spew** (spu), vi. and vt. To vomit; cast forth with loathing.

**sphere** (sfer), n. A globe; planet; circuit; province; rank.

**spheroid** (sfe'roid), n. A body nearly spherical.

**sphinx** (sfingks), n. A fabulous monster which proposed riddles to travellers, and slew those who could not solve them; a species of hawk-moth.

**spicy** (spi'si), a. Abounding in, or flavored with, spice; aromatic; piquant.

**spigot** (spig'ot), n. Perforated plug of wood, by which liquor can be drawn from a cask; faucet.

**spinach** (spin'aj), n. A garden vegetable.

**spinal** (spin'al), a. Pertaining to the spine or backbone.

**spindle** (spin'dl), n. Pin on which thread is wound as it is spun, or on which it is formed; pin on which anything turns.

**spindling** (spind'ling), a. Shaped like a spindle; slender and tapering.

**spinster** (spin'ster), n. A woman who spins; unmarried woman.

**spiracle** (spi'ra-kl), n. A breathing-hole.

**spiral** (spir'al), a. Like a spire; winding like the thread of a screw.

**spiritualism** (spir'it-yu-al-izm) n. Doctrine of the distinct existence of spirit.

**spiteful** (spit'fol), a. Malicious; desirous to vex or injure.

**spittle** (spit'tl), n. Saliva.

**spittoon** (spit-ton'), n. A vessel for receiving spittle.

**spleen** (splen), n. Spongy organ near the stomach; the milt; anger; melancholy.

**splendid** (splen'did), a. Showy; magnificent; famous.

**splendor** (splen'dur), n. Brilliancy; magnificence.

**splenetic** (sple-net'ik), a. Full of spleen; peevish.

**splice** (splis), v. To unite the strands of two ends of a rope.

**splinter** (splin'ter), n. A thin piece of wood.

**splutter** (splut'ter), v. To scatter drops about; to sputter.

**spoil** (spoil), v. To rob; to mar; to strip; to decay.

**spoliate** (spo'li-at), v. To pillage; to plunder; to rob.

**spoliation** (spo-li-a'shun), n. The act of plundering.

**sponsor** (spon'sur), n. Surety; baptismal godfather or godmother.

**spontaneous** (spon-ta'ne-us), a. Voluntary; unforced.

**spouse** (spowz), n. A married person; a husband or wife.

**spout** (spowt), n. A projecting mouth or pipe.

**sprain** (spran), n. Unusual strain of the ligaments of the joints.

**sprawl** (spral), v. To stretch out or struggle with the limbs; to fall or recline at length.

**spray** (spra), n. Small drops of water scattered by the wind; a shoot or branch of a plant.

**spread** (spred), n. Extent; compass; expansion.

**spree** (spre), n. Drinking carousal; a merry frolic.

**sprightly** (sprit'li), a. Gay; lively; active; vigorous.

**springy** (spring'i), a. Containing springs; elastic.

**sprinkle** (spring'kl), v. To scatter drops; to disperse.

**sprout** (sprowt), v. To germinate and shoot out; to bud.

**spruce** (spros), a. Neat; trim.

**spry** (spri), a. Nimble; active; alert.

**spunk** (spungk), n. Touchwood; spirit; mettle.

**spur** (spur), n. An instrument to hasten speed of horses; a projecting mountain; incitement; something projecting.

**spurious** (spu'ri-us), a. Not genuine; false; impure.

**spurn** (spurn), v. To kick; to reject with contempt.

**spurt** (spurt), v. To rush or issue out with force; to jet at intervals or suddenly.

**sputter** (sput'ter), v. To speak hastily; to throw liquid in scattered drops.

**squab** (skwob), n. Anything short and stout.

**squabble** (skwob'l), v. To debate peevishly. n. A wrangle.

**squad** (skwod), n. A company; a small party for drill.

**squadron** (skwod'run), n. Part of a fleet; a body of cavalry consisting of two troops.

**squalid** (skwol'id), a. Poverty-stricken; foul; dirty; filthy.

**squall** (skwal), n. A sudden gust of wind; a loud scream.

**squalor** (skwa'lur), n. Filthiness; coarseness; foulness.

**squander** (skwon'der), v. To dissipate; to spend lavishly.

**square** (skwar), a. Having four equal sides and right-angles; honest; fair.

**squash** (skwosh), n. Something soft and crushed; a plant and its fruit.

**squat** (skwat), v. To sit upon the heels; to settle on land without a title.

**squatter** (skwot'ter), n. One who settles on new land without title; one who squats.

**squaw** (skwa), n. An Indian word for wife.

**squeak** (skwek), v. To utter a short, sharp, shrill sound.

**squeamish** (skwem'ish), a. Nice; fastidious; scrupulous.

**squeeze** (skwez), v. To embrace closely; to press; to oppress.

**squelch** (skwelch), v. To crush; to suppress.

**squib** (skwib), n. A firework; a witty expression.

**squint** (skwint), v. To look obliquely or awry.

**squirm** (skwerm), v. To wind, twist, and struggle.

**squirt** (skwert), v. To eject liquid from a narrow opening.

**stability** (sta-bil'e-te), n. Firmness.

**stagnant** (stag'nant), a. Not flowing; still.

**stain** (stan), vt. To discolour; to disgrace.

**stair** (star), n. A step for ascending.

**stake** (stak), n. A sharpened stick of wood; wager; pledge.

**stalactite** (sta-lak'tit), n. A mineral in form of an icicle.

**stale** (stal), a. Vapid and tasteless. n. A decoy; a long handle.

**stalk** (stawk), n. The stem of a plant.

**stallion** (stal'yun), n. A horse for stock.

**stamen** (sta'men), n. Foundation; support.

**stamina** (stam'i-na), n. pl. Main strength of anything; native vigor.

**stammer** (stam'er), vi. To falter in speech.

**stampede** (stam-ped'), n. Sudden fright and running away of a number of horses, etc.

**stanch** (stanch), vt. To check the flow of, as blood.

**stanchion** (stan'shun), n. A stay; prop; supporting beam.

**stanza** (stan'za), n. Series of lines of poetry arranged acording to a pattern.

**staple** (sta'pl), n. Important or chief article of trade; fibre of wood, cotton, etc.

**starch** (starch), n. A white vegetable granular substance used for stiffening linen, etc.

**stare** (star), vi. To look fixedly, or with eyes wide open.

**starry** (star'i), a. Adorned with stars; proceeding from the stars.

**starvation** (starv-a'shun), n. Act of starving; state of being starved.

**starve** (starv), vi. To die of hunger; suffer extreme hunger or want.

**statement** (stat'ment), n. Narration; recital; account.

**statesman** (stats'man), n. One skilled in state affairs or the art of government.

**static** (stat'ik), a. Pertaining to statics; at rest or in equilibrium.

**station** (sta'shun), n. Place where a person or thing stands; post; office; rank; place where railway trains stop; police-office.

**stationary** (sta'shun-ar-i), a. Not moving; fixed; settled.

**stationery** (sta'shun-er-i), n. Articles sold by stationers.

**statistics** (sta-tis'tiks), n. pl. Collected facts and figures on any subject.

**statuary** (stat'yu-a-ri), n. Art of carving statues; a collection of statues; sculptor.

**statue** (stat'yu), n. Carved image, esp. of a human figure.

**statuesque** (stat-yu-esk')

a. Like, or suitable for, a statue.

**statuette** (stat-yu-et'), n. A small statue.

**stature** (stat'yur), n. Natural height of a person or animal.

**status** (stat'us, stat'-), n. Position; condition.

**statute** (stat'yut), n. A law; permanent rule.

**statutory** (stat'yu-to-ri), a. Enacted by statute.

**steadfast** (sted'fast), a. Firm; resolute; constant.

**steady** (sted'i), a. Firm; without motion; fixed; regular.

**steal** (stel), vt. To take by theft, or without notice; win or accomplish stealthily.

**stealth** (stelth), n. Act of stealing; secret action. **[stealthy]**

**steam** (stem), n. Vapor of boiling water; any exhalation.

**steel** (stel), n. Iron combined with carbon; an instrument of steel; steel instrument for sharpening knives.

**steeple** (ste'pl), n. Spire or tower of a church.

**steer** (ster), vt. To direct with the helm; guide.

**steer** (ster), n. A young ox.

**steerage** (ster'aj), n. Act of steering; apartment between decks for passengers.

**stellar** (stel'ar), a. Starry; relating to the stars.

**stellate** (stel'at), a. Like a star; radiated.

**stencil** (stensil), n. A thin plate with figures or letters cut out, through which color is rubbed.

**stenographer** (sten-og'ra-fer), n. One who writes in short-hand. **[stenography]**

**stentorian** (sten-to'ri-an), a. Very loud or powerful, as a voice.

**steppe** (step), n. Vast uncultivated plain in Eastern Europe and in Asia.

**stereoscope** (ster'e-o-skop), n. An optical instrument for exhibiting pictures.

**stereotype** (ster'e-o-tip), n. A solid metallic plate for printing.

**sterile** (ster'il), a. Barren; unfruitful; unproductive.

**sterling** (ster'ling), n. Designating English money; genuine.

**stern** (stern), n. The after part of a ship.

**stethoscope** (steth'o-skop), n. An instrument used to distinguish sounds in the thorax.

**stevedore** (ste've-dor), n. One whose occupation is to load and unload vessels.

**stew** (stu), v. To boil slowly.

**steward** (stu'ard), n. One who manages the affairs of another; a manager or attendant.

**sticky** (stik'i), a. Viscous; glutinous; tenacious.

**stifle** (sti'fl), v. To smother; to suppress; to choke.

**stigma** (stig'ma), n. A brand; mark of infamy; in botany, the top of a pistil.

**stiletto** (sti-let'o), a. Small dagger; an instrument for making holes.

**stimulant** (stim'u-lant), a. Increasing vital action.

**stimulate** (stim'u-lat), v. To excite; to rouse; to urge.

**stimulus** (stim'u-lus), n. Anything that rouses the mind or excites to action.

**stingy** (stin'ji), a. Niggardly; sordid; penurious.

**stipend** (sti'pend), n. Settling wages; allowance; salary.

**stipulate** (stip'u-lat), v. To bargain; to covenant.

**stir** (ster), v. To move; to rouse; to incite.

**stitch** (stich), v. To sew; to join.

**stockade** (stok-ad'), n. A breast-work formed of stakes.

**stoic** (sto'ik), n. One indifferent to pleasure or to pain. [stoicism]

**stoker** (sto'ker), n. One who fires a steam engine.

**stole** (stol), n. Garment reaching to the feet; long, narrow scarf worn by clergy.

**stolid** (stol'id), a. Dull; heavy; stupid; foolish.

**stomach** (stum'ak), n. The organ of digestion; appetite.

**stony** (ston'i), a. Made of, or full of stones; hard.

**stoppage** (stop'paj), n. A hinderance; obstruction.

**stopple** (stop'pl), n. A plug.

**storage** (stor'aj), n. Storing goods or price for so doing.

**stout** (stowt), a. Strong; lusty; corpulent; brave.

**stow** (sto), v. To lay up. [stowage]

**straddle** (strad'l), v. To walk widely; to stand or sit astride of.

**straggle** (strag'gl), v. To ramble; to rove; to separate.

**straight** (strat), a. Not crooked; upward; direct.

**strain** (stran), v. To stretch; to extend; to filter.

**strait** (strat), a. Narrow; not crooked; strict.

**strand** (strand), n. Shore or beach; one of the twists of a rope.

**strangle** (strang'gl), v. To suffocate; to choke.

**strapping** (strap'ping), a. Large; lusty; well-grown.

**stratagem** (strat'a-jem), n. Artifice; trick; deceit.

**strategy** (strat'e-ji), n. The science of conducting complicated military movements.

**stratify** (strat'i-fi), v. To form or lay into beds or layers.

**streak** (strek), n. A line of colour; a stripe.

**streamer** (strem'er), n. A flag.

**strengthen** (strength'en), vt. or i. To make or grow strong.

**strenuous** (stren'u-us), a. Eagerly pressing; active.

**stress** (stres), n. Force; importance.

**stretch** (strech), vt. To extend; to strain. [stretcher]

**strew** (stro, stroo), vt. To scatter.

**striated** (stri'at-ed), a. Streaked.

**strickle** (strik'l), n. An instrument for levelling corn in a measure.

**strict** (strikt), a. Severe; close; rigid.

**stricture** (strikt'ur), n. Contraction; criticism.

**stringent** (strinj'ent), a. Binding closely; pressing hard; urgent.

**stringy** (string'e), a. Ropy; fibrous.

**stripe** (strip), n. A line of a different colour; a lash.

**stripling** (strip'ling), n. A youth.

**structural** (struk'tur-al), a. Pertaining to structure.

**structure** (struk'tur), n. Form; frame; an edifice.

**struggle** (strug'l), vi. To strive; to endeavour.

**strumous** (stroo'mus), a. Having swellings in the glands.

**strumpet** (strum'pet), n. A prostitute.

**strychnine** (strik'nin), n. A deadly poison.

**stubble** (stub'l), n. Stumps of rye, wheat, &c.

**stubborn** (stub'orn), a. Inflexible in opinion.

**stucco** (stuk'o), n. A kind of fine plaster.

**stud** (stud), n. A small post; a set of horses; a button; a nail.

**studied** (stud'id), a. Premeditated.

**studio** (stu'de-o), n. The work-shop, especially of a sculptor; pl. **studios.**

**studious** (stu'de-us), a. Given to study.

**stultify** (stul'te-fi), vt. To make foolish.

**stupefy** (stu'pe-fi), vt. To make stupid.

**stupendous** (stu-pend'us), a. Astonishing; amazing.

**stupid** (stu'pid), a. Dull in understanding; insensible; foolish. [**stupidity**]

**stupor** (stu'por), n. Partial or entire insensibility; dulness; stupefaction.

**sturdy** (stur'di), a. Stout; robust; strong.

**sturgeon** (stur'jun), n. A large seafish.

**stutter** (stut'er), vi. To speak with interrupted articulation; stammer.

**Stygian** (stij'i-an), a. Pertaining to, or like, the river Styx; black; gloomy.

**style** (stil), n. Manner of expression in speech or writing; peculiar mode of execution of an artist; fashion; title; mode of reckoning time; tool for engraving; middle portion of a pistil.

**stylish** (stil'ish), a. Fashionable; showy. n. [**stylishness**]

**styptic** (stip'tik), a. Serving to stop bleeding.

**suasion** (swa'zhun), n. Act of persuading; persuasion.

**suave** (swav), a. Pleasant; bland; courteous. [**suavity**]

**subaltern** (sub-al'tern, sub-al-), a. Inferior; subordinate.

**subaqueous** (sub-a'kwe-us), a. Under water.

**subdue** (sub-du'), vt. To conquer; tame; soften.

**subjacent** (sub-ja'sent), a. Lying under or below.

**subjection** (sub-jek'shun), n. Act of subjecting; state of being subject or subjected. [**subjective**]

**subjugate** (sub'ju-gat), vt. To bring under power; conquer; subdue.

**subjunctive** (sub-jungk'tiv), a. Subjoined; expressing condition, supposition, or contingency.

**sublease** (sub-les'), n. Lease by a lessee to another.

**sublimate** (sub'li-mat), vt. To convert into vapor by heat, as a solid substance.

**sublime** (sub-lim'), a. Lofty; majestic; awakening awe. [**sublimity**]

**sublunar** (sub-lu'nar), a. Earthly; terrestrial.

**submarine** (sub-ma-ren'), a. Under, or in, the sea.

**submerge** (sub-merj'), **submerse** (sub-mers'), vt. To plunge under water; overflow.

**submission** (sub-mish'un), n. Act of submitting; humility; resignation.

**submissive** (sub-mis'iv), a. Willing to submit; yielding; humble.

**subordinate** (sub-or'di-nat), vt. To place in a lower order; make inferior or subject. [**subordina'tion**]

**suborn** (sub-orn'), vt. To procure privately or indirectly; cause to commit perjury. [**suborna'tion**]

**subscribe** (sub-skrib'), v. To attest; to assent. [**subscription**]

**subsequently** (sub'se-kwent-li), ad. In time following.

**subservient** (sub-serv'i-ent), a. Useful to promote.

**subside** (sub-sid'), v. To sink; to tend downward. [**subsidence**]

**subsidiary** (sub-sid'i-ar-i), a. Assistant.

**subsidize** (sub'si-diz), v. To furnish with a subsidy.
**subsidy** (sub'si-di), n. Aid in money; supply granted.
**subsist** (sub-sist'), v. To continue; to live; to maintain with food, etc. [**subsistence**]
**substance** (sub'stans), n. A being; essential part; matter; body; goods; property. [**substantial, substantiate**]
**substantive** (sub'stan-tiv), a. Noting existence; real.
**substitute** (sub'sti-tut), n. A person or thing put in place of another.
**subterfuge** (sub'ter-fuj), n. An evasion; a trick; a shift.
**subterranean** (sub-ter-ra'ne-an), a. Lying under the surface of the earth; underground.
**subtile** (sub'til or sut'l), a. Fine drawn; piercing; acute.
**subtility** (sub'til-ti), n. Artfulness; cunning.
**subtle** (sut'l), a. Sly; artful.
**subtract** (sub-trakt'), v. To withdraw; to deduct.
**suburban** (sub-ur'ban), a. Relating to or being in the outer edge of a city. [**suburbs**]
**subvert** (sub-vert'), v. To overturn; to overthrow; to ruin; to pervert.
**subway** (sub'wa), n. An underground way.
**succeed** (suk-sed'), v. To follow or come after; to prosper. [**success**]
**succession** (suk-sesh'un), n. A lineage; a series; order of events. [**successor**]
**succinct** (suk-singkt'), a. Shortened; concise; brief.
**succor** (suk'kur), v. To relieve; to assist; to aid.
**succotash** (suk'ko-tash), n. Food made of green corn and beans.
**succulent** (suk'ku-lent), a. Juicy; moist; full of juice.
**succumb** (suk-kum'), v. To sink under difficulty; to yield.
**suckle** (suk'l), v. To give suck to; to nurse at the breast.
**suction** (suk'shun), n. Act or power of sucking or drawing.
**sue** (su), v. To prosecute at law; to request; to petition.
**suet** (su'et), n. Fatty tissue.
**suffer** (suf'fer), v. To feel or bear what is painful; to allow; to tolerate; to bear patiently. [**sufferance**]
**suffice** (suf-fiz'), v. To be equal to; to satisfy; to be enough. [**sufficient**]
**suffocate** (suf'fo-kat), v. To choke; to stifle; to smother.
**suffrage** (suf'fraj), n. A vote or voice in voting; aid; support.
**suffuse** (suf-fuz'), v. To overspread or cover.
**sugar** (shog'ar), n. A sweet substance made from the sugarcane, etc.
**suggest** (sud-jest'), v. To intimate; to hint. [**suggestion**]
**suggestive** (sud-jest'iv), a. Containing a hint.
**suicide** (su'i-sid), n. Self-murder; a self-murderer.
**suit** (sut), n. A set; petition; courtship; action at law.
**suitable** (sut'a-bl), a. Fit; proper; agreeable; becoming.
**suite** (swet), n. A retinue.
**suitor** (sut'ur), n. One who sues; a petitioner; a lover.
**sullen** (sul'len), a. Morose; obstinate; gloomy; dismal.
**sulphur** (sul'fur), n. A yellow mineral substance; brimstone.
**sultry** (sul'tri), a. Very hot and close.
**summary** (sum'ma-ri), a. Short; concise.

**summer** (sum'mer), n. The hot season.

**summit** (sum'mit), n. The top; the highest point or degree.

**summon** (sum'mun), v. To call or cite by authority.

**sumptuary** (sump'tu-a-ri), a. Regulating expenses.

**sumptuous** (sump'tu-us), a. Costly; expensive; splendid.

**sunder** (sun'der), v. To divide; to part; to separate.

**sundry** (sun'dri), a. More than one or two.

**superabundant** (su-per-a-bun'dant), a. Being more than is enough; copious.

**superannuated** (su-per-an'-u-at-ed), a. Disqualified by age.

**superb** (su-perb'), a. Grand; magnificent; stately; showy.

**supercargo** (su-per-kar'go), n. One who has the care or sale of a cargo.

**supercilious** (su-per-sil'i-us), a. Dictatorial; arrogant.

**superficial** (su-per-fish'al), a. Pertaining to, or on, the surface; shallow; slight.

**superficies** (su-per-fish'ez, per'fi-sez), n. Surface; outside.

**superfluity** (su-per-flu'i-ti), n. Superabundance; quantity more than is needful. [**superfluous**]

**superimpose** (su-per-im-poz'), vt. To lay above.

**superinduce** (su-per-in-dus'), vt. To bring in over, or as an addition to, something else.

**superintendent** (su-per-in-tend'ent), n. An overseer; manager.

**superior** (su-pe'ri-or), a. Higher; surpassing others; above the influence of. n. One superior to others; chief. [**superior'ity**]

**superlative** (su-per'la-tiv), a. Most eminent; supreme.

**supernal** (su-per'nal), a. Relating to things above; celestial.

**supernatural** (su-per-nat'yu-ral), a. Above, or exceeding, the powers of nature.

**supernumerary** (su-per-nu'-mer-a-ri), a. Above the needful or regular number.

**supersede** (su-per-sed'), vt. To displace; take the place of; overrule.

**superstition** (su-per-stish'un), n. Over-credulity in matters of belief; excessive rigor in religious matters; false or absurd belief. [**superstitious**]

**supervene** (su-per-ven'), vt. To occur; take place.

**supervise** (su-per-viz'), vt. To oversee; superintend. [**supervis'ion**]

**supervisor** (su-per-viz'or), n. An overseer; inspector.

**supine** (su-pin'), a. Lying on the back; indolent; negligent.

**supplant** (sup-plant'), vt. To displace by artifice; undermine.

**supple** (sup'l), a. Pliant; flexible; fawning.

**supplement** (sup'le-ment), n. An addition. vt. To supply; add to.

**suppliant** (sup'li-ant), a. Entreating. [**supplicant**]

**supplicate** (sup'li-kat), vt. To entreat earnestly; petition.

**support** (sup-port'), vt. To sustain; keep up; endure; defend.

**supportable** (sup-port'a-bl), a. That may be supported.

**supposable** (sup-poz'a-bl), a. That may be supposed.

**suppose** (sup-poz'), a. To assume as true; imagine. [**supposition**]

**supposititious** (sup-poz-i-tish'us), a. Fraudulently

**substituted**; **not genuine**; spurious.

**suppress** (sup-pres'), vt. To put, or keep, down; conceal. [**suppression**]

**suppurate** (sup'u-rat), vi. or t. To generate pus.

**suppuration** (sup-u-ra'shun) n. A ripening into matter.

**supramundane** (su-pra-mun'dan), a. Above the world.

**supremacy** (su-prem'a-se), n. Highest authority.

**supreme** (su-prem'), a. Highest; chief.

**sural** (su'ral), a. Pertaining to the calf of the leg.

**surcharge** (sur-charj'), vt. To overcharge.

**surd** (surd), n. A quantity whose root can not be exactly expressed in number.

**sure** (shoor), a. Not liable to fail; certainly knowing.

**surety** (shoor'te), n. Certainty; security against loss; a bondsman.

**surf** (surf), n. Continual swell of the sea upon the shore.

**surface** (sur'fas), n. Outside; outer face.

**surfeit** (sur'fit), vt. To fill to satiety; cloy.

**surge** (surj), n. Swell of a great wave; billows.

**surgeon** (sur'jun), n. One who practises surgery. [**surgery**]

**surloin** (sur'loin), n. A loin of beef.

**surly** (sur'li), a. Morose; gruff; ill-tempered.

**surmise** (sur-miz'), vt. To imagine; suspect; conjecture.

**surmount** (sur-mount'), vt. To mount above; overcome; surpass.

**surname** (sur'nam), n. Name borne after the baptismal name.

**surpass** (sur-pas'), vt. To pass beyond; exceed; excel.

**surplice** (sur'plis), n. White robe worn by clergymen.

**surplus** (sur'plus), n. Overplus; excess beyond what is needful.

**surprise** (sur-priz'), vt. To come, or fall upon, unawares; strike with wonder.

**surreptitious** (sur'rep-tish'-us), a. Underhand; done by stealth or fraud.

**surrogate** (sur'o-gat), n. A deputy; delegate.

**surtout** (sur-toot'), n. A close-fitting overcoat.

**survey** (sur-va'), vt. To look over; contemplate; view; measure and estimate, as land. [**surveying**]

**surveyor** (sur-va'or), n. One who surveys; a measurer of land.

**survive** (sur-viv'), vt. To outlive.

**survivor** (sur-viv'or), n. One who outlives another.

**susceptible** (sus-sep'ti-bl), a. Capable of receiving impressions; that may be affected; impressible; sensitive.

**suspect** (sus-pekt'), vt. To mistrust; imagine to be guilty; conjecture.

**suspend** (sus-pend'), vt. To hang; cause to depend; delay; cause to cease for a time.

**suspense** (sus-pens'), n. State of being suspended; uncertainty; cessation. [**suspension**]

**suspicion** (sus-pish'un), n. Mistrust; conjecture; surmise of guilt. [**suspicious**]

**sustain** (sus-tan'), vt. To bear; endure; maintain; prove.

**sustenance** (sus'te-nans), n. Maintenance; food; nourishment.

**sutler** (sut'ler), n. One who follows an army and sells provisions, etc.

**suture** (sut'yur), n. A seam;

**swamp** (swomp), n. Wet, soft, spongy ground; a bog.

**swan** (swon), n. A large waterfowl.

**swap** (swop), v. To exchange; to barter.

**sward** (sward), n. Grassy surface of land; green turf.

**swarm** (swarm), n. A multitude; a cluster of bees.

**swarthy** (swarth'i), a. Of a dark or dusky hue.

**swath** (swath), n. A line or row of grass cut down.

**swathe** (swath), v. To bind with a cloth.

**swear** (swar), v. To appeal solemnly to God for the truth of what is stated; to take an oath; to use profane language.

**sweat** (swet), n. Wet or moisture from the skin.

**swelter** (swel'ter), v. To be pained with heat.

**swerve** (swerv), v. To deviate; to rove; to wander.

**swig** (swig), v. To drink greedily.

**swill** (swil), v. To drink greedily.

**swindle** (swin'dl), v. To defraud with artifice; to cheat. [**swindler**]

**swine** (swin), n. sing. and pl. A pig; hogs collectively. [**swinish**]

**switch** (swich), n. A flexible rod or twig; a movable rail.

**swivel** (swiv'l), n. A ring or link that turns on a neck.

**swoon** (swoon), v. To faint.

**swoop** (swop), v. To catch on the wing; to catch up.

**sword** (sord), n. A weapon with a long blade.

**sycamore** (sik'a-mor), n. The plane-tree; the button-wood; the Egyptian fig-mulberry.

**sycophancy** (sik'o-fan-si), n. Servile flattery; servility.

**syllable** (sil'la-bl), n. As much of a word as can be uttered by one effort.

**syllabus** (sil'la-bus), n. An abstract of a discourse.

**syllogism** (sil'lo-jizm), n. Argument of three propositions.

**sylvan** (sil'van), a. Woody; pertaining to the woods.

**symbol** (sim'bul), n. A type; emblem; memorial rite.

**symmetrical** (sim-met'ri-kal), a. Having due proportion.

**symmetry** (sim'me-tri), n. Adaptation of parts to each other; harmony.

**sympathize** (sim'pa-thiz), v. To feel with another. [**sympathy**]

**symphony** (sim'fo-ni), n. Unison or harmony of sounds; a musical composition.

**symposium** (sim-po'zi-um), n. A merry feast.

**symptom** (simp'tum), n. A sign; a token; indication.

**synagogue** (sin'a-gog), n. A Jewish place of worship.

**syncope** (sing'ko-pe), n. The omitting of a letter; a swoon.

**syndicate** (sin'di-kat), n. Office of a syndic; a body of men chosen to watch the interests of a company or to promote some enterprise.

**synod** (sin'od), n. A convention; an ecclesiastical council.

**synonym** (sin'o-nim), n. A word which has the same signification as another. [**synonymous**]

**synopsis** (sin-op'sis), n. A general view of things.

**syntax** (sin'taks), n. The correct arrangement of words in sentences.

**synthesis** (sin'the-sis), n. The act of joining; composition.

**syringe** (sir'inj), n. A tube for ejecting liquids.

**syrup** (ser'up), n. Sweet fluid.

**systematic** (sis-tem-at'ik), a. Formed or done according to system; methodical.

# T

**tabernacle** (tab'er-na-kl), n. A temporary habitation.

**tablature** (tab'la-tur), n. Painting on walls or ceilings.

**tableau** (tab'lo), n. A striking and vivid representation.

**tablet** (tab'let), n. A little table; a level surface; a disc-shaped pill; a lozenge.

**taboo** (ta-bo'), n. A prohibition.

**tabulate** (tab'u-lat), v. To reduce to tables or synopsis.

**tacit** (tas'it), a. Silent; implied, but not expressed.

**taciturn** (tas'e-turn), a. Habitually silent. [taciturnity]

**tackle** (tak'l), n. Machines for raising weights.

**tackling** (tak'ling), n. Rigging of ships; harness.

**tact** (takt), n. Nice perception or skill.

**tactical** (tak'tik-al), a. Pertaining to tactics.

**tactics** (tak'tiks), n. pl. The science and art of disposing military and naval forces.

**tactile** (tak'til), a. Susceptible of touch.

**tactual** (takt'u-al), a. Pertaining to touch.

**taffeta** (taf'e-ta), n. A glossy silk stuff.

**tail** (tal), n. The hinder part; end.

**tailor** (ta'ler), n. One who makes men's clothes.

**taint** (tant), vt. To infect; to corrupt.

**tale** (tal), n. A narrative; story; anything told; reckoning.

**talent** (tal'ent), n. An ancient weight, and also denomination of money (varying in different countries and times); natural or special gift; mental ability.

**talisman** (tal'iz-man), n. A magical charm; amulet.

**tallow** (tal'o), n. Fat of an animal separated by melting.

**tally** (tal'i), n. Account kept on a notched stick, or by score marks; anything that matches another.

**tally-ho** (tal'li-ho), n. A four-in-hand coach.

**Talmud** (tal'mud), n. The body of Hebrew laws, with Rabbinical comments.

**talon** (tal'on), n. Claw of a bird of prey.

**tamable** (tam'a-bl), a. That may be tamed.

**tambourine** (tam-bu-ren'), n. A shallow drum with but one skin.

**tandem** (tan'dem), adv. Harnessed one behind another, as horses.

**tangible** (tan'ji-bl), a. Perceptible by the touch; palpable; that may be realized.

**tangle** (tang'gl), vt. To unite or interweave confusedly; ensnared.

**tansy** (tan'zi), n. A bitter aromatic herb.

**tantalize** (tan'ta-liz), vt. To

# TANTAMOUNT 223 TELEPATHY

torment with baffled hope or desire.

**tantamount** (tant'a-mount), n. Equivalent.

**taper** (tap'er), n. Small wax candle, or light.

**tapestry** (tap'es-tri), n. Kind of hangings with embroidered figures.

**tapioca** (tap-i-o'ka), n. Starch obtained from the roots of a Brazilian plant.

**tapir** (ta'pir), n. A South American quadruped.

**tarantula** (ta-ran'tyu-la), n. A large venomous spider.

**tardy** (tar'di), a. Slow; sluggish; late.

**tare** (tar), n. Allowance for the weight of the vessel, etc., containing goods.

**target** (tar'get), n. A small round shield; mark to shoot at.

**tariff** (tar'if), n. System of duties on imports; table of such duties.

**tarnish** (tar'nish), vt. To sully; diminish the lustre or purity of.

**tarpaulin** (tar-pal'in), n. Tarred canvas.

**tarpon** (tar'pon), n. A large fish found in the Gulf of Mexico.

**tartar** (tar'tar), n. An acid salt deposited from wine; concretion on the teeth.

**Tartarean** (tar-ta're-an), a. Pertaining to Tartarus or the mythologic place of punishment after death.

**tassel** (tas'l), n. Ornamental knob with fringe attached.

**tasty** (tasti), a. Having good taste; in good taste.

**tatter** (tat'er), n. A torn piece; hanging rag.

**tattle** (tat'l), n. Trifling talk; gossip; scandal.

**tattoo** (tat-too'), n. Drumbeat or bugle-call to summon soldiers to their quarters at night.

**tattoo** (tat-too'), vt. To mark the skin with figures by pricking in some coloring matter.

**tautology** (ta-tol'o-ji), n. Needless repetition of words or ideas.

**tavern** (tav'ern), n. Public house for the entertainment of guests.

**tawdry** (ta'dri), a. Showy without taste; gaudy.

**taxicab** (tax'i-cab), n. An automobile used for hire by transient passengers.

**taxidermy** (taks'i-derm-i), n. Art of preparing and stuffing the skins of animals.

**tea** (te), n. A Chinese shrub, or an infusion of its leaves.

**teach** (tech), vt. To give knowledge to; instruct; instruct in; counsel.

**teachable** (tech'a-bl), a. That may be taught; docile.

**teamster** (tem'ster), n. One who drives a team.

**tear** (ter), n. A drop of the clear fluid from the eye.

**tear** (tar), vt. To part asunder violently; rend; lacerate.

**tease** (tez), vt. To comb or card; to vex; plague.

**teat** (tet), n. The nipple; dug.

**technical** (tek'ni-kal), a. Pertaining, or peculiar to, any art or craft.

**technology** (tek-nol'o-ji), n. A treatise on arts; explanation of terms or processes employed in arts.

**tedious** (te'di-us), a. Tiresome; irksome; slow.

**tedium** (te'di-um), n. Irksomeness; wearisomeness.

**tee** (te), n. A small heap of earth from which the ball is played in golf.

**telegram** (tel'e-gram), n. A telegraphic message. [telegraph]

**telepathy** (tel-ep'a-thi), n. Thought transference.

**telephone** (tel'e-fon), n. An instrument for conveying speech by electricity.

**telescope** (tel'e-skop), n. An optical instrument for viewing objects at a distance.

**temerity** (te-mer-i-ti), n. Rashness; contempt of danger.

**temperament** (tem'per-a-ment), n. Constitution; medium.

**temperance** (tem'per-ans), n. Moderation; sobriety. [temperate]

**temperature** (tem'per-a-tur), n. Degree of heat or cold.

**tempest** (tem'pest), n. Violent wind; a storm; commotion. [tempestuous]

**templar** (tem'plar), n. Student of law; a knight.

**temple** (tem'pl), n. An edifice for worship; flat side of the head above the cheek-bone.

**temporal** (tem'po-ral), a. Relating to this life; having limited existence; relating to the temples.

**temporary** (tem'po-ra-ri), a. Existing for a time; fleeting; transitory.

**temporize** (tem'po-riz), v. To comply with the times.

**tempt** (temt), v. To entice to evil; to allure; to provoke. [temptation]

**tenable** (ten'a-bl), a. That can be held or maintained.

**tenacious** (te-na'shus), a. Holding fast; grasping. [tenacity]

**tenant** (ten'ant), n. One who holds and rents property of another.

**tendency** (ten'den-si), n. Inclination; scope; aim; course.

**tendon** (ten'dun), n. A ligature of joints; a sinew.

**tendril** (ten'dril), n. The clasper of a vine, etc.

**tenement** (ten'e-ment), n. A house; anything held or occupied by a tenant.

**tenet** (ten'et), n. A position; opinion; principle.

**tenor** (ten'ur), n. Course; purport; a part in music.

**tense** (tens), n. Form of a verb to express time.

**tension** (ten'shun), n. Act of stretching; stiffness.

**tentacle** (ten'ta-kl), n. A filiform organ of certain insects for feeling or motion.

**tenuity** (ten-u'i-ti), n. Smallness; thinness.

**tenure** (ten'ur), n. A holding of lands or buildings.

**tepid** (tep'id), a. Lukewarm.

**tergiversation** (ter-ji-ver-sa'shun), n. A subterfuge.

**termagant** (ter'ma-gant), n. A virago.

**terminal** (ter'mi-nal), a. Being at or forming an end.

**terminate** (ter'mi-nat), v. To complete; to limit; to put an end to; to conclude. [termination]

**terminus** (ter'mi-nus), n. A boundary line; first or last station of a railroad.

**terrace** (ter'ras), n. A raised level bank; a gallery.

**terrapin** (ter'ra-pin), n. A large kind of turtle.

**terrestrial** (ter-res'tri-al), a. Belonging to the earth.

**terrible** (ter'ri-bl), a. That which may excite terror.

**terrier** (ter'ri-er), n. A species of hunting dog.

**terrify** (ter'ri-fi), v. To alarm; to frighten greatly.

**territory** (ter'ri-to-ri), n. A district of country under temporary government.

**terrorize** (ter'ur-iz), v. To fill with terror.

**terse** (ters), a. Elegant; neat.

**testament** (tes'ta-ment), n. A will; either of the two divisions of the Scriptures.

**testate** (tes'tat), a. Having left a will; disposed of by will. [**testator**]

**testify** (tes'ti-fi), v. To give testimony; to bear witness.

**testily** (tes'ti-li), ad. Fretfully; peevishly.

**testimonial** (tes-ti-mo'ni-al), n. A certificate; attestation. [**testimony**]

**testy** (tes'ti), a. Peevish.

**tetanus** (tet'a-nus), n. Lockjaw.

**tete-a-tete** (tat-a-tat), n. Head to head; in private.

**tether** (teth'er), v. To confine by a rope; to restrain.

**Teutonic** (tu-ton'ik), a. Relating to the ancient Germans.

**textile** (teks'til), a. Woven.

**textual** (tekst'u-al), a. Contained in the text.

**texture** (tekst'ur), n. Manner of weaving; the web woven.

**thatch** (thach), n. Straw for covering a roof.

**thaw** (thaw), vi. or t. To melt as ice or snow.

**theatre** (the'a-ter), n. A playhouse, a place of action or exhibition. [**theatrical**]

**theft** (theft), n. A felonious taking of property; thing stolen.

**theism** (the'izm), n. Belief in a God.

**theist** (the'ist), n. One who believes in the being of a God.

**theme** (them), n. Subject or topic.

**theocracy** (the-ok'ra-se), n. A government immediately directed by God.

**theologian** (the-o-lo'je-an), n. One versed in divinity.

**theorem** (the'o-rem), n. A proposition to be proved.

**theorist** (the'o-rist), n. One who theorizes, or is given to theory.

**theorize** (the'o-riz), vi. To form a theory; speculate.

**theory** (the'o-ri), n. Explanation or system of anything; unproved explanation of any series of phenomena; exposition of abstract principles; speculation.

**therapeutic** (ther-a-pu'tik), a. Pertaining to the healing art.

**thermal** (ther'mal), a. Pertaining to heat; warm.

**thermometer** (ther-mom'e-ter), n. An instrument for measuring degrees of temperature.

**thesaurus** (the-sar'us), n. A treasury; repository of information.

**thesis** (the'sis), n. An essay on any subject; literary or scientific exercise.

**thew** (thu), n. Muscle; brawn; sinew; (used chiefly in pl.).

**thief** (thef), n. One who steals. pl. **thieves.**

**thievery** (thev'er-i), n. The practice of stealing.

**thigh** (thi), n. Part of the leg between the knee and hip.

**thimble** (thim'bl), n. A metal cap to protect the finger in sewing.

**thistle** (this'l), n. A genus of prickly plants.

**thorax** (tho'raks), n. The chest in man or animals; middle part of the body in insects.

**thorough** (thur'o), a. Passing through; complete.

**thoroughfare** (thur'o-far), n. A way that may be passed through.

**though** (tho), conj. Admitting; even if; notwithstanding.

**thought** (that), pt. and pp. of **think.** n. Reasoning; reflection; meditation; an idea; consideration; opinion.

**thrash** (thrash), vt. To beat out grain.

**thread** (thred), n. A small

twist of silk, cotton, &c.; a filament.

**threadbare** (thred'bar), a. Worn out; common.

**threat** (thret), n. Denunciation of ill.

**threatening** (thret'n-ing), a. Indicating danger; imminent.

**thrift** (thrift), n. Frugality; prudence; profit.

**thrill** (thril), v. To pierce; to penetrate; to feel a quivering sensation.

**thrive** (thriv), v. To prosper; to grow rich; to succeed.

**throat** (throt), n. Fore part of the neck, in which are the windpipe and gullet.

**throb** (throb), v. To palpitate forcibly.

**throe** (thro), n. Extreme pain; agony; a pang.

**throne** (thron), n. A royal seat.

**throng** (thrang), n. A crowd of people. v. To crowd together.

**throttle** (throt'l), n. The windpipe.

**through** (thro), pret. From end to end; by means of.

**thrush** (thrush), n. A bird; ulcers in the mouth; aphthæ.

**thrust** (thrust), v. To impel; to push with force; to intrude. n. A hostile attack.

**thud** (thud), n. A stroke; a blow.

**thumb** (thum), n. The first and short thick finger of the hand.

**thump** (thump), v. To strike; to beat. n. A hard blow.

**thwart** (thwart), v. To oppose; to lie across; to traverse.

**thyme** (tim), n. A herb.

**tiara** (ti-a'ra), n. Ornamental head-dress; a diadem; the triple crown.

**tickle** (tik'l), v. To excite a thrilling sensation by the touch; to please by slight gratification; cause to laugh.

**tidal** (ti'dal), a. Pertaining to the tides.

**tidings** (ti'dingz), n. pl. Intelligence; news.

**tidy** (ti'di), a. Neat; ready. n. A fancy knitted cover on the back of chairs, etc.; a pinafore.

**tie** (ti), v. To bind; to fasten.

**tier** (ter), n. A row or rank.

**tighten** (tit'n), v. To make tight or close; to straighten.

**tile** (til), n. A plate of burned clay for roofing, etc.

**tillage** (til'aj), n. Culture and preparing of land.

**timid** (tim'id), a. Faint-hearted; fearful; wanting courage. **[timidity]**

**timorous** (tim'ur-us), a. Full of fear or scruples.

**tincture** (tingk'tur), n. Extract of a substance.

**tinder** (tin'der), n. An inflammable substance.

**tine** (tin), n. A tooth or prong.

**tinker** (ting'ker), n. A mender of vessels of metal.

**tinkle** (ting'kl), v. To make sharp sounds; to jingle.

**tinsel** (tin'sel), n. A kind of lace; something of slight value with false luster.

**tirade** (tir'ad), n. A violent and reproving declamation.

**tire** (tir), n. A band of iron for a wheel.

**tired** (tird), a. Weary; jaded.

**tissue** (tish'u), n. Cloth interwoven with gold, etc.

**tithe** (tith), n. Tenth of anything. v. To pay tithes.

**title** (ti'tl), n. An inscription; right; appellation of dignity.

**titter** (tit'er), v. To laugh

**titular** (tit'u-lar), a. Ex

isting in name or title only.
**toad** (tod), n. A reptile. [**toadyism**]
**tobacco** (to-bak'o), n. A plant.
**tocsin** (tok'sin), n. An alarmbell.
**toe** (to), n. One of the extremities of the foot.
**together** (too-geth'er), ad. In company.
**toil** (toil), vi. To work hard.
**toilet** (toil'et), n. A dressing table.
**toilsome** (toil'sum), a. Laborious; wearisome.
**tolerable** (tol'er-a-bl), a. That may be endured.
**tolerance** (tol'er-ans), n. Act of enduring.
**toll** (tol), n. Sound of a large bell rung slowly.
**toll** (tol), n. A tax for some liberty.
**tomahawk** (tom'a-hak), n. An Indian war-hatchet.
**tomato** (to-ma'to), n. A garden vegetable, and its fruit. pl. **tomatoes**.
**tomb** (toom), n. A grave; vault for the dead.
**tome** (tom), n. Volume of a work; a large book.
**to-morrow** (to-mor'o), n. Day after the present day.
**tongue** (tung), n. Muscular organ in the mouth used in speech and tasting; speech; language; anything like a tongue; point of land.
**tongue-tied** (tung'tid), a. Unable to speak freely.
**tonic** (ton'ik), a. Relating to tones; pertaining to the key-note; giving vigor to the system.
**to-night** (to-nit'), n. This night; night following this day.
**tonnage** (tun'aj), n. Weight in tons; cubical capacity of a ship in tons; duty by the ton.
**tonsil** (ton'sil), n. One of two appendages at the base of the tongue.
**tonsorial** (ton-so'ri-al), a. Relating to barbers or their craft.
**tonsure** (ton'shur), n. Act of clipping the hair.
**tontine** (ton-ten'), n. A financial scheme of which the gain accrues to the survivor or survivors.
**toothache** (tooth'ak), n. Pain in a tooth.
**topaz** (to'paz), n. A precious stone of a yellowish color.
**tope** (top), vi. To drink spirituous liquors.
**toper** (top'er), n. A tippler; drunkard.
**topic** (top'ik), n. A subject of discourse.
**topographer** (top-og'ra-fer), n. One skilled in topography.
**topple** (top'l), vt. and vi. To fall or pitch over; overthrow; tumble down; lean over as if about to fall.
**topsy-turvy** (top'si-tur'vi), a. and adv. Upside down; in confusion.
**torch** (torch), n. Light made of some combustible fastened to a staff; a burning brand.
**torment** (tor'ment), n. Extreme pain; torture; great annoyance; that which causes torment.
**torment** (tor-ment'), vt. To torture; afflict; annoy greatly.
**tornado** (tor-na'do), n. A violent storm or hurricane; cyclone.
**torpedo** (tor-pe'do), n. A kind of flat fish that gives electric shocks; apparatus for producing an explosion under water or the earth; small fulminating cracker.
**torpid** (tor'pid), a. Numb; sluggish; without feeling or emotion. [**torpor**]

**torrent** (tor'ent), n. A rushing stream.

**torrid** (tor'id), a. Burning; hot.

**torsion** (tor'shun), n. Act of twisting; recoil of anything twisted.

**tortoise** (tor'tis), n. A four-footed reptile inclosed in a hard case.

**tortuous** (tor'tyu-us), a. Winding; crooked; deceitful.

**torture** (tort'yur), n. Extreme pain; the infliction of great pain; torment.

**tory** (to'ri), n. A supporter of royal power; English conservative.

**total** (to'tal), a. Whole; complete. n. The whole amount; sum.

**totter** (tot'er), vi. To walk unsteadily; stagger; shake.

**touch** (tuch), vt. To come into contact with; perceive by feeling; reach to; relate to; influence; affect.

**tough** (tuf), a. Not easily broken; tenacious; strong; able to endure hardship.

**tour** (toor), n. A journey in a circuit; excursion. [**tourist**]

**tournament** (toor'na-ment), n. A mock fight, or martial sport, on horseback; contest of skill among several competitors.

**tourniquet** (toor'ni-ket), n. A bandage tightened by a screw, or other device, to check the flow of blood.

**tow** (to), vt. To draw through the water by a rope.

**tow** (to), n. The coarse fibres of flax or hemp.

**toward, -s** (to-ard, -z), prp. In the direction of; with respect to.

**toxicology** (toks-i-kol'o-ji), n. Science which treats of poisons.

**toy** (toi), n. A child's plaything; bauble; trifle.

**trace** (tras), n. A footprint; vestige; mark; one of the straps by which a vehicle is drawn. [**traceable, tracery**]

**trachea** (tra'ke-a), n. The windpipe.

**tracing** (tras'ing), n. Act of copying by drawing on thin paper a design seen through it; copy so produced.

**tractable** (trakt'a-bl), a. Easily managed; docile.

**tractate** (trakt'at), n. A treatise.

**tractile** (trak'til), a. That may be drawn out.

**traction** (trak'shun), n. Act of drawing or pulling.

**trade-wind** (trad'wind), n. A periodical wind.

**tradition** (tra-dish'un), n. The handing down of opinions or practices to posterity unwritten.

**traduce** (tra-dus'), v. To villify; to defame; to caluminate.

**traffic** (traf'ik), v. To buy and sell.

**tragedian** (tra-je'di-an), n. An actor of tragedy.

**tragedy** (traj'e-di), n. A dramatic poem representing an action having a fatal issue; any dreadful event.

**trail** (tral), v. To draw along the ground; to drag.

**train** (tran), v. To draw; to discipline; to educate.

**trait** (trat), n. A stroke; touch; a feature; the outline.

**traitor** (tra'tur), n. One who betrays his trust.

**tramp** (tramp), v. To travel on foot; to wander.

**trample** (tram'pl), v. To tread under foot; to insult.

**trance** (trans), n. A rapture; catalepsy; ecstasy.

**tranquil** (tran'kwil), a. Quiet; calm; undisturbed. [**tranquillity**]

**tranquilize** (tran'kwil-liz),

v. To render calm; to quiet.

**transact** (tras-akt'), v. To carry through; to manage; to perform; to conduct. [transaction]

**transcend** (tran-send'), v. To exceed; to surpass. [transcendent]

**transcribe** (tran-skrib'), v. To write over again; to copy. [transcription]

**transept** (tran'sept), n. The part of a church at right angles with the nave.

**transfer** (trans-fer'), v. To convey; to sell; to remove.

**transfer** (trans'fer), n. A conveyance; a removal.

**transfiguration** (trans-fig-u-ra'shun), n. Change of form or appearance.

**transfix** (trans-fiks'), v. To pierce through; to kill.

**transfusion** (trans-fu'zhun), n. Introduction of blood into the vessels of another.

**transgress** (trans-gres'), v. To pass over or beyond; to violate; to infringe. [transgression]

**transgressor** (trans-gres'-ur), n. An offender.

**transient** (tran'shent), a. Soon past; fleeting; momentary.

**transit** (tran'sit), n. A passing over or through; conveyance.

**transition** (tran-sizh'un), n. Passage; removal; change from one place to another.

**transitory** (tran'si-tor-i), a. Speedily vanishing; continuing a short time.

**translate** (trans-lat'), v. To remove; to interpret into another language.

**transmigrate** (trans'mi-grat), v. To pass from one country or body to another.

**transmission** (trans-mish'-un), n. Act of sending from one place to another; passage through.

**transmit** (trans-mit'), v. To send from one person or place to another.

**transmutation** (trans-mu-ta'shun), n. The change of anything into another substance.

**transom** (tran'sum), n. Crossbeam; a window over a door.

**transparency** (trans-par'en-si), n. The state of being transparent.

**transpire** (trans-pir'), v. To emit vapor through the pores; to become known.

**transplant** (trans-plant'), v. To plant in another place.

**transport** (trans'port), n. Conveyance; a ship for conveying goods, stores, etc.; ecstasy; rapture; rage.

**transport** (trans-port'), v. To carry; to banish; to ravish with pleasure or ecstasy. [transportation]

**transpose** (trans-poz'), v. To put each in the place of the other.

**transubstantiation** (tran-sub-stan-shi-a'shun), n. Changing into another substance.

**travail** (trav'al), v. To labor; to suffer in childbirth.

**travel** (trav'el), v. To make a journey or voyage. n. A passing through a country. [traveler]

**traverse** (trav'ers), ad. Crosswise; athwart.

**travesty** (trav'es-ti), n. A parody.

**trawl** (tral), v. To fish by dragging a net behind the vessel.

**treacherous** (trech'er-us), a. False; faithless perfidious. [treachery]

**treacle** (tre'kl), n. A saccharine fluid; molasses.

**tread** (tred), v. To step or walk on; to subdue; to trample. n. Manner of

**treadle** (tred'l), n. The part of a machine moved by the foot.

**treason** (tre'zn), n. A breach of faith or allegiance; disloyalty; treachery.

**treasure** (trezh'ur), n. Wealth.

**treat** (tret), vt. or i. To handle; to negotiate; to entertain.

**treatise** (tret'iz), n. A written discourse; a tract.

**treatment** (tret'ment), n. Usage; management; behaviour.

**treaty** (tret'e), n. An agreement or compact between parties, usually states.

**treble** (treb'l), a. Threefold.

**trefoil** (tre'foil), n. A three-leaved plant as clover.

**trellis** (trel'is), n. A structure or lattice-work of iron.

**tremble** (trem'bl), vi. To shake or quake; to quiver.

**tremendous** (tre-men'dus), a. Awful; frightful; terrible.

**tremor** (tre'mor, trem'or), n. Involuntary trembling.

**tremulous** (trem'u-lus), a. Trembling; shaking.

**trepan** (tre-pan'), n. A circular saw for perforating the skull.

**trepidation** (trep-id-a'shun), n. A trembling.

**trespass** (tres'pas), vi. To enter on another's property without right; to transgress. [**trespasser**]

**tress** (tres), n. A lock; ringlet of hair.

**trestle** (tres'l), n. A frame to support anything.

**tret** (tret), n. An allowance for waste.

**trey** (tra), n. The three at cards or dice.

**triad** (tri'ad), n. The union of three.

**trial** (tri'al), n. A temptation; legal examination; test.

**triangle** (tri'ang-gl), n. A figure of three angles.

**triangular** (tri-ang'gu-lar), a. Having three angles.

**tribe** (trib), n. A family; race; class.

**tribulation** (trib-u-la'shun), n. A great affliction.

**tribunal** (tri-bu'nal), n. A court of justice.

**tribune** (trib'un), n. A Roman magistrate; a platform.

**tributary** (trib'u-tar-e), a. Subject to tribute; contributing.

**tribute** (trib'ut), n. A tax on a conquered country.

**trice** (tris), n. A short time; an instant.

**trick** (trik), n. An artifice for the purpose of deception.

**trickery** (trik'er-e), n. Artifice; act of dressing up.

**trickish** (trik'ish), a. Knavishly artful.

**trickishness** (trik'ish-nes), n. Knavish practice.

**trickle** (trik'l), vi. To flow or drop gently.

**tricoloured** (tri'kul-erd), a. Of three colours.

**tricuspid** (tri-kus'pid), a. Having three points.

**trident** (tri'dent), n. A sceptre with three prongs.

**triennial** (tri-en'ne-al), a. Being every third year.

**trier** (tri'er), n. One who tries.

**trifle** (tri'fl), n. A thing of little value or importance.

**trifling** (tri'fling), a. Of little value or importance.

**trigger** (trig'er), n. Catch which when pressed releases the main-spring of a gun-lock.

**trigonometry** (trig-o-nom'e-tri), n. Science which treats of triangles and their measurement.

**Trinitarian** (trin-i-ta'ri-an),

**Trinity** — **Truculent**

**a.** Pertaining to the doctrine of the Trinity.

**Trinity** (trin'i-ti), n. Union of three Persons in one Godhead.

**trinket** (tringk'et), n. A small ornament.

**trinomial** (tri-nom'i-al), a. Consisting of three terms.

**trio** (tre'o), n. Combination of three; piece of music for three performers.

**tripartite** (trip'ar-tit), a. Divided into three parts; relating to three parties.

**tripe** (trip), n. Large stomach of the ox, etc., prepared for food.

**triphthong** (trif'thong), n. Union of three vowels in one syllable.

**triple** (trip'le), a. Threefold.

**triplet** (trip'let), n. Three of a kind or united; three lines rhyming together; three notes occupying the time of two.

**triplicate** (trip'li-kat), a. Threefold.

**tripod** (tri'pod), n. Stand, stool, etc., with three feet.

**trisect** (tri-sekt'), vt. To divide into three equal parts. [trisection]

**trisyllable** (tris-il'a-bl), n. A word of three syllables.

**trite** (trit), a. Worn out; hackneyed; commonplace.

**triturate** (trit'yu-rat), vt. To rub or grind to a powder. [tritura'tion]

**triumph** (tri'umf), n. Pomp or joy for victory or success; victory.

**triumvir** (tri-um'vir), n. One of three men united in office.

**triumvirate** (tri-um'vir-at), n. Government by triumvirs; association of three in office.

**trivial** (triv'i-al), a. Trifling; common; unimportant.

**triune** (tri'un), a. Being three in one.

**trochee** (tro'ki or -ke), n. Musical foot of a long and a short, or an accented and unaccented syllable.

**trolley** (trol'li), n. A long pole on the top of the trolley-car, connecting the electric current in the line overhead with the motor in the car.

**trombone** (trom'bon), n. A kind of musical instrument.

**trophy** (tro'fi), n. A memorial of victory.

**tropic** (trop'ik), n. The line that bounds the sun's declination north or south from the equator.

**troth** (trath), n. Faithfulness.

**trotter** (trot'ter), n. A trotting horse; a sheep's foot.

**troubadour** (tro'ba-dor), n. A lyric poet.

**trouble** (trub'l), v. To disturb; to grieve.

**trough** (traf), n. A long hollow vessel for water.

**trounce** (trowns), v. To punish severely; to cudgel.

**trousers** (trow'zerz), n. Long loose pantaloons.

**trousseau** (tro-so'), n. Collective lighter outfit of a bride.

**trout** (trowt), n. A river fish.

**trow** (tro), v. To think; to imagine; to conceive.

**trowel** (trow'el), n. A tool for spreading mortar.

**troy-weight** (troi'wat), n. Weight used by jewelers, etc.

**truant** (tro'ant), n. An idle youth.

**truce** (tros), n. A temporary peace; suspension of arms.

**truck** (truk), v. To barter; to exchange.

**truckle** (truk'l), v. To submit servilely.

**truculent** (truk'yu-lent), a

Fierce; savage; cruel. [truculence]
**trudge** (truj), vi. To travel on foot, esp. laboriously.
**true** (tru), a. Certain; faithful; according to fact; exact; correct; genuine; honest.
**truism** (tru'izm), n. An evident truth.
**trumpery** (trump'er-i), n. Empty talk; trifles; rubbish.
**trumpet** (trump'et), n. A wind-instrument of a martial character. [trumpeter]
**truncate** (trungk'at), vt. To cut short; maim.
**truncheon** (trunsh-un), n. A short staff; club; baton.
**trundle** (trun'dl), n. A wheel.
**trunnion** (trun'yun), n. One of the pivots on which a cannon, etc., rests.
**truss** (trus), n. A bundle; timber supporting a roof; a bandage for ruptures.
**tryst** (trist), n. An appointment to meet; meeting; place of meeting.
**tub** (tub), n. A pipe; long hollow cylinder.
**tuber** (tu'ber), n. A fleshy underground knob or root, as the potato.
**tubercle** (tu'ber-kl), n. A small knob; small mass of diseased matter.
**tubercular, tuberculous** (tuber'kyu-lar, -lus), a. Full of tubercles; characterized by, or affected with, tubercles.
**tubular** (tub'yu-lar), a. Having the form of, or consisting of, a tube.
**Tuesday** (tuz'da), n. Third day of the week.
**tuition** (tuish'un), n. Guardianship; instruction.
**tumble** (tum'bl), vi. To fall; roll; throw somersaults, etc.
**tumbler** (tum'bler), n. One who tumbles; drinking-glass without a foot; variety of pigeon.
**tumbrel** (tum'brel), n. Military wagon or cart.
**tumefy** (tu'me-fi), vt. and vi. To cause to swell; to swell. [tumefac'tion]
**tumid** (tu'mid), a. Swollen; inflated; bombastic. [tumid'ity]
**tumor** (tu'mor), n. A diseased swelling or morbid growth.
**tumult** (tu'mult), n. Commotion; uproar; violent agitation. [tumult'uous]
**tun** (tun), n. A large cask; measure of four hogsheads.
**tune** (tun), n. A melody; melodious or harmonious relation; order.
**tunic** (tu'nik), n. Ancient Roman under-garment; loose vestment.
**tunnel** (tun'el), n. Pipe for pouring liquors into bottles; funnel; artificial underground passage.
**turban** (tur'ban), n. An Eastern head-dress.
**turbid** (tur'bid), a. Muddy; not clear.
**turbine** (tur'bin), n. A horizontal water-wheel.
**turbulent** (tur'byu-lent), a. Tumultuous; disposed to disorder; unruly. [turbulence]
**tureen** (tu'ren), n. Large vessel for holding soup, etc.
**turf** (turf), n. Soil matted with roots of grass, etc.; sod; sward; peat; race-ground; horse-racing.
**turgescent** (tur-jes'ent), a. Swelling.
**turgid** (tur'jid), a. Swollen; pompous.
**turkey** (tur'ki), n. A large fowl, a native of America.
**turmoil** (tur'moil), n. Tumult; disturbance; harassing labor.
**turnip** (tur'nip), n. An esculent root.

**turnkey** (turn'ke), n. One who keeps the keys of a prison.
**turnpike** (turn'pik), n. A toll-gate; a road on which are turnpikes.
**turnstile** (turn'stil), n. A kind of turnpike in a footpath.
**turpentine** (tur'pen-tin), n. A resinous juice from pine trees.
**turpitude** (tur'pe-tud), n. Baseness.
**turret** (tur'et), n. A small tower.
**turtle** (tur'tl), n. A dove; a tortoise.
**tuscan** (tus'kan), a. Noting an order of architecture.
**tutelage** (tu'tel-aj), n. Guardianship; protection; care.
**tutelary** (tu'tel-ar-e), a. Guarding; protecting.
**tutor** (tu'tor), n. One who instructs.
**twaddle** (twod'l), vi. To prate.
**twain** (twan), a. Two.
**twang** (twang), vi. To sound with a quick, sharp noise.
**tweak** (twek), vt. To twitch.
**tweeds** (twedz), n. pl. Cotton or woolen goods of light fabric.
**tweezers** (twez'erz), n. pl. Nippers.
**twelfth** (twelfth), a. The ordinal of twelve.
**twelve** (twelv), a. Two and ten.
**twentieth** (twen'te-eth), a. The ordinal of twenty.
**twilight** (twi'lit), n. Light after sunset and before sunrise.
**twine** (twin), vt. and i. To twist; to wrap closely round.
**twinge** (twinj), vi. To feel sharp pain.
**twinkle** (twing'kl), vi. To sparkle.
**twirl** (twerl), vt. To move or whirl round.
**twist** (twist), vt. To wind, as one thread round another.
**twit** (twit), vt. To reproach.
**twitch** (twich), vt. To pull suddenly.
**twitter** (twit'er), vi. To make a noise as swallows.
**tympan** (tim'pan), n. A printer's frame for the sheets.
**tympanum** (tim'pan-um), n. Drum of the ear.
**typhoid** (ti'foid), n. A fever resembling typhus.
**typhoon** (ti-foon'), n. A tornado.
**typhus** (ti'fus), n. A fever characterized by great debility.
**typical** (tip'ik-al), a. Emblematical.
**typify** (tip'e-fi), vt. To represent by an emblem.
**typographer** (ti-pog'ra-fer), n. A printer.
**typographical** (ti-po-graf'ik-al), a. Pertaining to types or to printing.
**typography** (ti-pog'ra-fe), n. The art of printing.
**tyrannical** (ti-ran'ik-al), a. Despotic; cruel.
**tyrannicide** (ti-ran'e-sid), n. The killing or killer of a tyrant.
**tyrannize** (tir'an-iz), vi. To act as a tyrant.
**tyrannous** (tir'an-us), a. Cruel; arbitrary. [**tyranny**]
**tyrant** (ti'rant), n. An arbitrary ruler.
**tyro** (ti'ro), n. A beginner; a novice.

# U

**ubiquitary** (u-bik'we-tar-e), Existing every where.
**ubiquity** (u-bik'we'te), n. Existence every where.

**udder** (ud'er), n. The bag with the teats of a cow, &c.

**ugly** (ug'le), a. Not handsome; deformed.

**ukase** (u-kas'), n. Imperial decree.

**ulcer** (ul'ser), n. A sore that is attended with discharge. [ulcerate]

**ulterior** (ul-te'ri-ur), a. Lying beyond; distant; further.

**ultimatum** (ul-ti-ma'tum), n. Last or final proposition.

**ultimo** (ul'ti-mo), ad. In the last month.

**ultra** (ul'tra), a. and prefix. Beyond; extreme.

**umbrage** (um'braj), n. A shade; supposed injury; offense.

**umbrageous** (um-bra'je-us), a. Forming a shade.

**umbrella** (um-brel'la), n. A screen from rain or sun.

**umpire** (um'pir), n. A third person to whose sole decision a dispute is referred.

**un** (un). Negative prefix; chiefly prefixed to adjectives, participles and adverbs, used almost at pleasure.

**unanimity** (u-na-nim'i-ti), n. Agreement in opinion.

**unanimous** (u-nan'i-mus), a. Being of one mind.

**unappalled** (un-ap-pald'), a. Not daunted.

**unappreciated** (un-ap-pre'shi-a-ted), a. Not duly valued.

**unapt** (un-apt'), a. Not apt.

**unbecoming** (un-be-kum'ing), a. Improper; indecent.

**unbelief** (un-be-lef'), n. Infidelity; incredulity; scepticism. [unbeliever]

**unbosom** (un-boz'um), v. To reveal; to disclose.

**uncle** (ung'kl), n. The brother of one's father or mother.

**unctuous** (ung'tu-us), a. Oily; fat; greasy.

**under** (un'der), prep. Beneath; below; less.

**understanding** (un-der-stand'ing), n. The intellectual powers; judgment; sense.

**undertake** (un-der-tak'), vt. [pret. undertook; pp. undertaken] To take in hand.

**undertaker** (un-der-tak'er), n. One who undertakes.

**underwrite** (un-der-rit'), vi. To insure.

**underwriter** (un-der-rit'er), n. An insurer.

**undulate** (un'du-lat), vt. or i. To move backward and forward, as a wave.

**undulation** (un-du-la'shun), n. A waving motion or vibration. [undulatory]

**unction** (ung'shun), n. Act of anointing.

**unduly** (un-du'le), ad. Improperly; excessively.

**unearthly** (un-erth'le), a. Not terrestrial; not human.

**uneasily** (un-ez'e-le), ad. Without ease or quiet.

**uneasy** (un-ez'e), a. Restless; disturbed.

**unguent** (ung'gwent), n. An ointment.

**unicorn** (u'ni-karn), n. A fabulous animal.

**uniform** (u'ni-farm), n. The dress of a soldier. a. Similar to itself; not variable. [uniformity]

**unify** (u'ni-fi), v. To reduce to unity or uniformity. [unification]

**uniliteral** (u-ni-lit'er-al), a. Consisting of one letter only.

**unimpeachable** (un-im-pech'-a-bl), a. Free from guilt or stain; faultless.

**union** (un'yun), n. The act of joining; concord; confederation.

**unionist** (un-yun'ist), n. One who advocates or loves union.

**unique** (u-nek'), a. Sole; only; without an equal.

**unison** (u'ni-sun), n. Accordance of sound; concord.

**unit** (u'nit), n. One; a single thing or person.

**unitarian** (u-ni-ta'ri-an), n. One who denies the Trinity.

**unite** (u-nit'), v. To join two or more in one.

**unity** (u'ni-ti), n. State of being one; agreed; concord.

**universal** (u-ni-ver'sal), a. General; extending to all.

**universalism** (u-ni-ver'sal-izm), n. The doctrine or belief that all will be saved.

**universality** (u-ni-ver-sal'-i-ti), n. State of extending to the whole.

**universe** (u'ni-vers), n. Whole system of created things; the whole world.

**university** (u-ni-ver'si-ti), n. A corporation of teachers, or assemblage of colleges, for teaching the higher branches of learning.

**unkempt** (un-kempt'), a. Not combed; disordered.

**upas** (u'pas), n. A tree of Java yielding a poisonous juice.

**upbraid** (up-brad'), vt. To reproach; censure.

**upheave** (up-hev'), vt. To heave or lift up.

**upholster** (up-hol'ster), vt. To provide with cushions and covers, as furniture; make mattresses, etc.

**upholstery** (up-hol'ster-i), n. Articles supplied by upholsterers.

**uranography** (u-ran-og'ra-fi), n. A description of the heavens and heavenly bodies.

**Uranus** (u'ra-nus), n. A distant planet.

**urban** (ur'ban), a. Pertaining to a city.

**urbane** (ur-ban'), a. Polite; courteous; refined. [**urbanity**]

**urchin** (ur'chin), n. A hedgehog; a child.

**urge** (urj), vt. To impel; press earnestly; incite.

**urgent** (ur'jent), a. Pressing with importunity; calling for immediate attention; pressingly necessary. [**urgency**]

**urine** (u'rin), n. Liquid excreted by the kidneys. [**urinary**]

**urn** (urn), n. A kind of vase.

**usage** (u'zaj), n. Act of using; treatment; custom; habit.

**usher** (ush'er), n. An officer to introduce strangers, or walk before a person of rank; an under-teacher.

**usual** (u'zhu-al), a. Customary; common.

**usufruct** (u'zu-frukt), n. Right of using another's property without impairing the substance.

**usurer** (u'zhu-rer), n. One who practises usury.

**usury** (u-zhu-ri), n. Illegal interest for the use of money; act of taking illegal interest.

**utensil** (u-ten'sil), n. A household instrument or vessel.

**uterine** (u-ter-in), a. Pertaining to the womb; born of the same mother, but by a different father.

**utilitarian** (u-til-i-ta'ri-an), a. Pertaining to utility, or to utilitarianism.

**utilitarianism** (u-til-i-ta'ri-an-izm), n. Doctrine teaching that the standard of virtue is utility, or the promotion of human welfare.

**utility** (u-til'i-ti), n. Usefulness; profitableness.

**utopia** (u-to'pi-a), n. An ideal commonwealth; place or state of imaginary perfection. [**utopian**]

**utterance** (ut'er-ans), n.

Act or manner of speaking; expression; circulation.

**uxorious** (uks-o'ri-us, ugz-), a. Excessively, or submissively, fond of a wife.

# V

**vacancy** (va'kan-si), n. Emptiness; empty space; a void or gap; unoccupied situation; leisure.

**vacant** (va'kant), a. Empty; not occupied or filled; void of thought.

**vacate** (va-kat'), vt. To make or leave empty; abandon; annul.

**vacation** (va-ka'shun), n. Act of vacating; intermission of duty; recess.

**vaccinate** (vak'si-nat), vt. To inoculate with the cow-pox. [**vaccina'tion**]

**vaccine** (vak'sin), a. Pertaining to, or derived from, cows, or from vaccination.

**vacillate** (vas'i-lat), vi. To waver; fluctuate.

**vacuity** (va-ku'i-ti), n. Emptiness; void.

**vacuum** (vak'yu-um), n. Empty space.

**vagabond** (vag'a-bond), a. Wandering; without fixed habitation.

**vagary** (va-gar'i), n. A caprice; whim.

**vagrant** (va'grant), a. Wandering; unsettled. [**vagrancy**]

**vague** (vag), a. Unsettled; indefinite; uncertain.

**vain** (van), a. Fruitless; ineffectual; conceited; showy.

**vale** (val), n. A low ground; valley.

**valediction** (val-e-dik'shun), n. A saying farewell; farewell.

**valentine** (val'en-tin), n. A sweetheart chosen on St. Valentine's day, the 14th of February; a love-letter sent on that day.

**valet** (val'a, val'et), n. A body-servant.

**valetudinarian** (val-e-tu-di-na'ri-an), a. Sickly; infirm.

**valiant** (val'yant), a. Brave; intrepid; heroic.

**valid** (val'id), a. Firm; sound; of force; legal.

**valise** (va-les'), n. A travelling-bag; portmanteau.

**valley** (val'i), n. Low ground, esp. between hills; lowland.

**valor** (val'or), n. Courage; intrepidity. a. **valorous**.

**valuable** (val'yu-a-bl), a. Having value; costly; precious.

**valuation** (val-yu-a'shun), n. Act of fixing a value; value fixed.

**value** (val'yu), n. Worth; price; excellence.

**valve** (valv), n. One of the leaves of a folding-door; a lid, cover, or slide opening only one way; one of the pieces forming a shell. [**valvular**]

**vampire** (vam'pir), n. A fabled spectre; a bloodsucker; large blood-sucking bat.

**Vandal** (van'dal), n. One of a race of fierce barbarians; any one hostile to arts or letters; barbarian. [**vandalism**]

**vandyke** (van-dik'), vt. To ornament with points, as a collar, etc.

**vanguard** (van'gard), n. Troops preceding the main body; first line.

**vanilla** (va-nil'a), n. A tropical vine; its fruit, and a perfume extracted from it.

**vanish** (van'ish), vt. To

**vanity** (van'i-ti), n. Worthlessness; emptiness; empty pride; idle show.

**vanquish** (vang'kwish), vt. To conquer; overcome.

**vantage** (van'taj), n. Advantage.

**vapid** (vap'id), a. Spiritless; flat; insipid.

**vapor** (va'por), n. A body rendered gaseous by heat; steam; mist; exhalation. [**vaporize**]

**vaporous** (va'por-us), a. Like vapor; full of vapors.

**variable** (va'ri-a-bl), a. Changeable; unsteady.

**variance** (va'ri-ans), n. Disagreement; dispute. [**variation**]

**varicose** (var'i-kos), a. Morbidly enlarged, as a vein.

**variegate** (va'ri-e-gat), vt. To diversify with colors.

**variety** (va-ri'e-ti), n. Difference; diversity; number of different things; division less marked than a species; object differing from others of its kind.

**various** (va'ri-us), a. Different; diverse; several.

**varlet** (var'let), n. A footman; servant; knave.

**varnish** (var'nish), n. A liquid which forms a glossy coating by drying; polish; palliation.

**vascular** (vas'kyu-lar), a. Pertaining to, or containing, vessels.

**vase** (vas, vaz), n. An ornamental vessel; urn.

**vassal** (vas'al), n. A servant; dependant; feudal tenant.

**vaticinate** (va-tis'in-at), vt. and vi. To foretell; predict.

**vault** (valt), n. An arched roof; chamber with an arched roof; underground chamber.

**vault** (valt), n. A leap. vi. To leap.

**vaunt** (vant), vi. To boast. vt. To make a boast of.

**veal** (vel), n. Flesh of a calf.

**veer** (ver), vt. and vi. To turn; change direction.

**vegetable** (vej'e-ta-bl), n. A plant; plant, or a portion of it, used for food.

**vegetal** (vej'e-tal), a. Of or pertaining to plants.

**vegetate** (vej'e-tat), vi. To grow as a plant. [**vegetation**]

**vehement** (ve'he-ment), a. Passionate; eager; violent. [**vehemence**]

**vehicle** (ve'hi-kl), n. A carriage; conveyance.

**veil** (val), n. A covering; curtain; thin cloth to cover the face; cover; disguise.

**vein** (van), n. A vessel which conveys the blood back to the heart; streak in wood or stone; seam of mineral; train of thought; disposition.

**vellum** (vel'um), n. A fine kind of parchment.

**velocipede** (ve-los'i-ped), n. A light carriage for one person, propelled by the feet on treadles.

**velocity** (ve-los'i-ti), n. Swiftness; rate of motion.

**velvet** (vel'vet), n. A cloth made of silk or cotton, with a short close nap.

**venal** (ve'nal), a. That may be purchased; mercenary. [**venality**]

**vender** (ven'der), a. Seller.

**veneer** (ve-ner'), v. To inlay with thin pieces of wood.

**venerable** (ven'er-a-bl), a. Worthy of veneration.

**venerate** (ven'er-at), v. To revere; to respect. [**veneration**]

**vengeance** (venj'ans), n. Punishment for injury or offense; revenge.

**venial** (ve'ni-al), a. Pardonable; excusable.

**venison** (ven'i-zn), n The flesh of animals taken in hunting.

**venom** (ven'um), n. Poison; malice; spite.

**venomous** (ven'um-us), a. Poisonous; malignant.

**venous** (ve'nus), a. Pertaining to or contained in the veins.

**ventilate** (ven'ti-lat), v. To fan; to expose to air; to discuss; to circulate. [**ventilation**]

**ventilator** (ven'ti-la-tur), n. A contrivance to introduce pure air.

**ventricle** (ven'tri-kl), n. A cavity in an animal body.

**ventricose** (ven'tri-kos), a. Distended; swelling out.

**ventriloquism** (ven-tril'o-kwizm), n. Act or art of speaking so that the voice seems to come from a distance.

**venture** (ven'tur), v. To do or undertake; to risk.

**venturous** (ven'tur-us), a. Daring; fearless; bold.

**venue** (ven'u), n. Place of trial; neighboring place.

**veracious** (ve-ra'shus), a. Truthful. [**veracity**]

**veranda** (ve-ran'da), n. Roofed balcony; porch.

**verbatim** (ver-ba'tim), ad. Word for word.

**verbiage** (ver'bi-aj), n. Superabundance of words.

**verbose** (ver-bos'), a. Abounding in words; diffuse. [**verbosity**]

**verdancy** (ver'dan-si), n. Greenness.

**verdant** (ver'dant), a. Green; flourishing; fresh; soft; raw.

**verdict** (ver'dikt), n. The decision of a jury; judgment.

**verdigris** (ver'di-gres), n. Rust of copper.

**verdure** (ver'dur), n. Greenness; freshness of growth.

**verge** (verj), v. To tend downward; to approach.

**verification** (ver-i-fi-ka'shun), n. Act of proving.

**verify** (ver'i-fi), n. To prove to be true; to confirm.

**verisimilitude** (ver-i-sim-il'i-tud), n. Likeness to truth.

**veritable** (ver'i-ta-bl), a. Agreeable to fact; true.

**verity** (ver'i-ti), n. Truth.

**vermicular** (ver-mik'u-lar), a. Like a worm; spiral.

**vermifuge** (ver'mi-fuj), n. A medicine to destroy worms.

**vermilion** (ver-mil'yun), n. A beautiful red color.

**vermin** (ver'min), n. Any small noxious animals.

**vernacular** (ver-nak'u-lar), a. Peculiar or belonging to one's own country; native.

**vernal** (ver'nal), a. Belonging to the spring, or youth.

**versatile** (ver'sa-til), a. Variable; changing. [**versatility**]

**verse** (vers), n. A line of poetry; metrical arrangement and language; poetry; a stanza.

**vertebra** (vert'e-bra), n. A joint of the spine. pl. vertebrae.

**vertex** (vert'eks), n. The crown or top.

**vertical** (vert'ik-al), a. Being in the zenith; perpendicular.

**verticity** (ver-tis'e-te), n. Power of turning; rotation.

**vertiginous** (ver-tij'in-us), a. Giddy; turning.

**vertigo** (ver-ti'go), n. Swimming of the head.

**vesicate** (ves'e-kat), vt. To blister.

**vesicle** (ves'e-kl), n. A little bladder on the skin.

**vesper** (ves'per), n. The evening star; evening; Venus. pl. Evening service.

# VESSEL 239 VINDICATE

**vessel** (ves'el), n. A cask; a tube; a building for navigation.

**vestal** (ves'tal), a. Pertaining to Vesta; pure; chaste.

**vestibule** (ves'te-bul), n. The porch or entrance of a house.

**vestige** (ves'tij), n. A footstep; trace.

**vestment** (ves'ment), n. A garment.

**vestry** (ves'tre), n. A room for vestments in a church; a parochial committee.

**vesture** (ves'ur), n. A garment or articles worn.

**Vesuvian** (ve-su've-an), a. Pertaining to Vesuvius.

**veteran** (vet'er-an), a. Long exercised.

**veterinary** (vet'er-in-ar-e), a. Pertaining to the art of healing the diseases of domestic animals.

**veto** (ve'to), n. A prohibition.

**vexation** (veks-a'shun), n. Act of irritating; trouble. [**vexatious**]

**viable** (vi'a-bl), a. Capable of living, as a premature child.

**viaduct** (vi'a-dukt), n. A structure by which a way is formed from one road to another.

**vial** (vi'al), n. A small bottle; also written **phial**.

**viands** (vi'andz), n. pl. Meat dressed; victuals.

**vibrate** (vi'brat), vt. or i. To move to and fro. [**vibration**]

**vibratory** (vi'bra-tor-e), a. Consisting in oscillation.

**vicar** (vik'ar), n. Substitute; deputy.

**vicarious** (vi-ka're-us), a. Acting in place of another; deputed.

**vice** (vis), n. A blemish; fault; a kind of press; a Latin prefix, denoting in the place of.

**viceroy** (vis'roy), n. The substitute of a king.

**vicinage** (vis'in-aj), n. Neighbourhood.

**vicinity** (ve-sin'e-te), n. Neighbourhood.

**vicious** (vish'us), a. Immoral; wicked.

**vicissitude** (ve-sis'e-tud), n. Revolution; regular change.

**victim** (vik'tim), n. A living being sacrificed; a sacrifice.

**victimize** (vik'tim-iz), vt. To make a victim of.

**victor** (vik'tor), n. A conqueror.

**victorious** (vik-to're-us), a. Superior in contest.

**victory** (vik'to-re), n. Conquest; triumph; success.

**victual** (vit'l), vt. To supply with provisions.

**victuals** (vit'lz), n. pl. Food prepared for the table.

**videlicet** (vi-del'e-set), ad. To wit; namely; viz.

**vie** (vi), vi. To attempt to equal.

**view** (vu), vt. To see; to behold; to survey.

**vigil** (vij'il), n. Watch; nocturnal devotion; a fast.

**vignette** (vin-yet'), n. Engraving without a definite border.

**vigor** (vig'ur), n. Vital strength in animals or plants. [**vigorous**]

**vile** (vil), a. Base; depraved.

**vilify** (vil'i-fi), v. To defame; to degrade by slander.

**villa** (vil'la), n. A mansion.

**village** (vil'aj), n. A small collection of houses.

**villain** (vil'lin), n. A man extremely depraved. [**villainous, villainy**]

**vincible** (vin'si-bl), a. That may be overcome.

**vindicate** (vin'di-kat), v. To justify; to maintain. [**vindication**]

**vindicative** (vin-dik'tiv), a. Given to revenge; revengeful.

**vine** (vin), n. A climbing or trailing plant.

**vintage** (vin'taj), n. The harvest grape-gathering.

**vintager** (vin'ta-jer), n. One who gathers the vintage.

**violable** (vi'o-la-bl), a. That may be violated or injured.

**violate** (vi'o-lat), v. To break; to injure; to infringe; to ravish; to profane. [**violation**]

**violence** (vi'o-lens), n. Force.

**violent** (vi'o-lent), a. Forcible; outrageous, fierce.

**violet** (vi'o-let), n. A flower; a dark blue color.

**violin** (vi'o-lin), n. A musical instrument; a fiddle.

**viper** (vi'per), n. A kind of venomous serpent.

**virago** (ve-ra'go), n. Manlike woman; a termagant.

**virgin** (ver'jin), n. A maid.

**virginal** (ver'jin-al), a. Pertaining to a virgin. [**virginity**]

**virile** (vi'ril, vir'il), a. Pertaining to man; masculine.

**virility** (vi-ril'i-ti), n. Manhood.

**virtu** (ver'to), n. A love of the fine arts; curiosities.

**virtue** (vert'u), n. Strength; moral goodness; efficacy.

**virtuous** (vert'u-us), a. Morally good; chaste.

**virulence** (vir'u-lens), n. Extreme bitterness or malignity. [**virulent**]

**virus** (vi-rus). Poisonous matter.

**visage** (viz'aj), n. The face; look.

**viscera** (vis'er-a), n. pl. Organs in the abdomen or thorax; bowels. [**visceral**]

**viscid** (vis'id), a. Glutinous; sticky.

**viscount** (vi'kount), n. Nobleman next in rank below an earl.

**viscous** (vis'kus), a. Glutinous; sticky.

**vise** (vis), n. Instrument of two jaws, closing by a screw.

**visible** (viz'i-bl), a. That may be seen; perceptible.

**vision** (vizh'un), n. Act or sense of seeing; anything seen; imaginary sight; apparition; anything imaginary. [**visionary**]

**visitant** (viz'i-tant), n. One who visits; guest.

**visitation** (viz-i-ta'shun), n. Act of visiting; examination; infliction.

**visitor** (viz'i-tor), n. One who visits; an examiner.

**visor** (viz'or), n. Part of a helmet covering the face.

**vista** (vis'ta), n. View through an avenue; prospect; avenue.

**visual** (vizh'yu-al), a. Pertaining to sight.

**vital** (vi'tal), a. Pertaining, or essential, to life; very important. [**vitality**]

**vitiate** (vish'i-at), vt. To make vicious or defective; invalidate.

**viticulture** (vit'i-kult'yur), n. Cultivation of the vine.

**vitreous** (vit're-us), a. Pertaining to glass; of, or like, glass.

**vitrify** (vit'ri-fi), vt. and vi. To convert into, or become, glass, or a glassy substance.

**vitriol** (vit'ri-ol), n. A soluble sulphate of any metal (incorrectly used for sulphuric acid).

**vituperate** (vi-tu'per-at), vt. To censure or abuse violently. [**vitupera'tion**]

**vivacious** (vi-va'shus), a. Lively; active; sportive. [**vivac'ity**]

**vivid** (viv'id), a. Lively; life-like; brilliant; striking.

**viviparous** (vi-vip'a-rus), a. Producing young alive.

**vivisection** (viv-i-sek'shun), n. Dissection of a living animal.

**vixen** (viks'n), n. An ill-tempered woman; shrew.

**vizard** (viz'ard), n. Visor; mask.

**vocabulary** (vo-kab'yu-la-ri), n. A list of words; glossary; sum of words used.

**vocal** (vo'kal), a. Having a voice; uttered by, or pertaining to, the voice.

**vocation** (vo-ka'shun), n. Calling; occupation.

**vocative** (vok'a-tiv), n. Case used when a person or thing is addressed.

**vociferate** (vo-sif'er-at), vt. and vi. To cry aloud.

**vociferous** (vo-sif'er'us), a. Clamorous; noisy.

**vogue** (vog), n. Fashion; prevailing mode.

**voice** (vois), n. Sound uttered by the mouth; sound of anything; expressed opinion; vote; inflection of a verb indicating the relation of the subject.

**void** (void), a. Empty; destitute; null; unsubstantial.

**voidance** (void'ans), n. Act of voiding; state of being void.

**volatile** (vol'a-til), a. Evaporating quickly; flighty; airy; fickle.

**volatility** (vol-a-til'i-ti), n. Quality of being volatile; giddiness; levity.

**volatilize** (vol'a-til-iz), v. To make volatile.

**volcano** (vol-ka'no), n. A burning mountain ejecting lava and stones.

**volition** (vo-lish'un), n. The act of willing or choosing; the will.

**volley** (vol'li), n. An outburst of many things at once; a discharge of small arms.

**volplane** (vol'plan), v. To glide an aeroplane to earth.

**volubility** (vol-u-bil'i-ti), n. Fluency of speech.

**voluble** (vol'u-bl), a. Fluent in words; flowing smoothly.

**volume** (vol'um), n. A roll; a book; fulness of voice. [**voluminous**]

**voluntary** (vol'un-tar-i), a. Acting by choice; willing; free; music not prescribed by the ritual, as an introductory organ selection.

**volunteer** (vol-un-ter'), n. One who serves by choice.

**voluptuous** (vo-lup'tu-us), a. Luxurious; sensual.

**volution** (vo-lu'shun), n. A spiral turn or wreath.

**vomit** (vom'it), v. To eject from the stomach.

**voracious** (vo-ra'shus), a. Greedy to eat; ravenous.

**voracity** (vo-ras'i-ti), n. Greediness of appetite.

**vortex** (var'teks), n. A whirlpool; a whirlwind; a whirling motion.

**votary** (vo'ta-ri), n. One devoted to a pursuit.

**votive** (vo'tiv), a. Given by vow; promised by vow.

**vouch** (vowch), v. To call solemnly to witness; to warrant; to attest; to affirm.

**voucher** (vowch'er), n. One who vouches; a document that confirms anything.

**vouchsafe** (vowch-saf'), v. To yield; to condescend.

**voyage** (voi'aj), n. A passage by water.

**vulcanite** (vul'kan-it), n. Sulphur combined with India-rubber. [**vulcanize**]

**vulgar** (vul'gar), a. Common; low; mean; unrefined. [**vulgarity**]

**vulgate** (vul'gat), n. Latin version of the Scriptures.

**vulnerable** (vul'ner-a-bl), a. That may be wounded.

**vulture** (vult'ur), n. A large voracious bird of prey. [**vulturine**]

# W

**wafer** (wa'fer), n. A thin cake.

**waft** (waft), vt. To bear through a fluid.

**wage** (waj), vt. To lay a wager.

**wager** (wa'jer), n. Something laid; a bet.

**wages** (wa'jes), n. pl. Hire; reward of services.

**waggish** (wag'ish), a. Merry; droll.

**waggle** (wag'l), vi. To waddle.

**waif** (waf), n. Goods found, but not claimed.

**wail** (wal), vi. or t. To weep.

**wainscot** (wan'skot), n. A lining of rooms.

**waist** (wast), n. The part of the body below the ribs; middle of a ship.

**waistband** (wast'band), n. The band of trowsers, &c.

**waistcoat** (wast'kot), n. A garment worn under the coat.

**waive** (wav), vt. To relinquish.

**wallet** (wol'et), n. A bag or knapsack.

**waltz** (wawlts), n. A dance and a tune.

**wampum** (wom'pum), n. Shells or strings of shells used as current money by the native North American Indians.

**wan** (won), a. Having a pale and sickly hue.

**wane** (wan), vi. To decrease.

**wanness** (won'nes), n. A pale expression.

**wanton** (won'tun), a. Sportive; licentious.

**warble** (war'bl), vi. To sing in a quavering way; sing; chirp, as birds.

**warden** (ward'n), n. One who guards; a keeper.

**wares** (warz), n. pl. Goods; merchandise; commodities.

**warfare** (war'far), n. Military service; a struggle.

**warily** (war'i-li), ad. Prudently; cautiously.

**warrant** (wor'rant), n. An instrument of authority; a voucher.

**warrantable** (wor'rant-a-bl), a. Legal; justifiable. [warranty]

**warren** (wor'ren), n. A place for rabbits, fowls, fish, etc.

**warrior** (war'ri-ur), n. A military man; a soldier.

**wart** (wart), n. A small excrescence on the flesh.

**wary** (wa'ri), a. Cautious.

**waspish** (wosp'ish), a. Stinging; peevish; cross; petulant.

**waste** (wast), v. To diminish; to spend; to squander.

**weak** (wek), a. Wanting strength; feeble; dilute; inconclusive. [weakly]

**weaken** (wek'n), vt. and vi. To make, or become, weak.

**weakly** (wek'li), a. Weak in body or mind.

**weal** (wel), a. Prosperity; welfare.

**wealth** (welth), n. Riches; affluence; profusion.

**wean** (wen), vt. To accustom to do without being suckled; to reconcile to the want of anything; withdraw the affections.

**weapon** (wep'on), n. An instrument of offense.

**wearisome** (we'ri-sum), a. Tiresome; tedious.

**weary** (we'ri), a. Tired; fatigued; having the patience exhausted; causing weariness.

**weasel** (wez'l), n. Small carnivorous quadruped.

**weather** (weth'er), n. State of the atmosphere.

**weave** (wev), vt. To unite, as threads, to form a fabric; to make, as a fabric, out of threads.

**wedge** (wej), n. Piece of wood, metal, etc., sloping to an edge; ingot.

**Wednesday** (wenz'da), n. The fourth day of the week.

**week** (wek), n. A period of seven days.

**weekly** (wek'li), a. Happening, or coming, once a week.

**ween** (wen), vi. To think; fancy.

**weevil** (we'vil), n. An insect that destroys grain.

**weft** (weft), n. The woof of cloth; a web; a thing woven.

**weigh** (wa), v. To ascertain weight; to consider; to have weight; to raise the anchor.

**weight** (wat), n. Body of determinate mass; heaviness; importance.

**weighty** (wa'ti), a. Having weight; important.

**weir** (wer), n. Dam across a river; fence for catching fish.

**weird** (werd), a. Pertaining to witchcraft; wild and dreary.

**weld** (weld), v. To hammer into permanent union, as heated metal; to join together.

**welfare** (wel'far), n. Health; well-being; prosperity.

**welkin** (wel'kin), n. The sky; the vault of heaven.

**Welsh** (welsh), a. Pertaining to Wales or its people.

**welter** (wel'ter), v. To roll or wallow in mire.

**wen** (wen), n. A tumor.

**wench** (wench), n. A low coarse woman.

**westerly** (west'er-li), a. Toward or from the west.

**western** (west'ern), a. Being in the west.

**whack** (hwak), n. A blow.

**whale** (hwal), n. The largest of sea animals.

**whalebone** (hwal'bon), n. An elastic horny substance from the jaw of a whale.

**whaler** (hwal'er), n. A ship or person engaged in whaling.

**wharf** (hwarf), n. A pier or quay for landing goods.

**wharfage** (hwarf'aj), n. The fee for using a wharf.

**wharfinger** (hwarf'in-jer), n. The keeper of a wharf.

**wheat** (hwet), n. The finest kind of grain, which furnishes white flour for bread. [wheaten]

**wheedle** (hwe'dl), v. To coax or entice by soft words.

**wheel** (hwel), n. A circular body of wood or metal turning on an axis; a turning about.

**wheeze** (hwez), vi. To breathe hard.

**whelk** (hwelk), n. A pustule; a periwinkle; a kind of shell-fish.

**whelm** (hwelm), vt. To cover; to immerse; to bury.

**whelp** (hwelp), n. A puppy; a cub.

**whet** (hwet), vt. To sharpen by friction; to stimulate.

**whether** (hweth'er), pron. Which of the two.

**whetstone** (hwet'ston), n. A stone for sharpening tools.

**whey** (hwa), n. The thin part of milk.

**whig** (hwig), n. One of a political party.

**whim** (hwim), n. A freak of fancy.

**whimper** (hwim'per), vi. To cry with a whining voice.

**whimsical** (hwim'ze-kal), a. Full of whims.

**whine** (hwin), vi. To murmur in a plaintive tone.

**whir** (hwer), vi. To whirl.

**whirl** (hwerl), vt. To turn rapidly.

**whirligig** (hwerl'e-gig), n. A child's toy.

**whisk** (hwisk), n. A small besom.

**whisker** (hwisk'er), n. Long hair growing on the cheek.

**whisky** (hwisk'e), n. Spirit from grain.

**whisper** (hwis'per), vi. or t. To speak with a low voice.

**whist** (hwist), n. A game at cards.

**whistle** (hwis'l), vi. To utter sound with the breath.

**whitish** (whit'ish), a. Somewhat white.

**whitlow** (whit'lo), n. Suppurating inflammation at the edge or base of a nail.

**Whitsunday** (whit'sun'da), n. Pentecost; seventh Sunday after Easter.

**whittle** (whit'l), vt. To pare or cut with a knife.

**whiz** (whiz), n. A hissing sound.

**whoop** (hoop), n. A loud shout. vi. To utter a shout of scorn, joy, etc.

**whooping-cough** (hoop'ing-kof), n. A convulsive cough, in which the breath is caught with a shrill sound.

**width** (width), n. Extent from side to side; breadth.

**wield** (weld), vt. To use with full command; manage.

**wince** (wins), vi. To shrink; start back.

**winch** (winch), n. A crank; crank-handle.

**windlass** (wind'las), n. Revolving cylinder which winds up a cord or chain.

**windrow** (wind'ro), n. Ridge or row of hay or cut grain.

**windward** (wind'ward), Situated toward, or facing, the point from which the wind blows.

**winter** (win'ter), n. The cold season of the year; months of December, January, and February. vi. To pass the winter.

**wintery** (win'ter-i), a. Of, or like, winter; cold.

**wire** (wir), n. A thread of metal. vt. To bind or frame with wire.

**wiry** (wi'ri), a. Like wire; flexible and strong.

**wisdom** (wiz'dom), n. Right use of knowledge; judgment.

**wise** (wiz), a. Judging rightly; using knowledge well; learned; containing wisdom.

**wiseacre** (wiz'a-ker), n. A shallow pretender to wisdom.

**wistful** (wist'ful), a. Eagerly attentive; longing.

**witch** (wich), n. A woman who practises sorcery.

**witchcraft** (wich'kraft), n. Sorcery; magic. [witchery]

**withers** (with'erz), n. pl. Ridge between the shoulder-bones of a horse.

**witticism** (wit'i-sizm), n. A witty saying.

**witty** (wit'i), a. Having wit; droll; facetious.

**wizard** (wiz'ard), n. A magician; conjurer.

**wizen** (wiz'n), a. Shrunk; meagre.

**woe** (wo), n. Grief; misery; calamity.

**woful** (wo'ful), a. Sorrowful; wretched; calamitous.

**wolf** (wulf), n. A carnivorous animal allied to the dog. pl. **wolves**.

**wolverine** (wul-ver-en'), n. A carnivorous quadruped, the glutton.

**womb** (woom), n. Organ in which young are con-

**woodbine** (wud'bin), n. The honeysuckle.

**woodchuck** (wud'chuk), n. An American burrowing animal; ground-hog.

**woof** (woof), n. Threads that cross the warp in weaving.

**world** (wurld), n. The earth; mankind; society; present state of things; any planet.

**worthy** (wur'thi), a. Having worth; morally good; deserving.

**wound** (woond), n. A cut; injury; hurt.

**wrangle** (rang'gl), vi. To dispute noisily or angrily.

**wrapper** (rap'er), n. One who, or that which, wraps; covering; loose outer garment.

**wrath** (rath), n. Intense anger; fierce indignation.

**wrathful** (rath'ful), a. Full of wrath; angry; enraged.

**wreak** (rek), vt. To inflict.

**wreath** (reth), n. Something twisted; a garland.

**wreathe** (reth), vt. and vi. To twist; entwine.

**wreck** (rek), n. Destruction; destruction of a ship at sea; ruins of a ship; remains of anything ruined.

**wren** (ren), n. One of several genera of small birds.

**wrench** (rench), vt. To pull with a twist; twist violently; sprain.

**wrestle** (res'l), vi. To contend by grappling and struggling; strive.

**wretch** (rech), n. A miserable person; one sunk in vice.

**wriggle** (rig'l), vt. To twist to and fro.

**wright** (rit), n. A workman; artificer.

**wring** (ring), vt. To twist; force by twisting; compress; pain; extort.

**wrinkle** (ring'kl), n. A small ridge or fold; crease.

**wrist** (rist), n. Joint connecting the hand and arm.

**writ** (rit), n. Legal instrument or process. **Holy Writ**, the Scriptures.

**writhe** (rith), vt. and vi. To twist; turn violently.

**wroth** (rath), a. Very angry; exasperated.

**wry** (ri), a. Twisted; turned.

# X

**xanthin** (zan'thin), n. Yellow coloring matter of certain plants.

**xanthous** (zan'thus), a. Yellow; yellow-haired.

**xebec** (ze'bek), n. A small ship.

**x-rays** (eks-ras), n. Light emanating from an electrically excited vacuum tube; it penetrates many opaque substances. Discovered by Prof. Roentgen, of Wurzburg, Germany.

**xylography** (zi-log'ra-fi), n. Art of wood engraving.

# Y

**yacht** (yot), n. A light, swift sailing vessel for racing or pleasure.

**yahoo** (ya'ho), n. A low, boorish, or uneducated person.

**yawn** (yan), v. To gape; to open wide.

**yea** (ya), ad. Expressive of assent; verily; certainly.

**year** (yer), n. The time of one revolution of the earth in its orbit; twelve calendar months. [yearly]

**yearn** (yern), v. To feel pity, distress, or earnest desire; to long for.

**yeast** (yest), n. The froth of malt liquors in fermentation; a preparation which raises dough for bread.

**yelp** (yelp), v. To utter a sharp yell or bark.

**yeoman** (yo'man), n. A freeholder or farmer.

**yesterday** (yes'ter-da), n. The day last past.

**yew** (yo), n. An evergreen tree.

**yield** (yeld), v. To pay back; to give up, as a right; to concede; to produce; to afford; to submit.

**yoke** (yok), n. A framework of wood to connect oxen for work.

**yolk** (yolk), n. The yellow part of an egg.

**yore** (yor), n. The old time.

**youngster** (yung'ster), n. A young person; lad.

**youth** (yuth), n. State of being young; early life; a young person; young persons collectively.

**Yule** (yul), n. Christmas.

# Z

**zeal** (zel), n. Passionate ardor.

**zealot** (zel'ot), n. One full of zeal; a fanatic.

**zealous** (zel'us), a. Filled with zeal; ardent.

**zebra** (ze'bra, zeb-), n. African animal of the horse kind, marked with stripes.

**zenith** (ze'nith, zen'-), n. Point of the heavens directly overhead; greatest height.

**zephyr** (zef'ir), n. The west wind; a gentle breeze.

**zero** (ze'ro), n. The cipher 0; nothing; point from which a thermometer, etc., is graduated.

**zigzag** (zig'zag), a. Having short sharp turns.

**zinc** (zingk), n. A bluish-white metal.

**zodiac** (zo'di-ak), n. An imaginary belt in the heavens, in which the sun's path lies, and which contains the twelve constellations or signs.

**zone** (zon), n. A girdle; belt; one of the five climatic divisions of the earth.

**zoologist** (zo-ol'o-jist), n. One versed in zoology.

**zoology** (zo-ol'o-ji), n. Science which treats of animals. [zoolog'ical]

**zoophyte** (zo'o-fit), n. Name applied to animals resembling plants, as corals, sponges, etc.

**zouave** (zwav, zu-av'), n. One of a body of soldiers whose uniform resembles an Arab dress.

**zymotic** (zi-mot'ik), a. Pertaining to, or caused by, fermentation, or by some principle of disease acting like a ferment.